CHRISTMAS

***Celebrating the Christian History of
Classic Symbols, Songs and Stories***

**By
Angie Mosteller**

Christmas,
Celebrating the Christian History of Classic Symbols, Songs and Stories
Angie Mosteller
Printed in the United States of America

ISBN 978-0-9845649-0-3

Special thanks to the following contributors:

Grammatical Editing: Aarti Totlani
Content Editing: Julie Cochran
Graphic and Cover Design: Marta Studios, www.martastudios.com
Images used by permission: © iStockphoto LP 2006 and © 2007 JUPITERIMAGES, and its licensors. All rights reserved.
Music Engraving: Nish Music, www.nishmusic.com
Graphic Selection and General Review: Cheyenne Williams
Review: Tim Mosteller, Melody Essey and Eddie Essey

For more information on holiday history, please visit:
www.celebratingholidays.com

This book is dedicated to my husband Tim.
I thank God for the wonderful gift he gave me in you!

TABLE OF CONTENTS

A selection of the people and things most often depicted in images of Christmas.

Songs, *Carols, Hymns and Music of Christmas* *177*

A selection of music honoring Christ's birth.

Stories, *Tales and Verses of Christmas*

A variety of stories and poems that uniquely incorporate the symbols or themes of Christmas. Note that the approximate reading time is for the story only and does not include the background information.

INTRODUCTION

Dear Reader,

I have long been awed by the profound event of the first Christmas when the God of the Universe came to earth to dwell with us as a man. For many Christmases, I have pondered the magnitude of this great occasion, and with time, I became curious about the way in which we celebrate it in America. When I had children, my interest in the topic grew even more as I began to think about the kind of traditions that I wanted to incorporate into my family.

To be honest, there was a lot of confusion in my mind about how to celebrate Christmas. I was vaguely aware of claims about pagan influence on the holiday, particularly in regard to Christmas trees and Santa Claus, and I was completely ignorant about why things like candy canes, mistletoe and wreaths surrounded me during the Christmas season.

Thus began my adventure of researching the things of Christmas, and at the time, I had no idea how many hidden treasures lay before me. Initially, I had a modest goal of studying just a handful of symbols. However, I quickly became intrigued by the biblical relevance and the Christian history attached to many of these. With every nugget I found, I could not help but dig further. And each discovery seemed to lead to another. As my project grew, I started to organize my research into categories.

In the end, my project turned into a volume of 20 symbols, 20 songs (with music) and 20 stories (with text). I have also included a brief history of Christmas and some recommendations for further reading. I hope that the final result of my effort will prove to be a useful reference guide that you can use every Christmas season.

In regard to my process for selecting "classic" symbols, songs and stories, I chose to focus on those that are familiar to most Christians in the English-speaking world. Though many beautiful traditions exist around the globe, the information is just too voluminous to include in one book. I should also mention that, in an even more narrow focus, I took the liberty of adding a bit of U.S. history wherever relevant (since this is an area of personal interest for me).

In regard to my emphasis on "Christian history," please note that some of the entries in this book are not necessarily Christian in origin; however, I believe that in one way or another they all offer unique biblical relevance or inspiration to the Christian life. In summary, as you read through sections of this book, my prayer is that you will gain a more spiritually rich understanding of the symbols, songs and stories that surround you every Christmas. May they direct you to Jesus, the one whose birth we celebrate!

In His Service,

Angie

Source

THE ORIGIN & HISTORY OF CHRISTMAS

General History

General History

Christmas is a celebration of one of the most amazing events in history — the birth of Jesus Christ, the day that God himself entered the world as a man. The Bible teaches that Jesus "being in very nature God . . . made himself nothing, taking the very nature of a servant, being made in human likeness" (Philippians 2:6-7). An account of Christ's birth can be found in the gospels of Matthew (1:18-2:12) and Luke (1:1-2:20). "A Harmony of the Nativity Story" (a combination of Bible passages in chronological order) can be found on p. 323.

By the Middle Ages, Christians were honoring the remarkable event of Jesus' birth with an extended season that began with Advent (four Sundays before Christmas) and continued for the 12 Days after Christmas (up until Epiphany on January 6th). For more on the history of Advent, see p. 31, and for more on the history of the 12 Days of Christmas, see p. 35.

The time preceding Christmas used to be a solemn time of fasting, whereas the days after Christmas were the time of celebration. Christians looked forward to the Midnight Mass of Christmas Eve with great anticipation, because it marked the transition from fasting to feasting. This service known as "Christ's Mass" eventually became a description for celebrations of Jesus' birth throughout the world. The word *Christmas* comes from the old English term *Cristes Maesse*, meaning "Christ's Mass."[1]

Though the word *Christ* is commonly used as Jesus' name, it is actually a title. It comes from a Greek word that means "Anointed One" (the Hebrew word is "Messiah" — a term that Old Testament prophets used to describe the coming Savior). It should be noted that the abbreviated term *Xmas* does not necessarily take the "Christ" out of Christmas. The first letter of the Greek word for Christ (Χριστός) is "X" (pronounced "kai" in Greek), and it has been used among Christians throughout history to represent Jesus.

The word *Mass* comes from the Latin word *missa*, which means "dismissal." During the Middle Ages, the term became a general description for the Eucharistic service (when Christians partook of bread and wine in remembrance of the body and blood of Jesus).[2] The word gives insight into how medieval Christians may have understood at least one of the significant aspects of the Eucharist — they gathered together to remember the body and great sacrifice of Christ, so that they would be strengthened to go (or be "dismissed") back into the world to <u>be</u> the body of Christ. The apostle Paul told of this mystery when he wrote to believers in Corinth, "Now you are the body of Christ, and each of you is a part of it" (1 Corinthians 12:27).

How appropriate that the term *Christmas* calls to mind the body of Jesus who first entered the world in human flesh on this day. Furthermore, it serves to remind us that we are now to act as his body on earth!

---

[1] Martindale, Cyril Charles. "Christmas." The Catholic Encyclopedia. Robert Appleton Company, 1908. Retrieved July 20, 2008 from New Advent: http://www.newadvent.org/cathen/03724b.htm.

[2] Pohle, Joseph. "Sacrifice of the Mass." The Catholic Encyclopedia. Robert Appleton Company, 1911. Retrieved July 20, 2008 from New Advent: http://www.newadvent.org/cathen/10006a.htm.

The Days Before Christ's Birth, Prophecy

The Days Before Christ's Birth, Prophecy

Remarkably, long before his birth, the Bible gave several details about Christ. There are over 300 prophecies written about him in the Hebrew Scriptures (the Old Testament of the Bible); all of them were written at least 400 years before his birth. Here are just five of these prophecies and how they were specifically fulfilled by Jesus:

(1) Christ would come at a specific time in history.

> **"Know and understand this: From the issuing of the decree to restore and rebuild Jerusalem until the Anointed One, the ruler, comes, there will be seven 'sevens' and sixty-two 'sevens'. . . ." (Daniel 9:25, written in approximately 530 BC).**

The word *seven* is translated from the Hebrew word *shavua*. It can refer to days (meaning 7 days) or years (meaning a 7-year period). If we are to understand Daniel's prophecy in terms of years, then from Artaxerxes' decree in 445 B.C. to rebuild Jerusalem (as recorded in Nehemiah 2:1-20) to the time of the Anointed One, there should be a total of 483 years [(7x7)+(62x7)]. When factoring the Hebrew lunar year (sometimes called the "prophetic year") of 360 days, this prophecy points to the very generation in which Jesus lived. Some argue that it falls on the exact day of Jesus' triumphal entry (when Jesus entered Jerusalem and was greeted by the people as the King of Israel, John 12:12-19).

(2) Christ would come from the line of Judah.

> **"The scepter will not depart from Judah, nor the ruler's staff from between his feet, until he comes to whom it belongs and the obedience of the nations is his" (Genesis 49:10, written between 1446 BC and 1406 BC).**

This was the blessing that Jacob (also called Israel) gave to his son Judah. It is an interesting blessing to give to the fourth son. Yet history has revealed that the "scepter" did in fact pass to one of Judah's descendants. After 10 generations, the beloved David was made king over Israel. And Psalm 89 tells of God's plan for the line of David; verse 29 says, "I will establish his line forever, his throne as long as the heavens endure."

Up until at least the first century, the Jewish people expected the Messiah to come from the royal line of David. Interestingly, both Mary and Joseph were descendants of David. For more on the intriguing genealogy of Jesus, see pp. 324-327.

(3) Christ would be born of a virgin.

"Therefore the Lord himself will give you a sign. The virgin will be with child and will give birth to a son, and will call him Immanuel" (Isaiah 7:14, written in approximately 700 BC).

Immanuel means "God with us". In Jesus, God became a man. He was born to the virgin Mary (Luke 1:26-38).

(4) There would be a forerunner to Christ to prepare the way for him.

"A voice of one calling: 'In the desert prepare the way for the Lord; make straight in the wilderness a highway for our God'" (Isaiah 40:3, written in approximately 681 BC).

When John the Baptist began teaching in the desert, he drew great crowds. Priests came from Jerusalem to see if John claimed to be the Christ. When the priests asked John who he was, John said, "I am the voice of one calling in the desert, 'Make straight the way for the Lord'" (John 1:23).

(5) Christ would come from Bethlehem.

"But you, Bethlehem Ephrathah, though you are small among the clans of Judah, out of you will come for me one who will be ruler over Israel, whose origins are from of old, from ancient times" (Micah 5:2, written in approximately 700 BC).

The gospel of Matthew tells us that Jesus was born in Bethlehem during the time of King Herod. In fact, Herod asks his chief priests where the Christ was to be born. They replied without hesitation, "In Bethlehem in Judea" (Matthew 2:1-5). Clearly, this was common knowledge among Jewish scholars.

Additionally, it is interesting to note that Mary and Joseph were not residing in Bethlehem. They traveled there in response to a decree by Caesar Augustus; Joseph had to return to his place of ancestry for a census. While in Bethlehem, Jesus was born in divine fulfillment of prophecy.

The Day of
Christ's Birth,
December 25

The Day of Christ's Birth, December 25

Though the gospels of Matthew and Luke helped to spread knowledge of the Nativity story in the first century, neither writer provided an exact date for Christ's birth. Perhaps because the day was unknown, the earliest church records made no mention of a feast to honor it. Furthermore, it is likely that early Christians did not place any particular value on birthdays. In fact, Origen (185-254 AD), a Bible scholar from Alexandria, Egypt, had strong objections to birthday celebrations. He argued that only pagans celebrated their birthdays and that it would be sinful to observe the birthday of Jesus "as though He were a King Pharaoh."[1] To support his objection, Origen pointed to how Herod's birthday celebration had taken the precious life of John the Baptist (recorded in Matthew 14:1-12).

Origen's words were probably a response to Alexandrian Christians who were already celebrating birthdays and intending to honor that of Christ. By this time in history, most Christians came from Gentile backgrounds in which birthdays were an accepted part of culture, and it would have been natural for them to attach significance to the birthday of their Lord. Furthermore, believers were actively commemorating various saints on the day of their death (their birth into eternal life). Yet, Christ's death and resurrection marked the occasion that he, unlike any of the saints, *returned* to the eternal glory from which he had come. His birth was distinct and significant, because he left the glory of heaven to be born into the world as a man.

Interestingly, the first known attempt to apply a specific date to Christ's birth had been made by a preceding generation of Alexandrians. Clement (approximately 150-216 AD), who was Origen's predecessor as the head of the theological school in Alexandria, wrote around 200 AD: "There are those who have determined not only the year of our Lord's birth, but also the day; and they say that it took place in the twenty-eighth year of Augustus [3 BC] and in the twenty-fifth day of the month of Paschon [May 20]."[2] Clement offers no details to indicate whether this group of believers had a purely historical interest in the date or whether they intended to celebrate a feast in relation to it.[3]

What appears certain is that, prior to the days of Clement, Christians had shown little concern for identifying the date of Christ's birth or establishing a feast to honor it. It was not until the third century that various pockets of Christians began to show interest in the date, and it would take another century for the Church to begin celebrating it with some uniformity. Even then, the Eastern and the Western Churches remained divided on the date.

Conventional wisdom holds that Christians ultimately agreed to celebrate Christ's birth on December 25, because they wanted to counter popular pagan festivals. However, this may be historical myth. Even Encyclopedia Britannica acknowledges, "One of the difficulties with this view is that it suggests a nonchalant willingness on the part of the Christian church to appropriate a pagan festival when the early church was so intent on distinguishing itself categorically from pagan beliefs and practices."[4] Admittedly, some pagan practices were "Christianized" and became part of Christmas celebrations, but it appears that early Christians made a sincere effort to properly identify the date of Christ's birth, not just co-opt a pagan holiday.

Determining the Date:

In regard to the chronology of Christ's life, early church leaders were primarily concerned with determining the date of his death in order to establish the celebration of his resurrection (Easter). Since the Bible places Christ's death at the time of the Jewish Passover, the dating should have been easy. However, reconciling the Jewish lunar calendar (which has 12 months of 30 days each and adds an extra "month" every third year) with Greek and Roman calendars proved to be difficult. After much debate, the Eastern Church (which was using a Greek calendar) settled on April 6, and the Western Church (which was using a Roman calendar) settled on March 25 as the date of Christ's death. As we know, with time, the Western date prevailed and helped to determine the Sunday on which to celebrate Easter.

Interestingly, according to the Roman calendar, March 25 was also the spring equinox, a day that symbolized the "rebirth of the earth" and that some Christians believed marked the first day of creation. Hippolytus (170-235 AD), a Roman Christian, saw significance in the symbolism of Christ's death on the anniversary of creation, since it was Christ's redemptive death that allowed creation to be made new. Tertullian (160-235 AD), an African Christian, held the same view.[5]

By the third century, it appears that some Christians had started celebrating Christ's birth, as well as his death, on March 25, because in a book called *On Computing the Date of Easter* (written in 243 AD), the author makes a case against March 25 as Christ's birthday. As an interesting side note, this anonymous author made a case for March 28 as Christ's birth, because that would be the day that God created the lights in the sky (the fourth day of creation as recorded in Genesis 1:14-19); in other words, it would be the day on which the sun was born.[6] This argument reveals how important symbolism was to the ancient world.

So why were Christians celebrating Christ's birth and death on the same day (March 25)? Likely, an ancient Jewish tradition of "integral age"[7] or "whole year theory"[8] influenced this practice. The belief held that the life of a Jewish prophet began and ended on the same day. A third century Christian, Sextus Julius Africanus (180-250 AD), added an interesting component to this theory in his *Chronographiai* (221 AD). He argued that Christ's life began not at birth but at conception (note the pro-life implications). His case proves to be of particular relevance, because if Christ was conceived on March 25, he would have been born 9 months later on December 25, the date on which our discussion is focused.[9] Interestingly, the Church later recognized March 25 as the Annunciation (the date that Gabriel appeared to Mary to announce the birth of Christ and also believed to be the moment of conception) and December 25 as the birthday of Christ. Most Christians assume that the feast of the Annunciation was determined by taking the date of Christmas and counting back nine months; on the contrary, it was probably the reverse.[10]

The dating also fits well with the tradition that the angel Gabriel appeared to Zechariah during Yom Kippur, the Day of Atonement. The gospel of Luke records that while Zechariah was serving as priest, he was chosen by lot to go into the temple of the Lord. Gabriel appeared to Zechariah in the temple and told him that he and his wife Elizabeth would have a son (John the Baptist). Yom

Kippur typically falls in late September. If Elizabeth conceived immediately following Gabriel's announcement, then John would have been born in late June (tradition ascribes the date of June 24). We learn from the gospel of Luke that six months into Elizabeth's pregnancy (which would be March), the angel Gabriel appeared to Mary to announce the birth of Jesus. Assuming that Mary also conceived immediately following Gabriel's announcement, then Jesus would have been born in late December.

Though December 25 came to be widely accepted as the date of Christ's birth, scholars have long been debating its accuracy. Some say that shepherds would not be outside tending their flocks at this time of year; others point to the fact that even in modern times, shepherds in Palestine can be found tending flocks outdoors in December.[11] Some say that a census would not take place at this cold time of year; others argue that December would be the off-season for many trades and would be the most reasonable time for people to abandon their work to travel for a census. In the end, scholars have made a reasonable case for Christ's birth in nearly every month of the year. Though our modern sensibilities desire exactness in dating, let us consider Paul's words:

> "But when the time had fully come, God sent his Son, born of a woman, born under law, to redeem those under law, that we might receive the full rights of sons" (Galatians 4:4-5).

God sent his Son "when the time had fully come"; it was the exact time that God had planned since the beginning of the world.[12] Interestingly, it was probably the first time in human history when the message of Jesus could spread easily. The Romans had organized a system of roads, shipping ports, protection for travelers and a common language — all elements that would help to foster the spread of Christianity.

Though early Christian leaders made an effort to date Christ's birth with thoughtful consideration, bear in mind that Jesus was born in a period when time was referred to in terms of the "reign of so-and-so" and when both nature and symbolism played a role in dating significant events. St. Jerome (340-420 AD), an early church scholar, appealed to this symbolism to defend December 25 as the date of the Nativity: "Even nature is in agreement with our claim, for the whole world itself bears witness to our statement. Up to this day, darkness increases; from this day on, it decreases; light increases, darkness decreases."[13]

Pagan Influence:

If the dating of Christmas was influenced at all by pagan celebrations, the most likely candidate was a holiday established in 274 AD by the Roman Emperor Aurelian (around 214-275 AD) called *Dies Natalis Solis Invicti*, "The Birth of the Unconquered Sun," on December 25. However, it is equally possible that Aurelian was attempting to co-opt a date that already had significance for believers. According to history professor William Tighe, "The date had no religious significance in the Roman pagan festal calendar before Aurelian's time, nor did the sun play a prominent role in Rome before him."

By the time of Aurelian's reign, it appears that the god Mithras (originally a Persian deity who was said to be either the son of the sun or the companion of the sun) was earning popularity among traveling Roman soldiers.[15] Furthermore, the winter solstice, December 25 on the Roman calendar, held religious significance for a variety of cultures on the border of the empire. Though pagan customs varied widely in regard to the solstice, the shortest and darkest day of the year, they generally included solemn rituals to honor the sun and great festivities to celebrate the lengthening of the days. Aurelian decided to seize on an opportunity to bring the cult of the sun to the Roman Empire. Consider his possible motivation as described by professor Joseph Kelly, author of *The Origins of Christmas*:

"The emperor Aurelian ruled from 270 to 275. He feared that the empire was falling apart and needed a source of unity, such as a common religion. Recognizing that fewer and fewer people venerated the traditional gods, such as Jupiter and Venus, he hoped that monotheism might be the answer. Monotheism might also halt the challenge of a growing religion that he thought threatened the empire: Christianity.

"In 274 Aurelian instituted the cult of Sol Invictus, the Unconquered Sun. He built temples to the Sun, founded priesthoods, and tried to establish a solar theology. But he soon realized that his efforts would not stop Christianity, and in 275 he began to plan a persecution of the Christians, who were saved by the emperor's assassination."[16]

Interestingly, the cult did not die with Aurelian. The Emperor Constantine (272-337 AD) was a devotee of the sun before converting to Christianity.

Surely Aurelian was attempting to compete with Christianity, if not with Christmas itself. And, it appears that Christians dived into the ensuing propaganda war.[17] Records reveal how Christian leaders began to use sun imagery when referring to Christ: "Sun of Salvation," "Sun of Justice," "Sun of Righteousness" (a description used in Malachi 4:2), etc. And, over a century later, the war of words continued; Augustine (354 –430 AD), a theologian and Bishop of Hippo in North Africa, wrote of Christmas: "We hold this day holy, not like the pagans because of the birth of the sun, but because of him who made it."[18]

The reason that *Dies Natalis Solis Invicti*, "The Birthday of the Unconquered Sun," is often assumed to have influenced the dating of Christmas is that it was established in 274 AD, whereas the first clear record of *Dies Natalis Christi*, "The Birthday of Christ," as December 25 is an entry dated several years later — 336 AD (in a document called the *Chronograph of 354 AD*). The *Chronograph* is an almanac that lists, among other things, the burial dates for both Roman bishops and martyrs. Interestingly, the first date listed for martyrs is the birth of Christ on December 25. As professor

Kelly observes, "This inclusion may seem odd for a calendar of martyrs' feasts, but Christians considered the dates of death to be their birthdays into heaven, and thus the birthday of Christ made a fitting beginning for such a list."[19]

Unfortunately, the *Chronograph* makes no mention of how or when the date was selected. However, it is significant that Christ's birth was the first date listed among martyrs in calendrical order, not historical order. Thus, Christ's birth marked the beginning of the Christian liturgical calendar.[20] This could imply that the Roman church had accepted the date sometime earlier and that it was common knowledge.

Regardless, even if the dating of Christ's birth was owed in part to the pagan holiday, *Dies Natalis Solis Invicti*, "The Birthday of the Unconquered Sun," the influence was probably only secondary. It appears that the primary goal of the Church was to determine an appropriate date — one that Christians expected to be rich in symbolism. If this date, December 25, also happened to give the Church a sacred feast with which to counter pagan celebrations, then it was arguably the best possible choice for the day on which to honor Christ's birth.

---

[1] Hatch, Jane M. *The American Book of Days*. H.W. Wilson Company, 1978, p. 1142.

[2] Clement of Alexandria. *Ante Nicene Christian Library Translations of the Writings of the Fathers Down to AD 325, Part Four*. Edited by Alexander Roberts and James Donaldson. Kessinger Publishing, 2004, p. 445. Modern dates are drawn from Joseph Kelly's *The Origin of Christmas*, p. 57.

[3] Kelly, Joseph. *The Origins of Christmas*. Liturgical Press, 2004, p. 57.

[4] Encyclopedia Britannica. "Christmas." Retrieved August 05, 2008 from Encyclopedia Britannica Online: http://www.britannica.com/EBchecked/topic/115686/Christmas.

[5] Kelly, Joseph, p. 59.

[6] Kelly, Joseph, p. 60.

[7] Tighe, William. *Calculating Christmas*. Touchstone Journal, December 2003 issue.

[8] Kelly, Joseph, p. 59.

[9] Kelly, Joseph, p. 60.

[10] Kelly, Joseph, p. 60.

[11] Maier, Paul. *In the Fullness of Time*. Kregel Publications, 1997, p. 29.

[12] Maier, Paul. This is the basis for the title of the book "In the Fullness of Time."

[13] Witvliet, John D. and Vroege, David. *Proclaiming the Christmas Gospel, Ancient Sermons and Hymns for Contemporary Christian Inspiration*. Sermon by St. Jerome, Baker Books, 2004, p. 26.

[14] Tighe, William.

[15] Kelly, Joseph, p. 63.

[16] Kelly, Joseph, p. 63.

[17] Kelly, Joseph, p. 64.

[18] Hatch, Jane M., p. 1143.

[19] Kelly, Joseph, p. 69.

[20] Tally, Thomas J. *The Origins of the Liturgical Year*. Liturgical Press, 1986, p.85.

The Year of
Christ's Birth

The Year of Christ's Birth

The year of Christ's birth may seem obvious, since modern calendars note the years before his birth as *BC* (Before Christ) and the years after his birth as *AD* (*Anno Domini*, Latin for the "Year of the Lord"). Yet, Christ's birth did not fall perfectly between the two. A short review of how modern calendars were created will help to shed light on this surprising fact.

By the sixth century, there was a rapidly growing Christian population throughout the Western world. The existing Julian calendar was intimately tied to the pagan Roman Empire and counted its years in terms of *Anno Urbis Conditae*, Latin for "The Year of the Foundation of the City" (meaning Rome in 753 BC). Since the Roman Empire had collapsed in the fifth century, the Church recognized the need for a new calendar. A Scythian monk named Dionysius Exiguus was called to the task in 525 AD. Though Dionysius kept many of the Roman calendar elements in place (like days of the week and months of the year), he made a critical change to the way years were counted. Scholar Mark Kidger explains the process:

> "To set his calendar apart from its Roman predecessor, Dionysius decided to base it on the date of the birth of Jesus. . . . First, though, he had to calculate for himself the date of the Nativity. To do this, he followed precedent and used one of the best and most reliable measurements of time available to him: the reigns of the Roman emperors. By summing up the lengths of their reigns and calculating backwards, he was able to fix the date of the birth of Jesus by what appeared to be a most satisfactory method."[1]

Unfortunately, Dionysius made a few mistakes in his calculations. First, he forgot to account for the year zero; his calendar jumped from 1 BC to 1 AD. Second, Dionysius "excluded a four-year period during which Caesar Augustus reigned under his given name of Octavian, which he used for only a short part of his reign."[2] These two mistakes added up to a total of five years. According to Kidger, "If we assume that Dionysius made no other mistakes, Jesus would have been born in 5 BC — paradoxically, five years 'Before Christ.'"[3]

Additionally, historical records date King Herod's death shortly after an eclipse of the Moon, which was visible from Jericho, and before the feast of Passover (likely late March or early April in 4 BC). Herod was very much alive when Christ was born, making it unlikely that Jesus was born after 4 BC.

The arguments for an even earlier date for Christ's birth mainly center on the date of the census decreed by Caesar Augustus for which Mary and Joseph traveled to Bethlehem. History reveals three different decrees by Caesar Augustus for a census: one in 28 BC, another in 8 BC, and yet another in 14 AD. It is reasonable to imagine that Caesar's decree for a census in 8 BC could have taken three years to implement (thus going into effect in 5 BC).[4]

It seems ironic that our modern calendar erroneously dated Christ's birth (the very date for which it was designed). Regardless, the intention of the Church was clear — to identify the birth of Christ as a turning point in history, the beginning of the Church Age. And despite the pagan remnants of our calendar (see end notes regarding the days and months of the year), the God who transcends time entered human history to redeem time itself. Jesus' birth into the world initiated a Christian calendar which is centered on this marvelous event!

---

[1] Kidger, Mark. *Star of Bethlehem*. Princeton University Press, 1999, p. 44.

[2] Kidger, Mark. *Star of Bethlehem*. Princeton University Press, 1999, p. 45.

[3] Kidger, Mark. *Star of Bethlehem*. Princeton University Press, 1999, p. 45.

[4] Maier, Paul. *In the Fullness of Time.* Kregel Publications, 1997, p. 8.

DAYS OF THE WEEK: Though the concept of a seven day week has its origin in the creation account, the modern names of each day are rooted in various pagan beliefs. The following is an excerpt from Encyclopedia Britannica. "Week." Retrieved August 17, 2008 from Encyclopedia Britannica Online: http://www.britannica.com/EBchecked/topic/638786/week: "The days assigned by the Romans to the Sun, Moon, and Saturn were retained for the corresponding days of the week in English (Sunday, Monday, and Saturday) and several related languages. The other weekday names in English are derived from Anglo-Saxon words for the gods of Teutonic mythology. Tuesday comes from Tiu, or Tiw, the Anglo-Saxon name for Tyr, the Norse god of war. Tyr was one of the sons of Odin, or Woden, the supreme deity after whom Wednesday was named. Similarly, Thursday originates from Thor's-day, named in honour of Thor, the god of thunder. Friday was derived from Frigg's-day, Frigg, the wife of Odin, representing love and beauty, in Norse mythology.

MONTHS OF THE YEAR: The months of the year also have roots in paganism. The following information is drawn from Kidger. Mark. *Star of Bethlehem*. Princeton University Press, 1999, pp. 40-41: January gets its name from Janus, the two-headed god of gates who looked forward and backward at the same time. February is named after the Roman feast of Purification, Februa. March is named after the god Mars. April gets its name from a Latin word, *apero*, meaning "the latter" or "second" (March was actually considered the first month of the Roman year, so April would have been the second). May is named after Maia, the Goddess of increase. June is named after Juno, the sister of Jupiter. July is named after Julius Caesar. August is named after Augustus Caesar. The remaining months were named according to their position in the Roman calendar: *Sept*ember (the seventh month), *Oct*ober (the eighth month), *Nov*ember (the ninth month), and *Dec*ember (the tenth month).

The History
of Advent

The History of Advent

The term *advent* comes from the Latin word *adventus*, which means "coming." In the early Middle Ages, this term came to apply to a period of preparation for Christ's birth, his "coming" into the world, on Christmas day. One of the earliest traditions associated with this season was fasting.

In fifth century France, under the direction of Bishop Perpetuus of Tours (in office from 461-490 AD), Christians fasted between St. Martin's Day (November 11) and Epiphany (January 6).[1] Since this fast, known as St. Martin's Lent, excluded weekends, it added up to approximately 40 days. Thus, it was compared to Christ's time in the desert (Matthew 4:1-2) and the practice of Lent (the 40 days of fasting before Easter).* Though the original fast ended on Epiphany, it eventually culminated on Christmas day (as December 25 rapidly earned prominence among Christians). With time, the practice of fasting spread and came to be specifically associated with a period of preparation for Christmas.

In the sixth century, a more formal season of Advent began to take shape. By sanctioning the practice of fasting and by encouraging churches to devote several Sunday sermons to the subject of Christ's birth, Pope Gregory I (in office from 590-604 AD) has been credited with establishing the first clear form of an Advent season. However, Gregory granted "a certain latitude to the several churches as to the manner of [Advent's] observance."[2] Thus, for the next several centuries, the traditions of individual churches varied widely.

In regard to the length of Advent, by the 10th century, most churches recognized the season to include the four Sundays prior to Christmas Day. If Christmas Eve fell on a Sunday, it was considered the fourth Sunday. Or rather, the first Sunday since "these Sundays were then counted inversely, that is, the nearest to Christmas was called the first Sunday, and so on with the rest."[3]

In regard to the practice of fasting, by the 14th century, the tradition had largely been lost. Pope Urban V (in office from 1362-1370) required only that "all the clerics of his court should keep abstinence during Advent, without in any way including others, either clergy or laity, in this law."[4] Though fasting (an outward expression of penitence and preparation during the Advent season) is no longer formally practiced, customs associated with Advent wreaths have become a popular way to prepare for the "coming" (or Advent) of Jesus on Christmas Day. For more information on the history and traditions of the Advent wreath, see pp. 167-175.

It is also interesting to consider the twofold meaning of *Advent*. Christians celebrate the *coming* of Jesus into the world over 2,000 years ago but also wait expectantly for his *second coming*. After giving his last instructions to the apostles, Jesus ascended into heaven. The Book of Acts records:

> "[The apostles] were looking intently up into the sky as he was going, when suddenly two men dressed in white stood beside them. 'Men of Galilee,' they said, 'why do you stand here looking into the sky? This same Jesus, who has been taken from you into heaven, will come back in the same way you have seen him go into heaven'" (Acts 1:10-11).

The Latin term *adventus* is the translation of the Greek word *parousia*, which is often used in reference to the second coming of Christ. The Gospel of Matthew records Jesus' words about this coming, or parousia, as follows:

"For as lightning that comes from the east is visible even in the west, so will be the *coming* [the Advent] of the Son of Man. . . . all the nations . . . will see the Son of Man coming on the clouds of the sky, with power and great glory. And he will send his angels with a loud trumpet call, and they will gather his elect from the four winds, from one end of the heavens to the other. . . . No one knows about that day or hour, not even the angels in heaven, nor the Son, but only the Father. As it was in the days of Noah, so it will be at the *coming* [the Advent] of the Son of Man. So . . . be ready, because the Son of Man will come at an hour when you do not expect him" (Matthew 24:27-44).

Clearly, Jesus wants his people to be prepared for his return. Though he came first as a servant and a savior, he will come again as a ruler and a judge and will establish an eternal kingdom on a new earth. The Apostle Peter writes, "But in keeping with his promise we are looking forward to a new heaven and a new earth, the home of righteousness" (2 Peter 3:13). May believers "eagerly wait for our Lord Jesus Christ to be revealed" (1 Corinthians 1:7) and be ever ready for his second Advent!

---

[1] Gueranger, Abbot. *The Liturgical Year.* Translated by Laurence Shepherd. James Duffy, 1870, p. 24.

[2] Gueranger, Abbot, p. 28.

[3] Gueranger, Abbot, p. 28.

[4] Gueranger, Abbot, p. 26.

*The following information is drawn from Kelly, Joseph. *The Origins of Christmas*. Liturgical Press, 2004, p. 73-74: Since Easter Sunday developed into a traditional day to baptize new believers, many scholars believe that a pre-baptismal fast formed the basis for Lent. Interestingly, many Christians were also baptized on Epiphany (January 6th) -- a day that is still celebrated among Eastern Christians as the day of Christ's baptism. The pre-Epiphany fast that eventually formed the Advent season probably started as a pre-baptismal fast as well.

The Twelve Days
of Christmas

The Twelve Days of Christmas

The "Twelve Days of Christmas" are the days between Christmas and Epiphany (January 6). *Epiphany* comes from the Greek word "epiphaneia" which means "appearance," "manifestation" or "showing forth." Eastern Christians generally celebrate Epiphany as the day of Jesus' baptism (when Jesus was first revealed as God's Son), and western Christians celebrate it as the day the Wise Men first saw Jesus.

Since modern American celebrations take place between Thanksgiving and Christmas, we have all but lost the history associated with the twelve days of Christmas. In the past, the greatest celebrations of the season happened *after* Christmas. Authors Joe Wheeler and Jim Rosenthal note:

> "It was not so long ago that most everyone in Christian nations celebrated the twelve days following Christmas Day. Today, so many have ceased to observe these days that people lift their eyebrows in puzzlement when Shakespeare's *Twelfth Night* play is discussed or 'The Twelve Days of Christmas' is sung."[1]

A common misconception is that the twelve days of Christmas are the days *before* Christmas when they are actually the days *after* Christmas. Furthermore, the notion of the twelve days of Christmas is known to many Americans only by the popular carol of the same name. Ironically, though the importance of the actual twelve days of Christmas has been lost, the song has been infused with significant spiritual meaning that did not originally exist. There are widely circulated claims that the "true love" of the song refers to God and that each verse represents a point of Christian doctrine as follows:

1 Partridge in a Pear Tree (Jesus)
2 Turtle Doves (The Old and New Testaments)
3 French Hens (Faith, Hope and Love)
4 Calling Birds (The Four Gospels or the Four Evangelists)
5 Golden Rings (The First Five Books of the Old Testament, the "Pentateuch")
6 Geese A-Laying (The Six Days of Creation)
7 Swans A-Swimming (The Seven Gifts of the Spirit or the Seven Sacraments)
8 Maids A-Milking (The Eight Beatitudes)
9 Ladies Dancing (The Nine Fruits of the Spirit)
10 Lords A-Leaping (The Ten Commandments)
11 Pipers Piping (The Eleven Faithful Apostles)
12 Drummers Drumming (The Twelve Points of Doctrine in the Apostles Creed)

The idea that the carol was written with intentional Christian symbolism is probably a confusion of the song with another similar title, "In Those Twelve Days." The first four verses (out of 12 total) are as follows:

"What is that which is but one?
We have but one God alone
In heaven above sits on his throne.

"What are they which are but two?
Two Testaments, as we are told
The one is New, the other Old

"What are they which are but three?
Three persons of the Trinity,
The Father, Son and Ghost Holy.

"What are they which are but four?
Four Gospels written true,
John, Luke, Mark and Matthew."[2]

Verses 1, 2, 4, 8, and 10 of "In Those Twelve Days" share the same meaning as the supposed hidden message of "The Twelve Days of Christmas." But the fact is that "The Twelve Days of Christmas" probably had little relevance to the Christian significance of the celebration other than its association with a game played on Twelfth Night (January 5, the night before Epiphany). According to *The New Oxford Book of Carols*:

"This song derives from a traditional forfeits game which was played on Twelfth Night (hence the twelve days). Each player would have to remember and recite the objects named by the previous players and then add one more. [If a line was missed or confused, a forfeit would have to be paid.] The game was probably universal, but the song seems to be of Gallic origin."[3]

But the carol may not be entirely frivolous. According to Hennig Cohen and Tristram Potter, editors of *The Folklore of American Holidays*, "The Twelve Days of Christmas" contains a "charming example of medieval numerological wit."[4] Here is how it works:

"On the first day the true love gave one gift (a partridge in a pear tree), on the second day he gave three gifts (two turtle doves and a partridge in a pear tree), etc., so that on the twelfth day he gave seventy-eight fanciful gifts. . . . [In the end] that lady has received exactly 364 gifts – enough to last until next Christmas. A modern might ask, 'What about the 365th day?'; but I am sure that to the medieval mind there was no need for a gift from a mortal giver on Christmas Day itself."[5]

Truly, the greatest gift ever given to man was that of Jesus who came to earth on Christmas day. Yet, the days leading up to Epiphany are significant as well. For, through his appearance to the Wise Men, as well as through his baptism, Jesus revealed himself as the true King and Son of God who would ultimately bring "salvation to the ends of the earth" (Isaiah 49:6).

---

[1] Wheeler, Joe and Rosenthal, Jim, *St. Nicholas, A Closer Look at Christmas*. Thomas Nelson, 2005, p. 267.

[2] Keyte, Hugh and Parrott, Andrew, Editors. *The New Oxford Book of Carols*. Oxford University Press, 1992, p. 473.

[3] Keyte, Hugh and Parrott, Andrew, Editors. *The New Oxford Book of Carols*. Oxford University Press, 1992, p. 469.

[4] Cohen, Hennig and Coffin, Tristram Potter, Editors. *The Folklore of American Holidays, First Edition*. Gale Research Company, p. 402.

[5] Cohen, Hennig and Coffin, Tristram Potter, Editors.

Christmas
in America

Christmas in America

Throughout the course of the Middle Ages, Christmas was wholly supported by the Church and was thus celebrated festively around the world. It survived well through the Reformation and did not become a subject of controversy until the 17th century in England. At this point in history, the Christmas season had evolved into a time of excessive drinking and rioting which disturbed many Christians, particularly the Puritans. Of course, attitudes varied widely about how Christmas should be celebrated, and these conflicting views made their way to early American colonies. Though difficult times prevented indulgent celebrations for any of the initial settlers, some distinct differences arose between the early Northern and Southern colonies.

In the South, America's first clearly recorded Christmas was at Jamestown, Va., in 1607 (if we exclude a celebration in 1604 by French settlers when they unsuccessfully tried to establish a colony on St. Croix Island off the coast of Maine).[1] The Jamestown settlers departed from England on Dec. 19, 1606 and spent their first Christmas together on board their ship. Unfortunately, due to "unprosperous winds," the ship was "kept six weeks in the sight of England."[2] Many of the men were sea sick, but they made the best cheer they could. Little did they know that their first Christmas in America would prove to be much more difficult.

Jamestown was founded on May 13, 1607, but by Christmas of that year, only about 40 of the original 100 settlers had survived. Captain John Smith, their leader, was absent. He had undertaken the dangerous mission of securing food from the Native Americans. Thus, the first official Christmas on American soil was a solemn one commemorated in a simple wooden chapel.

Fortunately, after many trying years, conditions improved, and by 1624, Smith recorded:

> "The extreme winde, rayne, frost and snow caused us to keep Christmas among the savages where we were never more merry, not fed on more plenty of good Oysters, Fish, Flesh, Wilde Fowl and good bread, nor never had better fires in England."[3]

With time, as Jamestown and other newly established Southern colonies became prosperous, they developed a reputation for festive, hospitable and even lavishly decorated Christmas celebrations.

Compared to the South, New Englanders had quite a different view of Christmas. Many of these colonists had been appalled by the behavior (drunkenness, rioting, etc.) demonstrated during the Christmas season in their native England. From the time these Pilgrims arrived at Plymouth Rock and set foot in the New World in 1620, it appears that Christmas was essentially ignored.

William Bradford, governor of the Plymouth Colony, recorded how he had called his citizens out to work on Christmas of 1621, as was his custom. Some men who had recently arrived to the colony told Bradford that it was "against their consciences" to work on Christmas day. The governor said he would "spare them till they were better informed," but when he returned at noon, he found the men playing sports in the street. Here is what the governor recorded (he speaks in the third person as a historian):

> "So he went to them and tooke away their implements, and tould them that was against his conscience [notice how he uses their own words against them!], that they should play and others worke. If they made the keeping of it mater of devotion, let them kepe their houses, but ther should be no gameing or revelling in the streets. Since which time nothing hath been attempted that way, at least openly."[4]

Several years later, the "ban" on Christmas actually made it into the law books of the Massachusetts Bay Colony. For over 20 years (1659-1681), anyone caught celebrating Christmas was subject to fines. The law read as follows:

> "For preventing disorders, arising in several places within this jurisdiction by reason of some still observing such festivals as were superstitiously kept in other communities, to the great dishonor of God and offense of others: it is therefore ordered by this court and the authority thereof that whosoever shall be found observing any such day as Christmas or the like, either by forbearing of labor, feasting, or any other way, upon any such account as aforesaid, every such person so offending shall pay for every such offence five shilling as a fine to the county."[5]

Even after the ban was lifted, animosity toward Christmas celebrations remained among colonists for many more years. Sadly, much of the bad behavior that early New Englanders tried to prevent showed up anyway. However, good traditions made their way to our young nation as well. Immigrants from all over Europe were coming to America with long held Christmas traditions. In Germany, for example, Christmas had evolved into a time for family, giving and worship. Americans began to embrace such traditions, and the American Christmas started to take shape.

It was not until 1822 that Clement Clarke Moore, a minister and educator, reportedly wrote the poem now known as "'Twas The Night Before Christmas" (for the poem, its history and the dispute of its authorship, see p. 431). This poem is credited with popularizing St. Nicholas and making children an important part of Christmas. Furthermore, in 1843 Charles Dickens published the classic story *A Christmas Carol* which helped to solidify the perception of Christmas as a time of giving and hope (for an excerpt from this classic, see p. 313).

It is not surprising that the first three states to declare December 25 a legal holiday were Southern states: Louisiana (1831), Arkansas (1831) and Alabama (1836).[6] Other states would follow and by 1870, Christmas was declared a U.S. Federal holiday. At present, American Christians have, for the most part, returned to the ancient view as articulated by the respected theologian Augustine (354-430 AD): "So then, let us celebrate the birthday of the Lord with all due festive gatherings."[7] Surely it is good when Christians appropriately celebrate the birth of the one for whom they exist — Jesus Christ!

---

[1] Hatch, Jane M. *The American Book of Days.* H.W. Wilson Company, 1978, p. 1145.

[2] Barbour, Philip L., editor. *The Complete Works of Captain John Smith (1580-1631),* Volume I. University of North Carolina Press, 1986, p. 204.

[3] Smith, John. Contributor: John Milliken Thompson. *The Journals of Captain John Smith: A Jamestown Biography.* National Geographic Society, 2007, p. 114.

[4] Bradford, William. *Bradford's History of Plymouth Plantation, 1606-1646.* Edited by William T. Davis. Barnes & Noble Inc., 1908, pp. 126-127.

[5] Massachusetts Bay Colony. From the records of the General Court, May 11, 1659. Retrieved August 6, 2008 from *Massachusetts Travel Journal*: http://masstraveljournal.com/features/1101chrisban.html.

[6] Hatch, Jane M., p. 1146.

[7] Witvliet, John D. and Vroege, David. *Proclaiming the Christmas Gospel, Ancient Sermons and Hymns for Contemporary Christian Inspiration.* Sermon by St. Augustine, Baker Books, 2004, p. 31.

IMAGES OF CHRISTMAS

Angels

The term *angel* literally means "messenger," and it is in this prominent role that angels take part in the Christmas story. The angel who appeared to Zechariah (to announce the birth of John the Baptist) and to Mary (to announce the birth of Jesus) is identified by name as Gabriel. He said to Zechariah, "I am Gabriel. I stand in the presence of God, and I have been sent to speak to you and to tell you this good news" (Luke 1:19). Tradition holds that Gabriel is God's lead messenger angel and that it was he who appeared to Joseph and the shepherds in the Christmas story. Interestingly, Gabriel also appeared to the prophet Daniel more than 500 years before the birth of Jesus to outline the specific time in history that Christ, the Anointed One, would come (Daniel 9:20-27). See this prophecy addressed on p. 18.

In Matthew's account of the Christmas story, an angel appeared to Joseph in dreams on at least three different occasions to deliver messages. The first time, the angel said to Joseph, "Do not be afraid to take Mary home as your wife, because what is conceived in her is from the Holy Spirit. She will give birth to a son, and you are to give him the name Jesus [meaning "God saves"], because he will save his people from their sins" (Matthew 1:20-21). Then, after Jesus was born, the angel appeared again to tell Joseph to "take the child and his mother and escape to Egypt. Stay there until I tell you, for Herod is going to search for the child to kill him" (Matthew 2:13). After a time in Egypt, Joseph received his third visit by the angel, who told him to "take the child and his mother and go to the land of Israel, for those who were trying to take the child's life are dead" (Matthew 2:20).

In Luke's account of the Christmas story, an angel appeared to shepherds, saying, "Do not be afraid. I bring you good news of great joy that will be for all the people. Today in the town of David a Savior has been born to you; he is Christ the Lord" (Luke 2:10-11). This angel was then joined by a "great company of heavenly host" praising God (Luke 2:13). Surely, angels played a significant role in the Christmas story.

The Power of Angels

Understandably, images of angels have become a familiar symbol of Christmas. However, contrary to their depiction as gentle feminine creatures that top Christmas trees and hover over Nativity scenes, the Bible reveals angels as persons of tremendous strength. Psalm 103:20 refers to them as the "mighty ones" who do God's bidding. Consider the following . . .

(1) Angels have the power to make men blind or dumb.

Angels struck the men of Sodom with blindness.
"Then they (2 angels) struck the men who were at the door of the house, young and old, with blindness so that they could not find the door" (Genesis 19:10).

The angel Gabriel struck Zechariah dumb.

"And now you will be silent and not able to speak until the day this happens (the birth of John the Baptist), because you did not believe my words, which will come true at their proper time." (Luke 1:19-20).

(2) A single angel has the power to drive out masses of people from their land.

"Then the Lord said to Moses, 'Leave this place, you and the people you brought up out of Egypt, and go up to the land I promised on oath to Abraham, Isaac and Jacob, saying, 'I will give it to your descendants.' I will send an angel before you and drive out the Canaanites, Amorites, Hittites, Perizzites, Hivites, and Jebusites'" (Exodus 33:1-2).

(3) A single angel has the power to kill thousands of people.

A single angel killed 70,000 people with a plague.

"So the Lord sent a plague on Israel from that morning until the end of the time designated, and seventy thousand of the people from Dan to Beersheba died. When the angel stretched out his hand to destroy Jerusalem, the Lord was grieved because of the calamity and said to the angel who was afflicting the people, 'Enough! Withdraw your hand.' The angel of the Lord was then at the threshing floor of Araunah the Jebusite" (2 Samuel 24:15-16).

A single angel killed 185,000 Assyrian soldiers in one night.

"Therefore this is what the Lord says concerning the king of Assyria: 'He will not enter this city or shoot an arrow here. He will not come before it with shield or build a siege ramp against it. By the way that he came he will return; he will not enter this city,' declares the Lord. 'I will defend this city and save it, for my sake and for the sake of David my servant.' That night the angel of the Lord went out and put to death a hundred and eighty-five thousand men in the Assyrian camp. When the people got up the next morning—there were all the dead bodies!" (2 Kings 19:32-35).

In one account, an angel is described as "standing in the road with a drawn sword in his hand" (Numbers 22:23). In another account, the eyes of Elisha's servant were opened to see "horses and chariots of fire all around Elisha" (2 Kings 6:17) to protect him; most scholars believe that angels drove these chariots.

The strength of angels may sound terrifying, but it is great news for believers. After all, the holy angels follow the commands of a God who loves his people. The Bible says:

"If you make the Most High your dwelling — even the Lord, who is my refuge — then no harm will befall you, no disaster will come near your tent. For he will command his angels concerning you to guard you in all your ways; they will lift you up in their hands, so that you will not strike your foot against a stone" (Psalm 91:9-12).

The book of Genesis records how angels "grasped the hands" of God's chosen people (Lot and his family) to lead them away from destruction — in this case, the destruction of Sodom and Gomorrah (Genesis 19:16).

Be encouraged (consider the meaning of this word — endowed with courage) by the fact that angels, who are entrusted with so much power, protect those that love the Lord. Hebrews 1:14 asks, "Are not all angels ministering spirits sent to serve those who will inherit salvation?"

When speaking about children, Jesus said, "Their angels in heaven always see the face of my Father in heaven" (Matt 18:10). Though a belief in guardian angels was already prevalent among the Jews at this time, Jesus' words are often cited as confirmation of the concept. The Bible implies that angels have assignments not only to people, but to churches (Rev 1:20), nations (Daniel 10:13;12:1) and perhaps even nature (Revelation 7:1 speaks of four angels "holding back the four winds of the earth" and Revelation 16:5 speaks of "the angel in charge of the waters").

Thankfully, the powerful angels of heaven do the bidding of a God who loves his people, and they do not act in their own interest (as do the demons of hell). Though demons got their start as angels in heaven, they "did not keep their positions of authority but abandoned their own home" (Jude 6). Interestingly, an ancient Jewish tradition teaches that these angels rebelled against God when they learned of his plan to create man. They wanted no part in serving a species that was "lower" than them. A Christian version of this tradition is explained by philosopher Peter Kreeft:

> "God revealed to the angels his plan not only to create man but to incarnate himself in man, in Jesus. Satan and the other 'dignified' angels refused to accept this 'undignified' plan and bow to a God of flesh and blood. In [both] versions, the first sin [of the fallen angels] is pride, *Non serviam*, 'I will not serve.'"[1]

Revelation chapter 12 portrays an interesting picture of events in heaven. The Apostle John witnesses a pregnant woman who is about to give birth (presumably the virgin Mary). Then John sees an enormous dragon (Satan) whose tail sweeps a third of the stars out of the sky and flings them to the earth (an allusion to a third of the angels that fell from heaven). Satan is then hurled down to the earth "to make war against the rest of [the woman's] offspring – those who obey God's command-ments and hold to the testimony of Jesus" (Revelation 12:17).

Remember that heaven is not limited to chronological time as we know it. It appears that as a result of God revealing his "future" plan to the angels, many of them chose to abandon heaven. These demons have sought to destroy mankind ever since.

It is difficult to know what level of power demons are able to exercise on earth, but there are two points worth noting: (1) If demons make up only one-third of God's original angels, then there are two times as many good guys! And, (2) Satan, their leader, is not the opposite of God. He was created by God, and so his power will never rival that of the Lord. Author C. S. Lewis wrote the following:

> "There is no uncreated being except God. God has no opposite. No being could attain a 'perfect badness' opposite to the perfect goodness of God. . . . Devil is the opposite of angel only as Bad Man is the opposite of Good Man. Satan, the leader or dictator of devils, is the opposite, not of God, but of Michael."[2]

If Michael, the archangel, is indeed Satan's "opposite," be comforted by Revelation 12:7-9; it records a battle in which Satan and his angels "were not strong enough" for Michael and his angels. More importantly, be encouraged by the fact that Satan's power is no match for God's!

The Appearance of Angels

Several references in the Bible imply that angels in their natural state are spiritual beings and do not have physical or material bodies. This does not mean that they are without "form." Humans simply don't have the eyes to see their spiritual bodies. Thus, on several occasions, angels have assumed a physical body in order to communicate with men. These appearances range from breathtakingly glorious to ordinary.

The prophet Daniel offers one of the more detailed descriptions of a glorious appearance:

> "I looked up and there before me was a man dressed in linen, with a belt of the finest gold around his waist. His body was like chrysolite [a green colored mineral], his face like lightning, his eyes like flaming torches, his arms and legs like the gleam of burnished bronze, and his voice like the sound of a multitude" (Daniel 10:5-6).*

The Bible describes angels as dressing in white (John 20:12), their clothes gleaming like lightning (Luke 24:4), and wearing clean, shining linen with gold sashes around their chest (Rev 15:6). Though Daniel records that the angel Gabriel came to him in swift flight (Daniel 9:21), he does not describe him as having wings. The only classes of angels clearly described as having wings are the Seraphim (Isaiah 6:2) and the Cheribum (Exodus 25:20), two classes of angels that seem to guard and/or attend the throne of God. Regardless, wings have become a standard feature in our depiction of angels; perhaps they are simply a creative way to depict the speed by which angels travel. Similarly, halos are an artistic way to portray the "gleam" of angels and trumpets are a natural way to illustrate the heralding of important events (an activity which often involves angels).

The sight of angels in their glorious state must have been overwhelming. On seeing Gabriel, Daniel says that he was "terrified and fell prostrate" (Daniel 8:17). When Zechariah saw Gabriel, he was "startled and was gripped with fear" (Luke 1:12). Gabriel had to tell Mary not to be afraid (Luke 1:30).

In perhaps a less glorious state, three men appeared to Abraham in chapter 18 of Genesis. Two of the men were called angels (Genesis 19:1) and one was the Lord himself (Genesis 18:22). It should be noted that there are several instances in the Old Testament (prior to the birth of Jesus) in which God took on a temporary human form; in many of these cases, he was called the "angel of the Lord." Often we must rely on his words or actions to reveal his deity. The theological term for the appearances of God in human form is a *theophany*. Though the book of Genesis does not record anything stunning about the appearance of the three men, Abraham's response to them implies that he believed them to be very special visitors: he rushes to meet them, he bows low before them, he offers them water, rest and a generous meal.

Of all the recorded angelic appearances in the Bible, the most fascinating may be the most ordinary — so ordinary that humans do not even realize they have been visited by an angel. The Bible says, "Do not forget to entertain strangers, for by so doing some people have entertained angels without knowing it" (Hebrews 13:2).

The Actions of Angels

Though most people have not witnessed (or may not know that they have witnessed) an angel in physical form, angels most certainly serve as witnesses to human lives. It is possible that they are the ones who record the prayers and conversations of believers. The Bible says:

"Then those who feared the Lord talked with each other, and the Lord listened and heard. A scroll of remembrance was written in his presence concerning those who feared the Lord and honored his name" (Malachi 3:16).

Paul charges Timothy in the sight of God, Jesus and angels to follow his instructions (1 Tim 5:21). Paul also says that "because of the angels" Christians should have propriety in worship (1 Corinthians 11:10). Perhaps angels serve not only as witnesses to worship but as unseen participants.

It was angels that put God's law into effect (Acts 7:53; Gal 3:19), and it is angels that witness, along with the Lord, whether people follow it. Though they witness human sin, they do not desire to accuse men. The Bible says, "There is rejoicing in the presence of the angels of God over one sinner who repents" (Luke 15:10). How amazing that angels care about human salvation!

Furthermore, angels actively help humans in times of need: An angel brought food and water to Elijah in the desert when he was fleeing for his life (1 Kings 19:5-6); an angel came to the aid of Shadrach, Meshach and Abednego when they were thrown in a furnace (Daniel 3:24-28); an angel protected Daniel in the lion's den (Daniel 6:19-23); an angel opened the door of a jail to free Peter and other apostles (Acts 5:19); an angel appeared to Paul while stranded at sea to assure him of his safety (Acts 27:23-24). Even Jesus accepted the help of angels during his life on earth: Angels attended him after his 40-day fast and temptation (Matt 4:11), and an angel appeared to him and strengthened him right before his arrest and death (Luke 22:43). Over the centuries, innumerable stories recount how angels have helped believers. Some tell of "strangers" coming to the aid of believers in times of crises and disappearing without a trace. Others tell how unbelievers witness "strong men" at the side of the Christian whom they intended to harm.

We cannot know the extent to which angels protect us from harm on earth. However, there will come a time when our lives on earth must end, and most likely, angels will continue to play a role in our lives after death. Angels may, in fact, usher us into heaven when we die. Though told in the form of a parable, Jesus might have offered insight into life after death when he said, "The time came when the beggar died and the angels carried him to Abraham's side . . ." (Luke 16:22). How wonderful to be greeted when we die by angels who have watched over our lives, know us, care for us and escort us into the presence of the King of Kings.

At some point after death, "we will all stand before God's judgment seat" (Romans 14:10). It appears that angels will serve as witnesses during this time. Jesus said, "Whoever acknowledges me before men, the Son of Man will also acknowledge him before the angels of God" (Luke 12:8). After this judgment, heaven and earth will be made new. Peter wrote, "But in keeping with his promise we are looking forward to a new heaven and a new earth, the home of righteousness" (2 Peter 3:13). We will have new bodies on this new earth (see 1 Corinthians 15:35-58), and though in some way these bodies may resemble angels, we will not become angels. Perhaps a benefit of our new bodies on the new earth will be that we have eyes to see heaven. Perhaps the stairway between heaven and earth on which Jacob saw angels ascending and descending in his dream (Genesis 28:12) is something we will all see. Though we will not be angels ourselves, we will likely have the opportunity to freely interact with angels and even build friendships with them in eternity!

Angels and Jesus

It was "a great company of the heavenly host" (Luke 2:13) that heralded the birth of Christ. Imagine the wonder these angels must have felt at watching the Creator of the Universe descend to earth as a helpless baby. Though Jesus was superior to the angels, he was made "a little lower than the angels" (Hebrews 2:7), like mankind, for the sake of humanity. Imagine knowing the true identity of Christ and yet witnessing his most humble birth and his most ordinary Jewish upbringing. As Jesus grew into a man and began his ministry, the angels witnessed men hurling insults at, and ultimately crucifying, the author of life and salvation. Apparently, the work of Christ on earth was a mystery to the angels. When speaking of grace and salvation, the Bible says, "Even angels long to look into these things" (1 Peter 1:12). May our amazement surpass that of the angels, for we, unlike angels, are the recipients of this grace and salvation!

---

[1] Kreeft, Peter. *Angels (and Demons), What Do We Really Know About Them?* Ignatius Press, 1995, p. 119.

[2] Lewis, C.S. *The Screwtape Letters: With Screwtape Proposes a Toast.* Harper Collins, 1996, Preface.

*Some scholars believe that this was an instance of a theophany in which God himself took on temporary human form.

Bells

F or several centuries, bells have played a significant role throughout the Western world. For any given community, a bell was often the main form of communication and the only means of gathering the people of a village together quickly. In the days before watches were affordable, people relied on the toll of a bell to indicate the time of day. In fact, the word *clock* comes from the medieval Latin word *clocca*, which means "bell."

Today, bells have come to be strongly associated with churches and their respective religious functions. However, there are a variety of interesting ways that bells were used prior to the existence of the Christian Church.

Bells in Ancient Times

Though bells are often associated with Christianity and the West, their origin is much more ancient. The Catholic Encyclopedia records:

"That bells, at any rate hand-bells of relatively small size, were familiar to all the chief nations of antiquity is a fact beyond dispute. The archaeological evidence for this conclusion has been collected in the monograph of Abbé Morillot and is quite overwhelming. Specimens are still preserved of the bells used in ancient Babylonia and in Egypt, as well as by the Romans and Greeks, while the bell undoubtedly figured no less prominently in such independent civilizations as those of China and Hindustan."[1]

The use of bells is also found in the Old Testament of the Bible. Over 1,400 years before Jesus, Jewish priests were instructed to wear gold bells around the hem of their robe. The Bible taught that "the sound of the bells will be heard when he [the priest] enters the Holy Place before the Lord and when he comes out, so that he will not die" (Exodus 28:35). The Encyclopedia of Biblical Literature records:

"The sound of bells manifested that [the priest] was properly arrayed in the robes of ceremony which he was required to wear when he entered the presence-chamber of the Great King; and that as no minister can enter the presence of an earthly potentate abruptly and unannounced, so he (whom no human being *could* introduce) was to have his entrance harbingered by the sound of the bells he wore."[2]

It should be noted that the obstacle to freely approaching God is quite distinct from any obstacle to approaching an earthly ruler. Namely, it is sin that hinders people from freely approaching the Heavenly King. Furthermore, sin is so devastating and so pervasive among all humanity that even a priest would die should he fail to properly announce his presence, more specifically the presence of sin.

Thus, no person could freely approach God, because no person was without sin. No person, that is, until Jesus. He has become the eternal high priest who approaches God on behalf of mankind and who need not make any announcement of sin:

"Therefore, since we have a great high priest who has gone through the heavens, Jesus the Son of God, let us hold firmly to the faith we profess. For we do not have a high priest who is unable to sympathize with our weaknesses, but we have one who has been tempted in every way, just as we are—yet was <u>without sin</u>. Let us then approach the throne of grace with confidence, so that we may receive mercy and find grace to help us in our time of need" (Hebrews 4:14-16).

Christ became a mediator so that Christians could freely approach the throne of God. The presence of sin no longer needs to be announced by ringing bells. Jesus did "away with sin by the sacrifice of himself" (Hebrews 9:26), and as a result, believers have been declared holy. The Bible teaches that if you put your trust in Jesus, "you are a chosen people, a royal priesthood, a holy nation, a people belonging to God, that you may declare the praises of him who called you out of darkness into his wonderful light" (1 Peter 2:9).

Though the bells of Old Testament times announced the presence of sin, the bells of the New Testament Church announce freedom from sin. It is because Jesus came into the world to offer himself as the ultimate sacrifice for sin that "freedom rings."

Another mention of bells in the Bible came nearly 500 years before Jesus. Zechariah spoke of a day when Jerusalem would be secure and that God would strike the nations that fought against it (Zechariah 14:11-12). He wrote, "On that day HOLY TO THE LORD will be inscribed on the bells of the horses" (Zechariah 14:20). According to a commentary by John Gill, bells were used to train horses for war.

"Therefore they hung bells to their bridles, to [get them used to] noise, and to try if they could bear a noise, and the tumult of war, so as not to throw their riders, or expose them to danger; hence one that has not been tried or trained up to anything is called by the Greeks ακωδώνιστον [transliterated akodoniston], one not used to the noise of a bell, by a metaphor taken from horses, that have never been tried by the sound of bells."[3]

Zechariah foretold of a time of peace when the bells on horses would no longer be needed for the purpose of war. Thus, they were to be dedicated to the Lord. The sound of bells would no longer invoke thoughts of war but rather of joy and celebration in a time of peace. Similarly, the "jingle bells" and the "sleigh bells" that are associated with Christmas today have come to symbolize a time of joy.

It should be noted that the Hebrew word *mets-il-law* used for the bells on horses is also translated "rattle" or "tinkler." It is different than the Hebrew word *pah-am-one* used for the "bells" on the robe of the priests.[4] Interestingly, scholars now classify jingle bells and sleigh bells as "rattles" rather than bells. Surely, a spherical vessel with loose pellets is quite distinct from a church bell. Regardless, just as the rattle of horse bells signified a time of peace in Zechariah's day, modern "jingle bells" and "sleigh bells" serve as a reminder to worship the God who brought peace and joy to the world by giving his son Jesus Christ!

Bells in Churches

It appears that bells came to Europe by way of Irish Christian missionaries in the Middle Ages. In Celtic lands, bells were regarded with great veneration. They were carried into battles and solemn oaths were made upon them. The Catholic Encyclopedia records that "even though the earlier specimens are nothing but rude cow-bells, wedge-shape in form and made of iron plate bent and roughly riveted, still they were often enclosed at a later daye in cases or 'shrines' of the richest workmanship."[5]

Perhaps the most famous of bells in Ireland is that of St. Patrick (approximately 378-493 AD): the *clog-an-edachta* or "bell-of-the-will." Patrick, the first missionary to establish Christianity in Ireland, quite possibly used this bell to gather the Irish people together for the preaching and teaching of God's Word. Thus, the bell came to be associated with God's work in Ireland and to symbolize something sacred.

As Irish missionaries likely made the same use of bells as Patrick, the rest of the Western world would soon attach an equivalent religious significance to them. Prior to the influence of these Irish missionaries, it appears that Christians used a variety of other methods to gather together – gongs, trumpets, or drums. However, the Irish bell would eventually prevail in the Western world, and its shape would follow the same evolution as the bells in Ireland "passing from the small cow-bell of riveted iron to the cast bronze instrument of considerable size with which we are now familiar."[6]

By the eighth century, bells came to be viewed as an essential part of the church. At the same time, the craft of bronze casting grew considerably. Encyclopedia Britannica records that "although bronze casting was practiced in pre-Christian Europe, it was not resumed to any extent until the 8th century."[7] Concurrently, bell turrets were built, bells increased in size, and many churches had claim to two or more bells.

The ringing of church bells often signaled the time, and many communities depended on the bells in order to attend weddings, funerals or other services at the proper hour. In some cases, the sequence of tones and the number of bells rung could indicate several details about a service or feast that was about to commence. Additionally, bells were used within the church to indicate different parts of the service. This was particularly useful for parishioners who did not understand Latin (at a time when many church services were conducted exclusively in Latin). Most importantly, bells helped to identify when the sacrifice of the Eucharist was about to take place. Just like the bells on the garment of the Jewish priest would ring as he was about to enter the Holy and Holies and offer a sacrifice (Exodus 28:35), the bells in Christian Churches would ring as the priest prepared to offer the Eucharistic Sacrifice (the bread and wine of which Christians partake in remembrance of the body and blood of Jesus).

In summary, bells were used to communicate significant messages. A popular inscription found on bells reads as follows:

"I praise the true God, I call the people, I assemble the clergy;
I bewail the dead, I dispense storm clouds, I do honor to feasts."[8]

These verses, which have been attributed to monks, describe the many roles of a bell. The idea that a bell could "disperse storm clouds" reveals that Christians may have so deeply associated bells with the work of God that they assigned supernatural powers to them. In his poem "The Golden Legend," Henry Wadsworth Longfellow (1807-1882), the great American poet, portrays Lucifer (Satan) encouraging his demons to throw down a church bell:

"[Lucifer says,] Lower! lower!
Hover downward!
Seize the loud, vociferous bells, and
Clashing, clanging, to the pavement
Hurl them from their windy tower!

"[Demon voices reply,] All thy thunders
Here are harmless!
For these bells have been anointed,
And baptized with holy water!
They defy our utmost power."[9]

Longfellow portrays bells as such an important symbol of Christianity that Satan is determined to destroy them. How their ringing must frustrate him!

In regard to bells doing honor to feasts, the Catholic Encyclopedia records, "It became in time a recognized principle that the *classicum*, the clash of several bells ringing at once, constituted an element of joy and solemnity befitting great feasts."[10] Thus came the association with Christmas. Of all the Christian feasts, Christmas marks one of the most joyous celebrations. It is a time to recognize the great gift that God gave to the world, his son Jesus!

---

[1] Thurston, Herbert. "Bells." Catholic Encyclopedia. Robert Appleton Company, 1907. Retrieved July 20, 2008 from New Advent: http://www.newadvent.org/cathen/02418b.htm [2] Kitto, John and Alexander, William Lindsay, editors. The Encyclopedia of Biblical Literature, Volume 1. "Bell." Kessinger Publishing, 2003, p. 332.

[3] Gill, John. *The New John Gill Exposition of the Entire Bible (Commentary on Zech. 14:20).* Retrieved July 20, 2008 from Studylight: http://www.studylight.org/com/geb/view.cgi?book=zec&chapter=014&verse=02.

[4] Strong, James. *The New Strong's Exhaustive Concordance of the Bible.* Thomas Nelson Publishers, 1984, p. 123 (Hebrew Dictionary Reference Numbers 6472 and 4698).

[5] Encyclopedia Britannica. "Bell." Retrieved July 20, 2008 from Encyclopedia Britannica Online: http://www.britannica.com/EBchecked/topic/59546/bell.

[6] Thurston, Herbert.

[7] Encyclopedia Britannica.

[8] Thurston, Herbert.

[9] Longfellow, Henry Wadsworth. *The Poetical Works of Henry Wadsworth Longfellow.* Houghton, Mifflin and Company, 1886, pp. 139-140.

[10] Thurston, Herbert.

Candy Canes

The traditional Christmas candy cane is white with red stripes and flavored with peppermint. Though several accounts make their claim to be the "true story" of the origin of the candy cane, history reveals that, most likely, it took several centuries and the contributions of several countries for the candy cane to evolve into its current form.

The Shape

In their early form, candy canes began as plain white sticks. Though their origin is unknown, it appears that they were popular throughout Europe by the 17th century. The most widely recognized account of how the sticks came to be formed into canes credits the change to a German choirmaster. In 1670, the Cologne Cathedral in Germany hosted a living Nativity scene for its Christmas celebration. The choirmaster had great difficulty keeping the children of the choir in order, so he got creative.[1] Plain white candy sticks were popular with the children, and the choirmaster believed that if they were kept busy licking candy, they wouldn't chatter so much. But the choirmaster wanted more than just keeping the children quiet. He wanted them to learn something of the significance of the Nativity, so he appealed to a local candy maker to bend the sticks in the form of shepherd's staffs.

Legend holds that the choirmaster used his ingenious design to encourage the children to watch how the shepherds of the Nativity used their canes to direct the live animals. More importantly, the choirmaster could instruct the children to consider how Jesus became the "Good Shepherd" (John 10:11) who led his people (the sheep) and saved them from harm.

The shape and purpose of the shepherd's cane is significant. The design is meant to literally hook sheep by the neck in order to lead them to better nourishment (pastures, water, etc.) or to rescue them from harm. For nervous and fearful sheep, the sight of the shepherd's staff is a great comfort. Surely that is why the psalmist David could say to the Lord his shepherd, "I will fear no evil, for you are with me; your rod and your staff, they comfort me" (Psalm 23:4b).

The choirmaster's idea became so popular that the practice of passing out candy canes at living Nativity scenes spread throughout Europe. They could be used not only as a teaching tool, but to serve another practical purpose — their shape made them an ideal decoration to easily hang on a Christmas tree.

The Color

Reportedly, peppermint candies with red stripes first appeared in the Swedish town of Granna (known as the peppermint candy capital of the world) in the mid-19th century. Granna may well have influenced the addition of red stripes to candy canes by the early 20th century. Prior to this time, Christmas cards in both Europe and America portrayed plain white canes. However, by the early 20th century, candy canes began to appear on Christmas cards with their familiar red stripes.

In the 1920's, Bob McCormick, a Georgia confectioner, was credited with being the first American to distribute candy canes in large quantities. However, production was limited by the fact that the decorative striping of the candy cane had to be done by hand. Fortunately, by the 1950s, Bob's brother-in-law, a catholic priest named Gregory Keller, invented a machine to create the striping. Candy canes could then be made and distributed en masse. With time, "Bob's Candies" became the world's leading candy cane producer.[2]

Other popular stories credit American confectioners with actually inventing the candy cane. Although historical evidence conflicts with these claims,[3] it is possible that an American was the first to infuse the candy cane with extensive Christian symbolism.

The Symbolism

Beyond its shape, the candy cane does not appear to have been designed with any intentional Christian symbolism. Regardless, it has proven to be a useful teaching tool. It seems appropriate to use it as such, particularly if its original form was meant to teach children about Christ, the Good Shepherd. Below is a list of the symbolic meanings most often assigned to the candy cane:

Hard Candy: It is a reminder that Jesus is the Rock.

> "He alone is my rock and my salvation; he is my fortress, I will never be shaken" (Psalm 61:2).

Cane Shape: It is a reminder of the shepherd's staff. Consider the shepherds that came to worship Jesus at his birth, and think of how Jesus came to the world to be a shepherd of his people.

> Jesus said, "I am the good shepherd" (John 10:11).

The Letter "J" Shape: It is a reminder of the name of Jesus.

> "She will give birth to a son, and you are to give him the name Jesus [meaning "God saves"], because he will save his people from their sins" (Matthew 1:21).

Peppermint Flavor: It is a reminder of the gift of spices from the Wise Men.

> "They opened their gifts and presented him with gifts of gold and of incense and of myrrh" (Matthew 2:11).

White Candy: It is a reminder of purity and holiness. Consider the virgin birth of Christ, the sinless life of Christ and the holy life that Jesus wants his people to live.

"But just as he who called you is holy, so be holy in all you do" (1 Peter 1:15).

The Color Red: It is a reminder that Jesus became flesh and blood and spilled his blood to save his people.

"Since the children have flesh and blood, he too shared in their humanity so that by his death he might destroy him who holds the power of death – that is, the devil" (Hebrews 2:14).

The Stripes: It is a reminder of Jesus' suffering for the sake of his people

"He himself bore our sins in his body on the tree, so that we might die to sins and live for righteousness; by his wounds ["stripes" in King James Version] you have been healed. For you were like sheep going astray, but now you have returned to the Shepherd and Overseer of your souls"(1 Peter 2:24-25).

---

[1] Coffman, Elesha. "Raising Cane." *Christianity Today.* Retrieved July 20, 2008 from http://www.christianity-today.com/history/newsletter/christmas/cane.html.

[2] Farley's and Sathers Candy Company. "Bob's." Retrieved August 8, 2008 from http://www.farleysandsathers.com/About/WhoWeAre.asp?BrandID=1.

[3] Mikkelson, Barbara. "Candy Cane." Retrieved July 20, 2008 from Snopes.com: http://www.snopes.com/holidays/christmas/candycane.asp.

Christmas Trees

Though some scholars have attributed the origin of the Christmas tree to pagan celebrations, it is more likely that the modern Christmas tree has its roots in Christian practices. No one will disagree that pagans have long "worshipped and served created things rather than the Creator" (Romans 1:25) . . . yes, even trees. Lighted trees were certainly used in various pagan religious celebrations throughout history, but there is no evidence of any direct link between the pagan rituals and the Christmas tree.

The Origin of the Christmas Tree

Among the many accounts claiming to explain the origin of the Christmas tree, the three most popular are from Germany — making it the likeliest place of origin. The stories span from the 8th century to the 16th century; all three are rooted in historical fact and may be connected to one another.

(1) St. Boniface (672 – 754 AD), 8th Century:[1]

St. Boniface (birth name Winfried) was a missionary to some of the remotest tribes of Germany. He is probably best known for what is called the "Felling of Thor's Oak." It is said that upon entering a town in northern Hesse, Boniface learned that the people worshiped the god Thor. They believed that Thor resided in a great oak tree among them. Boniface determined that if he wanted to earn an audience with the people, he would have to confront Thor. He announced before the people that he was going to cut down the oak, and he openly challenged Thor to strike him down. Miraculously, as Boniface began to chop the oak, a mighty wind blew and hurled the tree to the ground. Tradition holds that a fir tree was growing in the roots of the oak, and Boniface claimed the tree as a symbol of Christ. Needless to say, the people stood in awe and readily accepted Boniface's message about the one true God.

Author Henry Van Dyke (1852-1933) offers a dramatic retelling of the story of St. Boniface in his historical fiction account, *The First Christmas Tree*. See p. 407.

(2) The Paradise Plays, 15th Century:[2]

Another possible source of the Christmas tree comes from medieval religious plays in Germany. Among the most popular of these plays was the "Paradise" play. It started with the creation of man, acted out the first sin, and showed Adam and Eve being expelled from Paradise (the Garden of Eden). It closed with the promise of a coming Savior, which made the play a particular favorite during the Christmas season. In the play, the Garden of Eden was most often represented by a fir tree hung with apples and surrounded by candles.

At one point, religious plays were suppressed in Germany, and the popular symbol of the Paradise play made its way into the homes of Christians. By the 15th century, Christians started to decorate their trees not only with apples (the symbol of sin and the need for a Savior) but with small white wafers (the symbol of Christ's body, the Savior). These wafers were later replaced by little pieces of pastry cut in the shape of stars, angels, bells, etc.

The connection between the Garden of Eden and Christmas is profound. The first sin in the Garden of Eden was eating from the tree of the knowledge of good and evil, and *wanting to be like God*. How did God address this sin? *God became a man* that we might be saved. And trees play a significant role in the entirety of the Christian story, for the temptation that brought sin into the world hung on a tree and the act that resulted in salvation from sin (Christ on the cross) hung on a tree. Furthermore, once sin entered the world in the Garden of Eden, Adam and Eve, and all mankind, were no longer permitted to eat of the tree of life. However, in eternity, Christ's work on the cross will give us "the right to eat from the tree of life" once again (Revelation 2:7).

For about 200 years, the use of the "Paradise Tree" during the Christmas season was limited to people living along the Rhine in Germany. With time, the tradition spread throughout Europe and beyond. German immigrants to Pennsylvania likely brought the practice to America.

(3) Martin Luther, (1483-1546 AD), 16th Century:

A third tradition about the origin of the Christmas tree attributes it to Martin Luther, the leader of the Reformation. Some say that on Christmas Eve, Luther was walking through the woods near his home. He was struck by the beauty of how the snow shimmered in the moonlight on the branches of the trees. In an effort to re-create the magnificent sight for his family, he cut down the tree, placed it in his home, and decorated it with candles.

Though Christmas trees may have already existed in homes throughout Germany at the time of Luther, it is possible that he did in fact conceive the idea of adding candles to their branches. He may have been erroneously credited with beginning the tradition of the Christmas tree itself simply because his followers were the ones to spread the custom around Europe as they fled persecution in Germany.

Oldest Records:

The two oldest recorded references to Christmas trees come from the Alsace region (in modern day France, but previously populated by Germans). The first record is a forest ordinance from Ammerschweier dated in 1561; it states that no person "shall have for Christmas more than one bush of more than eight shoes' length."[3] The second record is in a diary written in 1605; it states: "At Christmas time in Strassburg they set up fir trees in the rooms, and they hang on them roses cut of-many colored paper, apples, wafers, gilt [something the color of gold], sugar."[4]

The first record of candles on Christmas trees is from a Silesian duchess in 1611.[5] The Silesian region includes parts of modern day Poland, the Czech Republic and Germany. Interestingly, the

Reformation turned this region almost entirely Protestant,[6] which strengthens the case for German influence at the time.

Though there may be disagreement on when the tradition of Christmas trees first started, the case is certainly strong for both a German and a Christian origin. As might be expected, the popular carol "O Christmas Tree" ("O Tannenbaum" in German) also had its beginning in Germany.

Christmas Trees in America

It appears that the custom of Christmas trees was first introduced into America during the Revolutionary War (1775-1783) by Hessian troops who were homesick for Germany. By the early 1800s, German immigrants had brought the tradition to Pennsylvania. However, the practice did not become widespread until the mid-1800s when a picture of Queen Victoria's tree appeared in *Godey's Lady's Book*, an American publication considered to be the "fashionable women's magazine" of the day.[7] Queen Victoria and her husband, Prince Albert of Germany, made a practice of setting up an enormous and beautifully decorated tree during the Christmas season. The royal couple has since been credited with popularizing the custom of Christmas trees in both England and America.

By 1889, President Benjamin Harrison set up the first recorded White House Christmas tree, and in 1929, First Lady Hoover began the as yet unbroken custom of decorating an "official" White House tree.[8]

The Decorations of Christmas Trees

Note that early Christmas trees "were not of a uniform appearance. There were no mass-produced balls, lights, or tinsel, which left tree decorators to create their own imaginative displays."[9] By the late 19th century, however, such ornaments became available. Since then, bulbs and electric lights have even become a symbol of Christmas in their own right. See pp. 105-106 for more on electric lights.

Interestingly, God compares himself to a tree in the Bible. He says, "I am like a green pine tree; your fruitfulness comes from me" (Hosea 14:8b). This is a relevant analogy to consider during the Christmas season. The fruitful lives of Christians can serve as the "ornaments" that draw others to admire the "tree" – God himself!

---

[1] Encyclopedia Britannica. "St. Boniface." Retrieved August 8, 2008 from Encyclopedia Britannica Online: http://www.newadvent.org/cathen/02656a.htm.

[2] Weiser, Francis X. *Handbook of Christian Feasts and Customs*. Harcourt, Brace and Company, Inc., 1958, p. 99.

[3] Hatch, Jane M. *The American Book of Days*. H.W. Wilson Company, 1978, p. 1145.

[4] Hatch, Jane M., p. 1145

[5] Encyclopedia Britannica. "Christmas." Retrieved August 8, 2008 from Encyclopedia Britannica Online: http://www.britannica.com/EBchecked/topic/115686/Christmas.

[6] Encyclopedia Britannica. "Silesia." Retrieved August 8, 2008 from Encyclopedia Britannica Online: http://www.britannica.com/EBchecked/topic/544097/Silesia.

[7] Swartz Jr., B.K. *The Origin of American Christmas Myth and Customs*. Retrieved July 20, 2008 from Ball State University: http://www.bsu.edu/web/01bkswartz/xmaspub.html.

[8] The White House Historical Association. "White House Christmas Tree Themes." Retrieved July 20, 2008 from The White House Historical Association: http://www.whitehousehistory.org/whha_shows/holidays_christmas/index.html

[9] Myers, Robert J. *Celebrations, The Complete Book of American Holidays*. Doubleday and Company Inc, 1972, p. 333.

Colors, Red & Green

I t is interesting to consider that in many areas of the world, red and green are the only bright colors that survive in nature during the winter. In fact, at a time when most plants are barren, those that remain green and even blossom (eg: holly with its red berries and the poinsettia with its brilliant red leaves) captivate attention. Historically, magical powers have even been attributed to plants that could withstand the winter. Since the vibrant red and green colors of these plants have long had a meaningful association with winter, it seems natural that they would eventually become attached to the most significant celebration of the season, Christmas. The colors of red and green also have intriguing biblical relevance, particularly in so far as they represent life.

The Color Red

Throughout the Bible, the color red has a strong association with life and blood. Interestingly, the first human life in all creation was a man named "Adam." The name in Hebrew can be translated as "man" or "red." This man was created as the first of all human life on earth, but he also became the first to bring death to humanity.

When Adam and his wife Eve first sinned against God by eating of the forbidden fruit, they brought death into the world. Since man was the source of death, man would also have to be the solution in overcoming it. Herein lies the dilemma; only God himself could conquer death, and God was not a man. Human blood was required to reverse the consequence of human sin. For this reason, and beyond all comprehension, God chose to become a man, Jesus, with real flesh and blood.

This man Jesus is also called the last "Adam" (quite fitting in that he took on the "red" blood of humanity). He was born into the world to conquer death and give us life. The Bible says: "So it is written: 'The first man Adam became a living being'; the last Adam, a life-giving spirit" (1 Corinthians 15:45). Additionally, "For as in Adam all die, so in Christ all will be made alive" (1 Corinthians 15:22). How very amazing that Jesus was born into the world with real human flesh and blood: "Since the children have flesh and blood, he too shared in their humanity" (Hebrews 2:14).

The book of Leviticus records that "the life of a creature is in the blood" (17:14). For this reason, the Jewish people were not permitted to eat the blood of any creature. This sheds light on the significance of Jesus' words when he said, "I tell you the truth, unless you eat the flesh of the Son of Man and drink his blood, you have no life in you. Whoever eats my flesh and drinks my blood has eternal life, and I will raise him up at the last day" (John 6:53-54).

For hundreds of years, the Jewish people used the blood of animals to "cover" their sins. The blood of Jesus, however, was meant to do more than cover sins; it was given as a drink offering to purify man from the inside out. The prophet Isaiah foretold: "Though your sins are like scarlet, they shall be as white as snow; though they are red as crimson, they shall be like wool" (Isaiah 1:18). The color of red gives a visual of the sacrificial animal blood that was shed to cover and hide sin. In a sense, our sins were so drenched with blood that they were "like scarlet" and "red as crimson." Isaiah pointed to the future sacrifice of Jesus whose blood would not simply cover over sins; it would so effectively wash them away that his people would be "white as snow."

Though the red of blood is often associated with death, in the case of Jesus and all who believe in him, it always symbolizes life. Death could not conquer Jesus. He is alive, and his blood, real human blood, gives life to all who believe in him.

It should also be noted that red (or more specifically scarlet) was one of three colors (blue, purple and scarlet) prescribed by God for the clothing of Jewish priests. Many scholars believe that blue represented God in the heavens, red represented man, and purple (the combination of red and blue) represented Jesus. After Jesus' life on earth, the color red remained a significant liturgical color, and tradition holds that the good St. Nicholas wore red bishop vestments. Thus evolved the common Christmas depiction of Santa Claus in red. See p. 129 for more information on "Santa Claus."

The Color Green

The color green is used frequently throughout the Bible to describe living things in nature: leaves, grass, pastures, plants and trees. Yet, just as sin brought death into the world for man, it brought death and decay to all of nature. The course of nature follows the course of man. After time, all living things wither and die. However, Jesus came to redeem man back to life, and he will do the same for creation. The Bible teaches:

"The creation waits in eager expectation for the sons of God to be revealed. For the creation was subjected to frustration, not by its own choice, but by the will of the one who subjected it, in hope that the creation itself will be liberated from its bondage to decay and brought into the glorious freedom of the children of God. We know that the whole creation has been groaning as in the pains of childbirth right up to the present time. Not only so, but we ourselves, who have the firstfruits of the Spirit, groan inwardly as we wait eagerly for our adoption as sons, the redemption of our bodies" (Romans 8:19-23).

How fitting that the Bible uses the analogy of childbirth. For it is through the "pains of child-birth" that life is brought forth. And it is the birth of Jesus, "the firstborn over all creation" (Colossians 1:15), that will ultimately bring forth new life for all created things. Not only will human bodies be made new, there will also be "a new heaven and a new earth, the home of righteousness" (2 Peter 3:13).

May the colors of Christmas serve as a reminder of how all creation — from man, symbolized by red, to all of nature, symbolized by green — will be redeemed by Jesus for new and eternal life!

Doves

The dove has long been viewed as a symbol of peace. Surely, the concept of peace is relevant to Christmas. After all, Jesus was born into the world to bring peace between God and mankind. Consider the words of the angels to shepherds on the day of Christ's birth, "Glory to God in the highest, and on earth peace to men on whom his favor rests" (Luke 2:14).

Though the good news of Jesus' birth was said to be "for all the people" (Luke 2:10), it seems that the offer of peace was more exclusive; it was for "men on whom (God's) favor rests" (Luke 2:14). There are a handful of distinct occasions in history when God made an offer of peace through specific men; special covenants were made with Noah, Abraham, Moses and Jesus, and interestingly, the dove played a symbolic role in each case.

Though the Bible never mentions the color of the doves, they are generally depicted as white when symbolizing peace. Recall that Jesus commanded his disciples to be "innocent as doves" (Matthew 10:16). Perhaps because white is the color most often associated with purity and innocence, it is the most natural color in which to portray the dove.

Noah and the Dove

In the days of Noah, the Bible tells us that:

"God saw how corrupt the earth had become, for all the people on earth had corrupted their ways. So God said to Noah, 'I am going to put an end to all people, for the earth is filled with violence because of them. I am surely going to destroy both them and the earth. So make yourself an ark. . . . I am going to bring floodwaters on the earth to destroy all life under the heavens, every creature that has the breath of life in it. Everything on earth will perish. But I will establish my covenant with you, and you will enter the ark—you and your sons and your wife and your sons' wives with you'" (Genesis 6:12-18).

After many days in the ark, the "floodgates of the heavens" (Genesis 8:2) were closed, and Noah sent out a dove on three different occasions to determine the state of the earth. After the dove's second journey, it returned to Noah, and "in its beak was a freshly plucked olive leaf! Then Noah knew that the water had receded from the earth" (Genesis 8:11). Surely, God was offering peace to mankind through Noah and his family by giving them a fresh start on earth.

Interestingly, once Noah came out of the ark, he built an altar to the Lord. On it, he sacrificed a burnt offering of clean animals and clean birds (probably doves). The Bible records:

"The LORD smelled the pleasing aroma and said in his heart: 'Never again will I curse the ground because of man, even though every inclination of his heart is evil from childhood. And never again will I destroy all living creatures, as I have done'" (Genesis 8:21).

God made peace with man in confirming that he would never again destroy all the life on earth, and doves, here again, probably played a role in bringing about this message of peace.

Abraham and the Dove

Several generations later, God chose to establish a special relationship of peace with Abraham and his descendants:

"I will establish my covenant as an everlasting covenant between me and you and your descendants after you for the generations to come, to be your God and the God of your descendants after you. The whole land of Canaan, where you are now an alien, I will give as an everlasting possession to you and your descendants after you; and I will be their God" (Genesis 17:7-8).

Abraham would become the father of the Jewish people, a nation to whom God offered peace and relationship with himself. As a confirmation of his covenant to give them the land of Canaan, the Bible records the following ritual:

"So the Lord said to him, 'Bring me a heifer, a goat and a ram, each three years old, along with a dove and a young pigeon.' Abram brought all these to him, cut them in two and arranged the halves opposite each other; the birds, however, he did not cut in half. Then birds of prey came down on the carcasses, but Abram drove them away. . . . When the sun had set and darkness had fallen, a smoking firepot with a blazing torch appeared and passed between the pieces. On that day the Lord made a covenant with Abram, 'To your descendants I give this land . . .'" (Genesis 15:9-18).

Though this ritual seems odd, it appears to have been a common ancient practice. The *Tyndale Commentary on Genesis* records, "In its full form, probably both parties would pass between the dismembered animals to invoke a like fate on themselves should they break their pledge."[1] Consider the somber words of the Lord in the book of Jeremiah:

"The men who have violated my covenant and have not fulfilled the terms of the covenant they made before me, I will treat like the calf they cut in two and then walked between its pieces. The leaders of Judah and Jerusalem, the court officials, the priests and all the people of the land who walked between the pieces of the calf, I will hand over to their enemies who seek their lives. Their dead bodies will become food for the birds of the air and the beasts of the earth" (Jeremiah 34:18-20).

In the Abrahamic covenant, though God passed through the animals in the form of "a smoking firepot with a blazing torch" (Genesis 15:17), Abraham did not pass through the animals. God committed himself to a covenant in which he was the only party obligated to uphold it. Interestingly, "making a covenant" is more literally translated as "cutting a covenant"; the expression is derived from the cutting of animals.

The fact that God required specific animals of specific ages may imply that they had some symbolic significance. We will find later in history that each of these species, and none other, were prescribed for sacrifice in the temple. One interpretation is that God's instruction for a three-year-old-heifer, goat and ram was indicative of three "ages" or periods in history that were to come (possibly the periods of Abraham, Moses and Jesus).[2] Certainly the ram calls to mind Jesus, the Lamb of God, who would usher in the new and final covenant — a period after which no more covenants would need to be "cut." This theory sheds light on why neither the dove nor the pigeon were cut and why an age was not specified for them; they were meant to symbolize a new period of peace with God that would have no end.

As seen during Jesus' baptism, the Holy Spirit, the sign and seal of peace between God and man, was represented as a dove (Matthew 3:16). The pigeon (a term often used synonymously with "dove") has long been known for its ability to carry and deliver messages. Perhaps the pigeon is indicative of the message of Jesus being carried throughout the world.[3] The Bible says, "And this gospel of the kingdom will be preached in the whole world as a testimony to all nations, and then the end will come" (Matthew 24:14). As the good news of peace between God and man reaches the world, the time draws near when God's people will finally enter the promised land, the New Earth, where there will be eternal peace!

Moses and the Dove

Many generations after Abraham, his descendant Moses arrived on the scene. Moses was born in Egypt at a time when the Jewish people were enslaved. However, through a series of miraculous events, Moses was raised as a prince in Egypt. The Bible tells us:

> "By faith Moses, when he had grown up, refused to be known as the son of Pharaoh's daughter. He chose to be mistreated along with the people of God rather than to enjoy the pleasures of sin for a short time. He regarded disgrace for the sake of Christ as of greater value than the treasures of Egypt, because he was looking ahead to his reward" (Hebrews 11:24-26).

Ultimately, God chose Moses to lead the Jewish people out of Egypt and into the promised land. He commanded Moses to relay the following words: "Now if you obey me fully and keep my covenant, then out of all nations you will be my treasured possession" (Exodus 19:36). As part of this particular covenant, God revealed his laws to the Jewish people. Yet, knowing that they could not perfectly obey his law, God set up a system of animal sacrifices. Sin separated the people from God, and the sacrifices were designed to make peace with him. Essentially, the animals took upon themselves the consequence of sin, which is death. Throughout the book of Leviticus, doves were used as a sacrifice for sin, a sacrifice to renew peace with God.

Yet animal sacrifices would never be sufficient for permanent peace with God. The Bible says, "Day after day every priest stands and performs his religious duties; again and again he offers the same sacrifices, which can never take away sins" (Hebrews 10:11). The law was meant to reveal the need for a priest, Jesus, who could offer "for all time one sacrifice for sins" (Hebrews 10:12).

Jesus and the Dove

Once more, several generations passed before Jesus, another descendant of Abraham, was born. Before beginning his ministry on earth, Jesus was baptized. The Bible records that as Jesus came up out of the water, "the Holy Spirit descended on him in bodily form like a dove. And a voice came from heaven: 'You are my Son, whom I love; with you I am well pleased'" (Luke 3:22). How fitting that since the Holy Spirit is a sign of peace between God and man, and since it otherwise has no physical body, it would take on the form of a dove.

Ultimately, Jesus gave his life as a sacrifice for the sin of men. He made it possible for those who put their hope in him to receive the same Holy Spirit that descended on him, a sign and seal of peace between God and man. The Bible records:

"... by one sacrifice he (Jesus) has made perfect forever those who are being made holy. The Holy Spirit also testifies to us about this. First he says: 'This is the covenant I will make with them after that time, says the Lord. I will put my laws in their hearts, and I will write them on their minds.' Then he adds: 'Their sins and lawless acts I will remember no more.' And where these have been forgiven, there is no longer any sacrifice for sin' (Hebrews 10:14-18).

Jesus paid the final sacrifice for sin. He ushered in the final covenant of peace between God and man. When the angels spoke of the "peace to men on whom [God's] favor rests" (Luke 2:14), they spoke of Jesus and all those who believe in him. May images of doves during the Christmas season serve as a reminder of the Holy Spirit, who is the seal of peace with God. After all, true spiritual peace was the purpose for which Jesus was born into the world!

---

[1] Kidner, Derek. "Genesis." *Tyndale Old Testament Commentaries.* Inter-Varsity Press, 1967, p. 124.

[2] Burns, Bill. "Abraham's Revelation." Retrieved July 20, 2008 from Faith Tabernacle:http://ft111.com/abrahamsrevelation.htm.

[3] Burns, Bill.

Gifts

The Bible teaches, "Every good and perfect gift is from above, coming down from the Father of the heavenly lights" (James 1:17). Surely, no greater gift has ever been given to the world than Jesus:

> "For God so loved the world that he <u>gave</u> his one and only Son, that whoever believes in him shall not perish but have eternal life. For God did not send his Son into the world to condemn the world, but to save the world through him" (John 3:16-17).

Jesus, the Son of God, came into the world in genuine flesh and blood, and he willingly gave up this flesh and blood in death to save his people. This truth is recognized when believers eat of the bread (Christ's body) and drink of the wine (Christ's blood) of the Eucharist (a word derived from the Greek word *eucharistia* which means "good grace" or "good gift"). How fitting that many Christian churches refer to the bread and wine as "the Gifts."

Though the practice of giving gifts on Christmas seems like a natural response to God's great example, the history of giving on this holiday is not as obvious as one might expect.

The History of Gift Giving

The practice of gift giving has existed as long as humanity, and the Bible records several instances of it. The book of Genesis, records gifts used as a peace offering, (Jacob and Esau, Genesis 32:20), a request for marriage (Isaac and Rebekah, Genesis 24:53), a consolation (Abraham and his sons, Genesis 25:6), etc. Other books of the Bible record the use of gifts as offerings to God, tributes to kings, etc.

Gift giving was certainly not limited to people of God. In fact, it is possible that early Roman Christians borrowed from cultural practices of gift giving during December or New Year festivals and applied them to their celebration of Christmas. Certainly, gift giving had a natural association with Christmas, and Christians could appeal to the Wise Men (or Magi) for a precedent of giving in honor of Christ's birth.

However, in America, the practice of gift giving on Christmas seems to have developed out of the celebration of St. Nicholas Day. After his death on December 6 in the 4th century, stories of the generous Nicholas spread across Europe. See pp. 129-137 to learn more about St. Nicholas. By the 11th and 12th century:

> "All the legends of St. Nicholas having to do with his giving nature began to register in people's minds and bear fruit. . . . Throughout Europe, people began giving gifts in the name of St. Nicholas. [For example,] Nuns in France began the practice of surreptitiously leaving gifts for children at houses in the poorer parts of town on St. Nicholas Eve or St. Nicholas Day. Some were left in packages, others in stockings. Often included were good things to eat – such as fruits and nuts, or even oranges from Spain (a great luxury in those days)."[1]

The practice of gift giving on St. Nicholas Day, December 6, remains firmly rooted in many countries. However, in America, the tradition was transferred to Christmas (as was St. Nicholas). Since Christmas was the celebration of the birth of Christ (God's gift to the world) and since the Wise Men set a biblical precedent of giving during the season, the transfer was quite natural. In regard to St. Nicholas:

"The young Nicholas, when he made selfless giving (in secret and without desire for recognition) habitual in his life, an integral part of his character, inseparable from who he was, had no way of knowing that he was establishing himself as the post-apostolic link between the Magi and posterity, the torch-bearer who would keep selfless giving alive down through the ages. In fact, it is said that giving a 'Baker's Dozen' (13 for the price of 12) can also be traced to St. Nicholas."[2]

Though the tradition of giving gifts in American may not have a direct link to early Christmas celebrations, it is firmly rooted in Christian practice as demonstrated by the life of a godly man named St. Nicholas.

Biblical Gift Giving

St. Nicholas is a beautiful example of biblical giving; he gave to those in need and he gave in secret. The book of Proverbs records, "He who oppresses the poor to increase his wealth and he who gives gifts to the rich—both come to poverty" (Proverbs 22:16). Often the tendency to overlook the poor is rooted in the belief that the poor can give nothing in return; they certainly cannot increase our wealth. Yet, Jesus taught the following about giving:

"Then the King will say to those on his right, 'Come, you who are blessed by my Father; take your inheritance, the kingdom prepared for you since the creation of the world. For I was hungry and you gave me something to eat, I was thirsty and you gave me something to drink, I was a stranger and you invited me in, I needed clothes and you clothed me, I was sick and you looked after me, I was in prison and you came to visit me.'

"Then the righteous will answer him, 'Lord, when did we see you hungry and feed you, or thirsty and give you something to drink? When did we see you a stranger and invite you in, or needing clothes and clothe you? When did we see you sick or in prison and go to visit you?'

"The King will reply, 'I tell you the truth, whatever you did for one of the least of these brothers of mine, you did for me'" (Matthew 25:34-40).

Jesus taught that giving to those in need is actually credited to us as if we gave to HIM! Though people in need cannot return the favor, Jesus is one who can and will reward us on their behalf.

Consider the Wise Men who gave gifts to the poor Mary, Joseph and infant Jesus. Though they may not have lived to see an earthly reward for their generous gifts, their giving was recorded in God's Word to be remembered for all eternity. Surely they were also acknowledged and rewarded in heaven.

Ironically, in the Middle Ages, European monarchs used the example of the Wise Men to justify their demand for tributes:

> "Using the Bible as the rationale behind their demands, a host of kings and queens in Europe wrote into law that subjects were to provide annual Christmas tributes to their rulers. Thus, the very poorest people in Europe were required to give the best they had to the richest family in the land each year on December 25th. Soon lesser royals and government appointees were demanding Christmas tributes as well. The poor were deliberately being taken advantage of in the name of the Christian faith. Even the church had to pay the rulers. So rather than making the holidays a time of celebration and joy, the demands of many of Europe's elite put Christmas gifts in a rather bad light."[3]

Fortunately, the practice of oppressive demands on the poor at Christmas would decline over time. Yet, even when the practice could have been enforced, there were notable exceptions. Good King Wencelas, Duke of Bohemia (approximately 907-935 AD), was one of these exceptions. Rather than demanding tribute from his subjects and showing generosity to those who could help expand his territory and influence, he was known to practice biblical giving and to care for the poorest in his land. Surely Wenceslas was blessed in heaven for his generosity to the poor. See p. 345 for more on King Wenceslas.

Not only is it tempting to give exclusively to those who can offer something in return, giving can also be motivated by a wrong desire to get praise from others. For this reason, Jesus taught that giving should be done in secret:

> "Be careful not to do your 'acts of righteousness' before men, to be seen by them. If you do, you will have no reward from your Father in heaven. So when you give to the needy, do not announce it with trumpets, as the hypocrites do in the synagogues and on the streets, to be honored by men. I tell you the truth, they have received their reward in full. But when you give to the needy, do not let your left hand know what your right hand is doing, so that your giving may be in secret. Then your Father, who sees what is done in secret, will reward you" (Matthew 6:1-4).

The biblical principles of giving to the needy and giving in secret can certainly help to uproot any impurity that might otherwise motivate giving. When you give to the needy and when you give in secret, you reveal that you do not want anything in return.

Certainly the ultimate example of giving comes from God himself. Not only has he given his people life, relationships, talents, etc., but he also gave his son so that believers can spend eternity with him. The Bible says, "For the wages of sin is death, but the gift of God is eternal life in Christ Jesus our Lord" (Romans 6:23). Notice that eternal life is not the wage for good deeds. No, it is a gift of God. It is not something that is earned, and it is certainly not something that mankind deserves. God freely gives his people the gift of salvation and eternal life.

And God does not show favoritism. God first revealed this to the Apostle Peter at the home of Cornelius, a Gentile Roman military officer. Peter originally thought that the gift of salvation was only for the Jewish people. Yet, after a dream and the testimony of Cornelius, Peter proclaimed, "I now realize how true it is that God does not show favoritism but accepts men from every nation who fear him and do what it right" (Acts 10:34). Cornelius had recounted to Peter how an angel appeared to him saying, "Your prayers and gifts to the poor have come up as a memorial offering before God" (Acts 10:4). The angel further instructed Cornelius to call for the Apostle Peter so that he might hear about Jesus.

How interesting that Cornelius had the honor of being one of the first Gentiles to receive God's gift of salvation in part because he had remembered to give gifts to those in need. Cornelius did not show favoritism in his giving, and God chose Cornelius to reveal that he also did not show favoritism in giving his gift of salvation. Surely race, gender, intellect or riches play no part in God's gift of salvation, because God, unlike humans, is not concerned with what he can get in return. Rather, he is glorified when his people recognize how little they have to offer him.

In his letter to the church at Corinth, the Apostle Paul wrote:

"Brothers, think of what you were when you were called. Not many of you were wise by human standards; not many were influential; not many were of noble birth. But God chose the foolish things of the world to shame the wise; God chose the weak things of the world to shame the strong. He chose the lowly things of this world and the despised things—and the things that are not—to nullify the things that are, so that no one may boast before him. It is because of him that you are in Christ Jesus, who has become for us wisdom from God—that is, our righteousness, holiness and redemption. Therefore, as it is written: 'Let him who boasts boast in the Lord'" (1 Corinthians 1:26-31).

Should we feel tempted to boast about our abilities, riches, position, etc., consider how insignificant they are in comparison to the Almighty. May we rather boast about the glorious Lord who has freely given us the greatest gift imaginable, our salvation!

Wrapping Gifts

It appears that since the invention of paper in 105 AD, people have been wrapping gifts. There is something special about the expectation of seeing what is inside. Gifts that are wrapped thoughtfully often express something of the person who will receive the gift. It may be as simple as using a children's print for young ones, a masculine print for men, feminine bows for women, etc.

It seems that even God saw value in wrapping his gift to the world. Jesus came "wrapped" in the flesh of humanity, and this flesh reflected those who would receive him. He was "made in human likeness" and "found in appearance as a man" (Philippians 2:7-8). Yet, his glory was hidden. In fact, the Bible teaches that Jesus had "no beauty or majesty to attract us to him, nothing in his appearance that we should desire him" (Isaiah 53:2). The glory of Jesus was hidden in his human form so that it could rather be revealed in his people. We "open" God's great gift on earth as our hearts are opened to Jesus, so that his glory can shine through us. Yet, there is more. When we enter eternity, we will see God's great gift truly "unwrapped." The full glory of Jesus will shine. The Apostle John records the appearance of Christ in Revelation as follows:

> "[Jesus was] dressed in a robe reaching down to his feet and with a golden sash around his chest. His head and hair were white like wool, as white as snow, and his eyes were like blazing fire. His feet were like bronze glowing in a furnace, and his voice was like the sound of rushing waters. In his right hand he held seven stars, and out of his mouth came a sharp double-edged sword. His face was like the sun shining in all its brilliance. When I saw him, I fell at his feet as though dead. Then he placed his right hand on me and said: 'Do not be afraid. I am the First and the Last. I am the Living One; I was dead, and behold I am alive for ever and ever!'" (Revelation 1:13b-18a).

How wonderful it will be to see and understand the great value of God's gift and have all of eternity to gaze on his beauty and majesty. Though any gift we give this season will pale in comparison to the gift of Jesus, we can honor God by seeking ways to give in his name and for his glory.

---

[1] Wheeler, Joe and Rosenthal, Jim, *St. Nicholas, A Closer Look at Christmas*. Thomas Nelson, 2005, p.95.

[2] Wheeler, Joe and Rosenthal, Jim, p. 129.

[3] Collins, Ace. *Stories Behind the Great Traditions of Christmas*. Zondervan, 2003, p. 98.

Holly

S ome scholars believe that the name *holly* was derived from the word *holy*. The famous botanist William Turner (1508-1568), known as the "father of English botany," referred to holly as the "Holy Tree." It is also called "Christ's Thorn" throughout various parts of Europe. Other scholars maintain however that the word *holly* can trace its root to an Indo-European word meaning "prickly" or "to prick."

Regardless of the etymology of *holly*, Christians have identified a wealth of symbolism in its form. The sharpness of the leaves help to recall the crown of thorns worn by Jesus; the red berries serve as a reminder of the drops of blood that were shed for salvation, and the shape of the leaves, which resemble flames, can serve to reveal God's burning love for his people. Combined with the fact that holly maintains its bright colors during the Christmas season, it naturally came to be associated with the Christian holiday.

Though there are several hundred species of holly, the most common species found in Europe and America are evergreen (green all year long) and produce red berries. As a Christmas symbol, holly is generally portrayed as a small cluster of berries and leaves, so it may be surprising to learn that holly trees can grow to enormous heights (over 50 feet). Some even grow in the familiar shape of the Christmas tree – a spectacular sight when decorated by nature's own red berries.

Holly offers a striking contrast to the general barrenness of winter. It is rarely affected by even the most severe weather, and it appears to be immune to the infestation of insects. Thus, holly has understandably attracted the attention of many cultures throughout history and plays a part in a variety of legends. The most consistent theme in the range of traditions concerning holly is its association with celebration and merry-making. Even Shakespeare satirically states in his play "As You Like It":

"Heigh ho! sing heigh ho! unto the green holly:
Most friendship is feigning, most loving mere folly:
Then, heigh ho, the holly!
This life is most jolly."

More than just an empty festival and excuse to pretend "jolliness," Christmas offers real reason to celebrate. Christmas is meant to be truly merry.

Holly and Saturnalia

The use of holly at Christmas is often attributed to the ancient Roman celebration of Saturnalia. Romans believed that holly was sacred to the god Saturn. Thus, during Saturnalia, the feast celebrated in his name, holly could be found in abundance. Romans exchanged holly wreaths, carried holly in processions and even decorated images of Saturn with holly. Saturnalia was meant to be festive and merry.

Pliny the Elder (23-79 AD) helps to shed light on some additional reasons why holly may have been used in Roman festivities. Pliny was considered the standard authority for plant and animal life in his time. In his famous book *Historia Naturalis*, Pliny records that if holly was planted near a house or farm, it would defend it from lightning and witchcraft (on a side note, modern science has since discovered that the spines of holly can act as miniature lightning conductors, thereby protecting nearby objects).[1] Pliny also claimed that when the wood of holly was thrown at or near an animal, it would compel the animal to lie down beside it. Clearly, holly was thought to repel malice of all kinds (whether it was a natural disaster, dark magic or a vicious animal). Thus, as Romans celebrated festivities, holly was a symbol to them that nothing could hinder their merriment.

Since Saturnalia was generally celebrated between December 17th and 23rd, some scholars claim that it influenced Christmas celebrations. However, at least so far as holly is concerned, many different cultures used the plant as decoration or in winter festivities. It seems most reasonable to conclude that in the cold and dark of winter, people throughout history have sought to brighten homes and festivities with nature's beauty. Christians were no exception.

Holly and the Oak

The idea that holly repelled malice was held all throughout ancient Europe. In fact, Druids believed that the sharp leaves of holly offered protection against evil spirits. For this reason, Druid priests wore holly in their hair during mistletoe rituals. See pp. 114-115 for more on Druidism and mistletoe. Not only was holly believed to ward off evil spirits, it was thought to attract good spirits. Thus, it was also used in the home during the winter as a shelter for the spirits of the forest. The book *Observations on Popular Antiquities* records that in places where Druidism prevailed, "the houses were decked with evergreens in December, that the sylvan [wood or forest] spirits might repair to them, and remain unnipped with frost and cold winds, until a milder season had renewed the foliage of their darling abodes."[2] The most significant role of holly however seems to have been its association with the oak, the most sacred tree in the religion of the Druids.

Since oak helps to sustain the acidic soil in which holly prefers to grow, the two plants are often found together. Though holly is evergreen, it is often hidden among leafy oaks. It is not until the oak loses its leaves, that the presence of the holly begins to dominate the landscape. Thus, seasonal changes came to be characterized as a fight for supremacy between the "Oak King" and the "Holly King". The Oak King is said to rule from summer solstice to winter solstice and the Holly King for the other half of the year. Interestingly, these two characters show up in Mummers' plays (costumed performances thought to have originated in 18th century Great Britain or Ireland) during the Christmas season:

"The Holly King was depicted as a powerful giant of a man covered in holly leaves and branches, and wielding a holly bush as a club. He may well have been the same archetype on which the Green Knight of Arthurian legend was based and to whose challenge Gawain rose during the Round Table's Christmas celebrations [See p. 387 for the story *Sir Gawain and the Green Knight*]."[3]

If the plays maintain remnants of ancient practices, we may infer that the "war" between holly and oak was amicable and was merrily celebrated.

Holly and Ivy

Another common association in Great Britain is that of holly and ivy. It appears that in pre-Christian celebrations of the winter season, ancient people had great fun pitting boys and girls against each other in various games. The festivities culminated with a boy dressed in a suit of holly leaves and a girl in ivy joining together to parade around their village. The ritual symbolized the importance of male and female unity in order to perpetuate life throughout nature.

Over the course of several hundred years, it seems that the ritual was altered and had lost both its meaning and purpose. In 1779, a writer for *Gentleman's Magazine* recorded the following:

"Being on a visit Tuesday last in a little obscure village in this county (East Kent), I found an odd kind of sport going forward: the girls, from eighteen to five or six years old, were assembled in a crowd, and burning an uncouth effigy, which they called an Holly-Boy, and which it seems they had stolen from the boys, who, in another part of the village were assembling together, and burning what they called an Ivy-Girl, which they had stolen from the girls: all this ceremony was accompanied with loud huzzas, noise and acclamations. What it all means I cannot tell, although I inquired of several of the oldest people in the place, who could only answer that it had always been a sport at this season of the year."[4]

Though the meaning of holly and ivy rituals may have been lost, the association between the two plants, as well as the identification of holly with the masculine and ivy with the feminine, has persisted. In the 16th century song, "The Contest of the Ivy and the Holly," ivy is depicted as a woman and holly as a man. Some scholars believe this song influenced the Christmas carol, "The Holly and the Ivy" (believed to have first been published in 1710) in which holly is thought to represent the man Jesus and ivy is thought to represent the woman Mary. The words to the carol are as follows:

1. The holly and the ivy, Now both are full well grown.
Of all the trees that are in the wood,
The holly bears the crown.

Chorus:

Oh, the rising of the sun,
The running of the deer.
The playing of the merry organ,
Sweet singing in the quire.

2. The holly bears a blossom
As white as lily flower;
And Mary bore sweet Jesus Christ
To be our sweet Savior. ***Chorus***

3. The holly bears a berry As red as any blood;
And Mary bore sweet Jesus Christ
To do poor sinners good. ***Chorus***

4. The holly bears a prickle
As sharp as any thorn;
And Mary bore sweet Jesus Christ
On Christmas day in the morn. ***Chorus***

5. The holly bears a bark
As bitter as any gall;
And Mary bore sweet Jesus Christ
For to redeem us all. ***Chorus***

Here again, even as the carol walks through the redemption story, the chorus repeats the theme of merriment, "the playing of the merry organ." It is interesting to consider how a contest between the sexes was uniquely addressed in the Christmas story. Both sexes would prove to be critical to God's plan for salvation. God came into the world as a man, but he was born of a woman (on whom he was totally dependent in his early life). Ultimately, the Bible teaches, "There is neither . . . male nor female, for you are all one in Jesus Christ" (Galatians 3:28).

Over time, holly has become a much more prominent symbol of Christmas than it's ivy counterpart. And if holly is somehow representative of Jesus, then it seems appropriate to use it in celebrations of his birth.

Holly and America

Holly has been popular since the beginning of American history. The pilgrims noted its presence in Massachusetts when they landed in 1620. Its branches were said to have served the Native Americans with wood, and its berries were used as buttons.

Prior to the eighteenth century, before the introduction of turnips, holly was used as winter fodder for cattle and sheep. Some farmers even installed grinders to make the prickly leaves more pleasant for the animals. Cows seem to have thrived on holly and produced good milk and butter as a result. These were critically necessary to early Americans during the privations of winter.

Holly's hard white wood was also used to make chess pieces, tool handles and beautiful decorative inlays on furniture. Since folklore claimed that the wood was especially effective in controlling horses, most of the whips for ploughmen and horse-drawn coaches were made of holly. In the 1800s, holly was also used to make the spinning rod of looms. Since it could be sanded very smooth, holly wood was less likely than others to snag the threads of cloth.

Perhaps because of its contribution to early America, holly was said to be a favorite of George Washington. More than a dozen hollies planted by him are still in existence. Surely the presence of holly in America was evidence of God's provision, as well as a cause for rejoicing. It seems appropriate that holly would become a symbol of one of the most joyful celebrations of the year in America — Christmas.

And God is not only concerned with providing for the earthly needs of man (as he did with holly for early Americans), he is willing to go to great lengths to provide for our spiritual needs (as he demonstrated through the birth, death and resurrection of Jesus). As the angel said to the shepherds, the birth of Jesus was "good news of great joy" (Luke 2:10). Surely, Christmas offers every reason to rejoice.

A medieval calendar in the Church of Rome described Christmas Eve as *templa exornantur*, meaning "churches are decked."[5] As the tradition of decking "the halls with boughs of holly" continues in America, let us remember that it is the birth of Christ that makes the season jolly!

---

[1] Kendall, Paul. "Mythology and Folklore of the Holly." Retrieved July 20, 2008 from Trees for Life: http://www.treesforlife.org.uk/forest/mythfolk/holly.html.

[2] Brand, John and Ellis, Henry. *Observations on Popular Antiquities*, quoting words of Dr. R. Chandler, Chatto and Windus, 1900, pp. 278-279.

[3] Kendall, Paul.

[4] Brand, John and Ellis, Henry, pp. 318-319.

[5] Brand, John and Ellis, Henry, pp. 279.

Jesus

Whether in the arms of his mother or in a manger, images of Jesus as an infant abound at Christmas time. After all, he is the focus of our holiday; it is his birthday that we celebrate at Christmas. The idea that the King of all Creation would enter the world as a helpless child is astonishing. Yet, God made his intentions known through the prophet Zechariah over 400 years before the first Christmas when he said, "For I am coming, and I will live among you" (Zechariah 2:10). Additionally, Isaiah prophesied about Jesus over 700 years before his birth:

> "For to us a child is born, to us a son is given, and the government will be on his shoulders. And he will be called Wonderful Counselor, Mighty God, Everlasting Father, Prince of Peace" (Isaiah 9:6).

Not only did the Mighty God come as a child, he was born into the humblest of circumstances and with "no beauty or majesty to attract us to him, nothing in his appearance that we should desire him" (Isaiah 53:2). Truly the incarnation (God taking on flesh) is a great paradox. Consider the words of the great theologian Augustine (354-430 AD):

> "[He] was created of a mother, whom He created, was carried by hands which He formed; sucked at breasts which He had filled; cried in the manger in wordless infancy, He the Word, without whom all human eloquence is mute."[1]

His Humble Form

It may be an understatement to say that God did not take on the form or the circumstances in life that we might have expected. He was born into poverty, and his upbringing was quite ordinary. After Jesus began his ministry on earth, John the Baptist sent his followers to ask Jesus, "Are you the one who was to come, or should we expect someone else?" (Matthew 11:3). This question implies that even John the Baptist may have anticipated a different kind of "king."

The Bible foretold that Jesus would come from the line of David (Psalm 89:29) and would reign on David's throne (Isaiah 9:7). It is interesting to look back on the day that God chose David to be king. The Lord sent the prophet Samuel to David's house to anoint the new king. When Samuel saw David's brother Eliab, he thought surely that was the man whom God had chosen.

> "But the Lord said to Samuel, 'Do not consider his appearance or his height, for I have rejected him. The Lord does not look at the things man looks at. Man looks at the outward appearance, but the Lord looks at the heart'" (1 Samuel 16:7).

God chose David even though he was not initially what men expected of a king, and God used the opportunity to reveal that his priorities were quite different from man's. Surely it is not the appearance of man or the accomplishments of man that impress God. He could not have made this more evident than by the form he took on as a man. God is concerned with the heart, and he is pleased with a heart like King David of whom God said, "[He] followed me with all his heart" (1 Kings 14:8), and "I have found David son of Jesse a man after my own heart" (Acts 13:22).

His Flesh

The idea that God, the Creator of the Universe, would become a man is a remarkable mystery. So remarkable in fact that the attempt of finite minds to explain it has resulted in two dangerous errors throughout history. The first error is to believe that Jesus was *only* a man and not God. Yet, the Bible makes clear that Jesus was "in very nature God" (Philippians 2:6). Jesus himself stated, "I and the Father are one" (John 10:3). The other error is to believe that Jesus is *only* God and not a "real" man — that Jesus' body only appeared to be physical. Interestingly, as a way to test whether or not a prophet was from God, the Bible says, "This is how you can recognize the Spirit of God: Every spirit that acknowledges that Jesus Christ has come in the flesh is from God" (1 John 4:2).

Erroneous teaching about the nature of Jesus had become so prevalent in the 4th century that 318 bishops gathered together in Nicea in the year 325 AD to formulate a statement of faith, the Nicene Creed, for all Christians. It may be worth mentioning that St. Nicholas probably participated in this historic gathering. By 384 AD, a council of bishops met again to further develop the Creed. Here is an excerpt of the final Creed as it relates to Jesus:

"We believe . . . in one Lord JESUS CHRIST,
the only-begotten Son of God,
Begotten of the Father before all worlds;
Light of Light.
Very God of very God,
Begotten, not made,
Being of one substance with the Father;
By whom all things were made;
Who, for us men, and for our salvation,
    came down from heaven,
And was incarnate by the Holy Ghost of
    the Virgin Mary,
And was made man
He was crucified for us under Pontius Pilate;
And suffered and was buried;
And the third day he rose again,
According to the Scriptures;
And ascended into heaven,

And sitteth on the right hand of the Father
And he shall come again, with glory, to judge
    the quick and the dead;
Whose kingdom shall have no end."[2]

Here is the great paradox: The "God [who] is not a man" (Numbers 23:19) became a man for our sake; the God whom "no one has ever seen" (John 1:18) became a man for all to see. Jesus is "God the One and Only, who is at the Father's side, [and] has made him known" (John 1:18).

His Purpose

So why would God enter the world as a man? The Bible makes clear the great love and ultimate purpose for which Jesus came to earth. Ironically, he was born to die:

> "Since the children have flesh and blood, he too shared in their humanity so that by his death he might destroy him who holds the power of death—that is, the devil— and free those who all their lives were held in slavery by their fear of death. For surely it is not angels he helps, but Abraham's descendants. For this reason he had to be made like his brothers in every way, in order that he might become a merciful and faithful high priest in service to God, and that he might make atonement for the sins of the people." (Hebrews 2:14-17)

The consequence of sin is death, both physically and spiritually (meaning eternal separation from God). Only a sinless life could free mankind from this consequence, and the only man to live such a life was Jesus. When we put our faith in Jesus, his sinless life is "credited" to us, so that we no longer have to die spiritually. Jesus' perfect life on earth and his death on the cross are the only means by which humans can be saved from the consequence of sin. Recall that when the angel first appeared to Joseph in a dream, he said, "She [Mary] will give birth to a son, and you are to give him the name Jesus, because he will save his people from their sins" (Matthew 1:21). The name *Jesus* means "God saves."

Not only does Jesus save believers from sin, he helps them to resist the temptation to sin: "Because he himself suffered when he was tempted, he is able to help those who are being tempted" (Hebrews 2:18). Most Christians hesitate to compare their lives to that of Jesus. After all, he is God. Yet he lived his life on earth as a man. Certainly he experienced temptation as man, "for God cannot be tempted" (James 1:13). When speaking of Jesus, the Bible says, "For we do not have a high priest who is unable to sympathize with our weaknesses, but we have one who has been tempted in every way, just as we are—yet was without sin" (Hebrews 4:15).

Christians are to model their lives after Jesus not only in resisting temptation but in all that we do. When speaking of his "doings" (presumed to be his demonstrations of love, wisdom, miracles, etc.), Jesus said to his disciples, "I tell you the truth, anyone who has faith in me will do what I have been doing. He will do even greater things than these, because I am going to the Father" (John 14:12). Jesus implied that the great things he did on earth were in his humanity; after all, mere humans would be able to do even greater things. Jesus went on to explain that once he left earth, the Holy Spirit would come. The Bible teaches that the very same "spirit of him who raised Jesus from the dead is living in you" (Romans 8:11). It is through this spirit that believers can in fact live a life like Jesus. Therefore, "just as he who called you is holy, so be holy in all you do" (1 Peter 1:15).

Thomas à Kempis (1380-1471), a monk best known as the author of *The Imitation of Christ*, wrote, "He who is never away from us in the divine is with us in human nature."[3] Though believers may know in theory how deeply God cares for them, there is something so very comforting and personal in knowing that Jesus intimately understands human struggles; he experienced them first-hand. Consider words of Charles Spurgeon (1834-1892), a British pastor known as the "Prince of Preachers":

> "Behold the incarnate Son of God born of Mary at Bethlehem; what can this intend for us but grace? If the Lord meant to destroy us, He would not have assumed our nature. If He had not been moved with a mighty love to a guilty race, He would never have taken upon Himself their flesh and blood. . . . It is not in the power of human lips to speak out all the comfort which this one sign contains."[4]

In times of trouble, may we find comfort in knowing that there is no hardship that Jesus did not endure: He lacked riches, position, and beauty; he faced temptation; he endured great physical pain. He understands!

His Majesty

Jesus gave his life for mankind, and he intimately knows the difficulties of being human. Is there anyone who can be more fully trusted to rule over our lives? Consider the following challenge from Charles Spurgeon:

> "Are you willing to have Christ to govern you? Will you spend your lives in praising Him? You are willing to have Christ to pardon you, but we cannot divide Him, and therefore you must also have Him to sanctify you. You must not take the crown from His head, but accept Him as the monarch of your soul. If you would have His hand to help you, you must obey the scepter which grasps it."[5]

Regardless of how humbly Jesus appeared or how humans chose to respond to him, nothing changes the fact that he is the King of all Kings. Consider the words of John Calvin (1509-1564), theologian and preacher, on how the Christmas story reveals the majesty of Jesus:

95

"In the history which St. Luke narrates, on the one hand we learn how the Son of God emptied himself of everything for our salvation. On the other hand, we also learn that he left certain and infallible testimony that he was the Redeemer of the world who was always promised. Even though he took our condition, he was able to maintain his heavenly majesty. Both sides are shown to us here. For our Lord Jesus Christ is here in a manger and he is, as it were, rejected by the world. He is in extreme poverty without any honor, without any reputation, as if subjected to being a servant. Yet he is praised and honored by angels from Paradise. In the first place, an angel brings the message of his birth. Then the same angel is accompanied by a great multitude, even by an army, who are all present and appear as witnesses sent by God to show that our Lord Jesus Christ, being so humbled for the salvation of humanity, never stops being King of all the world and having everything under his dominion."[6]

One day, all of creation will bow to the King of Kings. As it is written:

"And being found in appearance as a man, he humbled himself and became obedient to death— even death on a cross! Therefore God exalted him to the highest place and gave him the name that is above every name, that at the name of Jesus every knee should bow, in heaven and on earth and under the earth, and every tongue confess that Jesus Christ is Lord, to the glory of God the Father" (Philippians 2:8-11).

AMEN!

---

[1] Augustine. *An Augustine Synthesis*. Arranged by Erich Przywara. Harper, 1958, p. 74.

[2] Christian Classics Ethereal Library. *The Nicene Creed*. Retrieved August 9, 2008 from http://www.ccel.org/ccel/schaff/creeds1.iv.iii.html.

[3] Witvliet, John D. and Vroege, David. *Proclaiming the Christmas Gospel, Ancient Sermons and Hymns for Contemporary Christian Inspiration*. Sermon by Thomas á Kempis. Baker Books, 2004, p. 102.

[4] Spurgeon, Charles Haddon. *Spurgeon's Sermons on Christmas and Easter*. Sermon Titled: "Immanuel – The Light of Life." Kregel Publications, 1995, p. 8.

[5] Spurgeon, Charles Haddon, p. 17.

[6] Witvliet, John D. and Vroege, David, Sermon by John Calvin, p. 122.

Light

I n the biblical account of creation, God's first command was to "let there be light" (Genesis 1:3). Prior to God's directive, "the earth was formless and empty, darkness was over the surface of the deep" (Genesis 1:2). Some scholars have understood the presence of darkness to indicate that sin had entered the universe, most likely through the fall of the angels, prior to the creation of the earth. Regardless of whether this was the case, God created a world with both light and darkness (day and night). Furthermore, God told the first man Adam, "You are free to eat from any tree in the garden; but you must not eat from the tree of the knowledge of good and evil, for when you eat of it you will surely die" (Genesis 2:16). This implies that good and evil existed, at least they could both be known, before the sin of man.

Mankind was given an opportunity to obey or disobey God. Perhaps obedience would have resulted in man's ever increasing glory. However, we can only speculate. For the first man and woman in God's creation, Adam and Eve, chose disobedience. They chose to listen to Satan, the serpent, and believe that they could be like God if they ate from the forbidden tree. This "original sin" of man resulted in darkness and death. Surely, this "darkness" was spiritual. For we know that light did not physically cease to shine in the world. Even Jesus said, "He (God) causes his sun to rise on the evil and the good" (Matthew 5:45).

Spiritual darkness and death are, in essence, separation from God, the true source of light. The Bible records that God is "resplendent with light" (Psalm 76:4) and "wraps himself in light as with a garment" (Psalm 104:2). As a consequence of their sin, Adam and Eve, and all their descendants after them, were banished from the presence of God in the Garden of Eden. They were thus cast into a world of spiritual darkness. Ultimately, only God could deal with the problem of sin; only God could reconcile mankind back to himself; only God could bring humanity back "out of darkness into his wonderful light" (1 Peter 2:9). This he accomplished by entering the world as a man. Regarding the birth of Jesus, the gospel of John records, "Light has come into the world" (John 3:19). Jesus himself said, "I have come into the world as a light, so that no one who believes in me should stay in darkness" (John 12:46). Surely, it is appropriate that our Christmas celebration be filled with light as we celebrate Jesus, the "light of the world" (John 8:12).

The Light of Fire

Since the beginning of time, man has enjoyed the light of the sun, the reflection of light from the moon, and the twinkle of light from the stars. However, it was the light of fire that proved to be particularly useful to man. Different from other lights, fire could be somewhat controlled to offer both light and warmth when needed. The Bible reveals that early in man's history, fire was also used to forge tools out of bronze and iron (Genesis 4:22). Additionally, fire was used to burn offerings to God. It is possible, even likely, that the first man, Adam, gave burnt offerings to God. We know that his sons, Cain and Abel, gave offerings, though fire is not specifically mentioned. The first clear biblical record of a burnt offering is that given by Noah upon exiting the ark (Genesis 8:20).

After the flood, Noah, the new father of all mankind, would be the first to establish the use of fire in religious ceremonies.

History reveals that fire continued to play a significant role in religion. However, many of Noah's descendants abandoned the true God and came to associate fire with their pagan rituals. One particularly interesting ritual in ancient mythology (related to the goddess Hertha) may shed light on some of the modern fantasy associated with Christmas.

Hertha Ritual:

In ancient mythology, various gods were said to descend from heaven through smoke and appear in burning fire. The Germanic people of Scandinavia are believed to have annually sought the blessing of their goddess Hertha (Bertha and Perchta are just a few of her alternate names). Various traditions portray her as "mother earth," goddess of the home and/or goddess of domesticity. Historian Alfred Hottes records:

> "During the Winter Solstice houses were decked with fir and evergreens to welcome her [Hertha's] coming. When the family and serfs were gathered to dine, a great altar of flat stones was erected and here a fire of fir boughs was laid. Hertha descended through the smoke, guiding those who were wise in saga lore to foretell the fortunes of those persons at the feast."[1]

Before the creation of the chimney, fires most likely burned in the middle of the home with smoke exiting through an opening in the roof. Legend holds that with the invention of the fireplace, "Hertha stones" were transformed into "hearthstones." Though Europe was already predominantly Christian by the time chimneys became common (in the 12th century or later),[2] it is possible that old Hertha folklore influenced the fantasy that would come to be associated with Santa Claus. In an ironic cycle of traditions, it is even possible that Hertha legends (and those surrounding other mythological gods), which cannot be dated precisely, were borrowed from ancient accounts of the one true God. The Bible records that God appeared to Moses "in flames of fire from within a bush" (Exodus 3:2), that he appeared to the Jewish people in a "pillar of fire" (Exodus 13:21) to lead them out of Egypt, and that when he appeared to Moses on Mount Sinai, "it was covered with smoke, because the Lord descended on it in fire" (Exodus 19:18).

Yule Logs:

Another interesting tradition associated with fire is the burning of the yule log. Though most scholars agree that the origin of the yule log can be traced to Northern Europe, many of the traditions, including the name *yule*, are a bit of a mystery. The term *yule* is thought to be associated with the Norse words *Jol* (a pagan winter feast) and *Hoel* (meaning "wheel").[3] Among pagans, the sun was viewed as a wheel of fire that would roll away from them and then turn back toward them in repeating cycles. Interestingly, the term *yuletide* is possibly derived from a word meaning "turning time of the sun." When the sun reached its farthest point "away" from the earth and the days were their coldest and darkest, pagans began their winter solstice rituals in the hope that the sun would turn back toward them. Perhaps the tradition of the yule log originated in the belief that a large and enduring fire would somehow draw the sun, the "wheel of fire" back toward the earth.

The burning of logs during the winter season was common in a variety of cultures. However, it appears that the traditions associated with the yule log originated in Scandinavia and were spread throughout Northern Europe. Though the rituals were initially pagan, in time they became distinctly Christian. Furthermore, since there is no historical evidence for a "Christmas Log" prior to the 16thcentury (a time by which Europe had long been Christianized), it is possible that Christians began a new tradition that had no real connection to the ancient pagan practice (other than the name "yule").[4]

Though Christian traditions varied widely, most of them agreed that the yule log was to be lit on Christmas Eve and was to burn continuously for the next 12 days of Christmas. In order to burn for 12 days, an enormous log and extensive labor were required. Over time and perhaps for practical purposes, the ritual was reduced to 12 hours and, with a few exceptions, was eventually lost altogether. For most Americans, a yule log is now best known in the form of a dessert (a custom that began in France where it is called the *Buche de Noel*).

The Light of Candles

Though candles appear to have existed in Egypt and Crete over 3,000 years before Christ,[5] the first biblical reference to candles (or "lamps") came during the Exodus of the Jews from Egypt (approximately 1446 BC – 1406 BC). In ancient times, the word *lamp* was used to describe a wick burning flame, so the term will be used here synonymously with *candle*.

Candles in the Temple:

During the Exodus, God commanded his people to make their first menorah. The Lord said, "Make a lampstand of pure gold. . . . Six branches are to extend from the sides of the lampstand – three on one side and three on the other" (Exodus 25:31-32). The people were then instructed to make seven lamps with wick trimmers and trays of pure gold (Exodus 25:37-38). The Israelites were told to bring "clear oil of pressed olives for the light" (Exodus 27:20) and the lamps were to burn "from evening till morning" (Exodus 27:21). The candles burned first in the Tent of Meeting until the Tabernacle was built; then they burned in the Tabernacle until the temple of God was built in Jerusalem. God said that the burning of the menorah candles was "to be a lasting ordinance among the Israelites for the generations to come" (Exodus 27:21).

With various exceptions, the candles did in fact burn throughout the course of many generations. In the second century BC, the candles were still burning until an evil ruler, Antiochus Epiphanes, forcibly stole them from the temple. A series of tragic events following this incident would ultimately lead to the first Hanukkah (a Jewish holiday that falls during the Christmas season). Interestingly, Dr. Cassel, a famous German scholar and Jewish convert, makes that case that the customs of Christmas are "significantly in accordance with those of the Jewish festival" of Hanukkah.[6] It should be noted that the German word for Christmas is *Weihnachten*; *weihen* means "to consecrate or dedicate", and *nacht* means "night"; this appears to correspond directly to the meaning of *Hanukkah* which is "dedication." Furthermore, since the origin of Hanukkah is very relevant to the topic of light (it is also called the "Festival of Lights"), and since it is a story of brave and godly people who prepare the way for the Messiah, it is worth exploring.

Hanukkah:

During the 400 years between Nehemiah's return to Jerusalem and the birth of Christ, history reveals that Israel came under the occupation of Greece during the conquests of Alexander the Great (356 BC – 323 BC). After his death, the empire was divided and ruled by various leaders. In 175 BC, Antiochus Epiphanes became a king. This period in history is recorded in the books of the Maccabees.

The first and second books of the Maccabees are considered "deuterocanonical," which means that they are not part of the Jewish Bible. Though they are included in Catholic and Orthodox Bibles, the books are not part of the biblical record of Protestants. Since many Christians are not familiar with them and since they have proven to be reliable historical sources, the Maccabees will be quoted extensively in order to give the history of Hanukkah.

The first book of Maccabees records how King Antiochus sought to strengthen control over his kingdom by Hellenizing (making Greek in customs, laws and religion) the people. He was ruthless in his dealings with Israel.

"He went up against Israel and came to Jerusalem with a strong force. He arrogantly entered the sanctuary and took the golden altar, the lampstand for the light, and all its utensils. He took also the table for the bread of the Presence, the cups for drink offerings, the bowls, the golden censers, the curtain, the crowns, and the gold decoration on the front of the temple; he stripped it all off. He took the silver and the gold, and the costly vessels; he took also the hidden treasures that he found" (1 Maccabees 1:20-23).

Thus, the candles could no longer burn in the temple of God, and this caused great mourning in Israel. And things would only get worse. Two years after Antiochus left Israel, he sent one of his officials who, along with a large force, totally destroyed the city of Jerusalem.

"Then the king wrote to his whole kingdom that all should be one people, and that all should give up their particular customs. All the Gentiles accepted the command of the king. Many even from Israel gladly adopted his religion; they sacrificed to idols and profaned the sabbath. And the king sent letters by messengers to Jerusalem and the towns of Judah; he directed them to follow customs strange to the land, to forbid burnt offerings and sacrifices and drink offerings in the sanctuary, to profane sabbaths and festivals, to defile the sanctuary and the priests, to build altars and sacred precincts and shrines for idols, to sacrifice swine and other unclean animals, and to leave their sons uncircumcised. They were to make themselves abominable by everything unclean and profane, so that they would forget the law and change all the ordinances. He added, 'And whoever does not obey the command of the king shall die.' In such words he wrote to his whole kingdom. He appointed inspectors over all the people and commanded the towns of Judah to offer sacrifice, town by town." (1 Maccabees 1: 41-51).

At this time, there lived a righteous priest named Mattathias. He and his sons were mourning the state of affairs in Israel when inspectors arrived in their city.

"The king's officers who were enforcing the apostasy came to the town of Modein to make them offer sacrifice. Many from Israel came to them; and Mattathias and his sons were assembled. Then the king's officers spoke to Mattathias as follows: 'You are a leader, honored and great in this town, and supported by sons and brothers. Now be the first to come and do what the king commands, as all the Gentiles and the people of Judah and those that are left in Jerusalem have done. Then you and your sons will be numbered among the friends of the king, and you and your sons will be honored with silver and gold and many gifts.' But Mattathias answered and said in a loud voice: 'Even if all the nations that live under the rule of the king obey him, and have chosen to obey his commandments, everyone of them abandoning the religion of their ancestors, I and my sons and my brothers will continue to live by the covenant of our ancestors. Far be it from us to desert the law and the ordinances. We will not obey the king's words by turning aside from our religion to the right hand or to the left.' When he had finished speaking these words, a Jew came forward in the sight of all to offer sacrifice on the altar in Modein, according to the king's command. When Mattathias saw it, he burned with zeal and his heart was stirred. He gave vent to righteous anger; he ran and killed him on the altar. At the same time he killed the king's officer who was forcing them to sacrifice, and he tore down the altar. Thus he burned with zeal for the law, just as Phinehas did against Zimri son of Salu. Then Mattathias cried out in the town with a loud voice, saying: 'Let every one who is zealous for the law and supports the covenant come out with me!'" (1 Maccabees 2:15-27).

So Mattathias and several others were forced to flee to the hills. Many innocent Israelites continued to lose their lives, so Mattathias and his friends determined they must organize an army to defend their people. Their work prospered, and their numbers increased. But the days of aging Mattathias were coming to an end, so he appointed his son Judas Maccabeus as the commander of the army. These "rebels" thus came to be known as the Maccabees.

Judas was a noble leader, and the fame of his army spread throughout the land. In battle after battle, Judas' army was greatly outnumbered in both men and weapons. But God gave them victory. After three years of struggle, Jerusalem was reclaimed.

"Then Judas and his brothers said, 'See, our enemies are crushed; let us go up to cleanse the sanctuary and dedicate it.' So all the army assembled and went up to Mount Zion. There they saw the sanctuary desolate, the altar profaned, and the gates burned. In the courts they saw bushes sprung up as in a thicket, or as on one of the mountains. They saw also the chambers of the priests in ruins. Then they tore their clothes and mourned with great lamentation; they sprinkled themselves with ashes and fell face down on the ground. And when the signal was given with the trumpets, they cried out to Heaven. Then Judas detailed men to fight against those in the citadel until he had cleansed the sanctuary. He chose blameless priests devoted to the law, and they cleansed the sanctuary and removed the defiled stones to an unclean place. They deliberated what to do about the altar of burnt offering, which had been profaned. And they thought it best to tear it down, so that it would not be a lasting shame to them that the Gentiles had defiled it. So they tore down the altar, and stored the stones in a convenient place on the temple hill until a prophet should come to tell what to do with them. Then they took unhewn stones, as the law directs, and built a new altar like the former one. They also rebuilt the sanctuary and the interior of the temple, and consecrated the courts. They made new holy vessels, and brought the lampstand, the altar of incense, and the table into the temple. Then they offered incense on the altar and lit the lamps on the lampstand, and these gave light in the temple. They placed the bread on the table and hung up the curtains. Thus they finished all the work they had undertaken. Early in the morning on the twenty-fifth day of the ninth month, which is the month of Chislev, in the one hundred forty-eighth year, they rose and offered sacrifice, as the law directs, on the new altar of burnt offering that they had built. At the very season and on the very day that the Gentiles had profaned it, it was dedicated with songs and harps and lutes and cymbals. All the people fell on their faces and worshiped and blessed Heaven, who had prospered them. So they celebrated the dedication of the altar for eight days, and joyfully offered burnt offerings; they offered a sacrifice of well-being and a thanksgiving offering. They decorated the front of the temple with golden crowns and small shields; they restored the gates and the chambers for the priests, and fitted them with doors. There was very great joy among the people, and the disgrace brought by the Gentiles was removed. Then Judas and his brothers and all the assembly of Israel determined that every year at that season the days of dedication of the altar should be observed with joy and gladness for eight days, beginning with the twenty-fifth day of the month of Chislev" (1 Maccabees 4:36-59).

So the candles of the Menorah once again gave light to the temple, and this Feast of Dedication (the word *Dedication* in Hebrew is *Hanukkah)* became an annual celebration in Israel. Though the book of Maccabees does not specify why the celebration was to last for eight days, a rabbinical commentary called the *Gemara* reveals that as the Maccabees prepared to rekindle the Menorah, they only found a small amount of holy oil: "The oil in the cruse was sufficient for only one day, but miraculously they kindled from it for eight days" *(Shabbat 21b)*. Eight days was the length of time needed to prepare additional oil qualified for use in the temple. Thus, the Maccabees lit the candle by faith, and as the traditional Hanukkah saying goes, "A great miracle happened there."

The first Hanukkah ensured that the temple was prepared to receive the Messiah less than two hundred years later. For it was in the temple of Jerusalem that Jesus was consecrated to the Lord and that his parents, Mary and Joseph, offered sacrifices according to the law. The Bible records:

"When the time of their purification according to the Law of Moses had been completed, Joseph and Mary took him to Jerusalem to present him to the Lord (as it is written in the Law of the Lord, 'Every firstborn male is to be consecrated to the Lord'), and to offer a sacrifice in keeping with what is said in the Law of the Lord: 'a pair of doves or two young pigeons'" (Luke 2:22-24).

Surely, a great light came to the temple that day, and Simeon, a righteous man, recognized it. He said, "For my eyes have seen your salvation which you have prepared in the sight of all people, a light for revelation to the Gentiles and for glory to your people Israel" (Luke 2:30-32).

The faith of the Maccabees also ensured that the temple was prepared for the Messiah to fulfill the prophecy of Malachi.

"'See, I will send my messenger, who will prepare the way before me. Then suddenly the Lord you are seeking will come to his temple; the messenger of the covenant, whom you desire, will come,' says the LORD Almighty" (Malachi 3:1).

The Bible records that during Jesus' ministry he entered the temple area at the time of Hanukkah.

"Then came the Feast of Dedication [Hanukkah] at Jerusalem. It was winter, and Jesus was in the temple area walking in Solomon's Colonnade. The Jews gathered around him, saying, 'How long will you keep us in suspense? If you are the Christ, tell us plainly.' Jesus answered, 'I did tell you, but you do not believe. The miracles I do in my Father's name speak for me, but you do not believe because you are not my sheep'" (John 10:22-26).

Josephus, a first century Jewish historian, records that Hanukkah was called the "Festival of Lights" (Antiquities XII, 7:7). How tragic that the "light of the world" (John 8:12), the one who outshone the light of the menorah, was present in the temple area during this festival, yet few had eyes to see him! Jesus said, "While I am in the world, I am the light of the world" (John 9:5). However, in his absence on earth, believers were to be the "body of Christ" (1 Corinthians 12:27) and the "light of the world." Jesus said to his disciples:

"**You** are the light of the world. A city on a hill cannot be hidden. Neither do people light a lamp and put it under a bowl. Instead they put it on its stand, and it gives light to everyone in the house. In the same way, let your light shine before men, that they may see your good deeds and praise your Father in heaven'" (Matthew 5:14-16).

Believers are to be the light of the world, and the symbolism of the menorah reveals this truth. Though the Hanukkah menorah holds nine candles (eight for each day of the celebration and a ninth that is used to light the others), the temple menorah holds seven candles. The book of Hebrews tells us that the temple is a "copy and shadow of what is in heaven" (Hebrews 8:5), and the book of Revelation uses the imagery of seven golden lampstands to depict seven churches (Revelation 1:20). These churches are thought to represent all believers in some way (throughout both time and geography). If this is the case, the temple menorah was a beautiful prophetic symbol of how the Messiah would one day live and shine through his people, the Church!

Electric Lights

Though fires and candles still burn brightly during the Christmas season in America, electric lights have become the most common source of illumination. Interestingly, electric Christmas lights trace their origin to an American Christmas tree in 1882. Just three years prior, Thomas Edison announced his invention of a long lasting light bulb. One of his employees, Edward Johnson, decided to apply the invention to his own family Christmas tree. Johnson created a string of 80 twinkling lights for his tree, a revolving box on which the tree stood, and additional lights for the ceiling above the tree.[7] Since few Americans had electricity in their homes, the display created quite a stir. A procession of people came to observe the tree, and the spectacle made news all across the country.

Electricity quickly became available to America's largest cities, but it would take several decades to reach rural American homes. Additionally, it was not until 1924 that Christmas lights became affordable for the average American. By this time, electric lights were a welcome change; many homes had been lost or damaged due to fires resulting from candle lit Christmas trees. The tradition of lighting a tree with candles quite possibly started in 16th century Germany, and though the custom had proved to be hazardous, the stunning beauty of a lighted tree was apparently deemed worthy of the risk.

Thankfully, electricity allowed Americans to more safely light their Christmas trees. In fact, Americans so much enjoyed their electric lights that by the 1930's, lights were decorating the exterior of homes, businesses, and virtually anything that could be strung with them.[8] The American Christmas quickly became a feast of lights.

Conclusion

Clearly light in the form of fire, candles and electric lights have all come to be intimately associated with Christmas. After all, the birth of Jesus signifies that "light has come into the world" (John 3:19). Yet, man did not have eyes to see the full splendor of this light. In fact, humanity still waits to gaze upon the true glory of Jesus when he makes all things new (heaven, earth and even human bodies). In the book of Revelation, the Apostle John records his vision of the new city of Jerusalem: "The city does not need the sun or the moon to shine on it, for the glory of God gives it light, and the Lamb [Jesus] is its lamp" (Revelation 21:23). How amazing that in our eternal home we will live by the light of God's glory!

_____

[1] Hottes, Alfred Carl. *1001 Christmas Facts and Fancies (1937)*. Kessinger Publishing, 2004, p. 59.

[2] Encyclopedia Britannica. "Chimney." Retrieved June 2, 2008 from Encyclopedia Britannica Online: http://www.britannica.com/eb/article-9024112.

[3] McClintock, John. *Cyclopedia of Biblical, Theological & Ecclesiastical Literature, Yule*. Harper & Brothers, 1889, p. 1012.

[4] Weiser, Francis X. *Handbook of Christian Feasts and Customs*. Harcourt, Brace and Company, 1958, p. 97.

[5] Encyclopedia Britannica. "Candle." Retrieved June 2, 2008 from Encyclopedia Britannica Online: http://www.britannica.com/eb/article-9019957.

[6] Dawson, William Francis. *Christmas: Its Origin and Associations*. E. Stock, 1902, pp. 16-17.

[7] Collins, Ace. *Stories Behind the Great Traditions of Christmas*. Zondervan, 2003, p.120.

[8] Hatch, Jane M. *The American Book of Days*. H.W. Wilson Company, 1978, p. 1147.

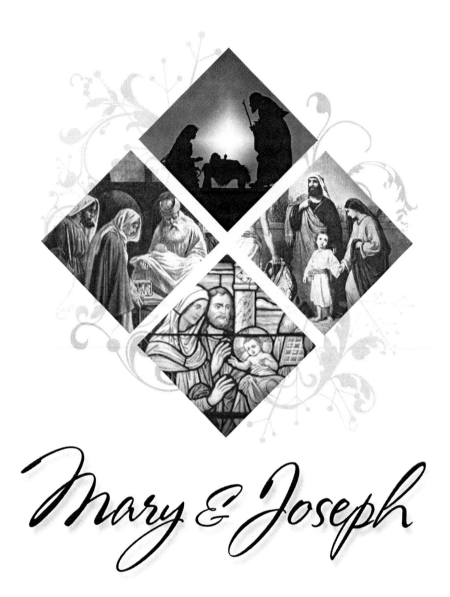

Mary & Joseph

During the Christmas season, Jesus is most often portrayed as an infant closely attended by his parents. Mary and Joseph are an essential part of the Nativity scene. They were the first of humanity to welcome the incarnate God into the world, and more profoundly, they were chosen to be his parents on earth.

Though Mary has taken a much more prominent role than Joseph in history, it is poignant to consider the monumental task assigned to Joseph. He was to lead Mary as a husband and Jesus as an earthly father. God confirms this leadership role by communicating solely with Joseph on four different occasions. The gospel of Matthew records that an angel of the Lord appeared to Joseph in dreams: telling him to take Mary as his wife (Matthew 1:20), telling him to escape with Mary and Jesus to Egypt (Matthew 2:13), telling him later to return to Israel (Matthew 2:19-20) and finally warning him not to settle his family in Judea (Matthew 2:22-23).

The Bible tells us little more of Joseph than that he was a carpenter (Matthew 13:55) and a "righteous man" (Matthew 1:19). We can infer that he cared deeply for Mary, because when he learned of her pregnancy during their betrothal, he had in mind to divorce her quietly so as not to "expose her to public disgrace" (Matthew 1:19). Historian Paul Maier gives a description of betrothal in biblical times:

> "This, the legal betrothal, was far more binding than the modern engagement. Only divorce could break it, and even though they were not yet married, had either Joseph or Mary been unfaithful to each other, it would have been deemed an adultery punishable by death [see Deut. 22:23]. Had Joseph died in the meantime, Mary would have been his legal widow."[1]

Joseph's intention of divorcing Mary quietly was meant to protect not only her reputation but also her life. One can only imagine the pain that Joseph endured as he struggled to understand Mary's apparent unfaithfulness to him. However, God saw fit to allow Joseph's character to grow in this suffering before he finally revealed that what was conceived in Mary was from the Holy Spirit.

In obedience to God, Joseph took Mary as his wife and became a father to Jesus. It is fascinating to consider that, as Jesus grew, he would have experienced the natural attachment that exists between a child and his parents. Surely, Jesus felt a deep and sincere love for Joseph, and thus would have suffered emotional pain at his death. Though the Bible never mentions Joseph's passing, he presumably died before Jesus began his earthly ministry An account of a 12-year-old Jesus at the Feast of Passover in Jerusalem makes reference to Joseph, but this is the last we hear of him (Luke 2:41-52). Considering the short life expectancy of biblical times, Joseph probably passed away early in Jesus' life. Additionally, wives were typically much younger than their husbands. Whereas Mary was believed to be an early teen when she gave birth to Jesus, Joseph was likely over thirty.

The young Mary had the honor of seeing Jesus grow "in wisdom and stature, and in favor with God and men" (Luke 2:52). But she would also witness her son suffer and die. Interestingly, Mary was the most probable source of information for the biblical account of the birth and childhood of

Jesus. She who "treasured up and pondered in her heart" (Luke 2:19 and 51) the events of Jesus' birth and childhood likely became the historian. Maier writes, "According to the earliest church tradition, it was Mary herself who told Matthew and Luke all about the Nativity, and it was they who wrote it down. And that is how we got the story of the first Christmas."[2]

Certainly, Mary played the most significant role of any woman in the gospel story. She "found favor with God" (Luke 1:30), and she was "blessed among women" (Luke 2:42). No human has ever experienced, nor will ever experience, the unique role Mary held as a virgin mother to the Son of God. As sin entered the world through the woman Eve, salvation for that sin entered the world through the woman Mary. She was the woman of whom God spoke when he told Satan:

"And I will put enmity between you and the woman, and between your offspring and hers; he will crush your head, and you will strike his heel" (Genesis 3:15).

Interestingly, the word used for offspring is "seed". Generally the Bible refers to the man's seed in the procreation of children. Yet, God foretold of a virgin birth when he spoke of "her seed." Isaiah also prophesied about Mary when he wrote, "The virgin will be with child and will give birth to a son" (Isaiah 7:14).

Christian tradition also draws parallels between Mary and the famed Ark of the Covenant, the chest in which the Ten Commandments were placed (Deuteronomy 10:1-5). Hebrews 9:4 reveals that the ark also contained "the gold jar of manna" and "Aaron's staff that had budded." Consider the following parallels as highlighted by author Steve Ray:

"In the ark was the law of God inscribed in stone; in Mary's womb was the Word of God in flesh. In the ark was the urn of manna, the bread from heaven that kept God's people alive in the wilderness; in Mary's womb is the Bread of Life come down from heaven that brings eternal life. In the ark was the rod of Aaron, the proof of true priesthood; in Mary's womb is the true priest."[3]

The old covenant of God's law was meant to reveal our sin, the consequence of which is death. God intended for the old covenant to reveal the need for a new one. Over 500 years before the birth of Jesus, Jeremiah recorded: "'The time is coming,' declares the Lord, 'when I will make a new covenant with the house of Israel and with the house of Judah'" (Jeremiah 31:31). Jesus came to be "the mediator of [this] new covenant, that those who are called may receive the promised eternal inheritance — now that he has died as a ransom to set them free from the sins committed under the first covenant" (Hebrews 9:15). Mary was chosen to be the vessel that held the fulfillment of God's great promise for a new covenant.

Yet Mary's great honor in carrying the "new covenant" would not come without hardship. Though Mary believed the angel Gabriel when he told her that she would give birth to a son (this is called the *Annunciation* and is found in Luke 1:26-38), who would have believed Mary's claim to virginity once her pregnancy became known? Perhaps to prepare and strengthen her for what was to come, Mary went to visit her relative Elizabeth. The angel Gabriel had told Mary that Elizabeth miraculously conceived a child in her old age and was in her sixth month of pregnancy. Mary "hurried to a town in the hill country of Judea" (Luke 1:39) to see Elizabeth. Surely this visit proved to be a time of encouragement. As a confirmation of Gabriel's message, Mary did indeed find that Elizabeth was pregnant. And on Mary's arrival, Elizabeth was filled with the Holy Spirit:

> "In a loud voice she exclaimed: "Blessed are you among women, and blessed is the child you will bear! But why am I so favored, that the mother of my Lord should come to me? As soon as the sound of your greeting reached my ears, the baby in my womb leaped for joy. Blessed is she who has believed that what the Lord has said to her will be accomplished!" (Luke 2:42-45).

Mary also responded to this meeting with joy. She said, "My soul glorifies [or magnifies] the Lord and my spirit rejoices in God my Savior" (this is the beginning of what is called the *Magnificat* and is found in Luke 1:46-55). Mary spent the following three months with Elizabeth before returning to Nazareth.

On arriving home, the Bible does not tell us whether any of Mary's most intimate family or friends in Nazareth believed her claim of virginity. We only know that Mary's dearly betrothed Joseph needed a personal visit from an angel to be assured of her innocence. Perhaps many agonizing days of isolation passed before Mary had Joseph, one other person in Nazareth, to believe that what was conceived in her was from the Holy Spirit. Once Joseph determined to take Mary as his wife, one can only imagine the suspicion and scorn that would have then surrounded the righteous couple.

When a decree by Caesar Augustus required that Joseph travel to Bethlehem for a census, perhaps Mary and Joseph welcomed the opportunity to leave their small town. But the 80-mile journey from Nazareth to Bethlehem would certainly have been an uncomfortable one for Mary in her advanced stage of pregnancy. To make matters worse, after a difficult journey, finding accommodations proved to be another challenging trial.

We learn that after arriving in Bethlehem, the time came for Mary to deliver her baby (Luke 2:6). Recall that Joseph had to travel to Bethlehem for the census, because this was the place of his ancestry. Surely, he would have relatives in Bethlehem. But for reasons not explicitly stated, Mary and Joseph did not stay with relatives. They had to seek shelter in an inn. The Bible simply tells us that there was "no room for them in the inn" (Luke 2:7). Perhaps the census had brought such a crowd to Bethlehem that there was truly no available shelter, or perhaps labor came too quickly to find either family or other acceptable accommodations. It is certainly possible that difficult travels could have sent Mary into early and fast-progressing labor, which would have put her and Joseph in the predicament of urgently needing shelter in a packed city. However, we cannot rule out the possibility that word had traveled to Bethlehem of Mary's "scandalous" pregnancy. In this case, relatives and innkeepers alike may have refused to offer decent shelter to Mary and Joseph. It is hard to imagine how room could not otherwise be made for a woman in labor.

The gospel of Luke records that Mary had to lay her baby in a manger, an animal's feeding trough (Luke 2:7); this implies that Mary gave birth in a stable. There is no indication that Mary and Joseph saw any glorious heavenly celebration. As far as we can tell from the biblical account, the birth of Christ was a quiet and humble event for Mary and Joseph. They were poor, alone and far from home. They had only a helpless infant to hold in their arms. Surely they had to wonder at God's plan.

Yet God did a unique thing; he used the testimony of humble shepherds to assure Mary and Joseph that he had not forgotten them. For "a great company of the heavenly host" (Luke 2:13) appeared to these shepherds, and they recounted the words of the angel who told them, "Today in the town of David a Savior has been born to you, he is Christ the Lord" (Luke 2:11). The sign they were told to look for was that the child would be wrapped in cloths and lying in a manger (Luke 2:7). Surely God confirmed through the account of these shepherds that he was well aware of the circumstances surrounding the birth of his Son. He had forgotten neither his Son nor his chosen servants Mary and Joseph. Rather, the birth had taken place just as he had intended. Furthermore, God may have used the testimony of the shepherds to secure shelter in Bethlehem for the holy family. All who heard the story "were amazed at what the shepherds said to them" (Luke 1:18), and by the time the Wise Men arrived in Bethlehem, they found Jesus and his mother Mary in a "house" (Matthew 2:11).

God did another unique thing in bringing Wise Men from the East to worship the infant Jesus (Matthew 2:1-12). Their purpose was two-fold. On the spiritual side, they revealed that people of all nations would worship Jesus. On the practical side, their gifts likely provided for the financial needs of Mary and Joseph. God would soon direct the new family to flee to Egypt, and travel would be costly.

God used other opportunities to confirm his plans to Mary and Joseph. In Jerusalem, the prophet Simeon and the prophetess Anna spoke marvelous things about the salvation and redemption that would come through Jesus (Luke 2:25-38). Also, an angel spoke on occasion to Joseph in dreams (as recorded above). Yet, Mary and Joseph would have to trust God's plan every day. There would surely be many days ahead that would be difficult, or maybe just mundane, when they would wonder why the life of the Son of God seemed so simple, so lacking in grandeur. Perhaps God was preparing them for this in the humble experience of the birth itself.

Though events on earth may seem insignificant, consider that the view from heaven may be dramatically different. When the Apostle John was permitted to witness the birth of Christ from a heavenly perspective, he wrote:

"A great and wondrous sign appeared in heaven: a woman clothed with the sun, with the moon under her feet and a crown of twelve stars on her head. She was pregnant and cried out in pain as she was about to give birth. . . . She gave birth to a son, a male child, who will rule all the nations with an iron scepter" (Revelation 12:1,2 and 5a).

What a contrast to the humble manger scene! Consider that as we serve God on earth, even in ways that seem trivial, we are part of a grand heavenly story. May we have a heart like Mary's to say, "I am the Lord's servant" (Luke 1:38).

----

[1] Maier, Paul L. *In the Fullness of Time*. Kregel Publications, 1997, p. 17.Kregel Publications, 1997, p. 17.

[2] Maier, Paul L., p. 86.

[3] Ray, Steve. "Mary, The Ark of the Covenant." Retrieved August 10, 2008 from Catholic Culture: http://www.catholicculture.org/library/view.cfm?RecNum=6811.

Mistletoe

There are a great variety of species of mistletoe; most of them are evergreen and bear their fruit (generally either red or white berries) in the early winter. Since so few plants remain green in the winter, mistletoe naturally came to be associated with the Christmas season.

The etymology of the word *mistletoe* is unknown, but some scholars believe that it is derived from the Old English *misteltan* (*mistel* meaning "dung" and *tan* meaning "twig"). Interestingly, mistletoe does in fact grow from "dung on a twig." A variety of birds make their nests in mistletoe on the branches of trees. These birds eat the berries of mistletoe and excrete living seeds, generally on branches in the near vicinity. These seeds then grow into new mistletoe plants!

The botanical name for the genus of mistletoe is *Phoradendron* (*phor* meaning "thief" and *dendron* meaning "tree" in Greek). As a partly parasitic plant, mistletoe does in fact act like a thief and "steal" nutrients from its host tree. It is only "partly" parasitic, because it has the ability to photosynthesize its own food and survive independently. However, mistletoe is generally found on trees, and it will use whatever means necessary to survive. It has been known to endure extremely harsh weather and even droughts by reaching deep beneath the tree bark of its host to drain water and minerals.

Likely due to its tenacity to survive, mistletoe came to play a prominent role in many pre-Christian traditions: Druidism, Norse mythology and Greco-Roman mythology. In each tradition, there is a common theme of protecting life.

Druidism

Druidism is a religion that is generally associated with the people of Gaul. The Romans referred to the region of Western Europe as Gaul. However, over time, the people of Gaul would migrate as far east as Asia Minor (recall that the Apostle Paul wrote a letter to the Galatians) and as far North as Ireland (where the term *gaelic* and its related term *celtic* are still used to describe ancient language and culture).

The Gallic religion is somewhat of a mystery. It appears that the people worshipped both nature and animals. They also had a set of gods loosely related to Greek gods. Part of the difficulty in understanding Gallic theology is that their Druid priests fervently guarded the secrets of their order. One of the few sources we have for understanding the role of mistletoe among Druids is Pliny the Elder (23-79 AD) who was considered the standard authority for plant and animal life in his time. Pliny records the following in his famous book *Historia Naturalis*:

"In treating of this subject, the admiration in which the mistletoe is held throughout Gaul ought not to pass unnoticed. The Druids, for so they call their wizards, esteem nothing more sacred than the mistletoe and the tree on which it grows, provided only that the tree is an oak. . . . For they believe that whatever grows on these trees is sent from heaven, and is a sign that the tree has been chosen by the god himself. The mistletoe is very rarely to be met with; but when it is found, they gather it with solemn ceremony. . . . After due preparations have been made for a sacrifice and a feast under the tree, they hail it as the universal healer and bring to the spot two white bulls, whose horns have never been bound before. A priest clad in a white robe climbs the tree and with a golden sickle cuts the mistletoe, which is caught in a white cloth. Then they sacrifice the victims, praying that God may make his own gift to prosper with those upon whom he has bestowed it. They believe that a potion prepared from mistletoe will make barren animals to bring forth, and that the plant is a remedy against all poison."[1]

According to Pliny the Elder, Druids believed that mistletoe had the power to protect life through healing and propagation. Some scholars believe that the practice of kissing under mistletoe originated with the Gallic notion that mistletoe helped to "bring forth" life through the union of male and female.

Norse Mythology

The term "Norse" is generally applied to the people of Scandinavia, so the terms will be used interchangeably. In Norse mythology, mistletoe played a prominent role in the story of Balder, the god of light. Balder was the son of Odin and Frigga, the supreme god and goddess (comparable to Zeus and Hera of Greek mythology or Jupiter and Juno of Roman mythology).

The myth of Balder tells how he became troubled by dreams that he would die. On learning of the dreams, his mother Frigga "extracted an oath from fire and water, from iron and all other metals, from stones, trees, diseases, beasts, birds, poisons, and creeping things, that none of them would do any harm to Balder."[2] Unfortunately, Frigga overlooked one thing, mistletoe, because she thought it was harmless. All was believed to be well among the gods, and they would often amuse themselves with throwing things at Balder (since nothing would hurt him). But Loki, an evil and mischievous god, undertook to harm Balder. He sought out mistletoe and persuaded the blind god Hoeder to hurl it at Balder. Sure enough, Balder died, and the entire world mourned for him.

Though mistletoe was the cause of Balder's death, it is believed that his story inspired a curious Scandinavian practice in which mistletoe would become a symbol of protecting life. Basically, when enemies met under mistletoe, they were obligated to drop their weapons and embrace. Perhaps in honor of Balder, Scandinavians would hesitate to needlessly harm one another. Surely, Balder's death was pointless and resulted only in sorrow. An embrace would further emphasize the commitment of good will between enemies in the presence of mistletoe. It is intriguing to consider the feared Vikings of old engaging in this practice, but even they may have recognized the need, on occasion, to honor and protect life. This ancient tradition may be another source for the modern custom of kissing when meeting under mistletoe.

Henry Wadsworth Longfellow (1807-1882), the great American poet, put an interesting spin on the death of Balder in his poem "Tegner's Drapa":

Balder the Beautiful,
God of the summer sun,
Fairest of all the Gods!
Light from his forehead beamed,
Runes were upon his tongue,
As on the warrior's sword.

All things in earth and air
Bound were by magic spell
Never to do him harm;
Even the plants and stones;
All save the mistletoe,
The sacred mistletoe!

Hoeder, the blind old God,
Whose feet are shod with silence,
Pierced through that gentle breast
With his sharp spear, by fraud
Made of the mistletoe,
The accursed mistletoe!

They laid him in his ship,
With horse and harness,
As on a funeral pyre.
Odin placed
A ring upon his finger,
And whispered in his ear.

They launched the burning ship!
It floated far away
Over the misty sea,
Till like the sun it seemed,
Sinking beneath the waves.
Balder returned no more!

So perish the old Gods!
But out of the sea of Time
Rises a new land of song,
Fairer than the old.

Over its meadows green
Walk the young bards and sing.

Build it again,
O ye bards,
Fairer than before!
Ye fathers of the new race,
Feed upon morning dew,
Sing the new Song of Love!

The law of force is dead!
The law of love prevails!
Thor, the thunderer,
Shall rule the earth no more,
No more, with threats,
Challenge the meek Christ.

Sing no more,
O ye bards of the North,
Of Vikings and of Jarls!
Of the days of Eld
Preserve the freedom only,
Not the deeds of blood![3]

Longfellow portrays Balder as a symbol of the transition between the death of the old gods and the beginning of the age of the true God. Mistletoe may have caused the death of "the law of force," but it ushered in "the law of love" in which the "deeds of blood" should cease. Thus, in both Scandinavian practice and in Longfellow's poem, mistletoe symbolized the protection of life.

Greco-Roman Mythology

Virgil (70 BC – 19 BC), the classical Roman author, is probably best known for his classic poem *Aeneid.* In this epic tale, the hero Aeneas desires to seek counsel from his deceased father in the land of the dead. Sibyl, a prophetess, advises Aeneas that he must seek a "golden bough (branch)" in order to have a successful journey. The difficulty would not be in entering the land of the dead but in returning from it. Thus, Aeneas seeks out the sacred branch. With the help of his mother Venus, disguised as two doves, Aeneas finds the sacred branch. His life is protected as he visits his father and then returns home.

Most scholars believe that the "golden bough" is mistletoe on the branch of a tree, since mistletoe can have a golden-like appearance. Interestingly, since the Middle Ages, Virgil's writing has come to be viewed as symbolic and even prophetic regarding many aspects of Christianity. Whether there is any merit to this claim or not, the image of a golden branch certainly calls to mind the many Old Testament references to Messiah as the "Branch" (Isaiah 4:2, 11:1; Jeremiah 23:5, 33:15; Zechariah 3:8, 6:12). Since the purpose of Virgil's golden branch was to save Aeneas from the land of the dead, the reflection of Jesus is further emphasized in the Christian mind. Additionally, the image of two doves directing Aeneas to the golden bough is fascinating. Doves recall both the law (doves were used as a sacrifice for sin) and the Holy Spirit (who descended on Jesus in the form of a dove). See p. 73 for more information about doves.

In regard to Christmas, it may be worth mentioning the verses of Virgil's *Eclogue 4*. Virgil speaks of a new age that will begin with the birth of a boy sent down from heaven:

"Now the last age by Cumae's Sibyl sung
Has come and gone, and the majestic roll
Of circling centuries begins anew:
Justice returns, returns old Saturn's reign,
With a new breed of men sent down from heaven.
Only do thou, at the boy's birth in whom
The iron shall cease, the golden race arise,
Befriend him, chaste Lucina; 'tis thine own
Apollo reigns. And in thy consulate,
This glorious age, O Pollio, shall begin,
And the months enter on their mighty march.
Under thy guidance, whatso tracks remain
Of our old wickedness, once done away,
Shall free the earth from never-ceasing fear.
He shall receive the life of gods, and see
Heroes with gods commingling, and himself
Be seen of them, and with his father's worth
Reign o'er a world at peace."[4]

Perhaps Virgil was not just a poet, but a prophet as well. He speaks of the boy who will "free the earth from never-ceasing fear." What greater fear does man have than death? Just like Aeneas, all men need a "golden branch" as protection from the land of the dead. This Branch is Jesus, the one "sent down from heaven."

Conclusion

Interestingly, many of the pre-Christian traditions surrounding mistletoe and its power to protect survived well into the Christian era. Mistletoe was hung over doors as protection from witches and demons, hung in cradles to protect infants from fairies and kept in homes as protection from fires. Surely, mistletoe has no power to offer such protection, but let it serve as a reminder of the one who truly can protect our lives and, more importantly, our souls. Consider the words of Psalm 91:

"'Because he loves me,' says the Lord, 'I will rescue him; I will protect him, for he acknowledges my name. He will call upon me, and I will answer him; I will be with him in trouble, I will deliver him and honor him. With long life will I satisfy him and show him my salvation'" (Psalm 91:14-16).

It is God who protects our lives and saves us for life eternal!

---

[1] Frazer, James George. *The Golden Bough, A Study in Magic and Religion*. MacMillan, 1900, p. 327.

[2] Bulfinch, Thomas. *Bulfinch's Mythology*. Harper Collins Publishers, 1991, p.299.

[3] Longfellow, Henry Wadsworth. *The Poetical Works of Henry Wadsworth Longfellow*. Houghton, Mifflin and Company, 1901, pp. 283-285.

[4] Virgil. *The Eclogues*. Kessinger Publishing, 2004, p. 14.

Nativity Scene

Records indicate that as early as the fourth century, churches were setting up manger scenes.[1] However, St. Francis of Assisi (1181-1226), a friar who is best known for founding the order of Franciscan monks, is credited with taking the scene beyond the walls of the church and popularizing it.[2]

St. Francis of Assisi was a fascinating man. It appears that in his youth he loved pleasure and spent money lavishly. But God was soon to capture his attention. At about 20 years of age, Francis took part in a small local battle. He was taken prisoner and was held for over a year. During this time of captivity, Francis determined to live a more noble and meaningful life, and once he was free, he set out to pursue a military career.

One night before heading off for war, Francis had a dream in which he saw a long hall hung with armor bearing the sign of the cross. He heard a voice say, "These are for you and your soldiers." Francis awoke feeling certain that he would achieve great success in battle. However, an illness detained his journey, and another dream persuaded him to return to Assisi in Italy.

After much reflection, Francis finally realized that God had been directing him to a spiritual life, and, setting pride aside, he humbly submitted. On noticing his changed demeanor and distracted mind, his companions teased him and asked if he had plans to be married. Francis replied, "Yes. I am about to take a wife of surpassing fairness." Sure enough, it was "Lady Poverty" to which he would devote his life.[3] Francis had been meditating on Scripture and was struck by Christ's commandment to leave all things and follow him. This became the rule of his life.

Though people scoffed at Francis initially, with time he would earn the love and respect of his generation, as well as many generations to follow. The popularity of Francis may largely be attributed to his winsome personality. The Catholic Encyclopedia says of Francis:

"Few saints ever exhaled 'the good odour of Christ' to such a degree as he. There was about Francis, moreover, a chivalry and a poetry which gave to his other-worldliness a quite romantic charm and beauty. Other saints have seemed entirely dead to the world around them, but Francis was ever thoroughly in touch with the spirit of the age."[4]

Francis delighted in humanity, animals, nature and song. In fact, it is believed that St. Francis and his friars were the first to compose Christmas carols. The word *carol* appears to come from the Middle English *carolen,* which means to "sing joyously." Carols were generally written as festive tunes that could be danced to. That Christmas carols would originate with Francis seems quite consistent with his character. He believed that man was created to rejoice in God.

Apart from his happy demeanor, the most prominent attribute for which Francis is remembered is his sympathy. Quite novel to the medieval world in which Francis lived, he showed a special affection for the poor, the sick and the fallen. It was probably his love for the poor that moved him to re-enact the Nativity scene that has become a familiar symbol of Christmas. Francis wanted to give a visual demonstration (remember that many people of his day were illiterate) of the poverty into which our Lord was born. He said that his wish was "to do something that will recall to memory the little Child who was born in Bethlehem and set before our bodily eyes in some way the inconveniences of his infant needs, how he lay in a manger, how, with an ox and an ass standing by, he lay upon the hay where he had been placed."[5]

In 1223 at Greccio, Italy, St. Francis received a manger, some straw and a few animals from his friend John Velita in order to accomplish his task. The simple scene, illuminated by the light of candles and torches (brought by men and women of the neighborhood) and accompanied by singing, surely accomplished the intended goal of visually revealing the humble circumstances into which Jesus entered the world. [6]

Over the centuries, Nativity scenes have evolved into much more elaborate displays that include Jesus, Mary, Joseph, Shepherds, Wise Men, an Angel (or Angels) and in some cases even the Star of Bethlehem. Though the scenes may not be perfectly historical (for example, the Bible records that the Wise Men arrived at a "house," not the manger), they continue to inspire worship of the newborn King, the Creator of the Universe, who entered his world in profound humility. Surely, this worship of the Lord is the end for which St. Francis labored.

Manger and Stable

Luke records that Mary "gave birth to her firstborn, a son [and] placed him in a manger" (Luke 2:7). The word *manger* is derived from a Latin verb *mandere* which means "to chew," and Webster's defines it as "a trough or open box in a stable designed to hold feed or fodder for livestock." The Bible never specifically mentions a stable, but the fact that Jesus was laid in a trough implies that Mary and Joseph must have been staying with animals. Simply put, "there was no room for them in the inn" (Luke 2:7), and the only other shelter available was probably that of animals.

Though the stable is typically depicted as a wooden structure, it was more likely a cave. In 150 AD, Justin Martyr (approximately 100-165 AD), a Christian philosopher and writer, recorded how Jesus was born in a cave that was used as a stable.[7] Additionally, in 326 AD, the Church of the Nativity was erected at the site of the cave that was traditionally held to be the birthplace of Christ. Interestingly, the manger may not have been made of wood either. Archeologists have excavated several stone mangers that date back to biblical times.[8] Though the stable and the manger are almost always made of wood in modern Nativity scenes, it is quite possible that they were both carved out of stone at the original scene.

The Bible does not tell us if in fact Mary and Joseph used hay to cushion the manger for their newborn infant, but it is reasonable to assume that they would seek to minimize both the roughness and filth of an animal trough. Assuming they were in a stable, hay would be a likely solution. The Bible simply says that Jesus was wrapped in cloths (Luke 1:7). One can only imagine what kind of cloth would be available in a stable. They could rather be called "rags," material discarded by people who deemed them fit only for animals. Surely we have a Savior who understands poverty and want. It is difficult to conceive of a more humble birth.

Ox and Donkey

Most people are surprised to find that there is no mention of either an ox or a donkey in the gospel records. It appears that Christians understood the prophecy of Isaiah (written approximately 700 years before the birth of Jesus) to apply to the birth of Christ: "The ox knows its owner and the donkey its master's *manger*, but Israel does not know, my people do not understand" (Isaiah 1:2-3).

As early as the second century, Christian art portrayed both ox and donkey at the birth of Christ. Knowing that Christ was laid in a manger, it is reasonable to expect that animals were present; however, whether an ox or a donkey were there, no one can be sure.

Note that the other people and elements of the Nativity scene are discussed in separate entries in this section: Angels, Jesus, Mary and Joseph, Shepherds, Star of Bethlehem and Wise Men.

---

[1] Thompson, Sue Ellen. *Holiday Symbols*. Omnigraphics, 1988, P. 70.

[2] Robinson, Paschal. "St. Francis." The Catholic Encyclopedia. Robert Appleton Company, 1909. Retrieved August 9, 2008 from New Advent: http://www.newadvent.org/cathen/06221a.htm. Much of the biography for St. Francis is drawn from this source.

[3] Robinson, Paschal.

[4] Robinson, Paschal.

[5] Thomas of Celano. *St. Francis of Assisi*. Translated from the Latin by Placid Herman. Franciscan Herald Press, 1963, p. 43.

[6] Thomas of Celano.

[7] Martyr, Justin. *Dialogue with Trypho*, Chapter LXXVIII. Retrieved August 9, 2008 from Christian Classics Ethereal Library: http://www.ccel.org/ccel/schaff/anf01.viii.iv.lxxviii.html.

[8] Maier, Paul L. *In the Fullness of Time*. Kregel Publications, 1997, pp. 38-41.

Poinsettias

Poinsettias are certainly a natural plant to associate with Christmas. They bloom during the Christmas season, and their star-shaped leaves call to mind both the star of Bethlehem and Christ himself who is called the "bright morning star" (Revelation 22:16).

The poinsettia, which is native to Mexico, is called *Cuitlaxochitl* (Star Flower) in the language of the Aztec people (an ethnic group that dominated central Mexico from the 14th to the 16th century). Apparently, poinsettias were so popular among the Aztecs that the last of their kings, Montezuma, had large quantities carried to what is now Mexico City (since they could not be grown in its high altitude).[1]

Even after the Spanish conquest of the Aztec Empire in the 16th century, the poinsettia retained its popularity in Mexico. However, since the country was Christianized through the influence of the Spaniards, the poinsettia came to be associated with one of the most significant Christian holidays — Christmas. A charming legend was spread throughout Mexico telling of how a simple weed was miraculously transformed into the first poinsettia plant on Christmas Eve. The plant soon came to be known in Mexico as the *Flores de Noche Buena* (Flowers of the Holy Night). See p. 431 for "The Legend of the Poinsettia."

The Botanical Name

The botanical name of the poinsettia is *Euphorbia Pulcherrima*. Carl Linnaeus (1707-1778), called the "Father of Taxonomy" because of his system for classifying organisms, is credited with naming the genus *Euphorbia*. Linnaeus had a passion for nature and a deep love for God. He believed that the study of living things revealed God's divine order. In the preface to a late edition of *Systema Naturae*, Linnaeus wrote that "the earth's creation is the glory of God, as seen from the works of Nature by Man alone."[2]

Linnaeus named the genus *Euphorbia* in honor of Euphorbus, a first century physician. Little is known of Euphorbus beyond his association with a plant from distant Africa, but it is believed that he used this African plant medicinally. On the other hand, Euphorbus' brother, Antonius Musa, was a much more distinguished physician who had a bronze statue erected in his honor.

Linnaeus was struck by the contrast between the legacies of Euphorbus and his brother Musa. The bronze statue of Musa had vanished, but Euphorbus' legacy of a remote plant had remained. Musa's name was attached to the creation of man, whereas Euphorbus' name was attached to the creation of God. Linnaeus wrote, "Where now is the statue of Musa? It has perished, vanished. But that of Euphorbus is perdurable, perennial, nor can it ever be destroyed."[3]

The name of the species, *Pulcherrima*, is credited to a German botanist by the name of Karl Ludwig Wilenow. Some accounts tell that while Wilenow was working in Mexico in the early 1800s, a poinsettia plant grew in through a crack in his greenhouse and blossomed before his eyes. He recognized it as a member of the Euphorbia family and christened the plant, *Euphorbia Pulcherrima*, meaning "most beautiful of the Euphorbias."[4]

The Popular Name

Joel Roberts Poinsett (1779-1851) was a physician, botanist and politician. In 1825, he became the first U.S. minister to Mexico (note that the term "ambassador" was not used until 1896 in the U.S.). Apparently, Poinsett injected himself so deeply in Mexican politics (until his recall in 1830) that the Mexicans coined the word *poinsettismo* to describe intrusive behavior.[5] Though his contribution *to* Mexico may have been questionable, Poinsett's contribution *from* Mexico proved to be an enduring one. Because of his interest in botany, Poinsett actively sought out new plant species during his stay. While visiting an area in Southern Mexico, Poinsett found the plant that was soon to carry his namesake. He sent samples of the plant home to his greenhouse in South Carolina and thus introduced the plant to the United States.

As the plant became increasing popular in the U.S., William Prescott (1796-1859), known as America's first "scientific historian," was asked to give the *Euphorbia Pulcherrima* a new name. Having recently completed the soon-to-be-famous book, "History of the Conquest of Mexico," Prescott had carefully documented Poinsett's discovery and thought it fitting to name the plant after him.[6]

The Flowers

Contrary to popular belief, the colorful leaves of the poinsettia are not petals of the flower; they are modified leaves, also called *bracts*. The flowers, called *cyathia*, are the small yellow structures found in the center.

Poinsettias are perennial plants that flower during the Christmas season. However, after their initial blossom, they need careful attention throughout the year in order to flower again. Because of the effort required, most experts advise to just "use it and lose it." Whether or not you agree, it is interesting to consider the care that a poinsettia plant requires in order to flower again. Since God is called the "gardener" (John 15:1), and the people of God are called "the garden of his delight" (Isaiah 5:7), perhaps it is worth exploring the careful attention that is required of a gardener.

So how does a gardener best tend to a poinsettia in order for it to blossom again? After Christmas, a poinsettia needs to be kept in a cool ventilated place. By the end of winter, it needs to be pruned and repotted. Like any plant, the poinsettia will then need an appropriate amount of water, sun and fertilizer. Note that though poinsettias need moist soil, sitting in water can do them harm. They must be allowed to drain out any excess water. Since the poinsettia is a "short-day plant," it will not flower until a few months after daylight shortens to 12 hours or less. Most experts advise that from the start of October to the end of November the poinsettia be kept in complete darkness for 15 hours a night. Any light exposure at all during the night can delay flowering.[7]

Clearly, a gardener must carefully tend to a poinsettia in order to see it flower again. It is interesting to consider how the poinsettia can reflect aspects of our own lives. First, though a poinsettia needs to absorb a fair amount of water, it also needs to let excess water flow out of it. If it sits in excess water, it will be damaged. In the same way, we need to allow God's living water to both fill our soul and flow out to others. Second, though a little cutting and pruning are to be expected, the poinsettia actually needs periods of complete darkness; even a small amount of incidental light can hinder it from flowering. During the dark and difficult times in life, there is comfort in knowing that the tender gardener desires for us to bloom, not to wither. We are meant to be "a planting of the Lord for the display of his splendor" (Isaiah 61:3)!

---

[1] Wolford, Ron. "The Poinsettia Pages, History." Retrieved August 10, 2008 from University of Illinois Extension: http://www.urbanext.uiuc.edu/poinsettia/.

[2] Waggoner, Ben. "Carl Linnaeus." Retrieved August 10, 2008 from University of California Museum of Paleontology: http://www.ucmp.berkeley.edu/history/linnaeus.html.

[3] Archer, Robert. "Euphorbia." Retrieved August 10, 2008 from PlantZAfrica: http://www.plantzafrica.com/plantefg/euphorbia.htm.

[4] Wolford, Ron.

[5] Encyclopedia Britannica. "Joel R. Poinsett.". Retrieved August 10, 2008 from Encyclopedia Britannica Online: http://www.britannica.com/eb/article-9060536.

[6] Wolford, Ron

[7] Wolford, Ron. "The Poinsettia Pages, Reflowering." Much of the information for reflowering is drawn from this source.

Santa Claus

The name *Santa Claus* is the English form of *Sinterklaas*, the Dutch name for St. Nicholas. Though the modern Santa Claus is associated with a world of fantasy, the historical St. Nicholas (around 270 AD - 343 AD) was a godly man known for his charity and generosity.

Nicholas was born in Patara (a harbor city in modern day Turkey) in the 270s AD to wealthy Christian parents. It is probable that Nicholas and his parents could trace their spiritual heritage to the Apostle Paul, who stopped in Patara on his third missionary journey 200 years earlier (Acts 21:1).

It is said that Nicholas' parents were devout believers who had long prayed for a child. When Nicholas was finally born, they devoted him to God. As an only child, Nicholas was raised with great affection and special attention. However, when Nicholas was still young (probably a teenager), a plague struck his city, and both of his parents died. Though a loss like this might turn some away from God, it seems to have drawn Nicholas closer to him. It also made the boy's heart tender to the suffering of others.

Nicholas was left with a large inheritance and decided that he would use it to honor God. He developed such a good reputation in his region that he was chosen as Archbishop of Myra (a harbor city just south and east of Patara) when he was in his early 20s, an indication that he must have demonstrated wisdom and maturity beyond his years.

During his service as Archbishop, a violent persecution of Christians began. Nicholas was almost certainly imprisoned during this time and was likely tortured for his faith. The persecution that began during the reign of the Roman Emperor Diocletian was carried on by his successor, Galerius, for a total of eight long years until …

> "By 311, Galerius had had enough. The most widespread persecution in Roman history had failed to force every knee to bow to Caesar and Roman gods. The people were outraged, the emperor's own guards were sullen about their role in this unrelenting bloodbath, and the Christians continued to choose torture or death rather than worship the emperor. *He – God?* What a laugh! Galerius was dying of a terminal illness and would soon be dead himself. His own wife had turned against his vindictive edict, imploring him to make peace with the all-powerful God of the Christians before it was too late. So Galerius finally caved in: he promulgated an edict of toleration, recognized Christianity as a 'lawful religion,' and contritely asked the Christians to pray for him in return for 'our most humble clemency.'"[1]

Christian leaders who endured this period of persecution earned a tremendous amount of admiration from believers and pagans alike. Had anyone questioned Nicholas' young age at his appointment as Archbishop, they would no longer express concern. Years of suffering for his faith had most certainly deepened his godly character in a manner worthy of respect.

Interestingly, following Emperor Galerius, Constantine, the first Christian Emperor, became the undisputed leader of the West. By 324 AD, Constantine claimed leadership of the entire empire and declared Christianity a legal religion. Once persecution ended and Christians gained new religious freedom, they started to face new challenges. Serious disagreements regarding doctrine began to erupt. Constantine recognized the need for unity among Christians, so in 325 AD he summoned bishops from all over the empire to meet in Nicea and discuss critical doctrinal issues. Nicholas of Myra is listed among the bishops in attendance at this meeting. Little could Nicholas have known that his name would one day be more recognized than any other in attendance at this council that developed the famous Nicene Creed (see pp. 93-94).

Stories of St. Nicholas

There are an overwhelming number of stories regarding Nicholas' generosity and even miracles. Three of the most popular are summarized below.

(1) Journey to Holy Land:

While on board a ship, Nicholas had a vivid dream of Satan cutting the ropes that supported the vessel's main mast. Nicholas interpreted the dream to mean that a storm was coming. He quickly alerted the sailors and assured them that God would protect them from death. Sure enough, a violent storm immediately followed the warning. In an effort to save the mast of the ship, one sailor was given the dangerous task of climbing it to secure the rope supports. The sailors below begged Nicholas to pray for the success of this effort. The ropes were successfully secured, but the sailor was thrown to his death on the deck below before he could climb back down. The storm gradually subsided, and though the sailors thanked God for their lives, they were overcome with grief for the loss of their companion. Nicholas felt compelled to ask God to return life to the dead sailor. God answered his prayer, and miraculously, the sailor awoke as if from a deep sleep.

On reaching the port, news of this miracle spread quickly. With time, Nicholas became the patron saint of sailors throughout the world; he even displaced the pagan gods Poseidon (the Greek name) and Neptune (the Roman name) in many regions. Since a number of American traditions regarding St. Nicholas come from Holland, it is interesting to consider that, as their patron saint of the sea, an image of St. Nicholas often stood on the bow of Dutch ships and would literally be the first thing to touch American soil when arriving in the U.S.

(2) Confrontation with Artemis:

Another miraculous story involves a confrontation with the goddess Artemis (the Greek name), also called Diana (the Roman name). Her name is mentioned in an account of the Apostle Paul's visit to Ephesus (another harbor city in modern day Turkey) in Acts 19. Her temple at Ephesus was one of the Seven Wonders of the World, and there was a great riot in the city when a group of men realized that Paul was leading people away from her worship.

In Myra, where Nicholas served as bishop, there was another great temple built for Artemis. Nicholas recognized that demonic power was at work in this temple, and he began to pray against it. Simeon Metaphrastes, a sixth century biographer, records how the altar in the temple collapsed and statues began to fall down. When the demons realized that they had been rendered powerless, they cried out to Nicholas, "You have been unjust to us. We did you no harm, and yet you send us away from our home. We had made this our home, while these misguided people adored us, and now where can we go."[2] Nicholas advised them to return to Hell's fire! It was the earnest desire of Nicholas that the people of Myra know the one true God, and he wanted nothing to hinder them.

(3) The Three Dowerless Daughters:

Perhaps the most well known story about the generosity of St. Nicholas involved a nobleman who had lost his fortune (in days of piracy, this could easily happen in a single attack). The pain of the loss was most poignant to the nobleman when he considered the future of his three young daughters. In those days, men would not propose marriage to women that were destitute. The options were grim. To survive, the father would have to sell his daughters as slaves or send them to work as prostitutes. At the point in which he could delay a decision no longer, the father determined that he would have to sacrifice the oldest of the daughters. Perhaps with her earnings, a small dowry for the other sisters could be saved. Word of this dreadful situation spread through the community. When it reached Nicholas, he decided to take action.

Determined to be anonymous, Nicholas secretly delivered a bag of gold to the oldest daughter. Some say that the gold was placed in her stockings as they hung to dry by the fire. Others claim that the bag was dropped down the chimney, but this is unlikely since chimneys were rare before the 12th century.[3] However since fires generally burned in the middle of homes, the roof would have had an opening through which smoke could escape. Perhaps Nicholas dropped the bag through this opening.

However it was delivered, there was great rejoicing in the home when it was found. The oldest daughter was dowered and happily married. And there was enough money to support the family until the second daughter came of age. At that point, the father boldly asked God for another miracle. Sure enough, a second bag of gold appeared in the same manner as the first. By the time the third daughter was ready for marriage, the father prayed again. This time, he was determined to discover his bene-factor. He kept watch night after night until the third bag was delivered. When the father finally heard someone approaching in the middle of the night, he rose and found that, sure enough, it was the man he had been waiting for. On learning the identity of the generous Nicholas, the aging father fell at his feet in gratitude. Nicholas raised him up, told him that God alone should be thanked, and begged that he tell no one. However, testimony of Nicholas' kindness could not be contained, and word would soon spread.

St. Nicholas and Christmas

After his death on December 6, 343 AD, a tradition of gift giving was begun in honor of the generous spirit of Nicholas. Some traditions taught that Nicholas would ride a horse down from heaven on December 5, St. Nicholas Eve, and distribute gifts to children that had been obedient to God. It is possible that Christians used St. Nicholas Day to replace old Northern European traditions. Folklore held that the mythological god Odin would host a great hunting party in the winter. Children would fill their boots with carrots or hay and set out to find Odin's flying horse Sleipner. Odin would thank the children for their kindness to Sleipner by replacing the horse's food with candy and gifts. Interestingly, Odin was often depicted as an old man with a long white beard. When the people of Northern Europe embraced Christianity, these practices naturally became associated with Nicholas, a saint whose giving spirit was celebrated in the winter. Dutch children still make a practice of filling their shoes with food for the horse of St. Nicholas, and it is possible that American stockings are a variation of the practice.

St. Nicholas Day is still observed on December 6 in many countries, but in others, America included, the practices associated with St. Nicholas' Day were combined with Christmas. It seems natural that a holiday celebrating giving would merge with the birth of Christ, the greatest gift ever given to the world. However, the merger happened to the dismay of many Christian leaders who thought that St. Nicholas drew too much attention away from Christ. In Germany, parents were encouraged to teach their children that the Christ Child was the gift-giver. The name *Kriss Kringle* is the English form of the German name *Christ-kindl* (Christ Child). Ironically, in America the name *Kriss Kringle* came to be used synonymously with St. Nicholas, St. Nick, Santa Claus and even the English name *Father Christmas*; all are associated with a white-bearded man in a red suit.

St. Nicholas in America

In Middle Age art, St. Nicholas was typically depicted as a tall, thin, bearded cleric. He was distinguished from other bishops by the three golden balls that he carried to represent the three bags of gold given to the dowerless daughters. This symbol helped the illiterate people of the day to differentiate St. Nicholas from other famous bishops of the past. So how did he evolve into the Santa that we know today in America?

Santa's red suit likely evolved from the red bishop's vestments worn by the Dutch Sinterklaas. Though the Dutch Sinterklaas rides a white horse across rooftops in Holland and is said to permanently reside in Spain, America's Santa rides a sleigh drawn by reindeer and makes his residence in the North Pole.

America may have adopted the idea of reindeer from Denmark where Santa's counterpart, Julemanden, uses reindeer to pull his sleigh. And just in case those of you in warmer climates thought reindeer were fictional, they are a real Arctic deer and do in fact pull sleighs. Though the idea for Santa's reindeer was probably borrowed, the "most famous reindeer of all" is uniquely American. Rudolph was invented in 1939 by Robert L. May as part of a marketing campaign at Montgomery Ward and Company.

> "Inspired by the story of the ugly duckling (and, according to a 1951 interview, by his own childhood frustrations), May decided his story would be about a young, outcast animal triumphing over adversity . . . . He wanted to connect the story to the myth of Santa Claus, and a reindeer seemed a natural choice. . . . May pondered the fact that Santa delivers his gifts at night and considered giving Rudolph large, bright eyes like headlights that could see in the dark, but decided that an oversized, red nose would seem a more credible source of mockery. . . . The story was an immense hit."[4]

When Johnny Marks composed the famous song "Rudolph the Red-Nosed Reindeer" in 1949 and when a popular television version was released, the story became firmly fixed "alongside Santa in the imaginations of American children."[5]

As for the North Pole, it served as the perfect explanation for why Santa was a competent traveler in the cold and snowy conditions of winter, and why he was never seen during the rest of the year. Additionally, in the 19th century, the North Pole "was on everyone's lips [and] reaching it [was] the equivalent of landing on the moon to that generation."[6] By the mid 1850s, New Yorkers had sent out several search-and-rescue expeditions to find the missing North Pole exploration team of the English admiral, Sir John Franklin. As a result, Americans and Britons alike felt an "almost proprietary interest in the North Pole."[7] Sadly, the skeletons of Franklin's team were found in 1859.

In regard to the appearance of America's Santa Claus, it is most often attributed to Dr. Clement Clarke Moore, a professor in the General Theological Seminary in New York. In 1822, he reportedly wrote a poem, "The Visit of St. Nicholas," now known as "'Twas The Night Before Christmas," not for publication but for his children. For more on the history of the poem, the debate on its authorship, and the text in its entirety, see p. 439.

Perhaps the motivation for creating a particularly jolly St. Nick was to affirm for children that they had "nothing to dread":

His eyes-how they twinkled! his dimples how merry!
His cheeks were like roses, his nose like a cherry!
His droll little mouth was drawn up like a bow,
And the beard of his chin was as white as the snow.

The stump of a pipe he held tight in his teeth,
And the smoke it encircled his head like a wreath.
He had a broad face and a little round belly,
That shook when he laughed, like a bowlful of jelly!

He was chubby and plump, a right jolly old elf,
And I laughed when I saw him, in spite of myself!
A wink of his eye and a twist of his head,
Soon gave me to know I had nothing to dread.

Though the poem drew a picture of Santa with words, Thomas Nast, a famous cartoonist, is credited with bringing Santa to life with pictures. From 1863 to 1886, Nast, who created the donkey and elephant symbols of the Democratic and Republican parties, drew a series of Christmas cartoons for *Harper's Weekly* that came to represent the modern image of Santa. Though Nast's early pictures depicted Santa as an elf, Santa grew to full size in his later pictures.

A Note on Fantasy

Determining how to address the subject of Santa Claus with children can be a sensitive topic for parents. The modern Santa Claus has devolved into a secularized figure surrounded by fantasy that can distract children from the real meaning of Christmas. First and foremost, follow your conscience. However, if you are unsure, below are some thoughts to consider.

First off, children love fantasy. That is why so many children's stories include talking animals, fairies, magic, etc. Fantasy can encourage both creativity and imagination in children. As they mature and begin to distinguish between fantasy and reality, parents can play an important role in helping to clarify what is true and what is fiction.

Beloved Christian authors, J. R. R. Tolkien and C. S. Lewis, both reputable scholars, are perhaps most famous for their work in the world of fantasy, and neither of them neglected the fantasy associated with Christmas. Tolkien, best known for his *Lord of the Rings* series, was a father of four. Over the course of 20 years, he wrote letters to his children in the name of Father Christmas (the English counterpart to Santa Claus). He included his own sketches of Father Christmas, the North Polar Bear and the North Pole (which he depicted as a literal pole). One year, the North Polar Bear, Father Christmas' somewhat clumsy assistant, had an incident that forced Father Christmas to move:

"It all happened like this: one very windy day last November my hood blew off and went and stuck on the top of the North Pole. I told him not to, but the North Polar Bear climbed up to the thin top to get it down – and he did. The pole broke in the middle and fell on the roof of my house, and the North Polar Bear fell through the hole it made in to the dining room with my hood over his nose, and all the snow fell off the roof into the house and melted and put out all the fires and ran down into the cellars where I was collecting this year's presents, and the North Polar bear's leg got broken. He is well again now, but I was so cross with him that he says he won't try to help me again. I expect his temper is hurt, and will be mended by next Christmas."[8]

Occasionally, even the North Polar Bear would send a letter to the children. He had to excuse "his bad English spelling from the fact that the language spoken at the North Pole was *Arctic*."[9] One year, the North Polar Bear got lost in Goblin caves (1932) and later "invented an alphabet from Goblin markings on the walls, and sent a short letter in it."[10] The children had great fun deciphering the letter.

C. S. Lewis, a friend of Tolkien, is probably best known for his *Chronicles of Narnia* in which he portrays a more serious Father Christmas. Though the White Witch had made it "always winter and never Christmas in Narnia,"[11] she was beginning to lose her powers. Here is an account of the visit of Father Christmas:

"It *was* a sledge, and it *was* reindeer with bells on their harness. But they were far bigger than the Witch's reindeer, and they were not white but brown. And on the sledge sat a person whom everyone knew the moment they set eyes on him. He was a huge man in a bright red robe (bright as hollyberries) with a hood that had fur inside it and a great white beard that fell like a foamy waterfall over his chest. Everyone knew him because, though you see people of his sort only in Narnia, you see pictures of them and hear them talked about even in our world — the world on this side of the wardrobe door. But when you really see them in Narnia it is rather different. Some of the pictures of Father Christmas in our world make him look only funny and jolly. But now that the children actually stood looking at him they didn't find it quite like that. He was so big, and so glad, and so real, that they all became quite still. They felt very glad, but also solemn."[12]

Father Christmas announces, "She [the White Witch] has kept me out for a long time, but I have got in at last. Aslan is on the move. The Witch's magic is weakening."[13] He proceeds to give gifts: a sword and shield to Peter; a bow, arrow and ivory horn to Susan; and a cordial and dagger to Lucy. He even delivers sugar, cream and tea "for the moment."[14] "Then he cried out, 'Merry Christmas! Long live the true King!' and cracked his whip, and he and the reindeer and the sledge and all were out of sight before anyone realized that they had started."[15]

Notice how the Father Christmas of Narnia calls attention to Aslan, the true King. Surely the intention of the real St. Nicholas was to direct people to his true King. He was a man who wholeheartedly gave his life to serving God, and he desired to give his Lord glory in all that he did.

The fact that American children are surrounded by images of Santa Claus during the Christmas season means that there are many opportunities to discuss the real St. Nicholas, a man whose life should inspire us to more fully serve God. Additionally, the miracles that St. Nicholas performed are far more wondrous than the mythical elements of the red-suited Santa who rides a sleigh through the sky; their purpose was to bring glory to God.

Furthermore, the idea of giving gifts in Santa's name is a useful practice. In essence, when we give gifts in Santa's name, we give them anonymously. Secret generosity is consistent with how St.

Nicholas gave gifts, and more importantly it follows Jesus' instruction to let our giving be done in secret. As Jesus said, "Your Father who sees what is done in secret will reward you." (Matthew 6:4).

[1] Wheeler, Joe and Rosenthal, Jim. *St. Nicholas, A Closer Look at Christmas*. Thomas Nelson, 2005, p.28. Much of the information on Santa Claus is drawn from this source.

[2] Wheeler, Joe and Rosenthal, Jim, p. 32.

[3] Encyclopedia Britannica. "Chimney." Retrieved June 2, 2008 from Encyclopedia Britannica Online: http://www.britannica.com/eb/article-9024112.

[4] Walsh, Joseph J. *Were They Wise Men or Kings? The Book of Christmas Questions.* Westminster John Knox Press, 2001, p. 9.

[5] Walsh, Joseph J., p. 9.

[6] Wheeler, Joe and Rosenthal, Jim, p. 190.

[7] Wheeler, Joe and Rosenthal, Jim, p. 190.

[8] Tolkien, J.R.R. *The Father Christmas Letters*. Edited by Baillie Tolkien. Houghton Mifflin Company, 1976, Letter written in 1925.

[9] Tolkien, J.R.R., Appendix.

[10] Tolkien, J.R.R., Appendix.

[11] Lewis, C.S. *The Chronicles of Narnia, The Lion, The Witch and the Wardrobe*. Harper Collins Publishers, 1982, p. 159.

[12] Lewis, C.S., p. 159.

[13] Lewis, C.S., p. 159.

[14] Lewis, C.S., p. 160.

[15] Lewis, C.S., p. 160.

Shepherds

At the birth of Jesus, the only recorded appearance of angels in the Bible was to shepherds. An angel says to them, "Do not be afraid. I bring you good news of great joy that will be for all the people. Today in the town of David a Savior has been born to you; he is Christ the Lord" (Luke 2:10-11). The message to the shepherds is both broad ("for all the people") and personal ("a Savior has been born to you"). Though the good news was for all the people, the Savior was ultimately born for those who would believe and respond.

Surely God knew in advance how the shepherds would respond to the announcement of Jesus' birth. They demonstrated an eagerness to embrace the good news; they hurried to find Jesus; they spread the word about him, and they glorified and praised God (Luke 2:16-20). Yet, it seems strange that the only appearance of a "great company of the heavenly host" was made to lowly shepherds, men who were living out in the fields tending sheep. Was there something significant to God about shepherding?

The Profession

Though shepherding was the most ancient profession of God's people, the Israelites, it was not a particularly desirable one. It was a dirty job, and apparently, it was considered "detestable" in some cultures. The Bible tells how Joseph prepared his brothers (now known as the fathers of the 12 tribes of Israel) for a conversation with Pharoah, the king of Egypt:

> "When Pharaoh calls you in and asks, 'What is your occupation?' you should answer, 'Your servants have tended livestock from our boyhood on, just as our fathers did.' Then you will be allowed to settle in the region of Goshen, for all shepherds are detestable to the Egyptians" (Genesis 46:33-34).

Goshen was an area on the periphery of society. Thus, the shepherds would be "outsiders." And it was only a matter of time before they were made slaves to the Egyptians.

When considering the shepherds of the Christmas story, historian Paul Maier said it well: "If resorting to symbolism . . . the shepherds stood for the cross-sectional, average Judean — quite literally, 'the man on the night shift.'"[1] Shepherds had a difficult job that earned no rank in society. Yet, God chose shepherds to receive the glorious angelic announcement of the birth of Christ.

The Character

God clearly saw significance in the role of shepherding. He used the term *shepherd* to describe the leaders of his people. He spoke of "rulers whom I commanded to shepherd my people Israel" (2 Samuel 7:7). Furthermore, leaders of the New Testament Church were called "shepherds of the church of God" (Acts 20:28) and "shepherds of God's flock" (1 Peter 5:2). What better example is there of selfless leadership than a shepherd who gently leads, nourishes, protects and cares for his sheep?

Interestingly, the term *shepherd* is used often to describe God himself. Jacob speaks of "the God who has been my shepherd all my life" (Genesis 48:15); David says, "The Lord is my shepherd" (Psalm 23:1); Isaiah describes God's tender leadership this way: "He tends his flock like a shepherd: He gathers the lambs in his arms and carries them close to his heart; he gently leads those that have young" (Isaiah 40:11).

That the title of *Shepherd* would be applied to God reveals that the role of the shepherd is praiseworthy. Truly it is the sheep that make the job dirty and "detestable" to any other than the shepherd who loves them. Who are the sheep? The Bible tells us that "the sheep" are actually the followers of God. A 20[th]century shepherd Phillip Keller writes, "Our behavior patterns and life habits are so much like that of sheep it is well nigh embarrassing."[2] Sheep are slow, weak, foolish, nervous, fearful, helpless and most importantly, totally dependent on their shepherd. The care of the shepherd profoundly impacts the condition of the sheep. Keller writes, "Under one man sheep would struggle, starve and suffer endless hardship. In another's care they would flourish and thrive content-edly."[3] Since humans are totally dependent on God, it is a wonderful blessing that Jesus, the "Chief Shepherd" (1 Peter 5:4), is a <u>good</u> shepherd.

The Good Shepherd

Approximately 700 years before the birth of Jesus, the prophet Micah foretold: "But you Beth-lehem Ephrathah, though you are small among the clans of Judah, out of you will come for me one who will be ruler over Israel, whose origins are from old, from ancient times. . . . He will stand and shepherd his flock in the strength of the Lord" (Micah 5:2-4). Jesus came to be our shepherd; he had tender compassion for us as "sheep without a shepherd" (Matthew 9:36). In his *Parable of the Lost Sheep*, Jesus reveals the length to which he would go for just one of his sheep:

"Suppose one of you has a hundred sheep and loses one of them. Does he not leave the ninety-nine in the open country and go after the lost sheep until he finds it? And when he finds it, he joyfully puts it on his shoulders and goes home. Then he calls his friends and neighbors together and says, 'Rejoice with me; I have found my lost sheep'" (Luke 15:4-6).

Jesus seeks out his sheep to care for them, so they "shall not be in want" (Psalm 23:1). There is no better "Shepherd and Overseer of your soul" (1 Peter 2:25). Jesus said, "I am the good shepherd. The good shepherd lays down his life for his sheep" (John 10:11). He says elsewhere, "Greater love has no one than this, that he lay down his life for his friends" (John 15:13). Thus, there is no greater love than that of the good shepherd who laid down his life for his sheep.

Not only did the shepherd lay down his life for his sheep, he actually became one himself. What a great mystery! The shepherd became a lamb in order to save his flock. The Bible says that believers are redeemed with "the precious blood of Christ, a lamb without blemish or defect" (1 Peter 1:19). Interestingly, the title most often applied to Jesus in the book of Revelation and the title that he carries into eternity is *"the Lamb."* At the end of time, "the Lamb at the center of the throne will be their shepherd; he will lead them to springs of living water. And God will wipe away every tear from their eyes" (Revelation 7:17).

For a historical fiction account about the shepherds of Bethlehem, see "A Bethlehem Shepherd" on p. 307.

———————————————

[1] Maier, Paul L. *In the Fullness of Time*. Kregel Publications, 1997, p. 44.

[2] Keller, Phillip. *A Shepherd Looks at Psalm 23*. Zondervan, 2007, p. 66.

[3] Keller, Phillip, p. 17.

Snowflakes

C hristmas comes just three or four days after the winter season officially begins. Since snow most often falls during this time of year in the Northern hemisphere, snowflakes have naturally come to be associated with Christmas in America. Though the naked eye can rarely appreciate the intricate beauty of snowflakes, technology (like photomicroscopes) has given us a window through which to see God's elegant designs.

The first known snowflake photographer, Wilson Bentley (1865-1931), wrote this:

"Under the microscope, I found that snowflakes were miracles of beauty; and it seemed a shame that this beauty should not be seen and appreciated by others. Every crystal was a masterpiece of design and no one design was ever repeated. When a snowflake melted, that design was forever lost. Just that much beauty was gone, without leaving any record behind."[1]

Yet, the Bible teaches that snow does in fact leave a "record" behind, and it accomplishes the purpose for which God sent it:

"As the heavens are higher than the earth, so are my ways higher than your ways and my thoughts than your thoughts. As the rain and the snow come down from heaven, and do not return to it without watering the earth and making it bud and flourish, so that it yields seed for the sower and bread for the eater, so is my word that goes out from my mouth: It will not return to me empty, but will accomplish what I desire and achieve the purpose for which I sent it" (Isaiah 55:9-11).

Additionally, believers need not fear that the beauty of snowflakes will be "forever lost." Beauty comes from God. He himself is the full embodiment of beauty, and he is eternal. In fact, the very thing that makes things in nature marvelous is that they reveal something of their Creator. Henry David Thoreau (1817-1862), a famous American author, wrote of snowflakes in his journal:

"How full of the creative genius is the air in which these are generated! I should hardly admire them more if real stars fell and lodged on my coat. Nature is full of genius, full of the divinity: so that not a snowflake escapes its fashioning hand."[2]

Snowflakes surely reveal both God's creative genius and his concern with even the smallest details on earth. And if God put so much care into the design of a snowflake, how much more does he care for man?

"Are not two sparrows sold for a penny? Yet not one of them will fall to the ground apart from the will of your Father. And even the very hairs of your head are all numbered. So don't be afraid; you are worth more than many sparrows" (Matthew 10:29-31).

What intimate concern for mankind. He knows the number of hairs on every head. Of all God's magnificent creation, it is man, and man alone, that was uniquely created in his image (Genesis 1:27); humans can think, reason, love, create, etc. And no other creature on earth can say, "God became one of us."

Unlike man, snowflakes have no genetic code to guide their construction; they appear to develop randomly as they fall through the sky. Yet, many of their characteristics are interesting to consider in comparison to humanity.

Their Creation

Interestingly, the creation of a snowflake begins with the "dust of the sky." Basically, as air temperatures cool, water vapor in the sky attaches to particles of dust in order to condense into water droplets. En masse, these droplets are what we see as clouds. As air temperatures continue to fall, water droplets freeze into snowflakes, and dust particles often play another role in providing a solid surface to help jump-start the freezing process. Dr. Ken Libbrecht, a professor at Caltech who has extensively researched snowflakes, records:

> "Once a droplet freezes into a miniature snowflake, it begins to grow and develop as water vapor condenses on its surface. . . . The frozen droplets will grow into full-sized snowflakes and drop out of the clouds. And, at the center of many snowflakes, too tiny for even the microscope to see, lies a solitary speck of dust that gave the crystal its start."[3]

The next time you see a snowman, consider that, roughly speaking, he got his start from the dust. Remember that man also was originally formed from the dust. In the account of creation, the Bible records that "the LORD God formed the man from the dust of the ground and breathed into his nostrils the breath of life, and the man became a living being" (Genesis 2:7).

Their Shape

When most people think of a snowflake, they envision a multi-branched snow star. Though snowflakes come in a variety of patterns, one thing they all have in common is their six-sided structure. The hexagonal form of water molecules is essentially transferred to the geometry of a growing snow crystal, and in the case of a snow star, six somewhat symmetrical branches will emerge.

In some rare cases, three sides of the hexagon will grow larger than the other and produce a triangular looking crystal. In other rare cases, two crystals combine, either through a collision or through twinning, to produce a twelve-branched snowflake. However, one thing that is not found in nature is a snow crystal with four, five, seven or eight sides. "The symmetry of the ice crystal does not allow such forms."[4]

It is intriguing that God designed the structure of water molecules with six-fold symmetry. As an element so essential to life, water molecules carry in their form an allusion to the Creation story. Consider that all of God's amazing creative work took place in six "days" and culminated in the creation of man.

Though "the heaven and the earth were completed in all their vast array" (Genesis 2:1) over a six day period, the seventh day is uniquely important:

> "By the seventh day God had finished the work he had been doing; so on the seventh day he rested from all his work. And God blessed the seventh day and made it holy, because on it he rested from all the work of creating that he had done" (Genesis 2:2-3).

There is something very significant about God's rest, and the Bible teaches that Christians can enter into it: "Now we who have believed enter that rest" (Hebrews 4:3). Interestingly, when God prohibited a generation of Jewish people from entering the Promised Land, he said, "They shall never enter my rest" (Psalm 95:11). This implies that God's rest is a place, and most Christians understand the true "promised land" to be Paradise, the eternal home for all believers.

May the six-fold symmetry of the snowflake be a reminder of the amazing creative work that God did in six days, and more importantly, that there is something more to come. Day seven signifies God's rest, and soon, believers will enter forever into this rest!

Their Imperfections

Snowflakes are generally illustrated with perfect symmetry. In nature, however, even approximate symmetry is the exception. Dr. Ken Libbrecht said this:

> "Symmetry is inherent in snow crystals, but it is fragile and never perfect. . . . If you examine a random sampling of falling snow . . . you will typically find that the majority of crystals are irregulars. . . . These crystals form under non-ideal conditions, with growth impeded by crowding from neighbors, crystal defects, midair collisions, sublimation [evaporation], and any number of other problems."[5]

Though symmetry is intrinsic to snowflakes, they form under "non-ideal conditions." Similarly, though God's perfect image is inherent in the design of man, we develop in a world full of sin. Like snowflakes, we are imperfect and quickly "melting" away. Yet, there is good news for us. The Bible teaches, "Though outwardly we are wasting away, inwardly we are being renewed day by day" (2 Corinthians 4:16). Thankfully, the difficulties of this world develop character in us, and perhaps this inward character will somehow manifest itself in our eternal bodies. May we look forward to eternity (a place of ideal conditions in which no sin will remain) when our unique beauty and God's perfect image in us will be fully revealed.

Their Color

In the Bible, the white color of snow is used to describe the appearance of Jesus in his glory. Daniel records, "His head and hair were white like wool, as white as snow, and his eyes were like blazing fire" (Revelation 1:14). The book of Revelation says of Jesus, "His clothing was as white as snow; the hair of his head was white like wool. His throne was flaming with fire, and its wheels were all ablaze" (Daniel 7:9).

The white of snow is also used to describe purity. The Lord speaks of purifying from sin, "Though your sins are like scarlet, they shall be as white as snow; though they are red as crimson, they shall be like wool" (Isaiah 1:18).

Interestingly, snow, made up of individual snowflakes, is not actually white; it is transparent. Individual snowflakes have no real color of their own. However, as light shines on snow, color is reflected evenly so that snow has the appearance of being white.

Consider that Jesus is "the true light that gives light to every man" (John 1:9). And just as light shines on a transparent snowflake to reflect pure white, the light of Christ shines on and through a transparent life to make it pure and "white as snow.

---

[1] Mullet, Mary. *The American Magazine. "The Snowflake Man."* Interview with Wilson Bentley, February 1925. Retrieved August 13, 2008 from Jericho Historical Society: http://snowflakebentley.com/mullet.htm.

[2] Thoreau, Henry David. *The Writings of Henry David Thoreau.* Houghton, Mifflin and Company, 1887, p.119.

[3] Libbrecht, Ken. *Ken Libbrecht's Field Guide to Snowflakes.* Voyageur Press, 2006, p. 32.

[4] Libbrecht, Ken. *The Snowflake, Winter's Secret Beauty.* Voyageur Press, p. 18.

[5] Libbrecht, Ken. *Ken Libbrecht's Field Guide to Snowflakes*, p. 12 and p. 99.

Star of
Bethlehem

When the Wise Men appeared before King Herod in Jerusalem, they asked, "Where is the one who has been born king of the Jews? We saw his star in the east and have come to worship him" (Matthew 2:2). Over the centuries, several theories have been proposed to explain this star. Though a single star may have miraculously and spontaneously appeared, it is interesting to consider that God might rather have been orchestrating the heavens over many centuries in order to communicate a unique message about Jesus. It seems reasonable to believe that a combination of signs in the heavens, rather than just a single star, led the Wise Men on their long journey to Jerusalem (and ultimately to Bethlehem) specifically seeking a "king of the Jews."

Perhaps, consistent with the Bible, God used special revelation for his people the Jews (e.g., the angelic announcement of Christ's birth to Jewish shepherds) but evidence in nature for the Gentiles (events in the sky for the Wise Men). In discussing the possible signs in the heavens, remember that it is God who controls the heavens and the earth; it is not the heavens that somehow control events on earth. Pope Gregory I (540-604 AD), said it well:

> "It is said of the star, 'Until it came to rest over the place where the child was' (Matt 2:9). It was not the child who was drawn to the star, but the star to the child; if you allow me to say so, the star did not influence the destiny of the child, but the child influenced the destiny of the star by his appearance. But let no talk of destiny come near the hearts of believers. Only the creator, who made human beings, directs their lives. Human beings were not made for the sake of stars, but stars for the sake of human beings." [1]

It is intriguing to consider the celestial events in the Middle Eastern sky at the time of Christ. Ancient records and astronomy both help to reconstruct the motion of the stars and planets over 2,000 years ago. Before examining some of the significant events in the sky, consider how astronomers communicate the location of certain activity in the heavens.

The sun and most of the planets move within a narrow band that stretches across the sky called the *zodiac*. Ancient astrologers divided the sky into 12 equal blocks through which the sun passed once each year. Each block was named after a constellation and most of us at least know the block or sign under which our birthday falls (Aries, Taurus, Gemini, Cancer, Leo, Virgo, Libra, Scorpio, Sagittarius, Capricorn, Aquarius and Pisces). These divisions of the sky are still used by modern astronomers to describe positions of the sun and planets. Note the difference between astronomy (the study of the movement in the heavens) and astrology (the study of how the movement in the heavens determines the future — thus the familiar horoscope for each of the zodiac signs).

Keep in mind that most modern scholars place the birth of Christ in approximately 5 BC. See more regarding the year of Christ's birth on p. 27. The Bible says that King Herod "gave orders to kill all the boys in Bethlehem and its vicinity who were two years old and under in accordance with the time he had learned from the Magi" (Matthew 2:16). Quite possibly, the Wise Men (also called "Magi") revealed to Herod that signs had appeared in the heavens a few years before Christ's actual birth. Thus, it seems appropriate to evaluate the signs in the sky back to 7 BC.

The Signs in the Heavens

The following signs are drawn from *The Star of Bethlehem, An Astronomer's View* by Mark Kidger.[2]

(1) Sign #1 (Conjunctions):

In the year 7 BC, three conjunctions took place in the zodiac block of Pisces. A *conjunction* is an astronomical term used to describe two celestial bodies that appear near one another in the sky (though they are in fact millions of miles apart).

Conjunction 1: On May 29 of 7 BC, Jupiter and Saturn passed each other (one slightly less than a degree to the north of the other) in Pisces.

Conjunction 2: On September 29 of 7 BC, Jupiter and Saturn passed each other again (one to the north and one to the south, moving in opposite directions) in Pisces.

Conjunction 3: On December 4 of 7 BC, Jupiter and Saturn met again in Pisces before slowly separating again.

Pisces is traditionally depicted by two fish and has long been associated symbolically with Palestine, more specifically with the Jews. Some ancient astrologers believed that the 12 zodiac signs represented 12 different countries, and ancient writings refer to Pisces as the "House of the Hebrews."[3]

Jupiter, the largest planet in our solar system, was considered to be a sign of royalty; it was known as the "King's Planet."[4] In Roman mythology, Jupiter was the supreme god and king (comparable to Zeus in Greek mythology and Marduk in Babylonian mythology).

Saturn, the second largest planet in the solar system, was considered to be a sign of protection and prosperity. In Roman mythology, Saturn was the god and protector of the harvest (comparable to Kronos in Greek mythology and Ninurta in Babylonian mythology). Interestingly, among the Jews, Saturn held messianic implications — "an old Jewish saying asserted that God has created Saturn to shield Israel."[5]

If the Wise Men sought to interpret celestial events, they could surmise that some imminent royal event was about to take place in Palestine that would bring protection and prosperity. Having the benefit of hindsight, the spiritual implications of these signs in the sky are evident. Jesus, the King of Kings, was born in Palestine, specifically in Bethlehem in Judea. In regard to protection, the Bible equates Jesus, the Anointed One, with a shield: "Look upon our shield, O God; look with favor on your anointed one" (Psalm 84:9). In regard to prosperity, the Apostle Paul wrote, "For you know the grace of our Lord Jesus Christ, that though he was rich, yet for your sakes he became poor, so that you through his poverty might become rich" (2 Corinthians 8:9).

(2) Sign #2 (Planetary Massing):

The following year, 6 BC, there was a massing of three planets in Pisces. In February of 6 BC, Mars joined Jupiter and Saturn in the constellation of Pisces. Mars was a sign of war in many cultures — perhaps because the red appearance of the planet invoked thoughts of blood and combat. In Roman mythology, Mars was the god of war (comparable to Ares in Greek mythology and Nergal in Babylonian mythology). This sign may have led the Wise Men to believe that the coming King of the Jews would bring both prosperity and war. Keep in mind that Jesus said he came to bring a sword into the world that would cause division even within families. Here are the words of Jesus:

> "Brother will betray brother to death, and a father his child; children will rebel against their parents and have them put to death. All men will hate you because of me, but he who stands firm to the end will be saved. . . . Do not be afraid of those who kill the body but cannot kill the soul. Rather, be afraid of the One who can destroy both soul and body in hell. Are not two sparrows sold for a penny? Yet not one of them will fall to the ground apart from the will of your Father. And even the very hairs of your head are all numbered. So don't be afraid; you are worth more than many sparrows. Whoever acknowledges me before men, I will also acknowledge him before my Father in heaven. But whoever disowns me before men, I will disown him before my Father in heaven. Do not suppose that I have come to bring peace to the earth. I did not come to bring peace, but a sword" (Matthew 10:21, 28-34).

Though the sword of which Jesus spoke may have had physical implications, the battle is surely spiritual. The apostle Paul wrote, "For our struggle is not against flesh and blood, but against the rulers, against the authorities, against the powers of this dark world and against the spiritual forces of evil in the heavenly realms" (Ephesians 6:12).

(3) Sign #3 (Occultations):

Several weeks later in 6 BC, there were two occultations of Jupiter and the moon. An *occultation* is when two celestial objects overlap. The difficulty with this sign is that the occultations could not be observed from either Babylon or Persia (the likeliest places of origin for the Wise Men). However, it is possible that the Wise Men knew how to calculate the motion of planets to some degree; they might have been able to predict that the occultations were due. Regardless, the symbolism of this sign is worth discussion.

On March 20 and April 17 of 6 BC, the Moon occulted Jupiter in the constellation of Aries. Most of us are familiar with the typical depiction of Aries as a ram. In the Bible, a ram was often used as a sacrifice for sins. Interestingly, when Abraham showed obedience to God by his willingness to sacrifice his son Isaac, God provided a ram in Isaac's place:

"But the angel of the Lord called out to him from heaven, 'Abraham! Abraham!' 'Here I am,' he replied. 'Do not lay a hand on the boy,' he said. 'Do not do anything to him. Now I know that you fear God, because you have not withheld from me your son, your only son.' Abraham looked up and there in a thicket he saw a ram caught by its horns. He went over and took the ram and sacrificed it as a burnt offering instead of his son. So Abraham called that place The Lord Will Provide. And to this day it is said, 'On the mountain of the Lord it will be provided'" (Genesis 22:11-14).

Most scholars agree that this biblical event foreshadowed how God would one day offer his son Jesus for us. Jesus would be the "ram" that would offer himself as the ultimate and final sacrifice for sin. Perhaps the occultation in the sky was predictive of the coming sacrifice. To further emphasize this possible meaning, consider the ancient beliefs regarding the moon:

"The cyclical process of disappearance and appearance of the moon is the basis of the wide-spread association of the moon with the land of the dead, the place to which souls ascend after death, and the power of rebirth. . . . The mythology of the moon emphasizes especially those periods when it disappears—the three days of darkness in the lunar cycle and eclipses."[6]

The association of the moon with death and rebirth is intriguing, particularly when applying the "three days of darkness" to Jesus' death and resurrection. "He [Jesus] then began to teach them that the Son of Man must suffer many things and be rejected by the elders, chief priests and teachers of the law, and that he must be killed and after three days rise again" (Mark 8:31). Note that the moon covered Jupiter, the "king star"; it was the "king" that disappeared from view for a time.

(4) Sign #4 (Planetary Pairing):

In 5 BC, two different pairings took place in Pisces. On February 20 of 5 BC, the moon passed close to Jupiter in the sky and sat just east of another pairing, Mars and Saturn in the constellation of Pisces. The combination of the moon and three planets in Pisces would surely affirm for the Wise Men that important activity was taking place, or about to take place, in Palestine.

(5) Sign #5 (A Nova):

After observing a series of significant astronomical events, the Wise Men probably looked intently for a final confirmation of the message they had witnessed in the heavens. The finale occurred in March of 5 BC. Chinese records make note of a star that was visible for more than 70 days. This length of visibility indicates that it was a brilliant nova (a star that suddenly increases in brightness). The Wise Men undoubtedly would have interpreted a bright new star in the heavens to mark the birth of a king. Understandably, this final sign would have started the Wise Men packing. Jerusalem, the capital of the Jewish world, was the logical place to travel. It would have been a 540-mile trip from Babylon and much farther from Persia (the two most likely places of origin for the Wise Men), but such a long journey would have seemed a small sacrifice to see the King to whom all of the heavens seemed to point.

After arriving in Jerusalem and speaking with King Herod, the gospel of Matthew tells us that the Wise Men "went on their way, and the star they had seen in the east went ahead of them until it stopped over the place where the child was. When they saw the star they were overjoyed" (Matthew 2:9-10). Matthew implies that the Wise Men had lost sight of the star for a time (since they were overjoyed at seeing it again). A logical astronomical explanation is that the brightness of the moon could have hidden the star for several days. Additionally, Matthew suggests that the Wise Men somehow followed the star from King Herod's palace to the house of Jesus in Bethlehem. Though first sighted in the east, the nova would have followed the natural motion of the heavens and gradually moved south in the dawn sky. Since ancient travel likely took place at dawn in desert regions, it would make sense that the Wise Men could follow the star in their journey south from Jerusalem to Bethlehem to see Jesus, the one who is called the "bright Morning Star" (Revelation 22:16).

In the words of astronomer Mark Kidger, "we find a series of events so unique that they can happen together only once in every several thousand years."[7] One has to take pause to consider the message of the heavens. May our response be like that of the Wise Men: They sought out Jesus despite great obstacles; they willingly gave him their treasure, and they humbly bowed down to worship him!

Depictions of Stars

Though stars are depicted in a variety of forms, perhaps the most common in America are the five-pointed pentagram, the six-pointed Star of David and the gleaming eight-pointed (or sometimes four-pointed) star.

(1) The Pentagram

The pentagram has long held a significant place in history and religion. This may, in part, be due to significant symbolic associations with the number five. There are five elements: earth, wind, water, light and fire; there are five senses; there are five extremities of the body (two arms, two legs, and a head); there are five fingers on each hand, and there are five toes on each foot.

Additionally, the pentagram reveals intriguing geometrical attributes. Some scholars think it has a sort of mathematical perfection. For example, within the pentagram, there are 10 different triangles; the ratio of the longer side to the shorter side in all ten of them results in "phi" (the golden ratio).[8]

For these reasons, Christians and pagans alike have attached significance to the pentagram. The Medieval Christian view is perhaps best described in the 14th century story, *Sir Gawain and the Green Knight*. The intriguing tale can be found on p. 387.

The noble Sir Gawain carried a shield engraved with a pentagram of red gold. The symbolism is described as follows:

> "First, he was proved faultless in his <u>five senses</u>, and secondly the knight was never at fault through his <u>five fingers</u>, and all his trust on this earth was in the <u>five wounds</u> which Christ received on the cross, as the Creed tells [the piercing of His two hands, His two feet and His side]. And wherever this man was beset in battle, his steadfast thought was upon this, above all else – that he should draw all his fortitude from the <u>five joys</u> which the gracious Queen of Heaven had in her child [the Annunciation, the Nativity, the Resurrection, the Ascension, and the Assumption]. . . . The fifth group of five [the virtues of knighthood] which I find the man displayed was generosity and love of his fellow men above all else, his purity and his courtesy were never at fault, and compassion, which surpasses all other qualities, these <u>five virtues</u> were more firmly attached to that man than to any other."[9]

(2) The Star of David

The symbol of the Star of David, also called the *Shield of David*, originated in antiquity. Though medieval Jewish mystics often referred to the *Magen David* (the shield of David) as a euphemism for God and though they "attached magical powers to King David's shield,"[10] it is unclear when the six-pointed star came to be associated with the shield. Of course, popular folklore teaches that this was in fact the shape of David's shield, but this cannot be authenticated.

The six-pointed star, which is so intimately connected with the Jewish people today, did not actually come into common use among the Jews until the 17th century. "The Jewish community of Prague was the first to use the Star of David as its official symbol, and from the 17th century on the six-pointed star became the official seal of many Jewish communities and a general sign of Judaism."[11]

See p. 146 for a brief discussion on the significance of the number six.

(3) The Eight-Pointed (and Four-Pointed) Star

The eight-pointed star is generally depicted as a cross with an "X" through it. Surely, the cross has carried significance for Christians ever since the crucifixion of Christ. The cross is a sign of God's amazing redemptive work for mankind. In some cases, stars are illustrated with only four points and appear like crosses in the sky. However, in the case of the eight-pointed star, the "X" is also significant. In the language of the New Testament, Greek, the word *Christ* begins with the letter "X" (Χριστός). It is marvelous to imagine the heavens filled with eight-pointed stars, all carrying the message of the Gospel: <u>Christ</u>, the "Anointed One," would come to die on a <u>cross</u> in order to save mankind from sin!

---

[1] Witvliet, John D. and Vroege, David. *Proclaiming the Christmas Gospel, Ancient Sermons and Hymns for Contemporary Christian Inspiration.* Sermon by Gregory the Great. Baker Books, 2004, pp. 52-53.

[2] Kidger, Mark. *The Star of Bethlehem, An Astronomer's View.* Princeton University Press, 1999.

[3] Kaufmanis, Karlis. "The Star of Bethlehem." *A Christmas Classic.* Augsburg Fortress, 1999, p. 35.

[4] Maier, Paul L. *In the Fullness of Time.* Kregel Publications, 1997, p. 54.

[5] Kaufmanis, Karlis, p. 35.

[6] Encyclopedia Britannica. "Moon Worship." Retrieved August 13, 2008 from Encyclopedia Britannica Online: http://www.britannica.com/EBchecked/topic/391399/moon-worship.

[7] Kidger, Mark, p.265.

[8] The "Golden Ratio" basically teaches that if "A" is the longer side and "B" is the shorter side, A+B/A = A/B = PHI.

[9] Barron, William Raymond. *Sir Gawain and the Green Knight.* Manchester University Press, 1998, pp. 65-67.

[10] Encyclopedia Britannica. "Star of David." Retrieved August 16, 2008 from Encyclopedia Britannica Online: http://www.britannica.com/EBchecked/topic/152589/Star-of-David.

[11] Encyclopedia Britannica. "Star of David."

Wise Men

Most people suppose that the Wise Men were three in number, were kings and were from the Orient — though none of these descriptions are given in the biblical narrative. The Christmas carol "We Three Kings of Orient Are" is the most likely source for perpetuating these popular, but probably erroneous, beliefs about the Wise Men.

The Number of Wise Men

First off, the number of Wise Men that made the trip to Bethlehem is not known; no number is mentioned in the biblical account (Matthew 2:1-12). The western tradition of three Wise Men is likely rooted in the fact that they delivered three gifts (gold, frankincense, and myrrh) to the infant Jesus. Many variations of names exist for these Wise Men, but the most common are Gaspar, Balthasar and Melchoir. According to historian Paul Maier, "These names arise first in the sixth century A.D., too late for any authenticity."[1] Eastern tradition, on the other hand, holds that there were 12 Wise Men.

In early drawings of the Nativity (found in Roman catacombs), some showed two Magi, some showed four. In writings, symbolic meaning was often attached to the number of Wise Men. For example, the Venerable Bede wrote, "Mystically, the three magi signify the three parts of the world, Asia, Africa and Europe."[2] For those that held there were 12 Wise Men, some asserted that they became Gentile apostles (paralleling the twelve Jewish apostles of the Gospel story).[3]

The Royalty of the Wise Men

The Greek New Testament refers to the Wise Men as *magoi*, most often translated as "magi, wise men, astrologers or magicians." There is no indication that these men were kings. Most likely, the Wise Men of the Nativity story came to be referred to as kings (and also depicted as riding camels) because of a prophecy written by Isaiah approximately 700 years before the birth of Jesus:

> "Nations shall come to your light, and kings to the brightness of your dawn. . . . A multitude of camels shall cover you, the young camels of Midian and Ephah; all those from Sheba shall come. They shall bring gold and frankincense and shall proclaim the praise of the Lord" (Isaiah 60:3-6).

The mention of gold and frankincense immediately brings to mind the gifts of the Wise Men, and it is reasonable to apply the prophecy to the Nativity story. Though Isaiah's words do not require that the gifts come from kings, it is quite possible that the Wise Men were sent as ambassadors of a king or kings. If we look to the Old Testament to better understand the role of wise men, we see that they were intimately connected to their kings and served as a primary source of counsel. Daniel, one of the wise men of Babylon, was made ruler over the entire province by King Nebuchadnezzar (Daniel 2:48), and was later placed in the highest position of authority under King Darius the Mede

(Daniel 6:1-3). Though the Wise Men of the Nativity story may have held important rank in their country, they were not kings.

The Home of the Wise Men

The Bible tells us that the Wise Men came from the East. Most scholars agree that they came from the Near East, either Babylon or Persia, not as far east as the Orient. Either way, the Wise Men would have traveled a great distance to see Jesus. It would have been a 540-mile trip from Babylon and much farther from Persia. So why would they journey so far to pay homage to a Jewish king? This question is most easily answered if we consider the possibility that the Wise Men could trace some of their beliefs back to a Jewish man named Daniel (yes, the Daniel of the Bible who escaped a lion's den unharmed).

Daniel, The Wise Man

The Bible records that Daniel served as a "wise man" in Babylon. During Daniel's lifetime, Babylon was ruled by several different kings; three of these kings actually gave honor to Daniel's God: Nebuchadnezzar (a Babylonian king), Darius (a Median king) and Cyrus (a Persian king). This is amazing when you consider that Daniel was a captive in a foreign land. Let's take a look at what these kings had to say about Daniel's God . . .

(1) Nebuchadnezzar (Babylonian King):

In the sixth century BC, the Babylonian army besieged Jerusalem and carried captives back to Babylon. Daniel was among a few young men from the royal family and nobility of Israel who was chosen to be groomed for the service of the Babylonian king Nebuchadnezzar.

After being trained for three years in Babylonian language and literature, Daniel, whose Babylonian name was Belteshazzar, entered the service of the king as a counselor or "wise man." When Daniel proved to be the only one who could interpret his dream, King Nebuchadnezzar "made him ruler over the entire province of Babylon and placed him in charge of all its wise men" (Daniel 2:48). Keep in mind that the "wise men" of Babylon consisted of magicians, enchanters, sorcerers, astrologers and diviners. Though Daniel always made clear that his abilities came from the one true God of heaven, he was called the "chief of the magicians" (Daniel 4:9). "Magician" has the same root as the word "Magi."

Nebuchadnezzar said to Daniel, "Surely your God is the God of gods and the Lord of kings" (Daniel 2:47). He later said, "I praised the Most High; I honored and glorified him who lives forever. His dominion is an eternal dominion; his kingdom endures from generation to generation" (Daniel 4:34b).

(2) Darius (Median King):

When Darius the Mede took control of Babylon:

> "It pleased [him] to appoint 120 satraps [similar to governors] to rule throughout the kingdom, with three administrators over them, one of whom was Daniel . . . Now Daniel so distinguished himself among the administrators and the satraps by his exceptional qualities that the king planned to set him over the whole kingdom" (Daniel 6:1-3).

Out of jealousy, the king's other officials plotted against Daniel and ultimately had him thrown into the lion's den. When he escaped unharmed, King Darius declared, "I issue a decree that in every part of my kingdom people must fear and reverence the God of Daniel. For he is the living God and he endures forever; his kingdom will not be destroyed, his dominion will never end" (Daniel 6:26).

(3) Cyrus (Persian King):

It is not known whether Daniel served in any formal capacity under Cyrus. Since Daniel was so highly esteemed by Darius, he may have naturally held his high position in the transition of the kingdom from King Darius to King Cyrus. The Bible simply states that "Daniel prospered during the reign of Darius and the reign of Cyrus the Persian" (Daniel 6:28).

When Cyrus became king, Daniel would have been in his 80s or 90s. We know that in his first year as king, Cyrus allowed the Jewish exiles to leave Babylon and return to Jerusalem to rebuild their temple. It is reasonable to suspect that Daniel greatly influenced Cyrus in this matter. Daniel's passion in regard to the desolate sanctuary, the Jewish people and the city of Jerusalem is evident in his prayer as recorded in Daniel 9. Ezra tells us that "the Lord moved the heart of Cyrus king of Persia to make a proclamation throughout his realm and to put it in writing" (Ezra 1:1b). Here is what Cyrus wrote:

> "The Lord, the God of heaven, has given me all the kingdoms of the earth and he has appointed me to build a temple for him at Jerusalem in Judah. Anyone of his people among you – may his God be with him, and let him go up to Jerusalem in Judah and build the temple of the Lord, the God of Israel, the God who is in Jerusalem" (Ezra 1:2).

It appears that Daniel left Babylon in the first year of the reign of Cyrus (Daniel 1:21), but he was not among those that returned to Jerusalem. Perhaps his age simply prevented him from completing the trip.

In summary, Daniel and his God were well known to kings of both Babylon and Persia. It is not difficult to imagine that the wise men of these regions would also have held Daniel in high regard and would have paid close attention to his prophecies. Remarkably, over 500 years before the birth of Jesus, Daniel outlined the details of the specific time in history that the Messiah would come (Daniel 9:20-27), see p. 18. Had the Wise Men of the Nativity story been familiar with this prophecy, they would have known the very generation in which to look for the birth of the King of the Jews. Interestingly, Suetonius (approx. 69 AD – after 122 AD), a Roman historian, recorded, "There had spread all over the East an old and established belief that it was fated for men coming from Judea at that time to rule the world."[4]

It is also worth mentioning a "wise man" that long preceded Daniel. Over 1,400 years before the birth of Christ, Moses recorded a story about a "magos" (singular for magi) whose name was Balaam. Balak, king of Moab, summoned Balaam to put a curse on Israel. Though Balaam practiced sorcery (Numbers 24:1), the Bible tells that the Spirit of the Lord came upon him to bless Israel instead of curse it. He also prophesied of the coming Messiah, "I see him, but not now; I behold him, but not near. A star will come out of Jacob, a scepter will rise out of Israel" (Numbers 24:17a). How interesting that it was in fact a star that would lead the Wise Men of the Nativity story to the King born in Israel!

The Gifts of the Wise Men

The Wise Men of the Nativity story have often been credited with beginning the tradition of gift giving on Christmas. Though the practice probably had another source, the Wise Men are in fact the first recorded people to present gifts to Jesus — gold, frankincense and myrrh. Early Church records reveal that these gifts have long been interpreted symbolically:[5]

(1) Gold is a sign of royalty and was believed to reveal Christ as <u>King</u>. When the Wise Men arrived in Jerusalem, they asked, "Where is the one who has been born king of the Jews?" (Matthew 2:2). Before his death, Jesus himself speaks of his kingship:

> "Jesus said, 'My kingdom is not of this world. If it were, my servants would fight to prevent my arrest by the Jews. But now my kingdom is from another place.'

> "'You are a king, then!' said Pilate.

> "Jesus answered, 'You are right in saying I am a <u>king</u>. In fact, for this reason I was born, and for this I came into the world, to testify to the truth. Everyone on the side of the truth listens to me'" (John 18:36-37).

(2) Frankincense (or incense) was often burned by priests as a sacrifice to God. The symbolism was thus two-fold: it revealed Christ as <u>God</u> (the Wise Men offered the incense to him) and his role as a <u>priest</u> (he would offer the final sacrifice of his own body and blood):

> "[Jesus] being in very nature <u>God</u>, did not consider equality with God something to be grasped, but made himself nothing, taking the very nature of a servant, being made in human likeness" (Philippians 2:6-7).

> "He [Jesus] had to be made like his brothers in every way, in order that he might become a merciful and faithful high <u>priest</u> in service to God, and that he might make atonement for the sins of the people (Hebrews 2:17).

(3) Myrrh was used for both anointing and embalming. The words *Messiah* and *Christ* both mean "Anointed One." Surely Jesus was anointed to come into the world to save God's people. But salvation would come at a great cost — the life of Jesus. Thus, myrrh is also believed to be predictive of <u>Christ's death</u>. John gives an account of how myrrh was used for Christ's burial:

> "He [Joseph of Arimathea] was accompanied by Nicodemus, the man who earlier had visited Jesus at night. Nicodemus brought a mixture of myrrh and aloes, about seventy-five pounds. Taking Jesus' body, the two of them wrapped it, with the spices, in strips of linen. This was in accordance with Jewish burial customs" (John 19:39-40).

On the practical side, it is interesting to consider that the gifts of the Wise Men most likely supplied the financial means that Mary and Joseph would need to travel to Egypt and back. The Bible records that:

> "When they [the Wise Men] had gone, an angel of the Lord appeared to Joseph in a dream. 'Get up,' he said, 'take the child and his mother and escape to Egypt. Stay there until I tell you, for Herod is going to search for the child to kill him.' So he got up, took the child and his mother during the night and left for Egypt, where he stayed until the death of Herod. And so was fulfilled what the Lord had said through the prophet: 'Out of Egypt I called my son'" (Matthew 2:13-15).

Certainly, the travel and stay in Egypt would have been costly, and we know that Mary and Joseph were very poor. Jewish law commanded that after a woman gave birth and completed her days of purification, she was to bring an offering (a lamb and a young pigeon or dove) for the priest to present to God on her behalf. But the law made an exception for the poor: "If she cannot afford a lamb, she is to bring two doves or two young pigeons" (Leviticus 12:8). Mary's offering, as recorded in Luke 2:24, reveals that she did not have the means to offer a lamb. What an intriguing paradox: The one who could not afford a lamb for her purification after birth had just given birth to the Lamb of God!

The Gentile Wise Men

Charles Spurgeon (1834-1892), a British pastor known as the "Prince of Preachers," said: "It was great mercy that regarded the low estate of the shepherds, and it was far-reaching mercy which gathered from lands which lay in darkness a company of men made wise to salvation."[6] God's extraordinary mercy for all of humanity is made evident in the Nativity story. He shows that he will reach far and wide to gather his people — rich or poor, Jew or Gentile.

Though it is possible that the Wise Men could trace their lineage to Jews (specifically those that were taken captive with Daniel), the vast majority of scholars believe that they were Gentiles (non-Jews). This would make the Wise Men the first among Gentiles to worship Jesus. The Bible foretold that the Messiah would be "a light for the Gentiles" and would "bring salvation to the ends of the earth" (Isaiah 49:6). Even Jesus said, "Many will come from the east and the west, and will take their places at the feast with Abraham, Isaac and Jacob in the kingdom of heaven" (Matthew 8:11). And how wonderful that God would include Gentiles in the very beginning of the Gospel story, from the very birth of Jesus.

Consider again that the Wise Men came from the East. Since the first sin in the Garden of Eden, the Book of Genesis implies that man began to move "east"; God placed angels on the "east-side" of the Garden of Eden, so that men could not enter back in (Genesis 3:24). Theologians have long interpreted references of eastward movement to symbolize distance from God. The Wise Men marked a turning point in this movement; they traveled <u>from</u> the East <u>toward</u> God. And through signs in the sky, God reached over a vast distance to draw these Wise Men to himself.

Remarkably, not only does God reach over immeasurable distances to bring his people to himself, he even sends their sins away "as far as the east is from the west" (Psalm 103:12). Note that there is <u>no end</u> to the distance between the East and the West on a sphere-shaped planet:

"For as high as the heavens are above the earth, so great is his love for those who fear him; as far as the east is from the west, so far has he removed our transgressions from us. As a father has compassion on his children, so the Lord has compassion on those who fear him" (Psalm 103:11-13).

How amazing that the same great love that extended over a vast distance to reach the Wise Men in the East is intended for all "who fear him."

---

[1] Maier, Paul L. *In the Fullness of Time*. Kregel Publications, 1997, p.48.

[2] Kidger, Mark. *The Star of Bethlehem, An Astronomer's View*. Princeton University Press, 1999, p. 172.

[3] Kelly, Joseph F. *The Origins of Christmas*. Liturgical Press, 2004, p. 96.

[4] Maier, Paul L., p. 50.

[5] Kelly, Joseph F., p. 94. In the second century, Irenaeus of Lyons, began a tradition of interpreting the gifts symbolically.

[6] Spurgeon, Charles Haddon. *Spurgeon's Sermons on Christmas and Easter*. Sermon Titled: "The Sages, the Star, and the Savior." Kregel Publicatoins, 1995, p. 19.

Wreaths

Though wreaths were well known throughout the ancient world, it appears that the people of Northern Europe were the first to specifically associate them with the winter season. For a region that experienced long hours of darkness and cold in the winter, wreaths brought a sense of hope into the home. These early wreaths were made of wheels (probably wooden wheels used on carts) decorated with greenery and candles.

The pagans of Northern Europe believed that the sun was a "wheel" that would roll away from them and then turn back toward them in repeating cycles.[1] Interestingly, the term *Yuletide* is possibly derived from a word meaning "turning time of the sun." When the sun reached its farthest point "away" from the earth and the days were coldest and darkest, pagans began their winter solstice rituals in the hope that the sun would turn back toward them. Perhaps the tradition of the wreath originated in the belief that a wheel filled with light and greenery would inspire the god of light to turn the wheel of the sun back toward earth. Then, the light of day could grow longer and the landscape could grow greener.

Even as Northern Europeans converted to Christianity, wreaths continued to decorate their homes during the winter season. With time, these wreaths became distinctly Christian in their symbolism. Since their circular shape had no beginning or end, they could serve as a reminder of the "Eternal God" (Genesis 21:33) and the life without end offered to "whoever believes in the Son" (John 3:36). Since wreaths were made of evergreens (trees that survive the "death" of winter), they could symbolize both the immortality of God and the souls of men. Lastly, the light of a wreath could represent Jesus, who said, "I am the light of the world" (John 8:12).

Another Christian tradition that began in Northern Europe was an association between the wreath and St. Lucy, or Lucia (283-304 AD). Her name means "light," and her feast day is observed on December 13 (though it originally fell on the winter solstice prior to the 16th century adjustments in the Gregorian calendar). Lucy, a contemporary of St. Nicholas, is celebrated for her commitment to purity, as well as for her generosity. One tradition tells how Lucy (at great personal risk) helped persecuted Christians who were hiding in the catacombs of Syracuse, Sicily. These underground burial places were dark, and light was required to travel through them. In order to free her hands to carry as much food, drink and other necessities as possible, Lucy attached lights to a wreath on her head. Lucy's feast day is still celebrated in Scandinavia where young girls wear a crown of lights on their head in her honor. See p. 381 for more on St. Lucy.

The idea of wearing a wreath on one's head would not have been foreign to St. Lucy. Throughout many regions of the ancient world, wreaths were worn like crowns. Generally, they served as a sign of honor or authority. In ancient Greece, wreaths were awarded to victorious athletes in the Olympic Games (beginning around 776 BC); they were also used to honor excellence in poetry and oration. In Ancient Rome, leaders wore wreaths much like the crown of a king. Julius Caesar (100 BC–44 BC), for example, is often depicted with a wreath of laurel around his head. Wreaths were also given as a crown of honor to Roman soldiers for distinction in battle.

At some point, it appears that the head ornament transitioned to a door or wall decoration in Greco-Roman society. Most likely, those who had received a crown of honor (athletes, poets, orators, leaders, soldiers, etc.) proudly hung their wreaths as a sign of their success. By the third century, common people had adopted the practice of hanging wreaths on doors. Perhaps because the tradition became superstitious (a wreath was believed to bring honor and success to a home or business), Tertullian (160-225 AD), a prolific Christian writer, condemned the practice as idolatry.

"But 'let your works shine,' saith He; but now all our shops and gates shine! You will now-a-days find more doors of heathens without lamps and laurel-wreaths than of Christians. . . . Idolatry is condemned, not on account of the persons which are set up for worship, but on account of those its observances, which pertain to demons."[2]

Though this ancient custom does not appear to have any association with the Christmas season, the practice of hanging wreaths may indeed have come from Greco-Roman society. Additionally, the use of a wreath as a crown and as a sign of authority, victory and honor are quite relevant to Christmas, for on this day the birth of Jesus, the King of Kings, is celebrated. Jesus said, "All authority in heaven and on earth has been given to me" (Matthew 28:18). And, he who was victorious over sin and death is "now crowned with glory and honor" (Hebrews 2:9).

The Lord is the only one truly worthy of wearing a crown. Yet, he desires to be a crown for his people. The Bible records that "the Lord Almighty will be a glorious crown, a beautiful wreath for the remnant of his people" (Isaiah 28:5).

Though wreaths decorate doors, windows, walls and fireplaces during the Christmas season in America, it is the tradition of the Advent wreath that carries the most significant Christian meaning. For more on the history of the Advent season, see p. 31.

The History of the Advent Wreath

A lovely and tangible way to prepare for the "coming" of Jesus is the Advent wreath. As discussed above, the wreath most likely had its origin in the winter traditions of the Northern Europeans. Though the earliest converts in this region would naturally come to associate their wreaths with Christmas, it is unclear how the wreaths came to be associated with Advent, the time of preparation for Christmas.

Though there is evidence to suggest that Christians in the Middle Ages may have used lighted wreaths as part of their spiritual preparation for Christmas, the first clear association with Advent is generally attributed to German Lutherans in the 16th century. However, another three centuries would pass before the modern Advent wreath took shape. Specifically, a German theologian and educator by the name of Johann Hinrich Wichern (1808-1881) is credited with the idea of lighting an increasing number of candles as Christmas approached.[3]

Wichern was passionate about urging Christians to minister to the physical and social, as well as spiritual, needs of people. He was a man who put his teaching into practice, and one of his many acts of social service included the founding of a home for poor children, the *Rough House*, in the city of Hamburg. Tradition holds that as Christmas approached each year, the children would daily inquire about its arrival. In 1839, Wichern ingeniously thought to use a wreath as a teaching tool. For each Sunday of Advent, Wichern positioned a large white candle in a wreath. For every other day in between, Wichern placed a small red candle in the wreath. Each day Wichern would light a candle and teach the children about Jesus. Thus, the children had a visual means to help them count the days until Christmas, and Wichern had an opportunity to help draw their focus to the purpose of Christmas. His idea was a success, and with time, it spread throughout Europe and on to North America.

Wichern's idea may also have influenced the modern Advent calendars that, beginning on December 1, count the days until Christmas. According to tradition, the Advent calendar was created by a Munich housewife for her children; the first commercial calendars were printed in Germany in 1851.[4]

The Candles of the Advent Wreath

Practices vary widely in regard to the type of evergreens used and the color of candles contained in the Advent wreath. Often, wreaths are decorated with the traditional Christmas colors of red and green. However, another common practice is to use purple and rose colored candles (a tradition originally unique to Catholics that has since grown in popularity). Generally, three purple candles and one rose candle light the Advent wreath, each being lit on successive Sundays. The rose candle is lit on the third Sunday (the second Sunday from Christmas if you count inversely).

Purple is believed to represent both royalty and repentance. In ancient times, purple dyes were so rare and costly that they came to be associated with kings. Thus, purple reminds us of the royalty of the coming King Jesus. In regard to repentance, there is an intriguing connection to God's royalty. For it is the very presence of the Holy King that makes one painfully aware of personal short-comings and penitent for them.

The pink candle most likely has roots in an association with Lent (as does the purple candle). For each of the seven solemn weeks of Lent, the church historically lit a candle on Sunday. The third Sunday of Lent was designated as a time to feast and remember the coming joy of the resurrection:

"In ancient times on this particular Sunday the Pope would honor a citizen with a pink rose, and as time passed the priests wore pink vestments on this day as a reminder of the coming joy. When the season of Advent was instituted, the church viewed it as a mini-Lent, a time for reflection and repentance (thus the purple). In so doing, the church adopted the first four candles of Lent and changed the third candle of Advent to pink in honor of the Lenten tradition."[5]

The third Sunday of Advent is also called *Gaudete* (Latin for "rejoice") Sunday. It symbolizes joy in the midst of our preparation, and marks the halfway point toward the coming of light into the world. The pink is likened to a faded purple color as though the light is beginning to shine through it. It is "like the first gleam of dawn, shining ever brighter till the full light of day" (Proverbs 4:18).

On Christmas Day (or Christmas Eve), one tradition replaces the purple and pink candles with white. However, a more common practice is to place a white candle, called "the Christ candle," in the middle of the wreath (leaving the purple and pink candles in place). The color white symbolizes the light, purity and holiness of Jesus. For "in him there is no darkness" (1 John 1:5) and "in him is no sin" (1 John 3:5).

Advent Wreath Traditions

Advent candles are commonly lit immediately before or after dinner and burn for approximately one hour. This is a wonderful time to read Scripture as a family and discuss the reason for the holiday season — the coming of Jesus.

Though a variety of meanings have been attached to each candle, two common traditions are (1) hope, peace, joy and love and (2) promise, prophecy, proclamation and presence. The selection of verses below incorporates these various meanings on their respective week of Advent:

Week 1: Light the first candle on the first Sunday of Advent (the fourth Sunday before Christmas). For the following six days, light this same candle. Consider allowing children to earn the honor of lighting the candle each day. The first candle is said to represent <u>hope</u> and the <u>promises</u> of a coming Savior. Discuss how this week's verses apply to the concept of hope.

(1.1) Promise to Abraham: God promised Abraham that all people on earth would be blessed through him. In Jesus, a descendant of Abraham, this promise was fulfilled. *"All peoples on earth will be blessed through you" (Genesis 12:3).*

(1.2) Promise to Isaac: God promised an everlasting covenant with Isaac (Abraham's son). In Jesus, a descendant of Isaac, this promise was fulfilled. God said to Abraham, *" 'Your wife Sarah will bear you a son, and you will call him Isaac. I will establish my covenant with him as an everlasting covenant for his descendants after him'" (Genesis 17:19).*

(1.3) Promise to Jacob (also called Israel): God promised Jacob that all people on earth would be blessed through him. In Jesus, a descendant of Jacob, this promise was fulfilled. *"All peoples on earth will be blessed through you and your offspring" (Genesis 28:14).*

(1.4) Promise to Judah: The Bible reveals that a descendant of Judah would be ruler over all the nations. Jesus, a descendant of Judah, is this ruler. *"The scepter will not depart from Judah, nor the ruler's staff from between his feet, until he comes to whom it belongs and the obedience of the nations is his" (Genesis 49:10).*

(1.5) Promise to the people of Israel: God promised that a Righteous One would be born out of the line of David. Jesus, a descendant of David, fulfilled this promise. *"'The days are coming,' declares the Lord, 'when I will fulfill the gracious promise I made to the house of Israel and to the house of Judah. In those days and at that time I will make a righteous Branch sprout from David's line; he will do what is just and right in the land'" (Jeremiah 33:14-15).*

(1.6) Promise Fulfilled: Jesus descended from the exact lineage that God promised. *"A record of the genealogy of Jesus Christ the son of David, the son of Abraham . . . there were fourteen generations in all from Abraham to David, fourteen from David to the exile to Babylon, and fourteen from the exile to the Christ" (Matthew 1:1 and 1:17).*

(1.7) Promise for All: The promise of Jesus is for all people; he offers hope! *"This mystery is that through the gospel the Gentiles are heirs together with Israel, members together of one body, and sharers together in the promise in Christ Jesus" (Ephesians 3:6).*

Week 2: Light the second candle on the second Sunday of Advent along with the first candle. For the following six days, light the first and second candle. The increase in light from week to week is meant to symbolize the coming of the light of the world, Jesus. The second candle is said to represent peace and the prophecies of a coming Savior. Discuss how this week's verses apply to the concept of peace.

(2.1) Prophecy About a Man That Will Crush Satan: In the first book of the Bible, written over 1400 years before Christ, God told Satan that the son of a woman would crush his head. Jesus fulfilled this prophecy. *"And I will put enmity between you and the woman, and between your offspring and hers; he will crush your head, and you will strike his heel" (Genesis 3:15).*

(2.2) Prophecy About a Virgin Birth: Over 700 years before Christ, the prophet Isaiah foretold that *Immanuel* (which means "God with us") would be born of a virgin. Jesus fulfilled this prophecy. *"Therefore the Lord himself will give you a sign: The virgin will be with child and will give birth to a son, and will call him Immanuel" (Isaiah 7:14).*

(2.3) Prophecy About the Identity of a Child: Over 700 years before Christ, the prophet Isaiah described the identity of Jesus. *"For to us a child is born, to us a son is given, and the government will be on his shoulders. And he will be called Wonderful Counselor, Mighty God, Everlasting Father, Prince of Peace" (Isaiah 9:6).*

(2.4) Prophecy About the Majesty of the Child: The prophet Isaiah further described Jesus and his majesty. *"Of the increase of his government and peace there will be no end. He will reign on David's throne and over his kingdom, establishing and upholding it with justice and righteousness from that time on and forever. The zeal of the Lord Almighty will accomplish this" (Isaiah 9:6-7).*

(2.5) Prophecy About the Birthplace of the Ruler: Over 600 years before Christ, the prophet Micah foretold that the Ruler would be born in Bethlehem. Jesus fulfilled this prophecy. *"But you, Bethlehem Ephrathah, though you are small among the clans of Judah, out of you will come for me one who will be ruler over Israel, whose origins are from of old, from ancient times" (Micah 5:2).*

(2.6) Prophecy About John the Baptist: Over 400 years before the birth of Jesus, the prophet Malachi foretold how a forerunner would prepare the way for Jesus. John the Baptist fulfilled this prophecy. *"'See, I will send my messenger, who will prepare the way before me. Then suddenly the Lord you are seeking will come to his temple; the messenger of the covenant, whom you desire, will come,' says the Lord Almighty" (Malachi 3:1).*

(2.7) Prophecy Fulfilled: Jesus is the only one that can bring <u>peace</u> with God. *"Therefore, since we have been justified through faith, we have peace with God through our Lord Jesus Christ" (Romans 5:1).*

Week 3: Light the third candle on the third Sunday of Advent along with the first and second candles. For the following six days, light the first, second and third candle. If using a pink candle, discuss the symbolism as mentioned above. This week, celebrate with joy that your hope in Christ is certain; prophecies about him are always fulfilled. "And we have heard the word of the prophets made more certain, and you will do well to pay attention to it, as to a light shining in a dark place, until the day dawns and the morning star rises in your hearts" (2 Peter 1:19). The third candle is said to represent <u>joy</u> and the <u>proclamations</u> regarding the coming Savior. Discuss how this week's verses apply to the concept of joy.

(3.1) Angelic Proclamation About John the Baptist: The angel Gabriel proclaimed to Zechariah that his son, John the Baptist, would prepare people for the coming of Jesus. *"Many of the people of Israel will he bring back to the Lord their God. And he will go on before the Lord, in the spirit and power of Elijah, to turn the hearts of the fathers to their children and the disobedient to the wisdom of the righteous—to make ready a people prepared for the Lord" (Luke 1:16-17).*

(3.2) Angelic Proclamation About Jesus: The angel Gabriel proclaimed to the virgin Mary that she would give birth to the Savior Jesus. *"You will be with child and give birth to a son, and you are to give him the name Jesus. He will be great and will be called the Son of the Most High. The Lord God will give him the throne of his father David, and he will reign over the house of Jacob forever; his kingdom will never end" (Luke 1:31-33).*

(3.3) Elizabeth's Proclamation About Jesus: Elizabeth, mother of John the Baptist, proclaimed that Mary carried the Lord in her womb. Even before his birth, John the Baptist made a unique proclamation about Jesus by leaping in his mother's womb.

"When Elizabeth heard Mary's greeting, the baby leaped in her womb, and Elizabeth was filled with the Holy Spirit. In a loud voice she exclaimed: "Blessed are you among women, and blessed is the child you will bear! But why am I so favored, that the mother of my Lord should come to me? As soon as the sound of your greeting reached my ears, the baby in my womb leaped for joy" (Luke 1:41-44).

(3.4) Mary's Proclamation About God: Mary proclaimed the great thing God had done in choosing her to give birth to Jesus. *"And Mary said: 'My soul glorifies the Lord and my spirit rejoices in God my Savior, for he has been mindful of the humble state of his servant. From now on all generations will call me blessed, for the Mighty One has done great things for me— holy is his name'" (Luke 1:46-49).*

(3.5) Zechariah's Proclamation About Jesus: Zechariah, father of John the Baptist, proclaimed his praise that Jesus would be the Redeemer and Savior. *"'Praise be to the Lord, the God of Israel, because he has come and has redeemed his people. He has raised up a horn of salvation for us in the house of his servant David (as he said through his holy prophets of long ago)'" (Luke 1:68-70).*

(3.6) Angelic Proclamation About Jesus: An angel proclaimed to Joseph that Jesus was conceived from the Holy Spirit and would save his people. *"An angel of the Lord appeared to him in a dream and said, 'Joseph son of David, do not be afraid to take Mary home as your wife, because what is conceived in her is from the Holy Spirit. She will give birth to a son, and you are to give him the name Jesus, because he will save his people from their sins'" (Matthew 1:20-21).*

(3.7) Prophetic Proclamation: Over 700 years before Christ, the prophet Isaiah announced that the Holy One of Israel would one day be among the people. Let us sing for joy that Jesus did indeed come to live with man! *"Shout aloud and sing for joy, people of Zion, for great is the Holy One of Israel among you" (Isaiah 12:6).*

Week 4: Light your fourth candle on the fourth Sunday of Advent along with the first, second and third candles. For the following days (however many there may be until Christmas), light all four candles. Combine the below verses, if necessary, in order to read all of them before Christmas. The fourth candle is said to represent love and the presence of the Savior. Discuss how this week's verses apply to the concept of God's love.

(4.1) His Presence Among Us: Over 400 years before Jesus, Zechariah foretold how God would one day come and live with men. *"'Shout and be glad, O Daughter of Zion. For I am coming, and I will live among you,' declares the Lord. 'Many nations will be joined with the Lord in that day and will become my people. I will live among you and you will know that the Lord Almighty has sent me to you'" (Zechariah 2:10-11).*

(4.2) His Presence as a Human: Jesus left the splendor of heaven to live on earth as a man. Therefore, *"Your attitude should be the same as that of Christ Jesus: Who, being in very nature God, did not consider equality with God something to be grasped, but made himself nothing, taking the very nature of a servant, being made in human likeness" (Philippians 2:5-7).*

(4.3) His Presence Declared by an Angel: When Jesus entered the world, a heavenly angel reported the news to shepherds. *"And there were shepherds living out in the fields nearby, keeping watch over their flocks at night. An angel of the Lord appeared to them, and the glory of the Lord shone around them, and they were terrified. But the angel said to them, 'Do not be afraid. I bring you good news of great joy that will be for all the people. Today in the town of David a Savior has been born to you; he is Christ the Lord'" (Luke 2:8-11).*

(4.4) His Presence Declared by the Heavens: Even the stars made known the presence of Jesus to Wise Men. *"After Jesus was born in Bethlehem in Judea, during the time of King Herod, Magi from the east came to Jerusalem and asked, 'Where is the one who has been born king of the Jews? We saw his star in the east and have come to worship him'" (Matthew 2:1-2).*

(4.5) His Presence Declared by Simeon: A righteous and devout man in Jerusalem named Simeon recognized the presence of the Savior. *"Simeon took him [the infant Jesus] in his arms and praised God, saying: 'Sovereign Lord, as you have promised, you now dismiss your servant in peace. For my eyes have seen your salvation, which you have prepared in the sight of all people, a light for revelation to the Gentiles and for glory to your people Israel" (Luke 2:28-32).*

(4.6) His Presence Declared by Anna: The prophetess Anna recognized the presence of Jesus, the Redeemer. *"There was also a prophetess, Anna. . . . She never left the temple but worshiped night and day, fasting and praying. Coming up to them (Mary and Jospeh) at that very moment, she gave thanks to God and spoke about the child to all who were looking forward to the redemption of Jerusalem" (Luke 2:38).*

(4.7) His Presence Motivated by Love: God sent Jesus into the world because of his great <u>love</u> for us! *"For God so loved the world that he gave his one and only Son, that whoever believes in him shall not perish but have eternal life. For God did not send his Son into the world to condemn the world, but to save the world through him" (John 3:16-17).*

Christmas Eve or Christmas Day: Replace all four candles with white candles and light them and/ or light a white candle in the center of the wreath. It is time to celebrate the birth of Christ, the "light of the world"! Read the following section from the gospel of John:

"In the beginning was the Word, and the Word was with God, and the Word was God. He was with God in the beginning. Through him all things were made; without him nothing was made that has been made. In him was life, and that life was the light of men. The light shines in the darkness, but the darkness has not understood it. There came a man who was sent from God; his name was John. He came as a witness to testify concerning that light, so that through him all men might believe. He himself was not the light; he came only as a witness to the light. The true light that gives light to every man was coming into the world. He was in the world, and though the world was made through him, the world did not recognize him. He came to that which was his own, but his own did not receive him. Yet to all who received him, to those who believed in his name, he gave the right to become children of God — children born not of natural descent, nor of human decision or a husband's will, but born of God. The Word became flesh and made his dwelling among us. We have seen his glory, the glory of the One and Only, who came from the Father, full of grace and truth" (John 1:1-14).

It may also be an appropriate time to discuss the twofold meaning of Advent. Christians celebrate the *coming* of Jesus into the world over 2,000 years ago but also wait expectantly for his *second coming*. After giving his last instructions to the apostles, Jesus ascended into heaven. The Book of Acts records:

"[The apostles] were looking intently up into the sky as he was going, when suddenly two men dressed in white stood beside them. 'Men of Galilee,' they said, 'why do you stand here looking into the sky? This same Jesus, who has been taken from you into heaven, will come back in the same way you have seen him go into heaven'" (Acts 1:10-11).

The Latin term *adventus* is the translation of the Greek word *parousia*, which is often used in reference to the second coming of Christ. The gospel of Matthew records Jesus' words about this coming, or parousia, as follows:

"For as lightning that comes from the east is visible even in the west, so will be the *coming* [the Advent] of the Son of Man. . . . all the nations . . . will see the Son of Man coming on the clouds of the sky, with power and great glory. And he will send his angels with a loud trumpet call, and they will gather his elect from the four winds, from one end of the heavens to the other. . . . No one knows about that day or hour, not even the angels in heaven, nor the Son, but only the Father. As it was in the days of Noah, so it will be at the *coming* [the Advent] of the Son of Man. So . . . be ready, because the Son of Man will come at an hour when you do not expect him" (Matthew 24:27-44).

Clearly, Jesus wants his people to be prepared for his return. Though he came first as a servant and a savior, he will come again as a ruler and a judge and will establish an eternal kingdom on a new earth. The Apostle Peter writes, "But in keeping with his promise we are looking forward to a new heaven and a new earth, the home of righteousness" (2 Peter 3:13). May believers "eagerly wait for our Lord Jesus Christ to be revealed" (1 Corinthians 1:7) and be ever ready for his second Advent!

---

[1] McClintock, John. Cyclopedia of Biblical, Theological & Ecclesiastical Literature, Yule. Harper & Brothers, 1889, p. 1012.

[2] Tertullian. *The Ante-Nicene Fathers, On Idolatry.* Edited by Alexander Roberts and James Donaldson. C. Scribner's Sons, 1903, p. 70.

[3] Das Rauhe Haus, "History, From 1832-1881." Retrieved August 15, 2008 from Das Rauhe Haus: http://www.rauheshaus.de/stiftung/geschichte.

[4] Encyclopedia Britannica. "Christmas." Retrieved August 15, 2008 from Encyclopedia Brittanica Online: http://www.britannica.com/EBchecked/topic/115686/Christmas.

[5] Tenny-Brittian, Bill. "Why Is There One Pink Advent Candle?" Retrieved August 15, 2008 from Home Church Network Association: http://www.hcna.us/columns/pink_advent_candle.html.

CAROLS, HYMNS, & MUSIC OF CHRISTMAS

Angels From the Realms of Glory

Angels From the Realms of Glory

Words: JAMES MONTGOMERY

REGENT SQUARE
Music: HENRY THOMAS SMART

With dignity ($\quad$ = 96)

1. An - gels from the realms of glo - ry, wing your flight o'er all the earth; ye who sang cre - a - tion's sto - ry, now pro - claim Mes - si - ah's birth:
2. Shep - herds, in the fields a - bid - ing, watch - ing o'er your flocks by night, God with man is now re - sid - ing, yon - der shines the in - fant light;
3. Sag - es, leave your con - tem - pla - tions, bright - er vi - sions beam a - far; seek the great de - sire of na - tions, ye have seen the na - tal star;
4. Saints, be - fore the al - tar bend - ing, watch - ing long in hope and fear, sud - den - ly the Lord, de - scend - ing, in His tem - ple shall ap - pear;
5. Though an in - fant now we view Him, He shall fill His Fath - er's throne. Gath - er all the na - tions to Him; ev' - ry knee shall then bow down.

Refrain

Come and wor - ship, come and wor - ship, wor - ship Christ, the new - born King!

Words by James Montgomery (1771-1854)

James Montgomery was born to a Moravian pastor in Scotland. The Moravian Church, a mainline Protestant denomination, is generally characterized by its commitment to Christian unity, worship and missions, and Montgomery's parents wholeheartedly embraced these ideals. When Montgomery was just 6 years old, his parents left him in the care of trusted friends at a Moravian settlement and set off as missionaries to the West Indies. Little did they know that they would never see their precious son again, for they perished in Barbados.[1]

At age 7, Montgomery began his formal education at a Moravian school in England, but it was not long before his interest in poetry became a distraction from his studies. Perhaps having lost his parents at a young age, Montgomery found a unique comfort in poetry. Though gifted in writing, he showed little interest in school, and the staff was eventually forced to dismiss him.

Since Montgomery had no parents, he was sent to work as an apprentice to a baker. After this unhappy attempt in a retail shop, a failed effort to find a publisher for his poems, and a period of aimless wandering, Montgomery took a position as a clerk in 1792 with Mr. Gales, publisher of the *Sheffield Register*.

With Gales, Montgomery found a mentor and a place where he could put his talent to work. However, just two years after Montgomery started his career, Gales had to flee to France. His newspaper had shown sympathy to the French Revolution, and as a result, he was threatened with political persecution in England.

In 1794, Montgomery took over the newspaper, and he would serve as the editor for the next 31 years. Though Montgomery changed the name of the paper to the *Sheffield Iris* and toned down its politics, he retained his mentor's love of liberty and concern for the oppressed (particularly the poor, the weak and those caught in slavery). He was imprisoned two times for libel, once for printing a song in honor of the storming of the Bastille and the second time for his "biased" coverage of a reform riot in Sheffield.[2]

Even while behind bars, Montgomery continued writing to champion the cause of the downtrodden. When he was 26 years old, he published a volume of poems called *Prison Amusements,* which were written during his time of confinement.

Over the course of the next several years, Montgomery put his pen to work in a variety of forms. All the while he, like his parents before him, was committed to serving God. In an 1860 preface to Montgomery's poetical works, author Robert Carruthers wrote, "He looked beyond the grave, but never neglected any form of suffering humanity or call of active duty and brotherly sympathy. . . . To all benevolent and missionary schemes, he lent a willing hand."[3]

In 1825, Montgomery relinquished ownership of the *Sheffield Iris* and devoted himself exclusively to religious writing. According to *The New Oxford Book of Carols*, Montgomery produced "some 400 hymns and skillfully adapted many more, in many cases his are the versions that are generally sung today."[4]

In regard to hymn writing, Montgomery took his work very seriously. He wrote, "Authors, who devote their talents to the glory of God, and the salvation of men, ought surely to take as much pains to polish and perfect their offerings of this kind, as secular and profane poets bestow upon their works."[5] Montgomery considered the "inestimable materials of hymns" to be "the truths of the everlasting Gospel, the very thoughts of God, the very sayings of Christ, [and] the very inspirations of the Holy Ghost."[6]

Interestingly, of all Montgomery's work, one poem called "Nativity" has stood the test of time. The poem was published in the *Sheffield Iris* on December 24, 1816, and would later become the text of the song "Angels, From the Realms of Glory." Montgomery's words beautifully sweep through history, from the beginning of time when angels "sang creation's story" (Job 38:7), to the glorious day when the Messiah "in His temple shall appear" (Malachi 3:1), to the end of time when "every knee shall then bow down" (Romans 14:11).

Music "Regent Square" by Henry Smart (1813-1879)

Henry Smart was a self-taught musician with a genius for organ music. Throughout his career, Smart served as the organist for a number of leading London churches. It was said that when he sought a position, other candidates would "quietly fade away."[7] Not only was Smart a gifted musician, he also designed and built some of the finest organs in England and Scotland.

During the last 15 years of his life, Smart was practically blind. Yet, he continued to play and write music with vigor. It was during this period that Smart composed a tune for a hymnal being compiled by Dr. Hamilton, pastor of the Regent Square Presbyterian Church in London. The tune thus acquired its name.

In England, Montgomery's poem was coupled with the French tune "Les Anges, Dans Nos Campagnes" (Americans use this tune for "Angels We Have Heard on High"). However, in the U.S. Montgomery's words found a perfect partner in Smart's magnificent tune.

Over the years, Smart's music has helped to stir the hearts of many generations as they "worship Christ the newborn King." Surely, even in blindness, Smart could see that "brighter visions beam afar."

---

[1] Montgomery, James. *The Poetical Works of James Montgomery: With a Memoir of the Author.* Memoir by Robert Carruthers. Little, Brown and Company, 1860, p. vii.

[2] Keyte, Hugh and Parrott, Andrew, editors. *The New Oxford Book of Carols.* Oxford University Press, 1998, p. 351.

[3] Montgomery, James. Memoir by Robert Carruthers, pp. xii – xiii.

[4] Keyte, Hugh and Parrott, Andrew, editors, p. 351.

[5] Music, David. *Hymnology, A Collection of Source Readings.* The Scarecrow Press, 1996, p.159.

[6] Music, David.

[7] Keyte, Hugh and Parrott, Andrew, editors, p. 351.

Angels We Have Heard on High

Angels We Have Heard On High

GLORIA
Words: ANONYMOUS
Translated by: JAMES CHADWICK
Music: FRENCH CAROL
Arranged by: EDWARD SHIPPEN BARNES

1. An - gels we have heard on high sweet - ly sing - ing o'er the plains,
2. Shep - herds, why this ju - bi - lee? Why your joy - ous strains pro - long?
3. Come to Beth - le - hem and see Him whose birth the an - gels sing;
4. See Him in a man - ger laid, whom the choirs of an - gels praise;

and the moun - tains in re - ply ech - o - ing their joy - ous strains.
What the glad - some ti - dings be? Which in - spire your heav'n - ly song?
come, a - dore on bend - ed knee, Christ the Lord, the new - born King.
Ma - ry, Jo - seph, lend your aid, while our hearts in love we raise.

Refrain

Glo - ri - a, in ex - cel - sis De - o!

Glo - ri - a, in ex - cel - sis De - o!

Words, Anonymous
Translated by James Chadwick (1813-1882)

The earliest known printed version of this song was in an 1842 French song book. Though the source of the song is unknown, it is believed to have originated in 18[th]century France.[1] The song was first translated into English in 1860 by James Chadwick, a Roman Catholic bishop.

Chadwick was born to an English father and Irish mother. Though he was born in Ireland, he was educated in England and spent the remainder of his life there. After attending Ushaw college, a combined college and seminary, and being ordained as a priest, Chadwick served for several years there as a professor in humanities (mainly teaching philosophy and theology). In 1866, Chadwick was elected bishop of Hexham and Newcastle and served in this capacity until his death.[2]

Chadwick's translation of "Angels We Have Heard on High" was said to be a "free imitation of the French."[3] Consider an example of a basic French to English translation:

"Les anges dans nos campagnes ont entonne l'hymne des cieux
Et l'echo de nos montagnes redit ce chant melodieux."

"The angels in our countryside sang the hymn of heaven
And the echo of our mountains reiterated this melodious song."

It takes a true poet to translate a masterpiece and retain its beauty. Perhaps angels themselves helped to inspire the translation. Chadwick was the kind of man who would have heard their voices. Judging by the topics of his publications, *St. Teresa's Own Words: Instructions on the Prayer of Recollection* and *Instructions How to Meditate*, to name a few, Chadwick was a man committed to prayer and meditation.

Conceivably, the shepherds of Bethlehem were also men committed to prayer and meditation. As they tended their flock in the vast plains by day and slept under magnificent stars by night, surely their hearts would be moved to reflect on the greatness of their Creator. It was to these shepherds that a great company of angels appeared to sing "Gloria, in Excelsis Deo" (Latin for "Glory to God in the Highest"); these were the words of the angels as recorded in Luke 2:14.

Praising God is what angels do. And though God's humble entrance into the human world brought no direct benefit to angels, they praised him for his supreme act of love toward mankind. "God in the highest" came down to earth in the "lowest" form in order to save humanity. Surely humanity, as recipients of God's amazing grace, should join the angels in singing glory to him!

Music "Gloria" Arranged by Edward Shippen Barnes (1887-1958)

Just as the origin of the words to this song is unknown, so also is the melody. Since it was common for text to be written for existing tunes, it is possible that the melody is even older than the words.[4]

The tune as we know it today was adapted and arranged by Edward Shippen Barnes. He was a talented organist who received training from gifted musicians at both Yale University and the Schola Cantorum in Paris. Having studied in France, it seems fitting that Barnes would arrange this traditional French carol.

After returning from France, Barnes devoted his talent to serving God as an organist in churches all across the U.S. (New York, Pennsylvania and California).[5] Barnes also composed organ symphonies, wrote a book on methods of organ playing and even served in the Naval Reserve during World War I. However, his most lasting contribution to humanity proved to be his musical arrangement for "Angels We Have Heard on High." After all, this music accompanies the voices of people who sing about their utmost purpose in life — bringing "glory to God in the highest."

---

[1] Keyte, Hugh and Parrott, Andrew, editors. *The New Oxford Book of Carols*. Oxford University Press, 1998, p. 638.

[2] Burton, Edwin. "James Chadwick." The Catholic Encyclopedia. Robert Appleton Company, 1908. Retrieved August 27, 2008 from New Advent: http://www.newadvent.org/cathen/03551c.htm.

[3] Keyte, Hugh and Parrott, Andrew, editors, p. 638.

[4] Keyte, Hugh and Parrott, Andrew, editors, p. 638.

[5] Hughes, Charles W. *American Hymns Old and New*. Columbia University Press, 1980, p. 113.

Away in a
Manger

Away in A Manger

Words: ANONYMOUS

MUELLER
Music: JAMES RAMSEY MURRAY

1. A - way in a man - ger, no crib for His bed, the
2. The cat - tle are low - ing the Ba - by a - wakes, but
3. Be near me, Lord Je - sus, I ask Thee to stay, close

lit - tle Lord Je - sus laid down His sweet head; the
lit - tle Lord Je - sus no cry - ing He makes. I
by me for - ev - er, and love me, I pray. Bless

stars in the sky____ looked down where He lay, the
love Thee, Lord Je - sus, look down from the sky and
all the dear chil - dren in Thy ten - der care, and

lit - tle Lord Je - sus a - sleep on the hay.
stay by my cra - dle 'til morn - ing is nigh.
take us to heav - en to live with Thee there.

Words, Anonymous

The words of this popular Christmas song are often attributed to Martin Luther. However, after doing extensive research, Richard Hill, distinguished head of the reference section of the Library of Congress in Washington D.C., discovered that the first two verses of the song were recorded without authorship in an 1885 American Lutheran publication called *Little Children's Book for Schools and Families.*[1]

The erroneous attribution to Luther appears to have come from James Murray (likely the author of the tune we know today). In 1887, Murray published *Dainty Songs for Little Lads and Lasses* in which he titled the song "Luther's Cradle Hymn" and noted that it was "composed by Martin Luther for his children, and still sung by German mothers to their little ones." Actually, German mothers knew nothing of the song at this time.[2] Murray probably confused "Away in a Manger" with another hymn that Luther wrote for his own family celebration of Christmas Eve. The hymn is titled, "Von Himmel hoch, da komm' ich her" ("From highest heaven, I come to tell"). Here are three of the 15 verses in the hymn:

"Awake, my soul! my heart, behold
Who lieth in that manger cold!
Who is this lovely baby boy?
'Tis Jesus Christ, our only joy.

"Ah, Lord, who all things didst create,
How cam'st thou to this poor estate,
To make the hay and straw thy bed,
Whereon the ox and ass are fed?

"Ah, Jesu, my heart's treasure blest,
Make thee a clean, soft cradle-nest
And rest enshrined within my heart,
That I from thee may never part."[3]

Hill believes that "Away in a Manger" most likely had its origin in one of the many dramatic presentations performed by American Lutherans in 1883 to mark the 400th anniversary of the birth of their founder. Most likely "Away in a Manger" was composed as a "simplified" version of Luther's hymn and was presented, for dramatic purposes, as a song (or poem) written by Luther.

Though Luther penned lovely verses for his children, and though he may have inspired the stanzas of "Away in a Manger," he did not write them. Hill's research concluded that we must put to rest "once for all the legend that Luther wrote a carol for his children, which no one else knew anything about, until it suddenly turned up in English dress four hundred years later in Philadelphia."[4] He added, "Luther can well afford to spare the honor."[5]

The third verse of "Away in a Manger" did not appear until 1892 in a Lutheran collection called *Gabriel's Vineyard Songs*. Ironically, even this later verse has questionable authorship. At one point, the secretary of the Lutheran Board of Education gave credit to John McFarland. However, this attribution is possibly the result of confusion between the man who supplied the verse for publication and the person who actually wrote it.[6]

Music "Mueller" by James Ramsey Murray (1841/2-1905)

As noted above, James Murray is held responsible for erroneously attributing the words of "Away in a Manger" to Martin Luther. Ironically, Murray's own authorship of the tune would be mistakenly assigned as well. In part, Murray was to blame for the confusion. He "signed the setting with his initials, thus giving the impression that he had merely arranged a melody by Luther."[7] On the other hand, as Murray's tune rapidly grew in popularity (more so than the other 40+ other tunes to which the song has been set), publishers were careless about researching the copyright.

The tune came to be called "Mueller," because at some point, publishers credited a Carl Mueller with its authorship. However, it appears that no such person existed. Hill writes that evidence makes it look "like the desperate hoax of an editor who, knowing full well that the melody was not composed by Luther, preferred to put down just any name, so long as it was vague enough, rather than attempt to establish the correct composer."[8] Murray himself claimed authorship, and unless evidence reveals the contrary, it is reasonable to assume that he truly composed the tune.

Murray was certainly a capable musician. He studied under many legendary teachers at the Musical Institute in North Reading, Mass. One of them was Lowell Mason who arranged the music for "Joy to the World" (see pp. 235-237). But Murray lived at a time of political unrest, and he ended up serving as an army musician in the American Civil War. During his time in the army, Murray became nationally famous for a sentimental song called "Daisy Deane"; he composed it in a Virginia camp in 1863. After the war, Murray taught and published music in a variety of positions.

By 1881, Murray began working for an Ohio publishing company, the John Church Company. He published several books of songs for Sunday schools and Gospel meetings. He also wrote a book on the basics of music and compiled a music dictionary. It was during his time at the John Church Company that he discovered the song "Away in a Manger" and had it published in 1887. It appears that Murray spent the remainder of his life working for this company and had the opportunity to see the song sweep across the nation.

Though Murray left behind a wonderful legacy with his music for "Away in a Manger," it is interesting to note that his life and musical activities are often overlooked in reference books on music and musicians. Additionally, little is known about his personal life and faith. He, like the author of the words, is left in obscurity.

It seems fitting that no real honor is given to either the author or the composer of "Away in a Manger." After all, the song is meant to turn attention to the God who humbly entered the world without honor or glory or even a "crib for a bed."

[1] Hill, Richard S. "Not So Far Away In A Manger, Forty-one Settings of an America Carol." Music Library Association, "Notes", December, 1945, Second Series, Vol. III, No. 1. Retrieved August 27, 2008 from Hymns and Carols of Christmas: http://www.hymnsandcarolsofchristmas.com/Hymns_and_Carols/Notes_On_Carols/away_in_a_manger.htm.

[2] Keyte, Hugh and Parrott, Andrew, editors. *The New Oxford Book of Carols*. Oxford University Press, 1998, p. 361.

[3] Keyte, Hugh and Parrott, Andrew, editors, pp. 201-202.

[4] Hill, Richard S.

[5] Hill, Richard S.

[6] Keyte, Hugh and Parrott, Andrew, editors, p. 361.

[7] Keyte, Hugh and Parrott, Andrew, editors, p. 361.

[8] Hill, Richard S.

Go, Tell It On the Mountain

Go, Tell It on the Mountain

Words: ANONYMOUS
Stanzas 1-3 Attributed to:
JOHN WESLEY WORK, JR.

Music: AFRICAN-
AMERICAN SPIRITUAL

Joyfully (♩ = 120)
Refrain

Go, tell it on the moun - tain, o - ver the hills and ev - 'ry - where;

go, tell it on the moun - tain that Je - sus Christ __ is born.

1. While shep - herds kept their watch-ing o'er si - lent flocks by night, be -
2. The shep - herds feared and trem-bled, when lo! a - bove the earth rang
3. Down in a low - ly man - ger the hum - ble Christ was born, and
4. When I __ was a seek - er, I sought both night and day, I

to Refrain

hold through - out the heav - ens there shone a ho - ly light. __
out the an - gel cho - rus that hailed our Sav - ior's birth. __
God sent us sal - va - tion that bless - ed Christ - mas morn. __
sought the Lord to help me and He showed me the way. __

194

Words Attributed to John Wesley Work Jr. (1871-1925)

At the end of the American Civil War, several schools were founded to meet the educational needs of freed slaves. One of these was the Fisk Free Colored School, named in honor of General Clinton Fisk who helped to secure old Union Army barracks in Nashville, Tenn. as facilities for the new institution. The first classes were held in January of 1866, and the first students ranged in age from 7 to 70. These students were said to share a "common experiences of slavery and poverty [as well as] an extraordinary thirst for learning."[1]

In August of 1867, the school was chartered as Fisk University, but its future remained uncertain. The financial needs of a university were vast, and the school quickly began accumulating debt. By 1871, a group of students, the now famous Jubilee Singers, set out on a mission to raise funds for their ailing school. In order to cover their traveling expenses, the singers departed with all of the university's financial resources. The principal of the school gave "all the money in his possession save one dollar, which he held back, that the treasury might not be empty."[2]

The Jubilee Singers knew that if their efforts failed, the school would close. Though they faced a variety of challenges, like being "shut out of hotels, railway waiting rooms and ships' cabins and excluded from some churches because of its members' colour,"[3] their performances gradually won them acclaim. As the Jubilee Singers toured the U.S. and Europe, they had the opportunity to perform before noted persons like Ulysses S. Grant, Mark Twain, and even Queen Victoria. Not only did the Jubilee Singers succeed in raising the funds needed to preserve the university, but they also introduced much of the world to the musical genre of the African-American spiritual.

Many of the members of this original group of Jubilee Singers also sang under the leadership of John Wesley Work in their local Nashville church choir. Work was a gifted artist who wrote and arranged music for his choir. His sons, John Jr. and Frederick, were undoubtedly raised in an environment surrounded by talented musicians.

John Wesley Work Jr. proved to be a competent scholar. In 1898, he graduated with a master's degree from Fisk University and was hired to teach Latin and Greek. His true passion, however, was evident in his work with music at Fisk, as well as in his publications. As early as 1889, Work Jr. was helping to organize singing groups at Fisk. Additionally, along with his brother Frederick, he began collecting and publishing spirituals. His first publication was in 1901 and titled *New Jubilee Songs as Sung by the Fisk Jubilee Singers*.

Though the Jubilee Singers had been singing "Go Tell It On the Mountain" since 1879, the song had yet to be published. Work Jr. authored the words of stanzas 1-3, coupled them with the popular refrain and published the piece as a solo song in 1907.[4] The fourth stanza was published in 1909 by Thomas Fenner in a book titled *Religious Songs of the Negro as Sung on the Plantations*. Interestingly, Fenner had been collecting plantation songs from students in Hampton, Va. for over 35 years. In an earlier publication, *Hampton and Its Students*, Fenner wrote:

"One reason for publishing this slave music is, that it is rapidly passing away. It may be that this people which has developed such a wonderful musical sense in its degradation will, in its maturity, produce a composer who could bring a music of the future out of this music of the past. At present, however, the freedmen have an unfortunate inclination to despise it, as a vestige of slavery; those who learned in the old time, when it was the natural outpouring of their sorrows and longings, are dying off, and if efforts are not made for its preservation, the country will soon have lost this wonderful music of bondage."[5]

Surely, Work Jr. rose to the task of being the "composer who could bring a music of the future out of the music of the past." Though it was a controversial task to promote songs born in the wretched days of slavery, Work Jr. unashamedly embraced the music of his heritage. In his book *Folk Song of the American Negro*, he wrote:

"In the Negro's mind his music has held, and still holds, positions of variable importance. In the darkness of bondage, it was his light; in the morn of his freedom, it was his darkness; but as the day advances, and he is being gradually lifted up into a higher life, it is becoming not only his proud heritage, but a support, and powerful inspiration."[6]

Work Jr. believed that the spirituals of slavery helped to make better men:

"The man, though a slave, produced the song, and the song, in turn, produced a better man. . . . What else could he be who had such ideals ever before him? How could a man be base who looked ever to the hills? Could a man cherish the idea of rapine whose soul was ever singing these songs of love, patience and God? Neither African heathenism nor American slavery could wholly extinguish that spark of idealism, set aglow by his Creator. This idealism, expressed in terms so beautiful and strong grew in power, and the possessor found himself irresistibly drawn and willingly striving to attain unto it."[7]

Though Work Jr. sought to live the "higher life," he also seemed to grasp the profound way in which God honors the humble. The words of his stanzas focus on the simple shepherds, the lowly manger and the humble Christ. Perhaps it was in the humility of bondage that slaves came to understand the significance of Jesus' birth in a unique way. For Christ came to "proclaim freedom" and "release the oppressed" (Luke 4:18). Surely, this is news worth telling "on the mountain, over the hills and everywhere." The Bible says:

"How beautiful on the mountains are the feet of those who bring good news, who proclaim peace, who bring good tidings, who proclaim salvation, who say to Zion, 'Your God reigns!'" (Isaiah 52:7).

Believers put their hope in a God who reigns and will one day set things right. This is not a message to keep to oneself!

Work Jr. devoted himself to spreading the good news found in African American spirituals, and his legacy continued not only in his music, but also in his sons. After graduating from Fisk University, his son John Wesley Work III went on to study at the Institute of Musical Art (now the Julliard School of Music). Work III developed an impressive resume in his lifetime and carried on the tradition of collecting folk songs. In 1960, he published *American Negro Songs and Spirituals*, which is considered a major contribution to musicology in its category. His brother Julian also became a professional musician and composer.

---

[1] Fisk University. "History of Fisk." Retrieved August 27, 2008 from: http://www.fisk.edu/page.asp?id=115.

[2] Work, John Wesley. *Folk Song of the American Negro*. Fisk University, 1915, p. 105.

[3] Bradley, Ian, editor. *The Penguin Book of Carols*. Penguin Books, 1999, p. 96.

[4] Work III, John Wesley. *American Negro Songs: 230 Folk Songs and Spirituals, Religious and Secular*. Courier Dover Publications, 1998, p. 215. John Work III made a note at the bottom of the song "Go Tell It on the Mountain" indicating that the verses were supplied by his father "in place of the original words which could not be found."

[5] Armstrong, Mary Frances, Ludlow, Helen Wilhelmina, and Fenner, Thomas P. *Hampton and Its Students*. G.P. Putnam's Sons, 1874, p. 172.

[6] Work, John Wesley. p. 110.

[7] Work, John Wesley. p. 110.

God Rest You
Merry, Gentlemen

God Rest You Merry, Gentlemen

Words: ANONYMOUS

CHESTNUT
Music: ENGLISH MELODY
Arranged by: JOHN STAINER

Heartily (♩ = 80)

1. God rest you mer - ry, gen - tle - men, let noth - ing you dis - may, re -
2. From God our heav'n - ly Fa - ther a bless - ed an - gel came; and
3. But when to Beth - le - hem they came where our dear Sav - ior lay, they
4. Now to the Lord sing prais - es all you with - in this place, and

mem - ber Christ our Sav - ior was born on Christ - mas day; To
un - to cer - tain shep - herds brought ti - dings of the same; how
found Him in a man - ger where ox - en feed on hay; His
with true love and broth - er - hood each oth - er now em - brace; this

Refrain

save us all from Sa - tan's pow'r when we were gone a - stray;
that in Beth - le - hem was born the Son of God by name;
moth - er Ma - ry kneel - ing un - to the Lord did pray;
ho - ly tide of Christ - mas doth bring re - deem - ing grace; O__ ti - dings of

com - fort and joy, com - fort and joy; O__ ti - dings of com - fort and joy.

Words, Anonymous

In the 1843 classic *A Christmas Carol,* Charles Dickens wrote:

"The owner of one scant young nose, gnawed and mumbled by the hungry cold as bones are gnawed by dogs, stooped down at Scrooge's keyhole to regale him with a Christmas carol; but at the first sound of

'God bless you, merry gentleman!
May nothing you dismay!'

Scrooge seized the ruler with such energy of action, that the singer fled in terror, leaving the keyhole to the fog and even more congenial frost."[1]

Indeed, the bitter cold was friendlier than Ebenezer Scrooge. Had he allowed the poor caroler to continue with the next verse, "Remember Christ our Savior . . ." and had he heeded the words of the carol, "Ebenezer could have saved himself quite an adventurous night."[2]

It comes as no surprise that "God Rest You Merry, Gentlemen" was chosen as "the Christmas carol of *A Christmas Carol*"[3]; it was arguably the most popular song of Dickens' era. Though the author is unknown, the carol was "a piece so often printed and sung in districts so widely separated [that] there are several variations in the different copies of [it]"[4] (notice Dickens' version of the words "God bless you" instead of "God rest you"). The first known published version of the carol was in William Sandys' *Christmas Carols, Ancient and Modern,* 1833. For more on Sandys, see pp. 284-285.

In addition to the variety of words associated with this carol, there is also tremendous confusion on the meaning, and even the punctuation, of the first line of the carol. For example, the Old English meaning of the word "rest" is perhaps best translated "keep"; the word "merry" is perhaps best translated as either "good spirits" or "strong." Additionally, the meaning of the first line changes significantly depending on where the comma is placed. The comma should be *after* the word "merry," as found in Sandys, not before it.

Thus, the original intent of the carol was that "God keep you in good spirits, gentlemen," not that God give rest to merry gentlemen. According to the *Penguin Book of Carols,* "It is not, as so often thought, addressed to merry gentlemen but rather to those who may be anxious."[5] As the first stanza of the carol reveals, there is a spiritual battle against evil. Yet, our hearts should not be troubled. As the words of the song say, "Christ our Savior was born on Christmas day to save us all from Satan's power." Surely, this news should keep believers in good spirits; it is a true tiding of "comfort and joy."

Music "Chestnut" Arranged by John Stainer (1840-1901)

A.L. Lloyd, a collector and researcher of folk songs, wrote of this tune: "In its sundry variants, it is [England's] commonest melody for *quête* songs" (a song that brings luck).[6] A number of related tunes existed throughout Europe by the 16th century, and Lloyd believed that though the tune most likely traveled to England from France, it may have originated further east and farther back in time.

The tune name "Chestnut" is derived from a 1651 book by John Playford called *The English Dancing Master* (a book that includes dance instructions and the music associated with each dance). This was the basis of the now "standard" arrangement by John Stainer.

Even as a young boy, Stainer's gift for music was apparent. He got his start in music as a singer in the choir of St. Paul's Cathedral, and by age 16, he took his first position as an organist at a school for church musicians.[7] Four years later, he was appointed to the position of organist at Magdalen College, Oxford where he served along side a chaplain by the name of H.R. Bramley (a man with whom Stainer would partner to publish several volumes of music).[8] After 16 years at Oxford, Stainer returned to the place where he started, St. Paul's Cathedral, to hold the prestigious position of organist. In all, Stainer worked as an organist for over 30 years until he had to resign due to failing eyesight.

All the while, Stainer was active in writing, researching, publishing and teaching a wide array of music. Though Stainer earned a reputation as an excellent organist and composer in his day, one of his most lasting contributions to modern music was his publication of *Christmas Carols New and Old*, produced in collaboration with Bramley. Together, Bramley and Stainer published three different volumes of Christmas music, and Stainer's arrangements became the standard version for not only "God Rest You Merry, Gentlemen" but many other beloved carols: "Good Christian Men Rejoice," "The First Noel" and "What Child Is This?"

By 1885, Durham University awarded Stainer with an honorary degree in recognition of his musical genius. Even Queen Victoria acknowledged Stainer's contribution to music in Britain, and he was knighted in 1888. The following year, Sir John Stainer became a professor of music at Oxford University where he spent the remainder of his life.

Interestingly, Stainer lost the use of one of his eyes in a childhood accident. For a brief period beginning in 1888, it appears that he lost the use of his other eye as well. Though this difficulty forced him to resign from serving as an organist, it also brought him back to Oxford as a professor. Thus, a new generation of students could benefit from a man who understood that music was intended to honor and "remember Christ our Savior."

[1] Dickens, Charles. *The Works of Charles Dickens*. Chapman and Hall, 1910, p. 17.

[2] Anderson, Doug. *God Rest You Merry, Gentlemen – Notes*. Retrieved on August 29, 2008 from Hymns and Carols of Christmas: http://www.hymnsandcarolsofchristmas.com/Hymns_and_Carols/Notes_On_Carols/god_rest_you_merry_notes.htm.

[3] Studwell, William. *The Christmas Carol Reader*. The Haworth Press, 1995, p. 133.

[4] Husk, William Henry. *Songs of the Nativity: Being Christmas Carols, Ancient and Modern*. J.C. Hotten, 1884, p. 27.

[5] Bradley, Ian, editor. *The Penguin Book of Carols*. Penguin Books, 1999, p. 100.

[6] Lloyd, A.L. *Folk Song in England*. International Publishers, 1967, p. 104.

[7] Encyclopedia Britannica. "Sir John Stainer." Retrieved August 29, 2008 from Encyclopedia Britannica Online: http://www.britannica.com/EBchecked/topic/562546/Sir-John-Stainer. Much of the biography of John Stainer is drawn from this entry.

[8] Keyte, Hugh and Parrott, Andrew, editors. *The New Oxford Book of Carols*. Oxford University Press, 1998, p. xxi.

Good Christian
Men, Rejoice

Good Christian Men, Rejoice

Words Attributed to: HENRY SUSO
Translated by: JOHN MASON NEALE

IN DULCI JUBILO
Music: GERMAN MELODY
Arranged by: JOHN STAINER

Words Attributed to Henry Suso (1295-1366)

At the age of 18, Henry Suso (Heinrich Seuse in German) submitted his life to God. He spent his subsequent years passionately seeking the Lord and meditating on spiritual things. In 1328, Suso published a devotional book called the *Little Book of Eternal Wisdom*. Surely, he could not have imagined that his book would become the most widely read meditation book in the German language for over 100 years. Though the book was intended for "simple men," the Catholic Encyclopedia records that Suso wrote "with rare skill, and contributed much to the formation of good German prose, especially by giving new shades of meaning to words employed to describe inner sensations."[1]

Yet, more widely known today than any of Suso's other work is the carol "Good Christian Men Rejoice" ("In Dulci Jubilo" in Latin). The song is generally attributed to Suso based on his autobiographical description of an encounter with angels. Note that Suso speaks in the third person and refers to himself as "the Servitor."

"After he had spent many hours in contemplating the joys of the angels, and daybreak was at hand, there came to him a youth, who bore himself as though he were a heavenly musician sent to him by God; and with the youth there came many other noble youths, in manner and bearing like the first, save only that he seemed to have some pre-eminence above the rest, as if he were a prince-angel. Now this same angel came up to the Servitor right blithely, and said that God had sent them down to him, to bring him heavenly joys amid his sufferings; adding that he must cast off all his sorrows from his mind and bear them company, and that he must also dance with them in heavenly fashion. Then they drew the Servitor by the hand into the dance, and the youth began a joyous ditty about the infant Jesus, which runs thus: 'In dulci jubilo,' etc. When the Servitor heard the dear name of Jesus sounding thus sweetly, he became so blithesome in his heart and feeling, that the very memory of his sufferings vanished. It was a joy to him to see how exceedingly loftily and freely they bounded in the dance. . . . This dance was not of a kind like those danced in this world; but it was a heavenly movement, swelling up and falling back again into the wild abyss of God's hiddenness."[2]

It is unclear whether the song was new to Suso or if it was already familiar to him. Either way, it is wonderful to consider that humans can join with the angels in singing this carol!

The earliest known source of the actual words and music of "In Dulci Jubilo" is from a manuscript dated around 1400 AD in which it is a single-stanza dance song. It is believed to be the oldest German macaronic hymn (a hymn that alternates between the languages of German and Latin). Over the course of the 15th century, additional stanzas were added, and the vernacular lines were recorded in a variety of German and Dutch dialects.[3]

Even though the words were not translated into English until several hundred years later, they remained coupled with their original music. The tune has retained its Latin name "In Dulci Jubilo" ("In Sweetest Rejoicing" in English), and though it may have a heavenly origin, its source is generally listed as an anonymous 14th century German melody.

Words Translated by John Mason Neale (1818-1866)
Music "In Dulci Jubilo" Arranged by John Stainer (1840-1901)

Neale was born to wealthy, well-educated, evangelical parents in London. However, the challenges that would largely characterize his life began early. When Neale was only 5 years old, his father died. Though this heavy loss was not easily forgotten, Neale determined to honor his father by diligently applying himself to his studies. And with the exception of mathematics, Neale proved to be a brilliant student. Though Neale was considered the best in his college class, he was forced to graduate without honors due to a "strange rule" that required distinction in math. Ironically, one year after he graduated, the rule was rescinded.[4]

Neale went on to a graduate seminary at Cambridge where he identified himself with a growing movement for revival in the Anglican Church. Unfortunately, once Neale was ready to accept a position in the Church, his weak lungs and overall ill health caused a delay. By 1846, when he was finally given an assignment, it was to an obscure position (the wardenship of Sackville College in East Grinstead) with a low salary. Quite possibly, the assignment was a consequence of Neale's association with the revivalist movement. Church leadership did not look favorably on this connection.

Neale's next challenge came as a result of establishing an organization called the "East Gristead Sisters" or "Sisterhood of St. Margaret," which was dedicated to helping the sick and suffering. An orphanage, a school for girls, and even a home for the "reformation of fallen women" were all started in connection with the sisterhood. However, for one reason or another, Neale faced tremendous criticism for establishing the group. The opposition culminated on at least one occasion in actual violence. Upon the death of one of the Sisters in 1857, rumors spread that she had been persuaded to give all her money to the Sisterhood and was then purposely sent to an area where she would catch the scarlet fever, of which she died. Neale and some of the Sisters were actually attacked and "roughly handled" at the funeral. According to John Julian, editor of *A Dictionary of Hymnology*, "To those who knew anything of the scrupulously delicate and honourable character of Dr. Neale, such a charge would seem absurd on the face of it; but mobs are not apt to reflect."[5]

More than likely, Neale had compassion for the "mob." Throughout his life, Neale demonstrated a sincere concern for others, especially those who were often overlooked by society at large. Consider just a handful of his publications: *Hymns for Children, Songs and Ballads for Manufacturers, Hymns for the Sick* and *Readings for the Aged.*

Neale was said to have a "happy mixture of gentleness and firmness."[6] Though he was committed to his convictions, he showed tremendous charity and patience to those who disagreed with him.

And he was not without a sense of humor. On one occasion, he was invited to assist a Mr. Keble and the Bishop of Salisbury on a new hymnal. During their meeting, Mr. Keble had to step out of the room to find some papers.

"On his return Dr. Neale said, 'Why, Keble, I thought you told me the *Christian Year* [the hymnal] was entirely original.' 'Yes,' he answered, 'it certainly is.' 'Then how comes this?' and Dr. Neale placed before him the Latin of one of Keble's hymns. Keble professed himself utterly confounded. He protested that he had never seen this 'original,' no, not in all his life. After a few minutes, Neale relieved him by owning that he had just turned it into Latin in his absence."[7]

Neale was certainly a master translator. Yet, he also had an "exquisite ear for melody [that] prevented him from spoiling the rhythm by too servile an imitation of the original."[8] His translations were definitely "free" and he faced criticism from Catholic leaders for altering the original Latin text when it did not conform to his theological views. Regardless, Neale was always true to his convictions, even if it relegated him to an obscure job, a low salary and criticism from nearly every corner of England.

Yet, even in the midst of opposition, Neale's talent was undeniable. In 1853, G. J. R. Gordon, Her Majesty's Envoy and Minister at Stockholm, gave a rare copy of the 1582 edition of *Piae Cantiones* to Neale and his friend Thomas Helmore.[9] The *Piae Cantiones* contained medieval songs from several European countries and was one of Finland's greatest musical treasures, yet it was unknown in England at the time. Neale and Helmore worked together to publish a dozen of these songs in their *Carols for Christmas-tide* (1853-1854); one of them is the now famous "Good Christian Men Rejoice." Helmore transcribed the tune and Neale offered the free translation of the Swedish/Latin text. Most hymnals today use John Stainer's arrangement which is also based on the *Piae Cantiones* and first appeared in *Christmas Carols New and Old* (1871). For more on Stainer, see p. 202.

Though his life was relatively short, Neale left an enduring contribution to English hymnody; it should be noted that he also translated "O Come, O Come Emmanuel." In the words of Archbishop Trench, a man that Neale deeply admired, it was "by patient researches in almost all European lands, [that Neale] has brought to light a multitude of hymns unknown before. . . . To him the English reader owes versions of some of the best hymns."[10] Because of Neale's efforts, we can rejoice in a rich variety of songs "with heart and soul and voice."

---

[1] McMahon, Arthur. "Blessed Henry Suso." The Catholic Encyclopedia. Robert Appleton Company, 1908. Retrieved June 27, 2008 from New Advent: http://www.newadvent.org/cathen/07238c.htm.

[2] Knox, Thomas Francis. Translated by W. R. Inge. *The Life of Blessed Henry Suso by Himself.* Kessinger Publishing, 2006, pp. 23-24.

[3] Keyte, Hugh and Parrott, Andrew, editors. *The New Oxford Book of Carols*. Oxford University Press, 1998, p. 198.

[4] Julian, John, editor. *A Dictionary of Hymnology*. Dover Publications Inc., 1957, p. 785. Much of the biography for John Mason Neale is drawn from this source.

[5] Julian, John, editor, p. 785.

[6] Julian, John, editor, p. 786.

[7] Julian, John, editor, p. 787 (quoting Moultrie).

[8] Julian, John, p. 787.

[9] Bradley, Ian, editor. *The Penguin Book of Carols*. Penguin Books, 1999, p. 110.

[10] Julian, John, p. 789.

Hark! the Herald
Angels Sing

Hark! the Herald Angels Sing

MENDELSSOHN

Words: CHARLES WESLEY

Music: FELIX MENDELSSOHN
Arranged by: WILLIAM HAYMAN CUMMINGS

1. Hark! the her-ald an-gels sing,___ "Glo-ry to the new-born King;
2. Christ, by high-est heav'n a-dored,___ Christ the ev-er-last-ing Lord;
3. Hail the heav'n-born Prince of Peace!___ Hail the Sun of Right-eous-ness!

peace on earth, and mer-cy mild,___ God and sin-ners rec-on-ciled!"
late in time be-hold Him come,___ off-spring of the Vir-gin's womb.
Light and life to all He brings,___ ris'n with heal-ing in His wings.

Joy-ful, all ye na-tions rise,___ join the tri-umph of the skies;___
Veiled in flesh the God-head see;___ hail th'in-car-nate De-i-ty,___
Mild He lays His glo-ry by,___ born that man no more may die,___

with th'an-gel-ic host pro-claim, "Christ is___ born in Beth-le-hem!"
pleased as man with man to dwell, Je-sus___ our Em-man-u-el.
born to raise the sons of earth, born to___ give them sec-ond birth.

Hark! the her-ald an-gels sing, "Glo-ry___ to the new-born King!"

212

Words by Charles Wesley (1707-1788)

Charles Wesley was the youngest and third surviving son of Samuel, an Anglican clergyman, and Susanna Wesley. Sadly, of their 19 children, 9 died in infancy. Yet, by all accounts, Susanna was a woman of remarkable character who was committed to the high call of motherhood. In her husband's absence, she wrote the following in a letter to him:

> "I cannot help but look upon every soul you leave under my care as a talent committed to me under a trust by the great Lord of all the families, both of heaven and earth. And if I am unfaithful to him or you in neglecting to improve these talents, how shall I answer unto him when he shall command me to render an account of my stewardship?"[1]

Having written these words when her sons, Charles and John, were about 3 and 7 respectively, she likely could not have imagined the depth of the talent that she was improving upon. Charles went on to publish more than 4,500 hymns (another 3,000 were left as manuscripts) and together with his brother John, founded the Methodist movement. The pair witnessed hundreds of people come to faith in Christ during their ministry across Great Britain.

At age 8, after being educated at home by Susanna, Charles entered the Westminster School in London. By age 18, he was elected to Christ Church College, Oxford, where he spent much of his time translating Greek and Latin classics into English verse. During his time in college, Charles helped to found the "Holy Club." Within its first year, Charles turned leadership of the club over to his brother John (who Charles believed to be a more gifted leader). The group met often to study the Bible and the classics. They also sought to live holy lives by taking communion often, fasting on Wednesdays and Fridays, serving the poor and working in prisons. Classmates derisively called the group "Methodists" because of their methodical habits of study and devotion. Though the group dissolved in 1735, when the Wesleys left on a missionary trip to America, it was considered the beginning of the Methodist movement.[2]

Commissioned by the Church of England, John and Charles sailed to America in 1735 as missionaries to the colony of Georgia. In 1737, John published the first hymnal in the American colonies, the *Charlestown Collection of Psalms and Hymns*. However, it appears that the Wesleys' missionary efforts were not warmly received. The brothers returned to England feeling discouraged and disillusioned. Fortunately, this sense of dismay would prove to be the impetus for a significant spiritual renewal that was soon to follow.

On his return to England, Charles began associating with a group of Moravians (a mainline Protestant denomination mainly characterized by its commitment to Christian unity, worship and missions). As a result of his interaction with the Moravians, Charles became convicted of the need to know Jesus personally and to surrender his life completely to the Lord. On May 23, 1738, Charles wrote, "[I] gave myself up, soul and body, to him."[3] Charles immediately wrote his first hymn, "Where shall my wondering soul begin?"

Hymnologists Harry Eskew and Hugh McElrath record of Charles:

"Before this turning point he, like John, was an ordained Anglican clergyman and, together with John, a missionary for a brief period to the Georgia colony. He was also a gifted poet. But it was not until he was catapulted into a deeply personal relationship to Jesus Christ as Redeemer and Lord that there was released in him the gift of sacred song."[4]

From the point of his conversion, hardly a day or experience would pass without it taking form in verse. And Charles' ministry efforts came to be motivated less by obligation than by genuine love for God and for mankind.

John had a separate conversion experience shortly after Charles, which set the two brothers on a course of ministry that would radically change lives. Little did the brothers know that they would be God's instruments of revival in their native country. England was ripe for spiritual awakening and much in need of the "light and life" that only Jesus could bring.

"The picture of England during the opening decades of the 18th century was a sorry one – morals were decayed, education was practically non-existent, sanitation was neglected, literature and the theater were debauched, intemperance was rampant, crime was widespread, politics were corrupt and the clergy were idle and uncaring. Into such a world came the Wesleys like a cleansing fire. The great organizer and promoter of the movement was John Wesley. But by all accounts much of the success of this remarkable religious awakening must be attributed to the singing of Charles Wesley's hymns."[5]

After their personal conversions, the Wesleys devoted themselves to spreading the message of God's love and power to transform lives in all social classes. Their audiences consisted of an odd combination of rich and poor, educated and unschooled, "fashionable" and low-class alike. And for those that could not otherwise hear their message, they spent time ministering to prisoners and even inmates of a dungeon for the insane.

Charles' academic training gave him a superb command of language. Yet his purpose in hymn writing was not to impress. His hymns were composed in order that men and women "might sing their way not only into experience but also into knowledge; that the cultured might have their culture baptized and the ignorant might be led into truth by the gentle hand of melody and rhyme."[6]

Surely Charles' songs had their intended effect. So many of them became and remain popular that they are too numerous to list. Among the best known are: "Love Divine, All Loves Excelling", "Christ the Lord is Ris'n Today," "Soldiers of Christ, Arise," "Rejoice, the Lord Is King" and "Jesu, Lover of My Soul." Yet, among all of his great songs, the beloved Christmas carol, "Hark the Herald Angels Sing," is probably the most popular. It appears in more hymn books than any other song.[7]

Though Charles' brother John adamantly opposed changes to Charles' original text, the hymn we sing today has endured a variety of alterations. In his 1779 preface to *A Collection of Hymns for the Use of the People Called Methodists*, John wrote:

"Many gentlemen have done my brother and me (though without naming us) the honour to reprint many of our Hymns. Now they are perfectly welcome so to do, provided they print them just as they are. But I desire they would not attempt to mend them; for they really are not able. None of them is able to mend either the sense or the verse. Therefore I must beg of them one of these two favours: either to let them stand as they are, to take them for better for worse, or to add the true reading in the margin, or at the bottom of the page; that we may no longer be accountable either for the nonsense or for the doggerel of other men."[8]

In addition to being a gifted poet, Charles Wesley was also a careful theologian. Understandably, his brother feared that alterations to his text could have devastating effects — not only to the elegance of Charles' poetry but to the biblical truths that were contained in it. Charles' hymns were generally full of Scripture and doctrine. Consider how the words "Hail the Sun of righteousness! Light and life to all He brings, ris'n with healing in His wings" draw from Scripture: "But for you who revere my name, the sun of righteousness will rise with healing in its wings…" (Malachi 4:2). Charles also incorporated essential doctrines of the Christian faith into his hymns:

(1) Jesus was born of a virgin ("offspring of the Virgin's womb").
(2) Jesus is God who became a man ("incarnate Deity").
(3) Jesus came that we might have eternal life ("born that man no more may die").
(4) Jesus will raise our dead bodies for life in the world to come ("born to raise the sons of earth, born to give us second birth").

Though "Hark the Herald Angels Sing" evolved through a series of changes, the song remains full of rich theological truths. Arguably, some of the changes have helped it maintain its popularity. When it was first published in *Hymns and Sacred Poems* (1739), it began "Hark how all the welkin rings, Glory to the King of Kings." *Welkin* is an old English term for "the vault of heaven." It was the Wesley brothers' friend, evangelist George Whitefield, who changed the words of the now familiar first line when he published the song in his 1753 collection, *Hymns for Social Worship*.[9]

Whether or not Charles would take issue with the changes made to "Hark the Herald Angels Sing," we will never know. We do know, however, that the purpose for which Charles wrote his poems and for which John published them has surely been accomplished with this beloved song. John wrote that hymns should serve "every truly pious reader as a means of raising or quickening the spirit of devotion, of confirming his faith, of enlivening his hope, and of kindling or increasing his love to God and man. When poetry thus keeps its place, as the handmaid of piety, it shall attain, not a poor perishable wreath, but a crown that fadeth not away."[10]

Music by Felix Mendelssohn (1809-1847)
Music "Mendelssohn" Arranged by W.H. Cummings (1831-1915)

Felix Mendelssohn was born in Germany into a line of genius. Moses Mendelssohn was a well-known philosopher; his son Abraham excelled in banking, and his grandson Felix proved to be a genius in music. Though inherited talent generally applies itself to the same "trade," biographer George Marek observed that the Mendelssohn's "possessed dissimilar and almost antithetical talents. One wrote books, one wrote loans, one wrote notes."[11]

Felix Mendelssohn's parents, Abraham and Lea, were Jewish converts to Christianity. Though their initial conversion may have been motivated in part by a desire to improve career opportunities and social standing, their beliefs eventually proved to be genuine, and they faithfully raised their children in the Lutheran Church. They also sought to give their children the best possible education, and having shown tremendous talent for music as a child, Mendelssohn had the opportunity to study with great teachers. Though he was naturally capable, he worked fervently to improve his skill. He labored at a feverish pace throughout his short life, and his efforts were evident in both the number of his performances and the breadth of his compositions. Mendelssohn is also credited with reviving the music of the renowned composers Bach and Schubert.

During his life, Mendelssohn's popularity extended well beyond the borders of his native Germany. He traveled extensively throughout Europe, and visited England at least 10 times. He was a particular favorite of Queen Victoria and her husband Prince Albert to whom he was "affectionately drawn."[12] Interestingly, the custom of playing the "Wedding March" from Mendelssohn's *A Midsummer Night's Dream* originated at the wedding of Queen Victoria's daughter, Princess Victoria, when she married Crown Prince Frederick of Prussia in 1858.

Though Mendelssohn was a master composer who had occasion to interact with some of the greatest intellectuals, artists and leaders of his time, he was also a man of humor, wit and great tenderness. He was deeply devoted to his wife and five children, and he had a particular attachment to his sister Fanny. She, like her brother, was especially gifted in music. In fact, some of Fanny's compositions were attributed to Felix, since it was not considered appropriate for women to have a career in music. Apparently, Fanny exercised a "powerful influence on the development of his inner musical nature," and when Mendelssohn learned of her death in May of 1847, it "would undermine his whole being."[13] His health and spirit deteriorated, and he passed away in November of the same year.

Fortunately, Mendelssohn's music did not pass away with him, and one piece known by his name is remembered every Christmas. In 1840, Mendelssohn composed a cantata for the Gutenberg Festival (an anniversary celebration of the invention of printing). Ironically, in a letter to his London publishers, Mendelssohn mentioned the possibility of adapting this music to a useful text, but added that "it will never do to sacred words."[14] Nevertheless, after his death, Mendelssohn's tune was indeed tied to sacred words — Wesley's "Hark the Herald Angels Sing." It should be noted that

Wesley's hymn, as found in *Hymns and Sacred Poems,* did not include music; church leaders generally selected music for psalms and hymns from a handful of common tunes.

An adaptation of Wesley's words with Mendelssohn's music was first published by W. H. Cummings in 1856 and gained national attention in England when it was included in R. R. *Chope's Congregational Hymn and Tune Book* (1857). Ten years prior, as a teenager, Cummings had been a singer for one of Mendelssohn's London performances. But he would never again have a chance to work with the musical master, since Mendelssohn passed away that same year. However, Cummings became a renowned English musician, tenor and organist, and used his talent to ensure that Mendelssohn's music would come alive again every holiday season.

It took over 100 years for Charles Wesley's words to find a permanent companion in Mendelssohn's tune. Though neither the author nor the composer would live on earth to see their work united, perhaps they join with the angels in the heavenly realms each Christmas and sing with us "Glory to the newborn King."

[1] Baker, Robert, and Landers, John M. *A Summary of Christian History.* B&H Publishing Group, 2005, p. 324.

[2] Eskew, Harry and McElrath, Hugh T. *Sing with Understanding.* Broadman Press, 1980, p. 122.

[3] Wesley, Charles. Contributor John R. Tyson. *Charles Wesley: A Reader.* Oxford University Press, 1989, p. 100.

[4] Eskew, Harry and McElrath, Hugh T., p. 122.

[5] Eskew, Harry and McElrath, Hugh T., p. 122.

[6] Routley, Erik. *Hymns and Human Life.* John Murray, 1952, pp. 71-72.

[7] Keyte, Hugh and Parrott, Andrew, editors. *The New Oxford Book of Carols.* Oxford University Press, 1998, p. 328.

[8] Music, David. *Hymnology, A Collection of Source Readings.* The Scarecrow Press, Inc., 1996, p. 143.

[9] Keyte, Hugh and Parrott, Andrew, editors, p. 328.

[10] Music, David, p. 143.

[11] Marek, George R. Gentle Genius, *The Story of Felix Mendelssohn.* Funk & Wagnalls, 1972, p. 7.

[12] Encyclopedia Britannica. "Felix Mendelssohn." Retrieved July 9, 2008 from Encyclopedia Britannica Online: http://www.britannica.com/EBchecked/topic/374785/Felix-Mendelssohn.

[13] Encyclopedia Britannica.

[14] Keyte, Hugh and Parrott, Andrew, editors, p. 328.

I Heard the Bells
On Christmas Day

I Heard the Bells On Christmas Day

Words: HENRY WADSWORTH
LONGFELLOW

WALTHAM
Music: JOHN BAPTISTE CALKIN

Thoughtfully (♩ = 88)

1. I heard the bells on Christ - mas day their
2. I thought how, as the day had come, the
3. And in de - spair I bowed my head: "There
4. Then pealed the bells more loud and deep: "God
5. Till, ring - ing, sing - ing on its way, the

old fa - mil - iar car - ols play. And wild and sweet the
bel - fries of all Chris - ten - dom had rolled a - long th'un -
is no peace on earth," I said, "for hate is strong and
is not dead, nor doth He sleep. The wrong shall fail, the
world re - volved from night to day a voice, a chime, a

words re - peat of peace on earth, good will to men.
bro - ken song of peace on earth, good will to men.
mocks the song of peace on earth, good will to men."
right pre - vail, with peace on earth, good will to men."
chant sub - lime, of peace on earth, good will to men.

Words by Henry Wadsworth Longfellow (1807-1882)

Henry Wadsworth Longfellow lived at a time when America was just beginning to establish a culture of its own, and he was the first U.S. poet to achieve widespread fame. Up until the 19th century, art, literature and music generally came from Europe, and Americans seemed reluctant to acknowledge talent on their own soil. Longfellow, however, proved worthy of recognition.

From his youth, Longfellow showed incredible academic aptitude, particularly in the areas of language and literature. In his senior year of college, Longfellow wrote to his father:

"I will not disguise it in the least. . . . The fact is, I most eagerly aspire after future eminence in literature, my whole soul burns most ardently after it, and every earthly thought centres in it. . . . I am almost confident in believing, that if I can ever rise in the world it must be by the exercise of my talents in the wide field of literature."[1]

By age 18, Longfellow graduated from Bowdoin College in Brunswick, Maine. Shortly thereafter, he was asked to serve as the school's first professor of modern languages, provided that he first study in Europe. During his time on the continent, he learned French, Spanish and Italian. When he returned to the United States in 1829, he dedicated his time to teaching, translating and writing.

Though Longfellow is credited with bringing great European work to American audiences, he unashamedly focused much of his original work on American history, traditions and landscapes. Longfellow was a true American at heart. He was a descendant of early English immigrants, John and Priscilla Alden of the Plymouth colony, whose love story was dramatized in his 1858 poem "The Courtship of Miles Standish." Additionally, Longfellow's maternal grandfather had served as a general in the Revolutionary War. Longfellow loved his native land, and this endeared him to the American people.

According to Encyclopedia Britannica, Longfellow's poetry is generally characterized by "sweetness, gentleness, simplicity, and a romantic vision shaded by melancholy."[2] The tone of sadness in Longfellow's work most likely found its source in the tender heart of a poet who had endured painful personal loss.

Shortly after his return to America, Longfellow fell in love with an old schoolmate, Mary Storer Potter. They were married in 1831. Three years later, Longfellow was offered a professorship at Harvard, and once again, he was sent to Europe to prepare for his job. This time, however, he had a young wife to accompany him. But the trip ended in tragedy. Mary died in Europe, and Longfellow returned to America heartbroken and alone to begin his new position at Harvard.

Fortunately, Longfellow found it in his heart to love again, and he courted Frances Appleton for seven years. Frances finally submitted to Longfellow's persistence and married him in 1843. The marriage was a happy one, but not without a difficult loss. The Longfellows' third child Fanny (named after her mother) died in infancy.

In time, however, three more daughters were born to join their two older brothers, and the Longfellow home, the famous Craigie House, became a gathering place for university students. Young people were drawn to the hospitality and warmth of the lively family.

Longfellow presided over the modern language program at Harvard for 18 years. During this time, he wrote several successful poems ("Hymn to the Night," "Psalm of Life," "Evangeline," etc). By 1854, he resigned from teaching and decided to focus exclusively on writing. He published the classic "Song of Hiawatha" in 1855 and "The Courtship of Miles Standish" in 1858.

Sadly, in 1861, tragedy struck again. Longfellow's wife Frances accidentally set her dress on fire and died of the burns. Longfellow was left as a single parent to his five young children, and he would have to learn to live the words of his poem, "The Light of Stars": "Know how sublime a thing it is to suffer and be strong."

In the same year, Longfellow's beloved country was in the beginning stages of Civil War. By March of 1863, 17-year-old Charles, Longfellow's oldest son, left home (without his father's knowledge) to join the Union Army. When Charles sought to enlist with the 1st Massachusetts Artillery, the commanding officer Captain McCartney (a family friend) wrote to his father requesting approval.[3] Willingly or not, Longfellow consented.

By early June, Charles came down with typhoid fever and malaria. He was sent home to recover. Though his illness caused him to miss the famous battle of Gettysburg, Charles returned to his unit in August of 1863. In November, during the battle of New Hope Church, Va., Charles was seriously injured. A bullet entered through his left shoulder, traveled across his back, and exited under his right shoulder. On December 1, Longfellow received word of Charles' injury and left at once to see him. One week later, Longfellow and his son made it home to begin Charles' long process of recovery.

It was during the Christmas season, in the midst of nursing his son, that Longfellow penned the words of his poem, "Christmas Bells." Two of the verses, which are generally omitted from the carol, focus on the great tragedy of the Civil War:

"Then from each black, accursed mouth The cannon thundered in the South,
And with the sound
The carols drowned
Of peace on earth, good-will to men!

"It was as if an earthquake rent The hearth-stones of a continent,
And made forlorn
The households born
Of peace on earth, good will to men!"

It was amid the devastation of war that the ringing of Christmas bells reminded Longfellow, "God is not dead, nor doth He sleep. The wrong shall fail, the right prevail!"

Surely our God lives, and he demonstrated his intimate concern for us by becoming a man. The Bible explains, "The reason the Son of God appeared was to destroy the devil's work" (1 John 3:8). And when he appears again, he will completely destroy evil by "the splendor of his coming" (2 Thessalonians 2:8). Righteousness will indeed prevail!

Tune "Waltham" by John Baptiste Calkin (1827-1905)

Over 10 years passed before Longfellow's poem was converted into a carol. Though the words have been joined to a variety of music, the predominant tune is that of John Baptiste Calkin, an English musician. Calkin came from a family of accomplished artists and worked as a professor at both the renowned Guildhall School of Music and the Croydon Conservatory in England. He also served as an organist and choirmaster at St. Columba's College in Ireland and at various other churches in London.

Calkin's tune, "Waltham," (a common town name in England),[4] was written in 1872. It is unknown who first paired it with Longfellow's words, but perhaps the anonymous person found the music to be "reminiscent of the ringing of bells."[5] As you sing the words of this moving carol, may they ring with hope in the God who can indeed offer true "peace on earth [and] good will to men."

---

[1] Arvin, Newton. *Longfellow: His Life and Work*. Boston: Little, Brown and Company, 1963, p. 13.

[2] Encyclopedia Britannica. "Henry Wadsworth Longfellow." Retrieved July 10, 2008 from Encyclopedia Britannica Online: http://www.britannica.com/EBchecked/topic/347476/Henry-Wadsworth-Longfellow.

[3] Carroon, Robert Girard. "The Christmas Carol Soldier." Loyal Legion Historical Journal, Fall 1998, Volume 55, No. 3. Retrieved August 30, 2008 from: http://suvcw.org/mollus/art005.htm.

[4] McCutchan, Robert Guy. *Hymn Tune Names, Their Sources and Significance*. Abingdon Press, 1957, p. 168

[5] Studwell, William. *The Christmas Carol Reader*. The Haworth Press, 1995, p. 166.

It Came Upon a Midnight Clear

It Came upon the Midnight Clear

Words: EDMUND HAMILTON SEARS

CAROL

Music: RICHARD STORRS WILLIS

Calmly (♪ = 126)

1. It came up-on the mid-night clear, that glo-ri-ous song of old, from an - gels bend - ing near the earth to touch their harps of gold; "Peace on the earth, good - will to men, from heav-en's all gra - cious King." The world in sol - emn still - ness lay to hear the an - gels sing.

2. Still through the clo - ven skies they come, with peace - ful wings un - furled, and still their heav-en - ly mu - sic floats o'er all the wea - ry world. A - bove its sad and low - ly plains they bend on hov - 'ring wing, and ev - er o'er its Ba - bel sounds the bless - ed an - gels sing.

3. Yet with the woes of sin and strife, the world has suf - fered long; Be - neath the an - gel strain have rolled, two thou - sand years of wrong. And man, at war with man, hears not, the love song which they bring; O hush the noise, ye men of strife, and hear the an - gels sing.

4. And ye, be - neath life's crush - ing load, Whose forms are bend - ing low, who toil a - long the climb - ing way with pain - ful steps and slow. Look now! for glad and gold - en hours, come swift - ly on the wing, O rest be - side the wea - ry road and hear the an - gels sing.

5. For lo, the days are has - t'ning on, by proph - et bards fore - told, when, with the ev - er cir - cling years, comes round the Age of Gold, when peace shall o - ver all the earth its an - cient splen - dors fling, and the whole world give back the song which now the an - gels sing.

Words by Edmund Hamilton Sears (1810-1876)

"It Came Upon a Midnight Clear" was one of the first Christmas carols to be written and composed by Americans. The author, Edmund Sears, was born in Massachusetts and claimed descent from one of the original Pilgrim Fathers. In his youth, Sears developed his love for poetry, and it is said that he was "fond of chanting Pope's *Iliad*."[1] By age 24, Sears authored his first Christmas poem, "Calm on the Listening Ear," while attending Harvard Divinity School. The words are strikingly similar to his later poem, "It Came Upon the Midnight Clear." Here is an excerpt:

"Calm on the listening ear of night
Come heaven's melodious strains,
Where wild Judea stretches forth
Her silver mantled plains.

"Celestial choirs from courts above
Shed sacred glories there,
And angels, with their sparkling lyres,
Make music on the air."

After graduating from Harvard in 1837, Sears wrote several religious books, served as editor for the Boston-based *Monthly Religious Magazine* (1859 to 1871), and worked as a pastor in various churches. According to music historian William Studwell:

"His longest pastorate was the Unitarian Church in rural Wayland, Massachusetts, where he stayed from 1848 to around 1865. Wayland was the locale for the idyllic and poetic environment which apparently helped precipitate the creation of his great 1849 poem."[2]

The poem "It Came Upon the Midnight Clear" was written in 1849 (and published the following year in the *Christian Register*).[3] Sears wrote his text at a time of great social unrest. Americans were still dealing with the effects of the Industrial Revolution; the Mexican-American War (1846-1848) had just recently concluded, and tensions over the issue of slavery in America were growing (these tensions of course led to the Civil War in 1861). To add to the chaos, in the same year that Sears wrote his poem, thousands of Americans, the "forty-niners," were rushing to California in search of gold. Perhaps this inspired Sears, whether consciously or not, to include three different references to gold in his carol ("harps of gold," "golden hours" and "Age of Gold").

The Unitarian Church, in which Sears was raised and then served as a pastor, was known for its efforts to improve social ills like poverty, injustice and war. Thus, it comes as no surprise that Sears' carol laments the "woes of sin and strife, the world has suffered long" and focuses on the angels' message of peace. Though the Unitarian Church was not orthodox in its overall theology, Sears parted from it in some critical ways. First off, he affirmed the Deity of Christ. In his book *Sermons and Songs of the Christian Life*, Sears wrote: "He [Jesus] is the revelation alike of perfect Divinity and perfect humanity."[4] Secondly, Sears understood that real change in society could only come as a result of spiritual change in individual souls. In 1854, he wrote in his book *Regeneration*:

"There is the indisputable fact that the old forms of belief and modes of operation have done about all they can do in renewing society. Misery and sin lie around the Church in solid masses, yea, within its inclosures. . . . [Thus] let the disciple who seeks the renewal of himself learn his relations to the personal and living Saviour."[5]

Surely, Sears recognized that the message of the angels on the night of Christ's birth was a message of spiritual peace. Without Christ and his life giving Spirit, man can never know the peace that God offers for the soul.

And there is more. In eternity, the true "Age of Gold," real and lasting peace will be manifest "over all the earth." Perhaps the "Babel sounds" of which Sears speaks will pass away. Recall that God "confused" the language of men in Babel because they used their common language for evil (Genesis 11:9). When sin is completed eradicated, perhaps we will all speak the same language once again (a language that even now may be buried in the depth of our soul) and join with the angels in singing praises to God in one united voice!

Music "Carol" by Richard Storrs Willis (1819-1900)

Richard Storrs Willis was born to a prominent family in Boston. He claimed descent from a distinguished Puritan, Nathaniel Willis, who immigrated to America in 1626. One hundred and fifty years later, Richard's grandfather founded the *Independent Chronicle* (published in the same building that Benjamin Franklin used as a printer!),[6] which helped to establish the family in both journalism and publishing for many years to come.

Richard received the best education that America had to offer, and when he entered Yale in 1837, he quickly earned distinction in literary and musical societies. During his time in college, he served as the president of the Beethoven Society and wrote compositions for the college orchestra and choir.[7] After graduating from Yale in 1841, Willis traveled to Germany and spent several years studying with some of the best known names in music; he also developed a close friendship with Felix Mendelssohn. For more on Mendelssohn, see pp. 216-217. Willis learned German perfectly and returned to Yale to teach the language for a brief period. Soon thereafter, he moved to New York to enter the world of journalism with which his family was so familiar.

Willis contributed to several publications, established a magazine for fine arts called *Once A Month*, and developed a reputation as a superb music critic. He also published several books and collections of music (his arrangement of "Fairest Lord Jesus" is still widely used). In 1850, one year after Sears composed his poem, Willis composed a tune called "Study No. 23" in his *Church Chorals and Choir Studies*. It was originally set to the hymn "See Israel's Gentle Shepherd Stand." How the tune came to be used with "It Came Upon a Midnight Clear" is not known. Some sources attribute the arrangement to Uzziah Christopher Burnap (1834-1900). A letter written by Willis simply states, "On my return from Europe in [1876], I found that it [the tune] had been incorporated into various church collections apparently to Edmund Sears text: 'It Came Upon A Midnight Clear.'"[8]

The tune later came to be called "Carol," suggesting that "it very capably fulfills its mission as an exponent of the spirit of Christmas."[9] Though "Willis never again duplicated the inspiration of his 1850 contribution to Christmas," it seems fitting that little "Study No. 23" would become his most "notable legacy to posterity."[10] It is a tune that helps us "hear the angels sing" their song of worship to God. Willis was passionate about the role of music in worshipping God. He wrote a book called *Our Church Music: A Book for Pastors and People*, in which he admonished Christians to understand the importance of singing. He concluded the book by reverently stating that the purpose of church music is "a holy one."[11]

---

[1] Bradley, Ian, editor. *The Penguin Book of Carols*. Penguin Books, 1999, p. 160.

[2] Studwell, William. *The Christmas Carol Reader*. The Haworth Press, 1995, p. 58.

[3] Hughes, Charles W., *American Hymns Old and New*. Columbia University Press, 1980, p. 112. Note that some sources indicate the poem was published in the same year it was written, 1849.

[4] Sears, Edmund. *Sermons and Songs of the Christian Life*. Noyes, Holmes, 1875, p. 325.

[5] Sears, Edmund. *Regeneration, 1854*. Kessinger Publishing, 2003, pp. 206-207.

[6] Stocking, William, and Miller, Gordon K . *The City of Detroit. Michigan, 1701-1922*. S.J. Clarke Publishing Company, 1922, p. 604.

[7] Hughes, Charles W., p. 599.

[8] Hughes, Charles W., p. 112.

[9] Studwell, William, p. 59.

[10] Studwell, William, p. 59.

[11] Willis, Richard Storrs. *Our Church Music: A Book for Pastors and People*. Dana, 1856, p. 133.

Joy to the
World!

Joy to the World!

Words: ISAAC WATTS

ANTIOCH
Music: ENGLISH MELODY
Arranged by: LOWELL MASON

With spirit (♩ = 108)

1. Joy to the world! the Lord is come, let earth re - ceive her
2. Joy to the earth! the Sav - ior reigns; let men their songs em -
3. No more let sins and sor - rows grow, nor thorns in - fest the
4. He rules the world with truth and grace, and makes the na - tions

King; _____ let ev - 'ry _____ heart _____ pre - pare _____ him _____
ploy. _____ While fields _____ and _____ floods, _____ rocks, hills, and _____
ground; _____ He comes _____ to _____ make _____ His bless - ings _____
prove _____ the glo - ries _____ of _____ His right - eous _____

room, _____ and heav'n and na - ture _____ sing, and _____ heav'n and na - ture
plains _____ re - peat the sound-ing _____ joy, re - peat the sound - ing _____
flow _____ far as the curse is _____ found, far _____ as the curse is _____
ness, _____ and won - ders of His _____ love, and _____ won - ders of His _____

(1) and heav'n and na - ture sing, and

sing, and _____ heav-en, and heav - en and na - ture sing.
joy, re - peat, _____ re - peat _____ the sound - ing _____ joy.
found, far _____ as, _____ far as _____ the curse is _____ found.
love, and _____ won - ders, won - ders of His _____ love.

heav'n and na - ture sing,

232

Words by Isaac Watts (1674-1748)

Isaac Watts was the oldest of nine children born in England to a father, also named Isaac, who was imprisoned on more than one occasion for dissenting from the doctrine of the Anglican Church. His mother, Sarah, supposedly sat on a stone outside the prison and nursed young Isaac while talking with her husband through the bars.[1]

Watts showed exceptional intellectual ability in his youth. By age 13, he had learned Latin, Greek, French and Hebrew. He also demonstrated his wit with rhyme at a young age. Once when asked to explain why he was disturbing the evening prayers, Watts described the mouse that was distracting him: "A mouse for want of better stairs, ran up a rope to say his prayers."[2] On this occasion (or possibly another), when he was being punished for his irritating rhymes, he said, "O father, do some pity take, and I will no more verses make."[3]

If Watts had been a member of the Church of England, he probably would have been sent to Oxford or Cambridge for college. Instead, he was enrolled at a school for "dissenters" in London. After leaving the Dissenting Academy at 19, Watts returned to his father's parish, Above Bar Congregational Church, in Southampton.

Both Watts and his father found church music to be uninspiring and monotonous. The congregational singing in English-speaking churches was limited to metrical psalms. Many Christians believed that it would be offensive to God to sing anything other than the actual words of Scripture. It was Watts' father who first challenged him to "write something better for us to sing."[4]

After Watts presented his first song, the congregation at his father's church responded with tremendous enthusiasm . . . so much so that they requested a new hymn every week. The next two years would become the richest hymn-writing period in Watts' life. After these two years, Watts moved to London to work as a tutor.

In London, Watts joined the Mark Lane Independent Church. On his 24th birthday in 1698, he preached his first sermon, and by 1702, he became the senior pastor. He retained this position for the remainder of his life and would become one of the best-known preachers in England.

Interestingly, Watts was also a reputable author of educational books on geography, astronomy, grammar and philosophy.[5] His books were widely used in universities in the 18th century. However, Watts is now best known for his hymns, which were motivated by a "fervent concern about the dismal state of congregational singing."[6] He wrote, "While we sing the Praises of our God in his Church, we are employ'd in that part of worship which of all others is the nearest a-kin to Heaven; and 'tis pity that this of all others should be perform'd the worst upon Earth."[7]

Watts published his first collection of hymns in 1706, *Horae Lyricae*. In the following year, 1707, he published *Hymns and Spiritual Songs*, which included the famous hymn, "When I Survey the Wondrous Cross." Watts' popularity quickly grew, and his verses caught the attention of the "beautiful and accomplished" Elizabeth Singer, a poet herself.[8]

"She told him in verse that, enchanted by his verse, her thoughts no longer occupy themselves with her old admirers and desired to meet him. Her wish was at last granted. But before her stood not even a moderately presentable Englishman, but a minute, sallow-faced anatomy with hook nose, prominent cheekbones, heavy countenance, pale complexion and small grey eyes. . . . But if on account of his plainness, she at first recoiled from him, the variety and charm of his conversation swiftly compensated for her disappointment, and she congratulated herself on having made the acquaintance of a man whose friendship would be as precious to her as his love was distasteful."[9]

Sadly, when Watts summoned up the courage to propose to Singer, she declined by saying, "Mr. Watts, I only wish I could say that I admire the casket as much as I admire the jewel."[10] Any wounds that resulted from this rejection appear to have "healed quickly and beautifully, and his subsequent friendship with Miss Singer proved to be one of the most pleasing episodes in his career."[11] However, he never again sought the companionship of a woman.

Watts poured his energy into his work, and with time, his labor began to take a toll on him physically. In 1712, he suffered a breakdown from which he never fully recovered. Though he asked his church to discontinue his salary, they decided to raise it and hire a co-pastor to assume many of the pastoral duties.

A wealthy family in Watts' congregation believed that fresh air and a change of scene would do him some good. In 1714, Sir Thomas Abney and his wife, Lady Abney, invited him to spend a week at their country estate. Watts ended up spending the remainder of his life with the Abneys, and the relationship proved to be beneficial to all. Watts developed a special affection for the three Abney daughters (Sarah, Mary and Elizabeth) and became a valuable part of their education. In 1715, he published a collection of songs for the girls, *Divine Songs for the Use of Children*, which became an English classic.

By 1719, Watts completed his work on the *The Psalms of David Imitated in the Language of the New Testament (*in which the famous words for "Joy to the World!" can be found). Watts paraphrased most of the 150 Psalms of the Bible and explained his approach as follows:

"Where the Psalmist describes Religion by the *Fear of God*, I have often joyn'd *Faith and Love* to it. Where he speaks of the Pardon of Sin, thro' the *Mercies of God*, I have added the *Merits of a Saviour*. Where he talks of sacrificing *Goats or Bullocks*, I rather chuse to mention the Sacrifice of *Christ the Lamb of God*. . . . Where he promises abundance of *Wealth, Honour and long Life,* I have changed some of these *typical* Blessings for *Grace, Glory, and Life Eternal*, which are brought to Light by the Gospel, and promised in the New Testament."[12]

It was his meditation on Psalm 98 that inspired "Joy to the World!" The resemblance is evident in verse 4: "Shout for joy to the LORD, all the earth, burst into jubilant song with music . . .

shout with joy before the LORD, the King" (Psalm 98:4). Though there is no explicit reference to Christmas, the words "the Lord is come" naturally came to be associated with the holiday.

Though Watts' hymns rapidly spread across England, their popularity did not come without controversy. They were derogatorily referred to as "Watts' Whims" or "songs of human composure." One man complained, "Christian congregations shut out divinely inspired Psalms and take in Watts' flights of fancy as if words of a poet were better than those of a prophet."[13]

In 1729, Benjamin Franklin was the first to publish Watts' Psalm paraphrases in U.S.,[14] and the controversy continued in America. Apparently, in 1789 (more than 40 years after Watts had passed away), a Reverend Adam Rankin rode on horseback from his home in Kentucky to the General Assembly of the Presbyterian Church in Philadelphia "to ask this body to refuse the great and pernicious error of adopting the use of Isaac Watts' hymns in public worship in preference to the Psalms of David."[15]

Fortunately, Watts' hymns survived the controversies, and he rightly earned the title "father of English hymnody"; it should be noted however that many others before him, like Nahum Tate (see pp. 301-302), "struggled toward a lyrical freedom within the tradition of scriptural paraphrase."[16]

Many of Watts' more than 600 hymns can still be heard in churches across the world; some of the most notable are: "When I Survey the Wondrous Cross," "O God, Our Help in Ages Past" and "We're Marching to Zion." Furthermore, Watts' work inspired many other great songwriters like John Newton (author of "Amazing Grace) and Charles Wesley (author of "Hark the Herald Angels Sing"). Even more than 100 years after Watts' death, the blind Fanny Crosby, who authored thousands of great American hymns, recounted how she came to faith in 1851 during a song by Isaac Watts. Crosby attended a revival service in New York, and when they sang Watts' hymn "Alas and Did My Savior Bleed," Crosby was struck by the words "Here Lord I give myself away." She recalled how her "very soul was flooded with celestial light."[17]

Music "Antioch" Arranged by Lowell Mason (1792-1872)

It took over a century for Watts' lyrics to find their current tune. It should be noted that Watts' *Psalms of David* did not include music. In 1836, Lowell Mason, an American hymn composer, published the words and music together for the first time in a booklet entitled *Occasional Psalm and Hymn Tunes* in which he attributed the tune to George Handel.

The first reliable record of the tune is from an 1833 British publication *Collection of Tunes* by Thomas Hawkes with the title "Comfort."[18] William Holford, a British choir conductor, in his popular tune-book, *Voce di melodia*, revised the tune around 1834.[19]

Though the earlier Hawkes publication listed the composer as "unknown," Holford attributed the tune to Handel "presumably because of the resemblance of the opening phrase to the choruses 'Glory to God' [piece #17] and 'Lift up your heads' [piece #33] in *Messiah*."[20] Additionally, the tune name "Comfort" is reminiscent of the opening words of *Messiah*, "Comfort Ye, Comfort Ye, my people" (piece #2). Yet, according to *The New Oxford Book of Carols,* "any resemblance to Handel was probably coincidental or, at least, unconscious."[21] Mason, like Holford, retained the attribution to Handel. As a student of classical composers, Mason obviously believed the piece was similar enough to Handel's work to be authentic.

Though Mason loved and studied music from his youth, he did not think he could make a living in the arts. Thus, he spent the first 15 years of his career in banking. It was in his spare time that he studied classical composers and even set his hand at writing original music. When he sent his first book of music to publishers in Philadelphia and Boston, it was flatly rejected on the grounds that Americans were not interested in classical work. Fortunately, a recently formed society called the *Boston Handel and Haydn Society* offered to publish the work in 1822. However, at Mason's request, his name did not appear on the title page. Mason said: "I was then a bank officer in Savannah, and did not wish to be known as a musical man, as I had not the least thought of ever making music a profession."[22]

Little did Mason know that his work would sell thousands of copies and be adopted by singing schools and church choirs alike. After witnessing the success of his work, Mason determined that it was time to dedicate more of his efforts to music. He moved to Boston where "he became a leader in the field of church and choral music."[23] He even became the president of the *Boston Handel and Haydn Society* in 1827. Five years later, Mason founded the Boston Academy of Music, and in 1838 he developed the first public school music program in the United States.[24] Over the course of his life, he published 20 different collections of hymns and composed tunes for great songs like "Nearer, My God, to Thee," and "My Faith Looks Up to Thee." He is suspected of arranging Handel's tune for "While Shepherds Watched Their Flocks" (see pp. 299-303) and may have even composed, not just arranged, the tune for Watts' hymn "When I Survey the Wondrous Cross."[25] Ultimately, Mason came to be known as the "father of American church music."

It seems fitting that both the "father of English hymnody" and the "father of American church music" would play a part in creating the most joyful of all Christmas carols, "Joy to the World!" Though "Mason's setting owes much to Holford's British version,"[26] Mason created his own beautiful arrangement. It is not clear why he changed the title of the tune to "Antioch" (the city in Syria where Jesus' disciples were first called Christians). According to *Hymn Tune Names*, Mason was known to select Bible names at random; furthermore, he may have been familiar with an old tradition (as preserved by Socrates, a 5th century historian): [27]

"Ignatius, martyred in A.D. 107, was led by a vision, or dream, of angels singing hymns antiphonally [when one side responds to another during a song or chant] to the Holy Trinity, to introduce antiphonal singing of hymns into the church at Antioch."[28]

This old tradition may have held significance for Mason, since he was trying to introduce a new kind of singing to American churches. Not only did he labor to bring the classical European form of music to America, he also encouraged congregational singing with an organ instead of using professional choirs. Furthermore, Mason may have looked to Watts, the author of the text for "Joy to the World!," as an example of how to introduce a new kind of singing to churches. In Watts' case, he pioneered the use of new poetic verse (instead of the exclusive use of Psalms).

Interestingly, the Psalms themselves say, "Sing to him a new song; play skillfully, and shout for joy" (Psalm 33:3). Though "Joy to the World" was inspired by an old Psalm, let us be grateful for the skill of the men that drew out of it a "new song" of joy with which to praise our Lord!

---

[1] Fountain, David Guy. *Isaac Watts Remembered.* Gospel Standard Publications, 1978, p. 7.

[2] Fountain, David Guy, p. 13.

[3] Bailey, Albert Edward. *The Gospel in Hymns: Backgrounds and Interpretations.* Scribner, 1950, p. 46.

[4] Osbeck, Kenneth W. *Amazing Grace.* Kregel Publications, 1990, p. 12.

[5] Encyclopedia Britannica. "Isaac Watts." Retrieved August 23, 2008 from Encyclopedia Britannica Online: http://www.britannica.com/EBchecked/topic/637744/Isaac-Watts.

[6] Osbeck, Kenneth, p. 333.

[7] Music, David. *Hymnology, A Collection of Source Readings.* From Watts' Preface to *Hymns and Spiritual Songs*, 1707. The Scarecrow Press, 1996, p.115).

[8] Fountain, David Guy, p. 44.

[9] Fountain, David Guy, p. 44.

[10] Fountain, David Guy, p. 45.

[11] Fountain, David Guy, p. 45.

[12] Music, David, From Watts' Preface to *Psalms of David*, 1719, p. 129.

[13] Abbey, John Charles. *Religious Thought in Old English Verse.* Sampson Low, 1892, p. 344.

[14] Hughes, Charles W. *American Hymns Old and New.* Columbia University Press, 1980, p. 588.

[15] Center for Church Music. *Isaac Watts.* Retrieved August 30, 2008 from Center for Church Music: http://songsandhymns.org/people/detail/isaac-watts.

[16] Eskew, Harry and McElrath, Hugh T. *Sing with Understanding.* Broadman Press, 1980, p. 118.

[17] Blumhofer, Edith L. *Her Heart Can See: The Life and Hymns of Fanny J. Crosby.* Eerdmans Publishing, 2005, p. 108.

[18] Keyte, Hugh and Parrott, Andrew, editors. *The New Oxford Book of Carols.* Oxford University Press, 1998, p. 274.

[19] Keyte, Hugh and Parrott, Andrew, editors, p. 274. It should be noted that a recently discovered source, *Psalmodia Britannica*, arranged by Charles Rider, includes the same revised version as Holford. Since it cannot be dated with certainly, it is not clear who was the first to make the revisions.

[20] Keyte, Hugh and Parrott, Andrew, editors, p. 274.

[21] Keyte, Hugh and Parrott, Andrew, editors, p. 274.

[22] Elson, Louis Charles. *The History of American Music.* The Macmillan Company, 1915, p. 39.

[23] Hughes, Charles W. *American Hymns Old and New.* Columbia University Press, 1980, p. 484.

[24] Hughes, Charles W., p. 485.

[25] Studwell, William. *The Christmas Carol Reader*. The Haworth Press, 1995, p. 123.

[26] Keyte, Hugh and Parrott, Andrew, editors, p. 274.

[27] McCutchan, Robert Guy. *Hymn Tune Names, Their Sources and Significance*. Abingdon Press, 1957, p. 42.

[28] McCutchan, Robert Guy, p. 42.

Messiah,

No.12 Chorus & No.44 Chorus

Messiah

Part I, No. 12 Chorus, "For Unto Us A Child Is Born"

Words Compiled by: CHARLES JENNENS
From: ISAIAH 9:6

Music: GEORGE FRIDERIC HANDEL

Messiah

Part II, No. 44 Chorus, "Hallelujah"

Words Compiled by: CHARLES JENNENS
From: REVELATION 19:6; 11:15; 19:16

Music: GEORGE FRIDERIC HANDEL

* Additional Lyrics:

Hallelujah! For the Lord God Omnipotent reigneth.
The kingdom of this world is become the Kingdom of our Lord,
And of His Christ,
And He shall reign for ever and ever.
King of Kings, and Lord of Lords,
And He shall reign for ever and ever. Hallelujah!

Music by George Frideric Handel (1685-1759)
Words Compiled by Charles Jennens (1700-1773)

Though George Frideric Handel showed undeniable talent in music as a youth (he was composing music before age 10), his father desired that he pursue a career in law. Sadly, when Handel was only 11 years old, his father passed away. Regardless, Handel determined to follow his father's wishes, and he enrolled as a law student at the University of Halle (his hometown in Germany) in 1702. It was not long, however, before Handel's interest in music drew him away from school and to the city of Hamburg, where he had the opportunity to perform in an orchestra.

By 1705, 20-year-old Handel presided over his first opera, *Almira*. Soon thereafter, his success drew him to Italy, the birthplace of great opera. Over the course of the following five years, Handel composed several pieces in Italy. By 1710, his opera, *Agrippina*, premiered in Venice; it was so widely acclaimed that Handel soon became known internationally as a master of Italian opera.

Handel traveled next to England. In 1711, he performed his opera *Rinaldo* for a London audience. He was greeted so enthusiastically that he determined to settle in London. Two years later, Handel was granted an annual allowance by Queen Anne, and by 1726 he became a British subject.

For several years, Handel composed most of the music for the operas performed at the King's Theatre in London. However, by 1726, Encyclopedia Britannica records, "the future of opera in the Italian style became increasingly uncertain in England. It went into decline for a variety of reasons, one of them being the impatience of the English with a form of entertainment in an unintelligible language [Italian] sung by artists of whose morals they disapproved."[1] Regardless, Handel continued to compose operas until 1741. A melody from his 1728 opera, *Siroë, King of Persia*, is used for the tune of "While Shepherds Watched Their Flocks By Night" (see pp. 299-303).

Handel also became instrumental in establishing a new genre, the *oratorio* (a large-scale musical production that included solo voices, chorus and orchestra but no costume, scenery or dramatic action) in the English language. His most popular oratorio is, of course, *Messiah*, written in 1741. In the few years prior to this phenomenal work, Handel had suffered a series of misfortunes. Due to the declining interest in opera, Handel's Italian opera company endured great financial loss and had to declare bankruptcy in 1737. In the same year, Handel suffered what appears to have been a mild stroke. Temporary paralysis, as well as difficulties with his vision, hindered his work for a time. Though Handel recovered physically and continued composing, he apparently battled depression. His involvement in establishing the *Fund for the Support of Decayed Musicians* (now the *Royal Society of Musicians*), founded in 1738, may be an indication that he was beset with concerns about his own future health and finances.

Perhaps the depth of Handel's depression was the very thing that drew him so intimately close to the Lord when he wrote *Messiah* in 1741. By all accounts, Handel had a spiritual experience that began when his friend, Charles Jennens, asked him to compose the music for a biblical *libretto* (the text of a musical work). Beginning with prophecies of the coming Messiah and ending with the final triumph of Messiah, Jennens had compiled a lengthy list of Scripture references as his text. Handel set to work at once, and in just over three weeks, he completed the masterpiece we know as *Messiah*. During this time, "a visitor is reported to have found the trembling composer sobbing with intense emotion, and after the 'Hallelujah Chorus' his servant is said to have seen tears streaming from his eyes."[2] Handel purportedly said of his experience, "Whether I was in the body or out of the body when I wrote it, I know not," and "I did think I did see all Heaven before me and the great God himself."[3]

Robert Manson Myers, author of *Handel's Messiah, A Touchstone of Taste*, wrote, "For the first time in musical history the mighty drama of human redemption was treated as an epic poem."[4] Unfortunately, few people have ever heard the full oratorio. It is a massive work consisting of three parts and 57 different pieces.[5] The first section of Part I begins with Old Testament prophecies about the coming Messiah and culminates in piece #12:

"For unto us a child is born, unto us a son is given: and the government shall be upon his shoulder: and his name shall be called Wonderful, Counsellor, The mighty God, The everlasting Father, The Prince of Peace" (Isaiah 9:6, KJV).

The oratorio continues through the birth, life, crucifixion, resurrection and ascension of Christ, and Part II culminates in his return, piece #44, the "Hallelujah Chorus." Part III of *Messiah* ends with the resurrection of the dead and Christ's eternal reign.

Interestingly, though *Messiah* has come to be intimately associated with Christmas, it was originally performed for Easter. Apparently, the Duke of Devonshire invited Handel to come to Dublin and produce concerts that would benefit various charities. The first performance of *Messiah* took place in Dublin on April 13, 1742. Perhaps because it debuted and was so often played for charitable purposes, it soon came to be associated with Christmas — a season of generosity.

In 1743, *Messiah* premiered in London's Covent Garden Theatre. It may be worth mentioning that the theater was owned by a man named John Rich, whose wife was a prominent convert of Charles Wesley.[6] For more on Wesley, see pp. 213-215. An association with the Rich family led to a friendship between Handel and Wesley, who would often dine together at the Rich home. In time, three of Wesley's hymns were set to music composed by Handel ("O Love Divine," "Rejoice, the Lord Is King" and "Sinners Obey the Gospel Word").

If Wesley attended one of the early performances of *Messiah* in London, he may have been in the same audience as King George II. A great custom, as recorded by Myers, began on that night:

"As the glorious strains of the 'Hallelujah Chorus' burst upon the awed assemblage, George II found himself so deeply affected by Handel's music (or so eager to shift his position) that he started to his feet. . . . Instantly his phlegmatic courtiers also rose, and since no Englishman may remain seated while his King is standing, the audience at once followed suit, thus inaugurating a custom which persists to the present day."[7]

Various explanations have been given for why the king stood during the "Hallelujah Chorus" (that he was hard of hearing and thought the national anthem was being played, that he was simply stretching his legs, etc.). However, it seems most reasonable to believe that he was truly moved by the magnificent music. The king's action also served as an interesting symbolic gesture (even if it was not intentional); it revealed that all people, including kings, should honor the true "King of Kings."

Handel continued to perform *Messiah* throughout the remainder of his life. He so passionately exerted himself that after his last performance of the great oratorio, he collapsed. He died soon thereafter to finally meet the "Lord of Lords" face to face!

---

[1] Encyclopedia Britannica. "George Frideric Handel." Retrieved August 29, 2008 from Encyclopedia Britannica Online: http://www.britannica.com/EBchecked/topic/254169/George-Frideric-Handel.

[2] Myers, Robert Manson. *Handel's Messiah, A Touchstone of Taste.* Octagon Books, 1971, p. 63.

[3] Myers, Robert Manson, p. 63.

[4] Myers, Robert Manson, p. 59.

[5] "An Appreciation and Explanation of Handel's Oratorio Messiah." Retrieved August 29, 2008 from Antipas Christadelphians: http://www.antipas.org/handel/midipage.html.

[6] Williams, Craven E. "Origins: Wesley and Handel." Retrieved July 20, 2008 from Greensboro College: http://www.gborocollege.edu/prescorner/handel.html.

[7] Myers, Robert Manson, p. 116.

O Come, All
Ye Faithful

O Come, All Ye Faithful

Words Attributed to: JOHN FRANCIS WADE
Translated by: FREDERICK OAKELEY

ADESTE FIDELES
Music Attributed to:
JOHN FRANCIS WADE

Words and Music "Adestes Fideles" Attributed to John Francis Wade (1711-1786)

The origin of this well-known Christmas carol remains a mystery. The earliest known manuscript of the tune is dated around 1740 and is attributed to John Francis Wade, a copyist and writer of music for the Roman Catholic Church. It appears that Wade resided primarily at the English College in France, a college established in 1568 to educate English Roman Catholics for the secular priesthood. However, "since most of the eighteenth-century documents and books of the English College were either confiscated or destroyed during the [French] Revolution, little information about Wade is available from what would have been its most likely source."[1] An obituary reveals that Wade was employed to teach "the Latin and Church song," and that his "beautiful manuscripts abound in our churches."[2] Wade was said to have used a lovely calligraphy on all of his work.

Though it is quite possible that Wade wrote both the music and the Latin text of the song, there is simply no way to confirm whether it is his original work or it was copied from another source. Interestingly, a similar tune appeared in a 1744 French comic opera, *Le Comte d'Acajou*. According to *The New Oxford Book of Carols*:

"The likeness is too close to be coincidental, and since at least one of Wade's manuscripts probably predates the play, or is at least coeval [the same age], it is possible that both tunes in fact derived independently from another source, as yet unidentified."[3]

On the other hand, the fact that the tune appeared in an opera close in both time and proximity to Wade's life may add credence to the possibility that he composed it. The use in comic opera may have been a parody of a new hymn.

What appears certain is that the song can trace its increase in popularity to a 1795 performance in the Portuguese Embassy Chapel of London (the same year in which the Latin text was first printed in America). The organist at the Embassy, Samuel Webbe, was a prominent Catholic musician who had connections with John Wade (as did many of the musicians of foreign embassy chapels in London).[4] Apparently, when Webbe performed the hymn in 1795, it made such an impression on the Duke of Leeds that the Duke commissioned the song to be played in the popular "Concerts of Ancient Music." The hymn was thus "repeated on many subsequent occasions, making [it] famous far beyond the Catholic circles to which it had been initially confined."[5]

Interestingly, the hymn came to be known as the "Porteguese hymn" which gave the impression that it had originated in Portugal. Vincent Novello, Webbe's successor as organist at the Portuguese Embassy Chapel of London, clarified this confusion in his *Congregational and Chorister's Psalm and Hymn Book*, 1843:

"This piece obtained the name of 'The Portuguese Hymn' from the accidental circumstance of the Duke of Leeds . . . having heard the hymn first performed at the Portuguese

247

Chapel and who, supposing it to be peculiar to the service in Portugal, introduced the melody at the Ancient Concerts, giving it the title of the 'Portuguese Hymn', by which appellation this very favourite and popular tune has ever since been distinguished; but it is by no means confined to the choir of the Portuguese Chapel, being the regular Christmas hymn 'Adeste Fideles', that is sung in every Catholic chapel throughout England."[6]

Though Novello clarified the confusion regarding a Portuguese origin, he further muddled the question of authorship. He attributed the melody to a John Reading in 1680, and noted that Reading was a pupil of Dr. Blow. According to *The New Oxford Book of Carols*:

"The John Reading taught by Blow was born in 1685/6, so Novello must have confused him with an earlier John Reading (d. 1692), organist of Winchester Cathedral. However, nothing extant by either Reading in any way resembles 'Adeste Fideles.'"[7]

As it is, unless a more ancient document is discovered, it seems reasonable to attribute both the words and music to John Wade. His tune name "Adeste Fideles" comes from the first words of the hymn in Latin, meaning "Be present (or near), ye faithful."[8]

Words Translated by Frederick Oakeley (1802-1880)

According to the Penguin Book of Carols, Frederick Oakeley was a "leader in choral revival" and a "pioneer of liturgical reform in the mid-nineteenth-century Church of England.[9] When he took a job at the Margaret Chapel in 1839, "he introduced the chanting of Psalms to Gregorian tones and Anglican chant, the singing of Tudor settings of the Communion service, and the use of hymns for feast days."[10] Sadly, Oakley was forced out of the Church of England because of his "ritualistic" practices. Soon thereafter, in 1845, he converted to Catholicism.[11]

Oakley's first translation began, "Ye faithful, approach ye." Though it was never published, it "achieved considerable popularity through its use at Margaret Chapel."[12] Later, Oakley tried his hand at translating the masterpiece again. This time, he began with the familiar line "O come, all ye faithful" and published it in F. H. Murray's *Hymnal for Use in the English Church* (1852). Since then, there have been dozens of other translations, and various editors have made alterations to Oakley's work. Regardless, all of the most popular English versions of the carol rely heavily on Oakley's translation.

It seems fitting that a song calling ALL the faithful together would include contributions from a variety of cultures. Consider that the song was originally written in Latin, composed by an Englishman living in France, propagated as a result of a performance in a Portuguese Chapel, and translated by an Anglican turned Catholic. Note how the song emphasizes beliefs embraced by Christians everywhere; the second line of the carol is particularly reminiscent of the words of the Nicene Creed:

"[We believe] in one Lord Jesus Christ, the only begotten Son of God, and born of the Father before all ages. (God of God) light of light, true God of true God. Begotten not made. . . . Who for us men and for our salvation came down from heaven. And was incarnate of the Holy Ghost and of the Virgin Mary and was made man."[13]

The "faithful" from around the world come from a diverse background of language and culture, yet we all share a set of core beliefs. Additionally, we share a common citizenship. The Bible tells us that "our citizenship is in heaven" (Philippians 3:20). So let "all ye citizens of heaven above" come together and "adore Him, Christ the Lord."

---

[1] Keyte, Hugh and Parrott, Andrew, editors. *The New Oxford Book of Carols*. Oxford University Press, 1998, p. 242.

[2] Keyte, Hugh and Parrott, Andrew, editors. The obituary is from the Laity's Directory, J.P. Coghlan, London, 1787.

[3] Keyte, Hugh and Parrott, Andrew, editors.

[4] Keyte, Hugh and Parrott, Andrew, editors.

[5] Keyte, Hugh and Parrott, Andrew, editors.

[6] Keyte, Hugh and Parrott, Andrew, editors.

[7] Keyte, Hugh and Parrott, Andrew, editors.

[8] McCutchan, Robert Guy. *Hymn Tune Names, Their Sources and Significance*. Abingdon Press, 1957, p. 36

[9] Bradley, Ian, editor. *The Penguin Book of Carols*. Penguin Books, 1999, p. 215.

[10] Bradley, Ian, editor.

[11] Bradley, Ian, editor.

[12] Bradley, Ian, editor.

[13] Wilhelm, Joseph. "The Nicene Creed." The Catholic Encyclopedia, V11. Robert Appleton Company, 1911. Retrieved August 31, 2008 from New Advent: http://www.newadvent.org/cathen/11049a.htm. Note that this is a literal translation of the Greek text of the Constantinopolitan form, the brackets indicate the words altered or added in the Western liturgical form.

O Come, O Come, Emmanuel

O Come, O Come, Emmanuel

Words: ANONYMOUS
Translated by: JOHN MASON NEALE

VENI EMMANUEL
Music: FRENCH MELODY
Arranged by: THOMAS HELMORE

Solemnly (♩ = 108)

1. O come, O come, Em - man - u - el, and ran - som cap - tive
2. O come, Thou Rod of Jes - se, free Thine own from Sa - tan's
3. O come, Thou Day - spring, come and cheer our spir - its by Thine
4. O come, Thou Key of Da - vid, come, and o - pen wide our
5. O come, O come, Thou Lord of might, who to Thy tribes on

Is - ra - el, that mourns in lone - ly ex - ile
ty - ran - ny; from depths of hell Thy peo - ple
Ad - vent here; dis - perse the gloom - y clouds of
heav'n - ly home; make safe the way that leads on
Si - nai's height in an - cient times didst give the

Refrain

here, un - til the Son of God ap - pear.
save, and give them vic - t'ry o'er the grave.
night and death's dark sha - dows put to flight! Re - joice! Re -
high, and close the path to mis - er - y.
law in cloud, and maj - es - ty and awe.

joice! E - man - u - el shall come to thee, O Is - ra - el.

252

Words, Anonymous
Translated by John Mason Neale (1818-1866)

John Mason Neale, translator of "O Come, O Come Emmanuel," wrote, "This Advent Hymn is little more than a versification of some of the Christmas antiphons commonly called the O's [or O Antiphons]."[1] The word *antiphon* comes from a Greek word meaning "opposite voice" and generally refers to one group responding to another during a song or chant.

Interestingly, the structure of the Psalms lends itself to an antiphonal method of singing and suggests that ancient Israelites sang this way. Though the earliest Christian churches may have adopted this form of worship from the Hebrews, Socrates, a 5th century church historian, credited Ignatius of Antioch (martyred in 107 AD) with introducing the antiphonal method of singing to the Eastern Church. Socrates recorded an old tradition that Ignatius had a vision of angels singing in alternate choirs and thus incorporated this form into worship.[2] St. Ambrose was credited with introducing antiphonal singing to the Western Church in the 4th century.[3]

The "O Antiphons" refer to the seven antiphons that begin with the word "O" and are recited during the "Octave," the eight days before Christmas. There is one antiphon for each day from December 17-23, with December 24, Christmas Eve, being reserved for the Christmas vigil. According to Dr. William Saunders, "The exact origin of the 'O Antiphons' is not known. Boethius (c. 480-524) made a slight reference to them, thereby suggesting their presence at that time. . . . [And] by the eighth century, they are in use in the liturgical celebrations in Rome."[4]

The Latin form of the "O Antiphons" is found in the Roman Breviary. Below are the Latin headings with an English translation.[5] Note how each antiphon highlights a title of the Messiah as prophesied in the book of Isaiah (written over 600 years before the birth of Christ).

O Sapientia: "O Wisdom, O holy Word of God, you govern all creation with your strong yet tender care. Come and show your people the way to salvation."

"The Spirit of the Lord will rest on him— the Spirit of wisdom and of understanding, the Spirit of counsel and of power, the Spirit of knowledge and of the fear of the Lord" (Isaiah 11:2).

O Adonai: "O sacred Lord of ancient Israel, who showed yourself to Moses in the burning bush, who gave him the holy law on Sinai mountain: come, stretch out your mighty hand to set us free."

"For the Lord is our judge, the Lord is our lawgiver, the Lord is our king; it is he who will save us" (Isaiah 33:22).

O Radix Jesse: "O Flower of Jesse's stem, you have been raised up as a sign for all peoples; kings stand silent in your presence; the nations bow down in worship before you. Come, let nothing keep you from coming to our aid."

"A shoot will come up from the stump of Jesse; from his roots a Branch will bear fruit" (Isaiah 11:1). *Recall that Jesse was the father of King David, from whom Jesus descended.*

O Clavis David: "O Key of David, O royal Power of Israel controlling at your will the gate of Heaven: Come, break down the prison walls of death for those who dwell in darkness and the shadow of death; and lead your captive people into freedom."

"I will place on his shoulder the key to the house of David; what he opens no one can shut, and what he shuts no one can open" (Isaiah 22:22).

O Oriens: "O Radiant Dawn, splendor of eternal light, sun of justice: come, shine on those who dwell in darkness and the shadow of death."

"The people walking in darkness have seen a great light; on those living in the land of the shadow of death a light has dawned" (Isaiah 9:2).

O Rex Gentium: "O King of all the nations, the only joy of every human heart; O Keystone of the mighty arch of man, come and save the creature you fashioned from the dust."

"For to us a child is born, to us a son is given, and the government will be on his shoulders. And he will be called Wonderful Counselor, Mighty God, Everlasting Father, Prince of Peace. Of the increase of his government and peace there will be no end. He will reign on David's throne and over his kingdom, establishing and upholding it with justice and righteousness from that time on and forever. The zeal of the Lord Almighty will accomplish this" (Isaiah 9:6-7).

O Emmanuel: "O Emmanuel, king and lawgiver, desire of the nations, Savior of all people, come and set us free, Lord our God."

"Therefore the Lord himself will give you a sign: The virgin will be with child and will give birth to a son, and will call him Immanuel" (Isaiah 7:14).

Interestingly, if we take the first Latin letter of each antiphon, ignoring the "O", and work our way back from the last to the first, it spells out "ERO CRAS." In Latin, this means "I shall be [with you] tomorrow."[6] This "hidden" meaning is revealed a little more each day as we draw closer to the birth of Jesus!

According to John Julian's *Dictionary of Hymnology*:

"Dr. Neale supposes [that around] the 12[th]century, an unknown author took five of these Antiphons, and wove them into a hymn in the following order: *O Emmanuel, O Radix Jesse, O Oriens, O Clavis David, O Adonai*. This hymn began with the line: 'Veni, veni, Emmanuel,' [O Come, o come, Emmanuel] and adding to each verse the refrain, which is not found in the original prose: 'Gaude, gaude, Emmanuel, Nascetur pro te, Israel' [Rejoice, rejoice, Emmanuel, shall come to thee O Israel]."[7]

Dr. Neale, a Latin scholar, found the full Latin text of the hymn in a book called *Thesaurus Hymnologicus* (1844) compiled by Professor Hermann Daniel in Germany. He published his first translation with the opening line "Draw nigh, draw nigh, Emmanuel" in *Mediaeval Hymns*, 1851. Neale's work was later altered to the familiar "O Come, O Come, Emmanuel" by the compilers of an 1859 trial copy of *Hymns Ancient and Modern*.[8] For more on Neale, see pp. 208-209.

Music "Veni Emmanuel" Arranged by Thomas Helmore (1811-1890)

Though some scholars believe that the tune may have its origin in the Gregorian chant of the eighth century, the oldest known record of the tune, according to *The New Oxford Book of Carols*, comes from a "French source, a fifteenth-century Franciscan processional, which was probably copied for a nunnery."[9] This source contains verses that were generally sung during the procession to a burial place after a funeral mass.

Another source in Lisbon, found and copied by Bishop Jenner in 1853, paired the French tune with the words of the hymn "Veni, veni Emmanuel." But since the original record (from which Jenner made his copy) has not yet been found, it cannot be dated, and the question remains open as to which text was originally sung to the tune. However, the editors of *The New Oxford Book of Carols* conclude, "The neat fit of the tune with, particularly, the repeated 'gaude' [rejoice] of the refrain makes us suspect that 'Veni, veni, Emanuel' was the original text."[10]

Bishop Jenner supplied his copy to Thomas Helmore who published the tune (along with Neale's translation) in *The Hymnal Noted, Part II* (1854). The tune name "Veni Emmanuel" comes from the first words of the Latin text.

Helmore, a friend of Neale's, was an ordained priest in the Church of England and played a major role in reviving ancient chant melodies along with the English translations of medieval Latin hymns. One of Helmore's most significant publications was *The Hymnal Noted*. He wrote that this work was "designed to supply the acknowledged want of an English Hymnal," and he claimed that "the omission, at the Reformation, of one entire portion of the ancient ritual [the hymns]" was nothing other than "injurious."[11] He believed that though the Reformers of the English Church desired for the hymns to be translated, the work had been left incomplete due to its difficulty. He said, "It was not so easy a task to translate verse as prose into the 'tongue understood of the people.'"[12] Fortunately, he found a master translator in John Mason Neale.

Helmore had a very high view of the role of music in worship, and he desired to revive congregational singing in the Church of England. However, he did not approve of the "new" style of hymns (presumably those of Watts and Wesley) that were being used for that purpose. He wrote:

> "The adoption in some places of an unecclesiastical, and secularized style, suited to the worst popular taste, and vulgar feeling, cannot too strongly be reprobated, as tending to bring down to the level of mere ordinary musical enjoyment, that portion of our worship on earth, which ought most to unite us to that of heaven."[13]

Helmore might not have guessed that the hymn, "O Come, O Come Emmanuel" would soon be published, and continues to be published, next to those of Watts and Wesley in nearly every collection of sacred Christmas music. Yet, the Bible instructs us to "worship the Lord with gladness; come before him with joyful songs" (Psalm 100:2). Whether old or new, if a song leads us to rejoice in the Lord, surely it honors him. So let us "Rejoice! Rejoice!," particularly during the Christmas season when we celebrate the birth of *Emmanuel* ("God with us").

---

[1] Neale, John Mason. *Mediaeval Hymns and Sequences*. J. Masters, 1867, p. 171.

[2] McCutchan, Robert Guy. *Hymn Tune Names, Their Sources and Significance*. Abingdon Press, 1957, p. 42.

[3] Encyclopedia Britannica. "Antiphon." Retrieved September 1, 2008 from Encyclopedia Britannica Online: http://www.britannica.com/EBchecked/topic/28480/antiphon.

[4] Saunders, William. "What are the 'O Antiphons'?" *Arlington Catholic Herald*. Retrieved September 1, 2008: http://www.catholiceducation.org/articles/religion/re0374.html.

[5] English Translation Drawn from: *Sourcebook for Sundays and Seasons, An Almanac of Parish Liturgy*. Liturgy Training, 2007, pp. 29-33.

[6] Keyte, Hugh and Parrott, Andrew, editors. *The New Oxford Book of Carols*. Oxford University Press, 1998, p. 45.

[7] Julian, John, editor. *A Dictionary of Hymnology*. Dover Publications Inc., 1957, p. 74. Note that the metrical form of the antiphons has not yet been traced earlier that the *Psalteroium Cantionum Catholicarum* (1710), p. 1721.

[8] Julian, John, editor, p. 74.

[9] Keyte, Hugh and Parrott, Andrew, editors, p. 45.

[10] Keyte, Hugh and Parrott, Andrew, editors, p. 45.

[11] Helmore, Thomas. *Accompanying Harmonies to The Hymnal Noted*. Novello, 1852, p. i.

[12] Helmore, Thomas, p. i.

[13] Helmore, Thomas, p. iv.

O Holy Night

O Holy Night

Words: PLACIDE CAPPEAU
Translated by: JOHN SULLIVAN DWIGHT

CANTIQUE DE NOEL
Music: ADOLPHE CHARLES ADAM

Words by Placide Cappeau (1808-1877)

As a young boy, Placide Cappeau tragically lost his hand in a shooting mishap with a friend. The family of Cappeau's friend was so distraught over the accident that they offered to partially finance Cappeau's education.[1]

Cappeau proved to be a very capable student. He studied at the Royal College of Avignon (where he won an award for drawing in 1825) and went on to earn degrees in both literature and law in Paris. After completing his studies, he returned to his hometown of Roquemaure, France to join the mayor, Guillaume Clerc, as a partner in the wine trade. Roquemaure was a port city on the Rhone River in the south of France that specialized in wine, and though Cappeau decided to pursue a career as a merchant, he maintained his love of literature and wrote poetry in his spare time. The local priest, Father Joseph Marie Gilles, must have been aware of Cappeau's gift with words, because in 1843 he asked Cappeau to compose a Christmas song to celebrate the upcoming restoration of the church organ.

When Mrs. Laurey (a singer and temporary resident in Roquemare) learned about Cappeau's song, she requested that her friend, Adolphe Adam, compose the music for it.[2] Mrs. Laurey intended to sing it for Christmas service of 1843. However, after returning to Paris to have a baby in July, Mrs. Laurey was not able to return to Roquemaure as intended that Christmas. In fact, she did not return for several years, and in October of 1846, Father Gilles died, never having heard Cappeau's words set to music. It was not until Christmas of 1847 that the song was finally performed by Mrs. Laurey at the church in Roquemaure.

Music "Cantique De Noel" by Adolphe Charles Adam (1803-1856)

Adolphe Charles Adam was the son of a talented musician, and when he entered the Paris Conservatoire in 1817 to study music, he proved to be gifted in his own right. However, his lax attitude toward the formal study of music was an annoyance to his teachers. Had it not been for a teacher by the name of Boieldieu who took interest in Adam and helped to develop his talent, his future may have taken a different course. It was Boieldieu who encouraged Adam to write music, and once Adam applied himself to this task, he proved to be a prolific composer throughout the rest of his life. He wrote operas, ballets, love songs, choruses, piano pieces, full orchestra pieces and a variety of religious pieces (including four masses).[3]

Adam's work was so successful that he was able to open his own opera house, the Opera National, in 1847. However, the political turmoil of the French Revolution of 1848, forced him to close it down just four months after opening its doors.[4] In addition to losing his fortune, Adam lost all of the money that he had borrowed. Yet, this hardship revealed his noble character. Adam said, "The loss of my fortune was not of great consequence to me. I know only one deprivation: that I could not as often receive my friends, my only and greatest pleasure."[5] Furthermore, he said, "I give thanks to God, in whom I firmly believe, of the favors, perhaps not well deserved, that he has bestowed on me; for, in spite of my misfortune in business, he left me with enough inspiration to compose works that I will attempt to produce in the best possible form."[6]

Adam committed to paying off his debts and spent the next several years doing so. Fortunately, he was still collecting royalties on previous pieces and was able to generate income from a variety of other sources; he worked as a music critic, wrote new compositions and taught music at his alma mater, the Paris Conservatoire. By 1852, he had paid off all his debts, and in 1856, he passed away.[7]

Though Adam's name is perhaps best known in association with his 1841 ballet, *Giselle*, his music for "O Holy Night" has proven to be his most popular and lasting legacy. Reportedly, Adam composed the carol in just a few days after receiving the request from his friend, Mrs. Laurey.[8] The fact that he did not even make allusion to the tune in his memoirs implies that he did not consider it to be one of his better works.[9] Yet, when the music was first played, and combined with Cappeau's words, it was an immediate success.

Controversy

Though the general population loved the song, it appears to have created a controversy among church leaders and music critics. By 1864, one writer for the *Review of Sacred Music* acknowledged the popularity of the song that was sung "in the streets, living rooms and café concerts."[10] However, his opinion was that it was "base and shallow" and "should make its way far from the church, where one could do extremely well without it."[11] For some people, the music was too "war-like"; for others, it was too "opera-like."

The controversy may also have been, in part, due to Cappeau's (the author of the words) growing reputation as a socialist. Recall that when he wrote his song in 1843, political tensions were brewing and would culminate in the French Revolution of 1848. Though socialists were working hard for universal suffrage and unemployment relief, they stood in opposition to the reigning monarch.

Furthermore, Cappeau's theological views were questionable. Reportedly, when he learned of the song's growing popularity, he wanted to change the words to better represent his beliefs. But the song had already "escaped" him and was sweeping across France. When Cappeau wrote the *Castle of Roquemaure, A Historical Poem in Twenty Songs* in 1876, his true beliefs were finally confirmed. He did in fact change the words to his song. Since our English translation is a loose one, you may not recognize the significance of Cappeau's changes. However, in the French language, Cappeau's original words made reference to the "God-man" and "original sin." Both were dropped in his revision. He wrote, "I had to modify what escaped me the first time on the original sin, in which I do not believe."[12] Furthermore, he clarified his understanding of the word "redeemer" by saying, "I admit Jesus is *like* [italics mine] a redeemer; he is a redeemer of inequalities, injustices, slavery and oppression of any kind."[13] Clearly, Cappeau did not recognize Jesus as the redeemer of sin.

Cappeau's changes to his original text imply that he wrote the song more as a service to the local priest, Father Gilles, than as a representation of his theological views. Fortunately, Cappeau's changes came too late, and the people of France managed to preserve the initial words. Though controversies surrounded the song long after the author and composer were dead, the carol continued to earn a cherished place in the hearts of its listeners, even if not in most church hymnals. Adam rightly called the song "the religious Marseillaise" (referring to the French national anthem), and the tune name "Cantique de Noel," the "Song of Christmas" in French, reveals how intimately it came to be associated with Christ and his birth.

Words Translated by John Sullivan Dwight (1813-1893)

John Sullivan Dwight is credited with introducing the song "O Holy Night" to America. Dwight was a descendant of the famous American preacher, Jonathan Edwards (1703-1758),[14] probably best known for his sermon "Sinners in the Hands of an Angry God" in which he emphasized the just wrath of God against sin in contrast to the amazing provision of grace for salvation. Dwight's father, Timothy Dwight (1752-1817), was equally famous. He served as a chaplain to George Washington in the Revolutionary War, as a pastor at the Connecticut Congregational Church in Greenville, and as a president of Yale from 1795 until his death in 1817. Furthermore, Timothy Dwight became a recognized leader in church music when he published an American version of Isaac Watts' psalms in 1801; in fact, the work came to be known as "Dwight's Watts."[15] Timothy Dwight included 33 of his own texts in the collection,[16] and his editor's version of Psalms 137, "I Love Thy Kingdom Lord" is the "earliest American congregational song remaining in common use.[17]

Though John Dwight came from a rich religious history, it appears that he abandoned the faith of his fathers during his years at Harvard Divinity School. Before graduating in 1836, he became deeply involved with the American Transcendentalist movement. A leading member of the movement, George Ripley, defined it as follows: "We are called Transcendentalists because we believe in an order of truth that transcends the sphere of external senses. Our leading idea is the supremacy of mind over matter."[18] Basically, Transcendentalists sought to attain an ideal spiritual state that "transcended" the physical world. They believed that the mind had direct access to spiritual truth apart from reason, religious doctrines or human institutions.[19]

In 1841, Dwight joined a transcendental commune called Brook Farm, founded by George and Sophia Ripley. In order to generate income and promote its philosophy, the commune established a day school. Dwight served as the director of this school, taught music and organized theatrical events. The commune also produced a journal called *The Harbinger* for which Dwight wrote regular columns on music. Dwight's writing revealed his transcendental belief that music, particularly classical, had a unique spiritual power. Handel's *Messiah* "seems to have been Dwight's favorite piece of music [because it] was filled with the 'pure, unlimited, humanity sentiment' that would someday lead to Universal Friendship."[20]

Though Brook Farm dissolved in 1847, Dwight continued to write for the *The Harbinger*. He also worked as a musical editor for various other magazines. In 1852, he founded *Dwight's Journal of Music*, which became one of the most influential musical publications of the 19th century.

A few years later, while seeking songs for his *Journal*, Dwight found and translated the French "Minuit Chrétiens" to "O Holy Night." The songs reception in America was quite similar to that in France. Although warmly received by the people, it was rarely printed in hymnals. Additionally, it proved to endure through the years in America just as it had in France. In fact, it was the first Christmas carol ever broadcast on the radio in the year 1906.[21]

Though the words of "O Holy Night" may have been written and translated by men who did not embrace historic Christianity, "What does it matter? The important thing is that in every way . . . Christ is preached" (Philippians 1:18). Jesus is the "Savior," the "King of Kings" and the night of his birth is truly HOLY!

[1] Durieu, René. L'auteur du "Minuit chrétiens." C. Lacour, 1997.

[2] Nova, Claude. "Histoire du Minuit chrétiens." Retrieved August 5, 2008: http://www.nimausensis.com/Gard/MinuitChretienNova.pdf. The history of this song has been reconstructed from recently discovered correspondence between Cappeau and his partner Mayor Guillaume Clerc. They have been reconciled with letters of Father Gilles and Mr. Laurey.

[3] Havard de la Montagne, Denis. *Minuit Chretiens, Une Partition D'Adolphe Adam*. Retrieved August 5, 2008 from: http://www.musimem.com/adam.htm.

[4] Feeney, Ann. "Biography of Adolphe Adam." Retrieved August 5, 2008 from All Music: http://www.allmusic.com/cg/amg.dll.

[5] Havard de la Montagne, Denis.

[6] Havard de la Montagne, Denis.

[7] Feeney, Ann.

[8] Studwell, William. *The Christmas Carol Reader.* The Haworth Press, 1995, p. 85.

[9] Havard de la Montagne, Denis.

[10] Havard de la Montagne, Denis.

[11] Havard de la Montagne, Denis.

[12] Havard de la Montagne, Denis.

[13] Havard de la Montagne, Denis.

[14] Hughes, Charles W. *American Hymns Old and New.* Columbia University Press, 1980, p. 378.

[15] Music, David W. *Hymnology, A Collection of Source Readings.* The Scarecrow Press, 1996, p. 189

[16] Music, David W., p. 189.

[17] Eskew, Harry and McElrath, Hugh T. *Sing with Understanding.* Broadman Press, 1980, p. 112

[18] Hillquit, Morris. *History of Socialism in the United States.* Funk & Wagnalls Company, 1910, p. 96.

[19] Bickman, Martin. "An Overview of American Transcendentalism." Retrieved August 5, 2008 from American Transcendentalism Web: http://www.vcu.edu/engweb/transcendentalism/ideas/definitionbickman.html.

[20] Delano, Sterling F. *The Harbinger and New England Transcendentalism: A Portrait of Associationism in America.* Fairleigh Dickinson University Press, 1984, p. 137.

[21] Collins, Ace. *Stories Behind the Best-Loved Songs of Christmas.* Zondervan, 2001, p. 138.

O Little Town
of Bethlehem

O Little Town of Bethlehem

Words: PHILLIPS BROOKS

ST. LOUIS
Music: LEWIS HENRY REDNER

Quietly (♩ = 96)

1. O lit - tle town of Beth - le - hem, how still we see thee lie! A -
2. For Christ is born of Ma - ry, and gath - ered all a - bove, while
3. How si - lent - ly, how si - lent - ly the won - drous gift is giv'n; so
4. O ho - ly Child of Beth - le - hem, de - scend to us, we pray; cast

bove thy deep and dream - less sleep the si - lent stars go by. Yet
mor - tals sleep, the an - gels keep their watch of won - d'ring love. O
God im - parts to hu - man hearts the bless - ings of His heav'n. No
out our sin, and en - ter in; be born in us to - day. We

in thy dark streets shin - eth the ev - er - last - ing Light; the
morn - ing stars to - geth - er pro - claim the ho - ly birth, and
ear may hear His com - ing, but in this world of sin, where
hear the Christ - mas an - gels the great glad ti - dings tell; O

hopes and fears of all the years are met in thee to - night.
prais - es sing to God the King, and peace to men on earth!
meek souls will re - ceive him still, the dear Christ en - ters in.
come to us, a - bide with us, our Lord Em - man - u - el.

Words by Phillips Brooks (1835-1893)

P hillips Brooks came from a long line of Puritans tracing back to John Cotton (1585-1652), a highly regarded New England minister. Brooks' parents, like many Puritans, became associated with the Episcopal Church in America and raised their children in this denomination. Brooks' home life was strict and religious, yet full of love. Three of Brooks' five brothers, like him, went on to be ordained as ministers in the Episcopal Church.

Brooks prepared for college at the Boston Latin School, America's oldest public school, and graduated from Harvard University in 1855, when he was just 20 years old. After an unhappy experience as a teacher at the Boston Latin School, Brooks decided to study for the ministry at Virginia Theological Seminary. When he graduated in 1859, he was appointed to a position at a small church in Philadelphia, the Church of the Advent. His teaching began to draw attention, and by 1861, he was sent to a larger church in the same city, the Church of the Holy Trinity. He remained there until 1869, providing moral strength to his congregation throughout the American Civil War and its aftermath.

Brooks upheld the cause of the North and passionately opposed slavery. He, along with thousands of others, was devastated by the news of Abraham Lincoln's death in 1865. When Lincoln's body was carried through Philadelphia en route to Illinois in a funeral procession, Brooks delivered a now famous eulogy on the great character of Lincoln. On the question of whether or not Lincoln was an "intellectual man," Brooks said the following:

"You are unable to tell whether in the wise acts and words which issue from such a life there is more of the righteousness which comes from a clear conscience or of the sagacity that comes from a clear brain.

"It is the great boon of such characters as Mr. Lincoln's that they reunite what God has joined together and man has put asunder. In him was vindicated the greatness of real goodness and the goodness of real greatness. The twain were one flesh.

"This union of the mental and moral into a life of admirable simplicity is what we most admire in children; but in them it is unsettled and unpractical. But when it is preserved into manhood, deepened into reliability and maturity, it is that glorified child-likeness, that high and reverend simplicity, which shames and baffles the most accomplished astuteness and is chosen by God to fill his purposes when he needs a ruler for his people, of faithful and true heart. Such as he had who was our President."[1]

Interestingly, Brooks' portrayal of Lincoln would prove to be an accurate description of his own life. And his words give insight into his sincere love for children, an affection that would largely characterize his life.

Not long after Lincoln's death, Brooks traveled to the Holy Land. Likely, he was in need of a retreat from war-torn America. In a letter to his father, Brooks tells how on Christmas Eve, he traveled on horseback from Jerusalem to Bethlehem.[2] He rode to the field outside Bethlehem in which the angelic announcement to the shepherds is said to have taken place, and he witnessed shepherds still "keeping watch over their flocks." That evening, he attended a five-hour (10 p.m. to 3 a.m.) service at the Church of the Nativity.

A few months later, while in Rome, Brooks wrote a letter to the "dear children" in the Sunday schools of his church in Philadelphia. In the letter he recalls his time in Bethlehem:

"I wish I could be with you in the Sunday-school. . . . For of all my friends in America there are none by whom I should be more sorry to be forgotten, or whom I should be more sorry to forget, than the circle who make up our schools and classes. I do not mind telling you (though of course I should not like to have you speak of it to any of the older people of the church) that I am much afraid the younger part of my congregation has more than its share of my thoughts and interest. I cannot tell you how many Sunday mornings since I left you I have seemed to stand in the midst of our crowded schoolroom again, and look about and know every face and every class just as I used to; nor how many time I have heard one of our home hymns ringing very strangely and sweetly through the different music of some far-off country. I remember especially on Christmas Eve, when I was standing in the old church at Bethlehem, close to the spot where Jesus was born, when the whole church was ringing hour after hour with the splendid hymns of praise to God, how again and again it seemed as if I could hear voices that I knew well, telling each other of the 'Wonderful Night' of the Saviour's birth, as I had heard them a year before [at his home church]; and I assure you I was glad to shut my ears for a while and listen to the more familiar strains that came wandering to me halfway round the world."[3]

By all accounts, it was this Christmas Eve experience that began to stir the now famous song "O Little Town of Bethlehem" in Brooks' heart. How fitting that the song was written for the children of whom he recalled so fondly when he was there. However, three years passed before the song that had been "singing in the soul of Phillips Brooks"[4] was finally written down for the Christmas service of the Sunday schools at his church.

Apparently, verse-writing was a regular habit with Brooks and was likely due, in large part, to an old family tradition.[5] Every Sunday as a child, Phillips and his brothers had to recite a new hymn before the assembled family. According to biographer Alexander Allen:

"In a little book, carefully kept by the father, there was a record of the hymns each child had learned, beginning with William, who had the advantage of age, and had learned the greatest number, followed by Phillips, who came next, and the record tapering down until John is reached, with a comparatively small number at his disposal. Most of them were from the old edition of the Prayer Book, then bound up with a metrical selection of Psalms and a collection of two hundred and twelve hymns. These hymns Phillips carried in his mind as so much mental and spiritual furniture, or as germs of thought; they often reappeared in his sermons, as he became aware of some deeper meaning in the old familiar lines."[6]

By the time Brooks went to college, he had some 200 hymns memorized. "His own mind and heart were stored with hymns to such an extent and in such a way that they were one of the real influences of his life."[7] Perhaps these hymns reminded Brooks of his happy childhood and served to cultivate in him a desire to write new hymns. His Christmas and Easter carols in particular reveal that "he entered into those festivals with a child's enthusiasm and joy."[8]

Brooks never married nor had children of his own, so he "took to his heart the children of others."[9] Though he was a man of towering physical presence, more than 6 feet 6 inches tall, "he not only loved children dearly, but liked to be their comrade and to get down on the nursery floor and romp with them."[10]

Surely, it pained Brooks to leave his church family in Philadelphia, but by 1869, Brooks' "leanings toward his native town and the urgency of repeated calls from there" led him to accept a position at Trinity Church in Boston.[11] Brooks' reputation as an "extraordinary orator" continued to spread, and he became "one of the most respected and accomplished ministers of the 19th century United States."[12]

By 1891, Brooks was elected as the sixth Episcopal Bishop of Massachusetts. But he did not hold this position for long. After a brief illness, he passed away in January of 1893. His death was a major event in Boston, and people of every denomination mourned the loss of a great man. Here is one tender account of how a child responded to news of his death:

"The morning after this great-lover of the Christ-child went Home, the mother of a little girl of five, who had been one of his special favorites, entered the room where the child was playing, and holding the little face between her hands, said tearfully, 'Bishop Brooks has gone to heaven.' 'Oh Mamma,' was the reply, 'how happy the angels will be!'"[13]

Music "St. Louis" by Lewis Henry Redner (1831-1908)

When Brooks wrote down his hymn, "O Little Town of Bethlehem" in 1868, he asked Lewis Redner, his church organist and superintendent of Sunday school to set it to music. Redner gave the following account of his composition:

"As Christmas of 1868 approached, Mr. Brooks told me that he had written a simple little carol for the Christmas Sunday-school service, and he asked me to write the tune to it. The simple music was written in great haste and under great pressure. We were to practice it on the following Sunday. Mr. Brooks came to me on Friday, and said, 'Redner, have you ground out that music yet to "O Little Town of Bethlehem"?' I replied, 'No,' but that he should have it by Sunday. On the Saturday night previous my brain was all confused about the tune. I thought more about my Sunday-school lesson than I did about the music. But I was roused from sleep late in the night hearing an angel-strain whispering in my ear, and seizing a piece of music paper I jotted down the treble of the tune as we now have it, and on Sunday morning before going to church I filled in the harmony. Neither Mr. Brooks nor I ever thought the carol or the music to it would live beyond that Christmas of 1868."[14]

According to Redner, the music was first christened with the name "St. Louis" in a Sunday school hymn and tune book called *The Church Porch*.[15] Redner made no comment as to why the tune was named as such. Quite possibly he was too humble to admit that it was named after him and that the French form of his name ("St. Louis" instead of "St. Lewis") was used so as not to embarrass him.

By all accounts, Lewis Redner truly was a "saint." Though he made a living in real estate, he devoted all of his spare time to serving in various churches. For 19 years, he served as both the organist and the superintendent of Sunday school at Holy Trinity Church. He, like Brooks, was not married and did not have any children of his own. Yet, he wholly committed himself to the children of his church. Not surprisingly, his devotion and leadership led to "a remarkable increase in attendance."[16] How fitting that Redner's most lasting legacy would be a tune that he composed for the beloved children of his Sunday school program and that honored the child most precious to him — Jesus!

---

[1] Newton, William Wilberforce. *The Child and the Bishop: Together with Certain Memorabilia of the Rt. Rev. Phillips Brooks*. J.G. Cupples, 1894, pp. 39-40.

[2] Brooks, Phillips. *Letters of Travel*. E.P. Dutton and Company, 1893, Letter Dated Dec 30, 1865, p. 69.

[3] Brooks, Phillips. Letter Dated February 19, 1866 from Rome, pp. 85-86.

[4] Allen, Alexander Viets Griswold. *Life and Letters of Phillips Brooks*, V2. E.P. Dutton and Co., 1900, p. 57.

[5] Benson, Louis Fitzgerald. *Studies of Familiar Hymns*. The Westminster Press, 1903, p. 8.

[6] Allen, Alexander Viets Griswold, pp. 214-215.

[7] Benson, Louis Fitzgerald, p. 9.

[8] Benson, Louis Fitzgerald, p. 9.

[9] Ninde, Edward Summerfield. *The Story of the American Hymn*. The Abingdon Press, 1921, p. 329.

[10] Benson, Louis Fitzgerald, p. 9.

[11] Benson, Louis Fitzgerald, p. 7-8.

[12] Studwell, William. *The Christmas Carol Reader*. The Haworth Press, 1995, p. 25.

[13] Ninde, Edward Summerfield, p. 333.

[14] Benson, Louis Fitzgerald, p. 4-5.

[15] Benson, Louis Fitzgerald, p. 6.

[16] Hughes, Charles. *America Hymns Old and New, Notes on the Hymns and Biographies of the Authors and Composers*. Columbia University Press, 1980, p. 530.

Silent Night

Silent Night

Words: JOSEPH MOHR
Translated by: JOHN FREEMAN YOUNG

STILLE NACHT
Music: FRANZ GRUBER

1. Si - lent night, ho - ly night. All is calm,
2. Si - lent night, ho - ly night. Shep - herds quake
3. Si - lent night, ho - ly night. Son of God,

all is bright 'round yon vir - gin moth - er and Child;
at the sight, glo - ries stream from heav - en a - far,
love's pure light. ra - diant beams from Thy ho - ly face,

ho - ly in - fant so ten - der and mild, Sleep in heav - en - ly
heav'n - ly hosts sing al - le - lu - ia; Christ, the Sav - ior is
with the dawn of re - deem - ing grace, Je - sus, Lord, at Thy

peace, Sleep in heav - en - ly peace.
born! Christ, the Sav - ior is born.
birth, Je - sus, Lord, at Thy birth.

Words by Joseph Mohr (1792-1848)

Joseph Mohr began life in very humble circumstances. He was born in Salzburg, Austria to an unwed mother and a mercenary soldier (who deserted both the army and Mohr's mother before his birth).[1] Despite the efforts of Mohr's mother to support her four illegitimate children by working as an embroiderer, their lives were marked by poverty.

Fortunately, a priest by the name of Johann Nepomuk Hiernle recognized young Mohr's potential for academics and music. Hiernle was able to secure an education for Mohr, as well as opportunities to sing and play the violin at various churches. Hiernle's efforts must have had a significant impact on Mohr. For when it came time to choose a career, he decided to follow in the footsteps of his mentor and become a priest himself. However, since Mohr was born illegitimately, he had to obtain special permission to attend seminary. Fortunately, approval was granted and Mohr was ordained as a priest in 1815.

Mohr's first official assignment was to serve as an assistant priest in Mariapfarr (1815-1817). It was during this time, in 1816, that he penned the words to "Silent Night."[2] Little is known about the circumstances that inspired the poem, but it is interesting to consider the historical context of the time. The Napoleonic Wars (1792-1815) had just come to an end, and in 1816, Bavarian occupation troops began to withdraw from Mariapfarr. Since the tumult of war was no longer raging across Europe, the nights could finally be silent, calm and peaceful. Though this earthly peace may have inspired Mohr's work, his words reveal that his deepest gratitude was for the "heavenly peace" that came through Christ the Savior.

Mohr's next assignment was as assistant priest in the village of Oberndorf. During his time there, his reputation as a "priest of the people" began to take shape. The church in Oberndorf, St. Nicholas Church, did not have living quarters for the priests. As a result, Mohr slept in the church caretaker's house without complaint. Furthermore, the economy of Oberndorf was largely based on the boating industry and the salt trade. The Napoleonic Wars had severely impacted business, and the town was suffering a depression. Since Mohr was raised in poverty, he understood what it meant to struggle. Not only could Mohr relate to the people of Oberndorf in their suffering, he did whatever he could to assist them. He had a generous heart and was eager to deny himself in order to provide for the needs of others.

Perhaps Mohr's popularity with the people of Oberndorf was the main source of tension between him and the parish priest Georg Heinrich Nöstler. According to the Silent Night Society:

> "Nöstler was critical of his young assistant priest, accusing him of 'neglecting his priestly duties, frequenting drinking locales, joking with persons of the opposite sex, and singing songs which do not edify.' The deacon of nearby St. Georgen, who served as overseer of the Oberndorfer priests, along with the town leaders in Oberndorf, responded in writing saying these accusations were unfounded."[3]

Despite Nöstler's criticism, Mohr's popularity would only increase when he introduced a new Christmas song to the parish in 1818. Church organist Franz Gruber gave an eyewitness account of the now famous event in his "Authentic Account of the Origin of the Christmas Carol, 'Silent Night, Holy Night!'" (1854):

> "It was the 24th of December of the year 1818, when the then assistant priest Joseph Mohr at the newly established parish of St. Nicholas in Oberndorf handed over to the organist represented by Franz Gruber (who at the time was also school teacher in Arnsdorf) a poem, with the request to write a fitting melody for 2 solo voices together with choir and for accompaniment by guitar."[4]

Gruber gives no explanation as to why he was asked to compose a tune in such haste or why Mohr requested it for guitar. Not surprisingly, a variety of romantic stories have been created to fill in the details. The most common tale is that the church organ had suddenly broken (some claim that mice had eaten through the organ wires, others claim that humidity had caused it to rust). Unfortunately, there is no evidence to either confirm or deny these claims. However, it is interesting to note that the song was soon to be carried throughout the immediate region by Carl Mauracher, a man well known for his skill in building and repairing organs; this fact is attested to by Gruber himself.[5] Documents reveal that Mauracher completely rebuilt the church organ of Oberndorf in 1825, and though there are no known records of work immediately following the performance of "Silent Night," the possibility certainly exists.

What is known for certain is that the song was well received by its first audience and would be heard by many more in the years to come. The song's debut was after Midnight Mass on Christmas Eve 1818 beside a Nativity scene in the side chapel of the church of St. Nicholas.[6] Mohr sang the tenor part and played the guitar, while Gruber sang bass. "According to Gruber, the song was met with 'general approval by all' in attendance (mostly shipping laborers, boat builders and their families)."[7]

According to music historian, William Studwell:

> "The place, St. Nicholas' Church in Oberndorf, Upper Austria, was admirably suited for a Christmas event, as its name implies, and also for a musical happening. The church was only 11 miles from historic Salzburg, which was the birthplace of the incomparable Wolfgang Amadeus Mozart as well as the location of the music festival won by the Von Trapp family singers in The Sound of Music."[8]

Though the Von Trapps would not appear on the scene for another century, it is interesting to note that the proliferation of "Silent Night" is largely credited to two family singing groups — the Rainer and Strasser Family Singers. Both families traveled extensively through Europe and sang "Silent Night" in their performances. Furthermore, on Christmas Day in 1839, the Rainers performed the song for the first time on American soil. By the turn of the century "Silent Night" had reached every continent on the globe (largely due to both Catholic and Protestant missionaries), and translations now exist in over 300 languages and dialects.[9]

Interestingly, Mohr remained at the church in Oberndorf (now a historic landmark because of his song) for only two years. From there, he would go on to serve over a dozen other communities. His longest assignment was also his last. He served as priest in Wagrain from 1837-1848 where "his impact with the parish was considerable and lasting, inspiring villagers to refer to him as a social reformer."[10] He created a fund to help poor children attend school (one that he was instrumental in building), and he administered a program to provide housing for the poor and aged. Mohr passionately served the people of Wagrain, who loved him dearly, until a lung disease took him home to "sleep in heavenly peace" in 1848.

Music "Stille Nacht" by Franz Xaver Gruber (1787-1863)

Franz Xaver Gruber was born in Upper Austria as the fifth of six children. In his youth, Gruber complied with learning his father's trade (linen weaving), even though his heart was set on music. Fortunately, the local schoolteacher recognized Gruber's talent and trained him in music. Eventually, Gruber's father released him from the family business so that he could pursue a career as a schoolteacher. Interestingly, in Gruber's day, schoolteachers often served as organists in their local church. By 1807, Gruber was working the combined jobs of schoolteacher, church caretaker and organist in Arnsdorf

In 1816, Gruber began "moonlighting" as organist at the newly established parish of Oberndorf, shortly before the arrival of Joseph Mohr. Most likely, Gruber was hoping to obtain a permanent position as both organist and schoolteacher in Oberndorf. Though Gruber's school in Arnsdorf was said to be one of the best run in the district, attendance was dismal. Arnsdorf was a farming community and "the farmers preferred keeping their children at home to help with the many chores of running a farm."[11]

Though Gruber never obtained a teaching position in Oberndorf, his dream of dedicating himself solely to music became a reality in 1835. He was appointed choir director and organist for the parish church of Hallein. During his time at Hallein, Gruber created a wide range of musical compositions. Though he would later characterize "Stille Nacht" (the words for "Silent Night" in German) as "a simple composition,"[12] of all his work, it would prove to be the most enduring.

Words Translated by John Freeman Young (1820-1885)

The first English translation of the song, "Stilly Night, Holy Night," was made in 1858 by Emily Elliott in England.[13] Of the many later English translations, John Freeman Young's is the most popular. Though the original poem included six verses in German, Freeman created a free translation of just three of them (verses 1, 6 and 2).

In 1841, Young began his college studies in science at Wesleyan University. However, after converting to the Episcopal Church, he decided to study for the priesthood. He transferred to Virginia Theological Seminary (the same school that Phillips Brooks, author of "O Little Town of Bethlehem," would attend a decade later) and graduated in 1845.

Young's first assignment was to St. John's Church in Tallahassee, Fla. He was ordained as a priest there in 1846 and "was one of only two clergymen in active parochial service in the entire state," serving until December 15, 1847.[14] From Florida, Young served in various positions across the country (Texas, Mississippi, Louisiana and New York) until he was consecrated as the Bishop of Florida in 1867.

Young's accomplishments in Florida were remarkable, especially considering the circumstances into which he accepted his position of leadership. According to historian Douglas D. Anderson:

"The church in Florida had been so devastated by the effects of the Civil War [1861-1865] that the Committee on the State of the Church wrote that it was a 'wonder' that the church in Florida still had 'an organized existence at all.' Bishop Young described that time as 'a struggle for life.' But through his diligent efforts, from 1875 to 1885 the church expanded from 20 parishes or missions and 14 clergy at work — to 48 congregations ministered to by 36 clergy."[15]

Young's experience, prior to becoming Bishop, prepared him well for the task in Florida. First off, his interest in church architecture equipped him with the knowledge he would need to oversee the construction of new churches throughout the state:

"While at Trinity Church in New York, Bishop Young met Richard Upjohn, the architect who had designed [it]. Upjohn had published a book containing detailed plans and instructions with which small congregations could build churches. Gothic in style, they looked like a church and felt like a church. In Florida many churches were built in Upjohn's Carpenter Gothic style throughout [Young's] diocese."[16]

Furthermore, Young had experience in working to overcome barriers of denomination — experience that would later help him to address the barriers of race and language in Florida. Young had served as the "secretary of the Russo-Greek Committee of the General Convention, and edited the papers issued by them in furtherance of the intercommunion between the Eastern, Anglican, and American churches."[17] His worked proved to be so valuable that he was awarded a Doctorate in Sacred Theology from Columbia College in 1865.

Most likely, Young viewed music as a valuable means through which to unite believers. He dedicated much of his time to "collecting and translating the great Christian hymns of various churches," and in 1862, he was appointed to the Joint Committee on Hymnody and Metrical

Psalmody.[18] It was in the year 1859, that Young published a pamphlet titled *Carols for Christmas Tide*. The first of the seven carols in this publication was his English translation of "Silent Night."

Though Young left behind a great legacy with his translation of "Silent Night," he left an even greater legacy through his work as bishop. He started schools, helped to revive a university, established a church for blacks, organized a Spanish language church for Cuban immigrants and helped to develop missions work to Cuba. It appears that he also published a pamphlet containing 25 hymns in Spanish.

Bishop Young's successor, Edwin Gardner Weed, third Bishop of Florida, said the following about Young:

"Throughout the Diocese I have learned how his care extended to the minutest details. His taste is to be seen everywhere. I venture to say there is not a Diocese in the American Church, with as many temples of worship, constructed with the same reference to the true principles of architecture. He was not only a wise and educated master-builder, however; his foresight was markedly shown in the selection of places for the erection of church buildings. When you consider what a wilderness Florida was when he was consecrated, and when you consider, also, how the Church has kept ahead of immigration, and how the population has followed and clustered round the places which he selected, as centers of worship, we must pay him the homage due the wise statesman. Not satisfied with planting and establishing the Church in the most remote districts, he did not rest till he had given the people a love of true Church music, and had instructed them in the proper rendering of the ritual."[19]

During a visit to New York, Young was stricken with pneumonia and passed away. After almost 40 years of serving his Lord in ministry, Young could finally gaze firsthand on the "holy face" of "love's pure light."

---

[1] Stille Nacht Gesellschaft (Silent Night Society) in Austria. Retrieved September 12, 2008 from: http://www.stillenacht.at/en/mohr.asp. Most of the biographical and historical data for "Silent Night" are drawn from this source.

[2] Many sources claim that Mohr penned the words of the song "Silent Night" on the day that it was first performed, Christmas Eve, 1818. However, a score autographed by Mohr was discovered in 1995 with the following note: "Text by Joseph Mohr - confirmed by my own signature - assistant priest 1816." Historians believe that the note was written between 1820 and 1825 and that 1816 refers to the year in which Mohr created the text. This autographed score also indicates "Melody by Fr. Xav. Gruber" proving conclusively that he composed the tune.

[3] Stille Nacht Gesellschaft (Silent Night Society) in Austria. Retrieved September 12, 2008 from: http://www.stillenacht.at/en/mohr.asp.

[4] Stille Nacht Gesellschaft (Silent Night Society) in Austria. These are the words of Franz Xaver Gruber which he wrote on December 30, 1854 in his "Authentic Account of the Origin of the Christmas Carol, 'Silent Night, Holy Night!'" Retrieved September 12, 2008 from: http://www.stillenacht.at/en/origin_song.asp

[5] Stille Nacht Gesellschaft (Silent Night Society) in Austria. These are the words of Franz Xaver Gruber which he wrote on December 30, 1854 in his "Authentic Account of the Origin of the Christmas Carol, 'Silent Night, Holy Night!'" Retrieved September 12, 2008 from: http://www.stillenacht.at/en/spreading_song.asp.

[6] Bradley, Ian, editor. *The Penguin Book of Carols*. Penguin Group, 1999, p. 300.

[7] Stille Nacht Gesellschaft (Silent Night Society) in Austria. Retrieved September 12, 2008 from: http://www.stillenacht.at/en/origin_song.asp.

[8] Studwell, William. *The Christmas Carol Reader*. The Haworth Press, 1995, p. 87.

[9] Stille Nacht Gesellschaft (Silent Night Society) in Austria. Retrieved September 12, 2008 from: http://www.stillenacht.at/en/spreading_song.asp.

[10] Stille Nacht Gesellschaft (Silent Night Society) in Austria. Retrieved September 12, 2008 from: http://www.stillenacht.at/en/mohr.asp.

[11] Stille Nacht Gesellschaft (Silent Night Society) in Austria. Retrieved September 12, 2008 from: http://www.stillenacht.at/en/gruber.asp.

[12] Stille Nacht Gesellschaft (Silent Night Society) in Austria. Retrieved September 12, 2008 from: http://www.stillenacht.at/en/gruber.asp.

[13] Bradley, Ian, editor, p. 301.

[14] Anderson, Douglas D. "Biography of John Freeman Young." Retrieved September 13, 2008 from Hymns and Carols of Christmas: http://www.hymnsandcarolsofchristmas.com/Hymns_and_Carols/Biographies/john_freeman_young.htm.

[15] Anderson, Douglas D.

[16] Anderson, Douglas D.

[17] Anderson, Douglas D.

[18] Anderson, Douglas D. Note that much of Young's work was published posthumously by Rev. John Henry Hopkins, Jr., *Great Hymns of the Church (New York, 1887)*.

[19] Pennington, Edgar Legare. "John Freeman Young, Second Bishop of Florida." Church Missions Publishing Company, 1939, p. 63.

The First Noel

The First Noel

Words: ANONYMOUS
First Published by: DAVIES GILBERT

Music: ENGLISH MELODY
First Published by: WILLIAM SANDYS
Arranged by: JOHN STAINER

cold win - ter's night _____ that was _____ so deep.
so it con - tin - ued both day _____ and night.
fol - low the star _____ wher - ev - er it went.
o - ver the place _____ where Je - sus lay.

Refrain

No - el, _____ No - el, No - el, No - el, _____

born is the King _____ of Is - ra - el.

Verse 5
Then did they know assuredly
Within that house the King did lie;
One entered in them for to see,
And found the Babe in poverty.
Refrain

Verse 6
Then enter'd in those wise men three,
Full reverently upon their knee,
And offer'd there in His presence,
Their gold, and myrrh and frankincense.
Refrain

Verse 7
Between an ox stall and an ass,
This Child truly there He was;
For want of clothing they did Him lay
All in a manger, among the hay.
Refrain

Verse 8
Then let us all with one accord
Sing praises to our heavenly Lord,
That hath made heav'n and earth of nought,
And with his blood mankind hath bought.
Refrain

Verse 9
If we in our time shall do well,
We shall be free from death and hell;
For God hath prepared for us all
A resting place in general.
Refrain

Words, Anonymous
First Published by Davies Gilbert (1767-1839)

The etymology of the word "noel" is uncertain. Some scholars believe that it is a contraction of the French word *nouvelles* (tidings or news) as in *les bonnes nouvelles* (the good news) of the Gospel; others believe that it is a corruption of the word *Yule* (a pagan winter feast).[1] Webster's dictionary indicates that the word is drawn from the Latin *natalis* (birth). If Webster's is correct, than music historian Kenneth Osbeck points out that the "repetition of the joyous 'noel' in the refrain is equivalent to our singing 'happy birthday' to someone."[2] Regardless of its etymology, the word "noel" has come to be used synonymously with "Christmas."

It should be noted that the original English spelling of the word is "nowell." Though the eventual alteration to "noel" has led some to erroneously believe that the song's origin is French, it is almost certainly an old English folk song.[3] The first publication of the words, without music, was in the 1823 revised edition of *Some Ancient Christmas Carols* by Davies Gilbert. Though the words are thought to have their roots in the 15th century, they were drawn from a collection of carols, called the Hutchens manuscript, prepared for Gilbert around 1816.[4]

Davies Gilbert was born in the county of Cornwall, the most southwesterly region of England, and was the son of a curate (a term generally used for an assistant priest or a deacon in the Anglican Church) at St. Erth Parish.[5] His original name was Davies Giddy, but he would later take his wife's last name (Gilbert) in order to inherit her uncle's large Sussex estate.

Gilbert received his early education in Cornwall before traveling to Oxfordshire for college. Shortly after earning a degree in 1789 from Pembroke College at Oxford, Gilbert returned to his hometown in Cornwall. In 1804, he began a successful career as a Member of Parliament, representing Helston (1804-1806) and Bodmin (1806-1832), two different towns in the county of Cornwall. Gilbert married in 1808 and took his wife's name in 1817.

As a member of the British Parliament for almost 30 years, Gilbert had the opportunity to promote his interests in science, art and history. Among his notable activities was his mentorship of the famous English chemist, Humphry Davy, who "discovered several chemical elements (including sodium and potassium) and compounds, invented the miner's safety lamp [to minimize the fatal accidents to coal miners caused by their lamps exploding], and became one of the greatest exponents of the scientific method."[6] Gilbert offered Davy the use of his library, as well as access to one of the best available laboratories for chemistry.

Gilbert was also a member of many reputable and exclusive organizations. Namely, he was elected to the Society of Antiquaries in 1820, and he served as the president of the Royal Society, the oldest and most prestigious scientific society in Britain, from 1827 to 1830. Though Gilbert published work in a variety of fields, "his 1822 publication of *Some Ancient Christmas Carols*, together with the second edition in 1823, marks his place of importance to the history of Christmas carols. These 20 carols, however modest their number, are the first collections published in the age of Victorian England."[7]

Gilbert's collection of carols was much more than a removed, academic effort on his part. In the preface to his first collection, Gilbert spoke sentimentally of the carols that were "sung in Churches on Christmas Day, and in private houses on Christmas Eve, throughout the West of England, up to the latter part of the late century." He said:

"The Editor is desirous of preserving them in their actual forms, however distorted by false grammar or by obscurities, as specimens of times now passed away, and of religious feelings superseded by others of a different cast. He is anxious also to preserve them on account, of the delight they afforded him in his childhood, when the festivities of Christmas Eve were anticipated by many days of preparation, and prolonged through several weeks by repetitions and remembrances."[8]

Interestingly, it appears that Gilbert's native Cornwall, the "West of England," was somewhat isolated from the views that had permeated much of the rest of the country in regard to Christmas. Beginning in the 16th century, Puritan views about Christmas rapidly spread across England, and the holiday transformed from a lively celebration to a time of somber reflection. Songs and carols with "sensual appeal"[9] were flatly rejected. At one point, the celebration of Christmas in England was actually banned. But remote Cornwall remained immune to many of the cultural trends that swept across the rest of England. *The New Oxford Book of Carols* records:

"In [Cornwall] some aspects of the medieval age lived on until the later eighteenth century, when Methodism, the decline of the Cornish language, and improved transport began to reduce the county's isolation. A richer soil for the growth and retention of folksongs and customs could hardly be imagined, and Cornwall has been beyond doubt the prime British source of folk carols."[10]

Gilbert probably recognized that Cornwall would gradually lose its identity as new cultural trends made their way across the county border. As new songs were being introduced to churches across England (largely through the efforts of the Methodist and Evangelical movements), for better or for worse, old songs were being cast off. Understandably, Gilbert wanted to preserve the joyful songs of his childhood.

Though Gilbert was praised for his efforts in rescuing many old carols from obscurity, the words of "The First Noel" have received their fair share of criticism. They have been described as "crude poetry" and as "a sincere, devout attempt of a peasant to put the Christmas story into rhyme."[11] Various examples are cited to demonstrate that the author of the text lacked knowledge of the biblical narrative of Christ's birth: "The second verse refers to the shepherds, instead of the wise men, seeing the star, and that the star was 'shining in the east,' when it logically had to be in the western sky."[12] Furthermore, though the first verse in Gilbert's version says "certain" shepherds, other versions specify "three" shepherds. Since the biblical record does not indicate any particular number of shepherds, this may reveal further naiveté on the part of the original author.

Keep in mind that if the words were in fact written in the 15[th]century, it was a time when very few people had access to the Bible. Most would rely heavily on their memory of the story as it had been told to them. Understandably, minor deviations from the biblical record could easily occur. It should be noted, however, that the author may have appealed to an old tradition when he made reference to the shepherds seeing the star. Phillips Brooks, author of "O Little Town of Bethlehem," mentions in a letter to his father that during his trip to Bethlehem, he "rode out of town to the field where they say the shepherds saw the star."[13] It seems reasonable to believe that the shepherds did in fact see the same star that drew the Wise Men from the East. After all, the shepherds spent their nights out in the field in full view of the sky; they may well have been amateur astronomers.

Whether the words of "The First Noel" are "crude poetry" or not, Gilbert's effort to preserve them has certainly "afforded delight" to many generations, as they did for him in his childhood. Amazingly, the lyrics as recorded by Gilbert have remained virtually intact (with only slight alterations). And if a humble, uneducated peasant did in fact write the words of the carol, it seems quite fitting. After all, "The First Noel" was announced to humble shepherds, and they were the first to wish a happy birthday to the "King of Israel."

Music, Anonymous
First Published by William Sandys (1792-1874)
Arranged by John Stainer (1840-1901)

Ten years after its appearance in Gilbert's collection (without music), the tune for "The First Noel" was published in William Sandys' *Christmas Carols, Ancient and Modern* (1833). Though Sandys was a lawyer by trade, he had a fervent interest in history, particularly in music and Christmas. He, like Gilbert, was a member of the exclusive Society of Antiquaries. Though he was born in London, Sandys, like Gilbert, was also "a member of a well-known family of Cornish gentlefolk."[14] In fact, "there was even a distant family connection, for Davies Gilbert was one of the coheirs of the Barony of Sandys."[15]

At the conclusion of his lengthy 143-page introduction to *Christmas Carols, Ancient and Modern,* Sandys speaks of his visits to Cornwall:

"But it is time to close this introduction which has imperceptibly almost, extended to a length that the subject will not sanction. We are apt to think that other persons take as much interest in our hobbies as ourselves, and therefore ride them unsparingly. Not that this has been any particular hobby, but rather an occasional amusement during some visits to the West of England [Cornwall], to collect any carols I could meet with. These gradually accumulated, and it was my intention, a few years since, to have printed a few of the most popular, but this was superseded by Mr. D. Gilbert having about the same time published his first edition. My number however still increasing, and the practice appearing to get more neglected every year, which will hereafter increase the difficulty of obtaining specimens, I determined to hazard the ensuing selection from a very large number of all descriptions."[16]

Sandys published the words for 80 carols (one of which is the popular "God Rest You Merry, Gentlemen") and the music for 18 tunes. As a result, he would become the first major collector of Christmas carols in the 19th century and a primary source for many subsequent collectors.[17] Furthermore, Sandys' publication, along with his book titled *Christmas-tide: its History, Festivities and Carols* (1852), would help to redefine Christmas in Victorian England.

Ironically, in a preface to a collection of works drawn from Gilbert and Sandys, the editor, Sir Richard Terry, noted that they both lacked basic knowledge about music and lived in a time when "the pursuit of music was considered 'no occupation for an English Gentleman.'"[18] In fact, both Gilbert and Sandys may have hired others to do their music notations. According to *The New Oxford Book of Carols*, the tunes in Sandys' collection were "amateurishly lithographed, with major omissions and mistakes."[19]

Our modern arrangement of "The First Noel" was made by John Stainer in *Christmas Carols Old and New* (1871) in which he "smoothed away all the rough places of the tune as given by Sandys."[20] For more on Stainer, see p. 202. Yet despite Stainer's fine work, the tune, like the words, has been criticized. Musicologist Erik Routley "describes the song as 'rather terrible' and points out that when it is sung in full, one two-line phrase is repeated twenty-seven times. 'It is repetitive to the point of hideous boredom.'"[21]

Further criticism has come from the suspected evolution of the tune. First off, it has a strong melodic link with Cornish wassail songs.[22] Wassail is a drink, and in its historic form, it is best compared to mulled ale (an alcoholic beverage heated with various spices). Thus, the tune may have descended from a "drinking song." Secondly, it appears to be pieced together from fragments of other songs. Though the tune is very similar to a version of the song discovered in 1913 (beginning "Nowell and Nowell"), there are also strains from an old English folk song titled "On Christmas Night All Christians Sing." Furthermore, the editors of *The New Oxford Book of Carols* suspect that as the song was transmitted orally, various voice parts were blended (for example, treble parts were infiltrated by the tenor tune). Thus when the song was finally documented, what began as a "mishearing" ended up "as a tune notated in someone's manuscript."[23]

Whatever professionals may say about the tune, it has rightly earned a permanent place in Christmas worship. Even if it has a connection to old drinking songs, men like Martin Luther and John Wesley believed that "the devil should never have all the good tunes,"[23] and this one has been claimed for a holy purpose. It gives us a joyful means by which to sing through the events of the marvelous Nativity story, culminating in the wonderful news: "Born is the King of Israel!"

[1] Dawson, William Francis. *Christmas: Its Origin and Associations.* E. Stock, 1902, p. 9.

[2] Osbeck, Kenneth. *Joy to the World! The Stories Behind Your Favorite Christmas Carols.* Kregel Publications, 1999, p. 86.

[3] Studwell, William. *The Christmas Carol Reader.* The Haworth Press, 1995, p. 63.

[4] Keyte, Hugh and Parrott, Andrew, editors. *The New Oxford Book of Carols.* Oxford University Press, 1998, p. 482.

[5] Anderson, Douglas D. *Biography of Davies Gilbert.* Retrieved September 14, 2008 from Hymns and Carols of Christmas: http://www.hymnsandcarolsofchristmas.com/Hymns_and_Carols/Biographies/davies_gilbert. htm.

[6] Encyclopedia Britannica. "Sir Humphry Davy" Retrieved September 14, 2008 from Encyclopedia Britannica Online: http://www.britannica.com/EBchecked/topic/152896/Sir-Humphry-Davy-Baronet/1741/Early-life#ref=ref172322.

[7] Anderson, Douglas D.

[8] Gilbert, Davies. *Some Ancient Christmas Carols.* John Nichols and Son, 1822, Preface.

[9] Keyte, Hugh and Parrott, Andrew, editors, p. 677.

[10] Keyte, Hugh and Parrott, Andrew, editors, p. 680.

[11] Studwell, William, p. 64.

[12] Studwell, William, p. 64.

[13] Brooks, Phillips. *Letters of Travel.* E.P. Dutton and Company, 1893, Letter Dated December 30, 1865, p. 69. Brooks' reference to "they" is not clear, but it seems that he is referring to the people living in Bethlehem.

[14] Keyte, Hugh and Parrott, Andrew, editors, p. 681.

[15] Keyte, Hugh and Parrott, Andrew, editors, p. 682.

[16] Sandys, William. *Christmas Carols, Ancient and Modern.* R. Beckley, 1833, Preface pp. cxlii-cxliii.

[17] Anderson, Douglas D. "Biography of William Sandys." Retrieved September 14, 2008 from Hymns and Carols of Christmas: http://www.hymnsandcarolsofchristmas.com/Hymns_and_Carols/Images/Sandys/ william_sandys.htm

[18] Terry, Sir Richard R., editor. *Gilbert and Sandys' Christmas Carols.* Burns, Oates & Washbourne, 1932, p. vi.

[19] Keyte, Hugh and Parrott, Andrew, editors, p. 681.

[20] Keyte, Hugh and Parrott, Andrew, editors, pp. 482.

[21] Bradley, Ian, editor. *The Penguin Book of Carols.* Penguin Books ,1999, p. 318 (quoting from Routley, Erik. *The English Carol.* Oxford University Press, 1959, p. 96.).

[22] Keyte, Hugh and Parrott, Andrew, editors, pp. 482.

[23] Keyte, Hugh and Parrott, Andrew, editors, pp. 482-483.

[24] Escew, Harry and McElrath, Hugh T. *Sing with Understanding.* Broadman Press, 1980, p. 125.

We Three Kings
of Orient Are

We Three Kings of Orient Are

THREE KINGS OF ORIENT
Words and Music: JOHN HENRY HOPKINS, JR.

Stately (♩ = 132)

1. We three kings of Or - i - ent are, bear - ing gifts we trav - erse a - far,
2. Born a king on Beth - le - hem plain, gold I bring to crown Him a - gain,
3. Frank - in - cense to of - fer have I, in - cense owns a de - i - ty nigh;
4. Myrrh is mine; its bit - ter per - fume breathes a life of gath - er - ing gloom;
5. Glo - rious now be - hold him a - rise, King and God and Sac - ri - fice;

field and foun - tain, moor and moun - tain, fol - low - ing yon - der star.
King for - ev - er, ceas - ing nev - er o - ver us all to reign.
prayer and prais - ing, all men rais - ing, wor - ship Him God on high.
sor - r'wing, sigh - ing, bleed - ing, dy - ing sealed in the stone - cold tomb.
heav'n sings hal - le - lu - jah: hal - le - lu - jah the earth re - plies.

Refrain

O_____ star of won - der star of night, star with roy - al beau - ty bright,

west - ward lead - ing, still pro - ceed - ing, guide us to thy per - fect light.

Word and Music "Three Kings of Orient" by John Henry Hopkins Jr. (1820-1891)

As mentioned in the discussion about Wise Men (see pp. 158-159), this song has been effective in perpetuating the belief that the Wise Men were three in number, were kings and were from the Orient. However, none of these descriptions are given in the Bible, and they may all be inaccurate. Regardless, the song is an American Christmas treasure, and it was one of only a handful of works to travel from the U.S. to Britain in the 19th century. In fact, it was "the sole North American contribution to [England's popular publication] *Christmas Carols, New and Old* in 1871."[1]

The song was written and composed by John Henry Hopkins Jr., son of John Henry Hopkins Sr. (1792-1868), the eighth presiding bishop of the Episcopal Church in the United States. Hopkins Jr. was born in Pittsburgh as one of 13 children. After earning his undergraduate degree at the University of Vermont in 1839, he moved to New York City to work as a reporter and prepare himself for a career in law. He returned to school in 1845 to earn a masters degree from the University of Virginia, but soon thereafter, he abandoned a career in law in order to follow his father's footsteps into ministry. Hopkins chose to enter the General Theological Seminary in New York where Clement Clark Moore, reputed author of "'Twas the Night Before Christmas," worked as a professor (see pp. 440-442). Moore was also the son of a bishop, Benjamin Moore, who served the Episcopal Diocese of New York.

After graduating from seminary in 1850, Hopkins held a variety of positions; he worked as a deacon, the first teacher of music at General Theological Seminary, a priest and an editor of the *Church Journal*. Of his extensive service, music historian Charles Hughes notes, "his distinctive contribution to his church was in the arts. . . . His talents for design were expressed in stained glass, Episcopal seals and other church forms. His hymn texts and tunes show him as a poet and musician."[2]

Two of Hopkins musical publications *Carols, Hymns and Songs* (1863) and *Canticles Noted with Accompanying Harmonies* (1866) enjoyed considerable success. He also published a number of hymns collected and translated by John Freeman Young (famous for his translation of "Silent Night," see pp. 275-277) in *Great Hymns of the Church* (1887). Hopkins and Young were "old and dear friends," and since Young was not able to complete his work due to his responsibilities as Bishop of Florida, his dying request was that Hopkins see his work "through to the press."[3]

Though many of Hopkins' original songs gained popularity, the song that would outlast all others was "We Three Kings of Orient Are." Some sources indicate that Hopkins wrote the song as part of a Christmas pageant for the General Theological Seminary (where he served as a music teacher). Other sources indicate that the song was intended for a family celebration. Every year, Hopkins' extended family would gather together at his father's house in Vermont for the holidays. Though Hopkins did not marry or have children of his own, he dearly loved his nieces and nephews, and he may have written the song for their pleasure and entertainment. Of course, it is possible that Hopkins wrote the song with both venues in mind — the Christmas pageant, as well as his family gathering. Though the work was composed in 1857, it was not published until 1863 in Hopkins *Carols, Hymns and Songs*.[4]

Hopkins' publication reveals that he wrote his song for the voices of three "Wise Men." Verses 1 and 5 were intended for a trio, and verses 2, 3 and 4 were designed as solos (verse 2 was assigned to Gaspard, verse 3 to Melchoir and verse 4 to Balthazar — variant spellings for the most common traditional names given to the Wise Men). Hopkins wrote, "Men's voices are best for the parts of the Three Kings, but the music is set in the G clef for the accommodation of children."[5]

Though we don't have any details on the first dramatization of the song, *The New Oxford Book of Carols* makes an interesting point about modern performances. Often, the song is sung as the Wise Men present their gifts to Jesus. The words, however, indicate that the Wise Men are "traveling, looking forward to the King."[6] Even the tune "imparts the sensation of continuous motion analogous to the long journey of the Wise Men."[7]

The words of the song convey more than just the hope of meeting a king; they describe the unique identity of a particular King. Hopkins artistically incorporates an ancient tradition that the gifts of the Wise Men symbolically reveal Christ's identity: Gold represents his royalty, frankincense represents his priesthood and deity, and myrrh represents his role as the Messiah and the sacrifice for sin (see more on pp. 161-162). Hopkins also remembers to draw attention to the miraculous event in the sky. By focusing the refrain on the "star of wonder," he emphasizes how even the heavens point to the "perfect light."

Apart from the first line of the song, Hopkins' accurately gives an account of the Wise Men as found in Matthew 2, and he effectively incorporates foundational truth about Jesus into his lyrics. Perhaps in honor of Hopkins' expressed wish to leave his text unaltered, it has remained, for the most part, in its original form. In his preface to *Carols, Hymns and Songs* (1863), he wrote:

"Compilers of other Collections are at liberty to transfer any of the pieces in this little volume, provided they leave what they take *unaltered*. If any change be made in either words or music without my permission, I shall prosecute the offender to the extent of the law."[8]

Though various publications have made minor alterations to the text (the original text is included here), the first words remain intact despite their errors. A more accurate rendering might be "Wise Men From the East We Are," but the words are now virtually impossible to change. Though most people probably could not sing this song in its entirety by memory, they generally remember the first line. The title of the tune, by the way, *Three Kings of Orient*, is derived from the first line and was the name given by Hopkins in his original publication.

Despite the errors perpetuated by the first line of the song regarding the identity of the Wise Men (their number, their position, and their place of origin), the focus of the song is really on the identity of the one they sought to worship, the glorious "King and God and Sacrifice." May we join with the Wise Men in seeking and worshipping him!

[1] Bradley, Ian, editor. *The Penguin Book of Carols*. Penguin Books, 1999, p. 377.

[2] Hughes, Charles W. *American Hymns Old and New, Notes on the Hymns and Biographies of the Authors and Composers*. Columbia University Press, 1980, p. 436.

[3] Hopkins Jr., John Henry, editor. *Great Hymns of the Church*. James Portt & Company, 1887, Preface.

[4] Hughes, Charles W., p. 263

[5] Hopkins Jr., John Henry. *Carols, Hymns and Songs*. Church Book Depository, 1863, p. 12.

[6] Keyte, Hugh and Parrott, Andrew, editors. *The New Oxford Book of Carols*. Oxford University Press, 1998, p. 358.

[7] Studwell, William. *The Christmas Carol Reader*. The Haworth Press, 1995, p. 77.

[8] Hopkins Jr., John Henry. *Carols, Hymns and Songs,* Preface.

What Child is This?

What Child Is This?

Words: WILLIAM CHATTERTON DIX

GREENSLEEVES
Music: ENGLISH MELODY
Arranged by: JOHN STAINER

1. What Child is this, who, laid to rest, on Mary's lap is sleep-ing? Whom
2. Why lies he in such mean es-tate where ox and ass are feed-ing? Good
3. So bring him in-cense, gold, and myrrh, come peas-ant, king to own him; the

an-gels greet with an-thems sweet, while shep-herds watch are keep-ing?
Christ-ian, fear, for sin-ners here the si-lent Word is plead-ing.
King of kings sal-va-tion brings, let lov-ing hearts en-throne him.

This, this is Christ the King, whom shep-herds guard and an-gels sing;
Nails, spear shall pierce him through, the cross be borne for me, for you.
Raise, raise the song on high, the Vir-gin sings her lul-la-by.

haste, haste to bring him laud, the Babe, the Son of Ma-ry.
Hail, hail the Word made flesh, the Babe, the Son of Ma-ry.
Joy, joy for Christ is born, the Babe, the Son of Ma-ry.

Words by William Chatterton Dix (1837-1898)

William Chatterton Dix was born in Bristol, England. His father John Ross Dix (1800-1865) was a reputable surgeon, as well as a prolific writer. Dix's father mainly published short biographies of notable people in literature, ministry and politics; one book focused exclusively on his favorite English poet, "The Life of Thomas Chatterton" (1851). It was in honor of this poet that William Dix received his middle name.

Like his father, Dix grew to love literature. Though his education at the Bristol Grammar School (comparable to a K-12 school in the U.S.) was designed to prepare him for a commercial career, the school offered a well rounded education, and Dix was trained in the liberal arts. Despite his interest in literature, Dix proved to be ambitious, and after completing his education, he took a position managing a marine insurance company in Glasgow, Scotland. However, soon thereafter, he became seriously ill and was confined to bed for an extended period of time. This was a devastating blow to an energetic man in his early 20s, and Dix fell into a deep depression. It was in his sorrow that he met God in a new and intimate way, and the heart of a poet was more fully formed in him.

Dix began to write verses during his illness, and one of the songs he penned at this time was "As With Gladness Men of Old" (1860); it is still sung during the Christmas season. Once Dix recovered from his illness, he returned to work and remained there for many years to come. But he continued to write, and over the course of his life, he produced more than 40 beautiful hymns. He published a collection of his work in *A Vision of All Saints, and Other Poems* (1871) and wrote *The Pattern Life or, Lessons for Children from the Life of our Lord* (1885). Of all his fine work, the song "What Child Is This?" has proven to be the most enduring, at least in America; it is rarely sung anymore in Dix's native England.[1]

Dix's song "What Child Is This?" written around 1865, asks "one of the most important questions ever to confront the human mind";[2] essentially, the question is: "Who is Jesus?" Dix was probably familiar with how depression can cause a debilitating self focus that asks questions like: "Why is this happening to <u>me</u>? Why doesn't anybody care about <u>me</u>? Who am <u>I</u> anyway?" Yet, as we learn to raise our eyes beyond ourselves and up to heaven, despair begins to melt away. Asking the question, "Who is Jesus?," focuses our attention on him and away from the "worries of this life" (Matthew 13:22). Perhaps it was this very question that helped to draw Dix out of his depression. Recognizing and responding to the reality of Jesus' identity can have a powerful effect. John MacArthur, author and pastor, writes:

"The answers [to this question] are myriad. Some have said He was a good and wise teacher. But good and wise teachers do not claim to be the God of the universe. Some say He was a classic example of human virtue. But good examples don't spend their time with prostitutes, drunkards, dirty politicians, and social riffraff. Some say He was a religious madman. But delusional minds and self-styled religious leaders don't speak the clear profound, gracious words He spoke – nor do they offer up their lives for others. Some think he was a deliberate deceiver. But a deceiver who died would stay dead. Some say He was only a myth and that the whole story is just a legend. But myths don't set the calendar for all of human history."[3]

What child is this? The carol answers with a profound paradox. On the one hand, he is just a "babe, the son of Mary," born in humble circumstances, human just like us. On the other hand, he is the "Word made flesh," salvation for mankind, the King of the Universe! Understanding who Jesus is requires a response. In the words of Dallas Willard, noted author and professor of philosophy, "When we see Jesus as he is, we must [either] turn away or else shamelessly adore him."[4]

Music "Greensleeves" arranged by John Stainer (1840-1901)

The tune "Greensleeves" was first registered in England in the year 1580 as a ballad entitled "A New Northerne Dittye of the Lady Greensleeves."[5] The oldest copy of the song reveals that it was about a lover lamenting his rejection by the Lady Greensleeves:

"Alas, my love, you do me wrong,
To cast me off discourteously.
For I have loved you well and long,
Delighting in your company.

"Greensleeves was all my joy
Greensleeves was my delight,
Greensleeves was my heart of gold,
And who but my lady greensleeves."[6]

There is evidence to suggest that when the song was registered, the tune (as well as different variations of the words) had already attained popularity in England. It appears that the song existed during the life of Henry VIII (1491-1547), and there are even claims that Henry composed it. The attribution is unlikely, however, and may stem from confusion with "Green Grow'th the Holly," a song that Henry may in fact have authored. According to music historian William Studwell:

"King Henry VIII of England (1491-1547) is a figure of both great fame and enormous notoriety. He is well known for his major role in the development of early modern England and in the conversion of England to Protestantism. He is equally well known for his egotism, his indulgent lifestyle, and his many wives. Lesser known, though, was his skill in sports and music. . . . It is quite possible that Henry composed the tune for 'Green Grow'th the Holly' and quite doubtful that he was responsible for 'Greensleeves.' If this immodest man had written 'Greensleeves,' it seems unlikely that its 'anonymous' label would ever have surfaced. The chances are much better for his being erroneously attributed as the author than for his authorship being overlooked or forgotten. Perhaps the presence of 'Green' at the beginning of the titles of both songs was a factor in the genesis of this myth."[7]

Most likely the tune was "one of several melodies that developed over the standard Italian dance basses which came to England around 1550."[8] It attained such popularity that "there is scarcely a collection of old English songs in which at least one may not be found to the tune of *Green Sleeves*."[9] Even Shakespeare (c.1564-1616) mentions the tune in his play *The Merry Wives of Windsor,* written around 1602. His character Mistress Alice Ford refers to the tune, and his comic knight, Sir John Falstaff, exclaims, "Let the sky rain potatoes! Let it thunder to the tune of *Green Sleeves*."[10]

It is not clear who joined Dix's lyrics with the tune *Greensleeves*. It may have been John Stainer (see p. 202) whose arrangement in *Christmas Carols Old and New* (1871) popularized the song. Regardless of who was responsible for the marriage, it is interesting to consider the difference between the old and new words. In complete contrast to the Lady Greensleeves, who cast off love discourteously, is a God who demonstrated his great love with action. He entered the world and willingly gave up his life to offer salvation to those who believe in him. May his people "with loving hearts enthrone him."

---

[1] Keyte, Hugh and Parrott, Andrew, editors. *The New Oxford Book of Carols.* Oxford University Press, 1998, p. 355.

[2] MacArthur, John, Eareckson Tada, Wolgemuth, Robert and Bobbie. *O Come, All Ye Faithful.* Crossway Books, 2001, p. 51.

[3] MacArthur, John, Eareckson Tada, Wolgemuth, Robert and Bobbie, p. 51.

[4] Williard, Dallas. *The Divine Conspiracy: Rediscovering Our Hidden Life in God.* Harper Collins, 1998, p. 19.

[5] Chappell, William. *The Ballad Literature and Popular Music of the Olden Time.* Chappell & Co., 1859, p. 227.

[6] Chappell, William, p. 230.

[7] Studwell, William. *The Christmas Carol Reader.* The Haworth Press, 1995, p. 36.

[8] Bradley, Ian, editor. *The Penguin Book of Carols.* Penguin Books, 1999, p. 382.

[9] Chappell, William, p. 232.

[10] Shakespeare, William. *The Merry Wives of Windsor: A Comedy.* G. Bell and Sons, 1886, Act II, Scene I, p. 28 and Act V, Scene V, pp. 115-116.

While Shepherds Watched Their Flocks

While Shepherds Watched Their Flocks

Words: NAHUM TATE

CHRISTMAS
Music: GEORGE FRIDERIC HANDEL

Moderately (♩ = 96)

1. While shep-herds watched their flocks by night, all seat-ed on the
2. "Fear not!" said he, for might-y dread had seized their trou-bled
3. "To you in Da-vid's town, this day is born of Da-vid's
4. "The heav'n-ly Babe you there shall find to hu-man view dis-
5. Thus spake the ser-aph, and forth-with ap-peared a shin-ing
6. "All glo-ry be to God on high, and to the earth be

ground, the an-gel of the Lord came down, and
mind; "Glad ti-dings of great joy I bring to
line the Sa-vior, who is Christ the Lord, and
played, all mean-ly wrapped in swath-ing bands, and
throng of an-gels prais-ing God, who thus ad-
peace; good will hence-forth from heav'n to men be-

glo-ry shone a-round, and glo-ry shone a-round.
you and all man-kind, to you and all man-kind!"
this shall be the sign, and this shall be the sign."
in a man-ger laid, and in a man-ger laid."
dressed their joy-ful song, ad-dressed their joy-ful song.
gin and ne-ver cease, be-gin and nev-er cease!"

Words by Nahum Tate (1652-1715)

The hymn "While Shepherds Watched Their Flocks" first appeared in the *Supplement* (1700) to *The New Version of the Psalms of David* (1696) produced by Nicholas Brady and Nahum Tate. Though the hymn is not attributed, it "seems to have been universally assumed from the time of the hymn's earliest appearances" that it was written by Nahum Tate.[1]

Tate was the son of an Irish Protestant clergyman named, literally, Faithful Teate. Both of his grandfathers were clergymen as well. Faithful Teate was forced to flee during the Irish Rebellion of 1641, and he spent a number of years in England. As a result, Nahum Tate's "whereabouts during his childhood are uncertain; he seems to have spent periods of time in both England and Ireland."[2]

After graduating from Trinity College in Dublin in 1672, Tate decided to pursue a literary career. He moved to London and published his first book of poems in 1677 (having altered his last name from "Teate" to "Tate"). He began writing plays the following year. Though his first few plays were not successful, he "seized a treasure" when he began reworking some of Shakespeare's neglected plays.[3] His version of King Lear, with a happy ending, was remarkably successful. For 150 years, audiences preferred Tate's version to the original Shakespearean tragedy.

Tate's next major literary effort was his contribution to the second part of John Dryden's poem *Absalom and Achitophel* (1682), a political satire. Dryden (1631-1700) was an influential poet, literary critic and playwright, who dominated the literary life of England to such a degree that the period came to be known as the "Age of Dryden." It is significant that Dryden actually encouraged Tate to write the sequel to his poem. Clearly, Dryden recognized Tate's aptitude in poetry.

Tate continued to write plays and even wrote the words for a successful opera, *Dido and Aeneas* (1689). His contributions to the arts were so significant that in 1692, Tate was named poet laureate of England; he held this position for 22 years, serving during the dual reign of William and Mary (1689-1694), the sole reign of William (1694-1702) and the subsequent reign of Queen Anne (1702-1714).

Tate's next major contribution to poetry was for the Church of England. In collaboration with Nicholas Brady, a high-profile clergyman and royal chaplain, Tate produced *A New Version of the Psalms of David* (1696). For over 100 years, the Church of England had relied on the *Sternhold and Hopkins Psalter* (1562) for corporate worship. "In contrast to the strict metrical rendering of the *Old Version* of Sternhold and Hopkins, the *New Version* made a freer and more polished literary paraphrase of the psalms."[4]

The *New Version* was dedicated to King William who, with his council in 1696, judged it as "allowed and permitted to be used in all Churches, Chappels, and Congregations, as shall think fit to receive the same"; it was also recommended by the Archbishop of Canterbury and many other church leaders.[5] The *Supplement* of the *New Version* was authorized by Queen Anne in 1703.[6] Yet, despite these significant endorsements, Brady and Tate were not spared from controversy. In fact in

301

his *Essay on Psalmody* (1710), Tate had to spend considerable energy responding to criticism of the *New Version*. It was condemned for being "flourished with wit and fancy," being too "gay and fashionable," and "breaching the uniformity" that existed when there was just one version of the psalms.[7] Reportedly one old man said, "David speaks so plain that we cannot mistake his meaning, but as for Mr. Tate and Brady, they have taken away my Lord, and I know not where they have laid him."[8]

Clearly, the *New Version* was not universally accepted at first; according to *The New Oxford Book of Carols*, it "was used primarily by those who were most ready to sing hymns along with the psalms, particularly the churches of London. Indeed the polished metrical hymns of Tate and Brady seemed much more like hymns than those of older psalters."[9] However, with time, the *New Version* would prove to be remarkably successful. Having been sanctioned by monarchs and church leaders alike, it was "routinely bound up with copies of *The Book of Common Prayer* [and] disseminated across the country."[10] Furthermore, Tate and Brady are credited with paving the way for men like Isaac Watts who "struggled toward a lyrical freedom within the tradition of scriptural paraphrase."[11] For more on Watts, see pp. 233-235.

Tate's metrical paraphrase of Luke 2:8-14, "While Shepherds Watched Their Flocks" (originally titled "Song of the Angels"), was one of 16 hymns that appeared in the 1700 *Supplement* of the *New Version*. It was the only Christmas hymn to gain official approval in the Church of England until Charles Wesley's hymn "Hark the Herald Angels Sing" was added in a 1782 edition of the *New Version*.

Tate showed unique genius in writing the lyrics of his Christmas hymn. Not only did he carefully paraphrase the biblical narrative of the angelic appearance to shepherds (as recorded in Luke 2:8-20), he demonstrated great insight in selecting the passage. The Church of his day was exclusively singing psalms of David (the famous shepherd of Bethlehem who later became king of Israel). In a cautious attempt to introduce a New Testament hymn, Tate wisely chose a passage that drew a connection to David. Tate's paraphrase of Luke 2:11 is: "To you in David's town this day is born of David's line the Savior who is Christ the Lord." The long-awaited descendant of King David (Jesus) was born in the town of David (Bethlehem). Furthermore, Tate selected the biblical passage that recorded the first Christmas song in history — the "joyful song" sung by "angels praising God." According the *The New Oxford Book of Carols*, Tate's work is the first known and "one of the finest" hymnic descriptions of this great event.[12]

Though Tate was respected for his modesty and good nature, he apparently fell victim to excessive drinking; he was also accused of unwise spending habits. These flaws of character may be explained by the possibility that when Queen Anne died in 1714, Tate was suddenly and unexpectedly cut off from his financial means of 22 years. Sadly, Tate's life ended the following year in a debtor's refuge in London. Though he died penniless, Tate left posterity with a rich and beautiful legacy of worship.

Music "Christmas" by George Frideric Handel (1685-1759)

"While Shepherds Watched Their Flocks By Night" was written in common meter, which allowed for a wide number of tunes to be drawn upon. According to *The New Oxford Book of Carols:*

"No other hymn has been sung to so many tunes and settings. . . .The hymn's common measure was only one reason for its vast number of tunes. Another was its status in the Church of England as the only legally authorized Christmas hymn."[13]

Over 100 tunes have been identified in printed sources, and there were probably more.[14] Yet the tune most widely sung in the U.S. is adapted from a melody in the opera *Siroë, King of Persia*, composed by George Frideric Handel (1685-1759) and first performed in 1728. For more on Handel, see pp. 242-244. No one is certain who married the words and the music, but the editors of *The New Oxford Book of Carols* suspect it was Lowell Mason. For more on Mason, see pp. 235-237. Since the hymn beautifully retells the Gospel story about the first song to ever praise the birth of Christ, the tune is appropriately named "Christmas."

---

[1] Keyte, Hugh and Parrott, Andrew, editors. The New Oxford Book of Carols. Oxford University Press, 1998, p. 143.

[2] Corman, Brian. "Nahum Tate". *The Literary Encyclopedia*. Retrieved September 22, 2008: http://www.litencyc.com/php/speople.php?rec=true&UID=4317.

[3] Corman, Brian.

[4] Escew, Harry and McElrath, Hugh T. *Sing with Understanding*. Broadman Press, 1980, p. 109.

[5] Escew, Harry and McElrath, Hugh T.

[6] Julian, John, editor. *A Dictionary of Hymnology*. Dover Publications Inc., 1957, p. 919.

[7] Julian, John, editor. The quotes are from a vigorous protest written by Beveridge in 1710 against the *New Version*.

[8] Millar, Patrick. *The Story of the Church's Song*. Originally Published in 1927. Read Books, 2007, p. 100.

[9] Escew, Harry and McElrath, Hugh T.

[10] Keyte, Hugh and Parrott, Andrew, editors. *The New Oxford Book of Carols*. Oxford University Press, 1998, p. 143.

[11] Escew, Harry and McElrath, Hugh T., p. 118.

[12] Escew, Harry and McElrath, Hugh T., p. 118.

[13] Keyte, Hugh and Parrott, Andrew, editors.

[14] Bradley, Ian, editor. *The Penguin Book of Carols*. Penguin Books, 1999, p. 396.

Stories

TALES & VERSES OF CHRISTMAS

A Bethlehem Shepherd

The Background
Bodie and Brock Thoene, Contemporary
Historical Fiction, First Century Story

The following account is an excerpt from the book *First Light*, part of the A.D. Chronicles series by Bodie and Brock Thoene (a wife and husband team). The story is "historical fiction" and is set during the first century in which Jesus lived. Historical people play key roles, and though fictional details fill in the gaps of the historical record, they do not contradict the facts.

The Thoenes are exceptionally talented writers in their genre. Brock is a history enthusiast with advanced degrees in both history and education, and Bodie is a gifted writer with degrees in journalism and communications. Together they have produced over 45 works of historical fiction. The Thoene's writing experience, respective skill sets, and personal interest in Judaism have all combined to uniquely equip them for their series on the life of Christ. They bring the ancient biblical record to life like no other, carefully weaving together historical records, ancient traditions and creativity to produce literary masterpieces.

Admittedly, it is easy to read through the Bible and forget that it contains stories about real people with real emotions and struggles (many not unlike our own). Imagine what it must have been like to see and know Jesus during his life on earth. To help give us insight into the people and events of this period, the Thoenes skillfully develop a character named Zadok, a shepherd in first century Bethlehem. Though he was blessed to experience the glorious angelic announcement of Christ's birth, he was soon thereafter to endure an unthinkable tragedy -- Herod's decree to "kill all the boys in Bethlehem and is vicinity who were two years old and under" (Matthew 2:16). Most likely, the real shepherds of Bethlehem were all touched in some way by this horrific event.

In the below excerpt, the fictional character Zadok is called before the Sanhedrin (a council of Jewish leaders) to be questioned about Jesus after he had begun his earthly ministry. When Zadok comes to stand before the Sanhedrin, he is identified as the Chief Shepherd of Israel. Interestingly, the shepherds near Bethlehem probably tended sheep that were sacrificed in the Jerusalem temple for the sin of the people. Thus, it is reasonable to imagine that one of the shepherds of the Nativity story could have risen to play a "chief" role among shepherds.

There are several other characters that are mentioned by name in the following excerpt. One is Gamaliel, a historical person who is mentioned in the book of Acts as a teacher of Judaism to the Apostle Paul (Acts 22:3) and as a respected member of the Sanhedrin (Acts 5:34). Tradition holds that he was the son of Simeon, the man who was moved by the Spirit to find the infant Jesus in the temple courts; Simeon held Jesus and said, "Sovereign Lord, as you have promised, you now dismiss your servant in peace. For my eyes have seen your salvation" (Luke 2:29-30). Another character is Peniel, a fictional name given to the blind man that Jesus healed in John 9:1-41. Lastly, note that Jewish names are used for John the Baptist (Yochanan the Baptizer) and Jesus (Yeshua).

May you be moved by this account of Christ's birth as told by a Bethlehem shepherd!

The Story
Reading Time: 10 minutes

The three-story structure called Nicanor Gate towered above Peniel's porch. Besides framing the division between the Court of Women and the Court of the Israelites, the massive archway also housed offices and conference rooms.

The lesser Sanhedrin usually held it's meeting in the Chamber of Hewn Stone, west of the sanctuary proper. Due to ongoing renovations in that hall, today's assembly of twenty-three members plus witnesses and guests convened in a second-floor chamber directly over Peniel's head.

Any speaker addressing the assembly stood at an angle between two windows. An overhanging cornice deflected the sound downward, so Peniel, with his acute hearing, took in every word as if he had been in the room himself.

This afternoon Gamaliel addressed the company. "Given the disturbances throughout the land," the rabbi said, "it is important for us, as elders of Israel, to understand what is taking place. Many times in the past, popular leaders have arisen, and many of them have claimed the title *Messiah.* Some have lost their followers and faded away; others have brought bloody retribution on their heads. But never in our history have so many been spoken of in connection with the Holy One of Israel as has lately been true. The rebel, bar Abba, has been proclaimed by some. So was Yochanan the Baptizer. And so has Yeshua of Nazareth."

Peniel heard the murmuring within the chamber swell in volume and hostility until it bubbled from the window.

"Decrying such claims as mere rabble-rousing and deploring them as politically dangerous doesn't serve any good purpose," Gamaliel chided. "There remain two fundamental questions: Is it possible that the true Messiah is alive? And if so, who is he?"

"How can we know?" a strident voice unknown to Peniel demanded.

"All the signs are in place," Gamaliel responded. "Here is one simple, straightforward indication: Just as it was fourteen generations from Avraham to David and fourteen generations from David to the Exile, so also have passed another fourteen generations from the Exile to our own day."[1]

The sounds of scoffing did not escape Peniel's notice. Then came a sharper rebuke from the high priest. "But Messiah will reveal himself by unmistakable signs, not like any of these imposters!"

"My father, Simeon, of revered memory," Gamaliel replied, "told me that he held the infant Messiah in his arms...here, on this sacred mountain."

The level of whispered commentary dropped dramatically.

"My father said it happened about the same time that King Herod, the butcher king, destroyed the genealogy records stored in the Temple archives-an infamous deed that many in this assembly may recall. Some thirty or thirty-two years ago it was, yet my father's words remain with me: These are the words Simeon spoke to Adonai, 'Sovereign Lord, as you have promised, you may dismiss your servant in peace. For my eyes have seen your salvation.'"[2]

"Then where is he?" Caiaphas insisted. "He would be old enough to be known to us all."

Peniel could almost hear Gamaliel's nod. "Though my father is not living to speak on his own behalf," Gamaliel said, "there is one here whom my father called the first witness: Zadok, Chief Shepherd of Israel."

After calls of welcome subsided, Peniel heard Zadok's gruff country twang: "I haven't spoken of these things before because of a vow binding me to silence. I've only lately been freed of that bond, so yer among the first to hear my story. It was on this wise: Thirty-two years ago this lambing season was the census decreed by Caesar Augustus. And everyone went to his own town to register. Now a man named Joseph went up to Bethlehem, because he belonged to the house and line of David's."

Murmurs of remembrance accompanied Zadok's words.

"He went there to register with Mary, who was pledged to be married to him and was expecting child. While they were there, the time came for the baby to be born, and she gave birth to her first-born, a son. She wrapped him in cloths and placed him in a manger, because there was no room for them in the inn."

Peniel imagined the scene. It must have been very hard to travel during the wet season of the year. And with the whole country in flux because of the Roman census, it was easy to imagine how a young, poor couple might find themselves in an awful predicament, like having a baby in a stable.

"I was on duty in the fields," Zadok continued. "I was a young shepherd attached to getting the Temple sacrificial lambs ready for Passover. About the middle watch of the night something amazing happened: An angel appeared to us. Not just to me, but to all the shepherds in charge of Temple flocks with me."

There was a lull in both Zadok's testimony and in the response of his audience. Skeptical men of the world were inclined to discount miraculous visions, yet the history of the Jews was full of such tales. Nor was the Chief Shepherd of Israel a voice to be taken lightly.

Zadok resumed, apparently satisfied that no immediate rebuttal was coming. "This angel appeared, surrounded by the glory of the Lord. I don't mind tellin' y', I was frightened! Terrified! Bright as sun at noonday, he was. With shining face and booming voice. And he said, 'Do not be afraid. I bring you good news of great joy that will be for all the people. Today in the town of David a Savior has been born to you; he is Christ the Lord.'"

The hum of comment overflowed the room like water from a too full basin, so much so that Zadok raised his voice to be heard over the top of it: "'This will be a sign to you,' the angel said. 'You'll find the baby wrapped in cloths and lying in a manger.' Then suddenly a great company of the heavenly host appeared with the angel, praising God and saying, 'Glory to God in the highest, and on earth peace to men on whom his favor rests.'"

"Why have we never heard this before?" challenged a deep, angry voice.

"I heard it," Peniel heard Gamaliel respond. "From my father. But in courtesy to our guest, let

Zadok finish. Save your questions for after."

The muttering simmered down again.

Zadok continued, "Now after the angels left, we shepherds said to each other, 'Let's go to Bethlehem and see this thing that has happened, which the Lord has told us about.' So we hurried off and found Mary and Joseph and the baby, who was lyin' in the manger. It was just as the angel said."[3]

"The next day we took the lambs here to the Temple. Did we speak of it? What do y' think? We told everyone! When the delivery was made we stayed here in the courts, tellin' the story over and over. Old Simeon, Gamaliel's father, was one who came and listened and listened. He quizzed me special, to see if he could find any prank to my tale, or if we had drunk too much wine and dreamed it. But he could not, because we spoke the truth! Later he told me that he himself met the young couple and held the baby when they brought him here for his circumcision."

"Then who is he?" many voices clamored. "If the learned Rabbi Simeon was there to hear him named, who is he? Is he alive today?"

"A moment more," Zadok insisted. "My story's not yet finished. My wife, Rachel, and I gave the family a place to live...." Zadok's words trailed away, but not before Peniel detected that the shepherd was in the grip of powerful emotion. When Zadok spoke again, Peniel heard the tremor of grief. "Herod likewise heard about the birth. But he wanted no rival king of Israel, not even a future one if not of his own choosin'! So he sent his butchers to slaughter the boy babies two years and younger. Burst in at night they did, and they killed...they murdered...my babies, my own dear sons!" At the memory a sigh as gaping as a grave escaped the shepherd.

"I fought them...to no use," Zadok finished. "Left me with this scar on my face to remember it, every day for the rest of my life."

"But the child?" Caiaphas hissed. "Was he killed? What become of him? Did he escape?"

Controlling his voice with evident struggles, Zadok answered, "The boy's father was warned in a dream to take his family and flee to Egypt. I alone knew their destination; I alone knew their secret. And I have kept it all these years."[4]

Again there was silence in the chamber as the assembly, and Peniel, took it in. Zadok might have saved his children, his own flesh and blood, if he had betrayed the whereabouts of the baby. He had protected a stranger, but at a horrific cost.

Finally the elders could stand the suspense no longer. One after another, several of them shouted, "Who is he? Where is he? Tell us!"

Peniel too was anxious to hear the conclusion.

"He's alive," Zadok declared. "He walks among us and has released me from my vow. He is... Yeshua of Nazareth."

The torrent of derision, wonder, disbelief, and exclamation drowned every previous comment. The tumult was so furious that passersby on the steps of Nicanor stopped to stare up at the window. The uproar buried conversations taking place around the courtyard.

Several minutes passed before the racket subsided, and then Peniel heard an oily, placating tone address Zadok. "Clearly the Chief Shepherd can be excused for such an ill-timed joke. Obviously he does not know that comments in support of Yeshua the charlatan are expressly forbidden."

Zadok's voice again quavered in the grasp of intense passion, but Peniel recognized this expression as barely controlled rage. "Do y' think I'm jokin'?" Zadok thundered. "Not a day of my whole life has passed since, that I have not longed to see that baby grown a man and come into his own! Still more: Do y' imagine I'd change my story to suit the likes of you? to change the truth for a lie because of fear of yer disapproval? By the Almighty, if I did not waver then, why would I draw back now?"

Inwardly Peniel applauded the old man. What power in his words, his convictions! How impressed Peniel was with the way Zadok stood up to them.

"Anyone supporting the claims of Yeshua of Nazareth will be put out of the synagogue," the high priest warned. "We make allowance for you, as Chief Shepherd, because of your age, your good service, and your painful family history. But you are strictly enjoined to keep it to yourself. You may not speak of it to anyone else, under pain of severe penalty."

Zadok's words were daggers, lancing a precise, razor-sharp response. "His secret I have kept for two and thirty years, no matter what penalty was applied. I will do as he wills, if it is to speak or no, whenever and wherever he chooses, and no threats will stop me!"

Taken from *First Light* by Bodie and Brock Thoene. Copyright © 2003 by Bodie and Brock Thoene. Used by permission of Tyndale House Publishers, Inc. All rights reserved.

---

[1] Matthew 1:17

[2] Luke 2:29-30

[3] Luke 2:1-15

[4] Matthew 2

A Christmas Carol,
The End of It

The Background
Charles Dickens, 1812-1870
Classic, 19ᵗʰ Century Story

Charles John Huffam Dickens was born in England to John Dickens and Elizabeth Barrow. Though Dickens' paternal grandparents were servants, "their position in the household of a rich landowner was a senior one which gave [Dickens' father] many advantages, some of which may have been damaging to his future;" essentially, Dickens' father became acquainted with a life that "made him feel that he himself was a gentleman, occupying a higher social position than he was fated to inhabit."[1]

Dickens' father began a career at the Navy Pay Office and was introduced to Elizabeth Barrow through a friend at work. The couple fell in love, married and had eight children; Charles was the second born, and his childhood appears to have been a happy one. He was initially educated by his mother who, by all accounts, was a lively person and an imaginative storyteller, and though Charles' father was a committed family man, he was also financially careless. He tried to live a lifestyle that he could not afford, and by 1823, the family finances were in crisis.

A defining moment for Dickens came in 1824 when at age 12 he was sent to work in a factory. His job consisted of sticking labels on bottles of shoe polish. Shortly thereafter, his father was imprisoned for debt. For lack of other options, the rest of the family (except Charles) joined him in prison. With the little money that Charles earned during his long days at work, he was able to rent a room and provide some money to his family. According to his biography in the *Literary Encyclopedia*:

> "There is no doubt that this experience had the most profound effect on Dickens' character and inner life. The disruption of his family, his expectations of being properly educated, his sense of himself as destined for some kind of respectable job and position in society were all swept aside in the degradation of being reduced to the status of a little labourer."[2]

During this time, "the seeds of ambition were sown," and Dickens determined "never to share the fate of his father."[3] He also developed a deep compassion for others, particularly lost or abandoned children, who were often left to work in the dreadful conditions that he experienced first hand. Furthermore, Dickens would carry into adulthood a disdain for anyone who took advantage of others in the pursuit of wealth or power.

Fortunately, after only a few months in prison, Dickens' father obtained an inheritance and secured his release from prison. But Dickens' mother did not immediately remove him from his factory work, and he would never completely forgive her for this. Eventually, he was able to return to school, but after only two more years of education, Dickens' family was evicted from their home for unpaid rent.[4] This time, Dickens would enter the workforce permanently at age 15. Luckily, he was able to get a decent job working as a lawyer's clerk, and in his spare time, he learned shorthand, which later secured him a job as a staff reporter for the *Morning Chronicle* newspaper. From this point forward, Dickens' family would often rely on him for financial support.

On his 18th birthday, Dickens acquired a pass to the British Museum, and he began a rigorous program of self-education. He also regularly attended the theater and organized his own amateur productions on the side. This same year he fell in love with Maria Beadnall, but her parents did not approve of him (either socially or financially). Consequently, they sent her off to school in Paris. This was another experience that would profoundly impact Dickens' writing. According to the *Literary Encyclopedia,* "It fuelled his determination to succeed while serving as yet another example of how money, class and power made their way into even the apparent privacy of the emotional life."[5] But Dickens did not waste much time mourning. Shortly after "losing" Maria, he met and married Catherine Hogarth and eventually had ten children with her.

Marriage appears to have had a positive effect on Dickens, and his career as a journalist began to expand into more creative writing. Beginning in 1833, he started to publish short essays in newspapers and magazines under the pseudonym "Boz." Dickens mainly wrote about lower middle class life in London, and his popular work was first collected and published in 1836 as *Sketches by Boz.* Dickens' next project, the *Pickwick Papers,* was a comic work "concerning the misadventures of a group of urban middle class gentlemen in attempting country pursuits for which they had no skills."[6] The work was published in 19 monthly parts from 1836 to 1837 and turned out to be a phenomenal success. It was one of the best sellers in the history of English literature, and it established Dickens as the most popular writer of his time.

From then on, Dickens began actively producing novels. Most of them were serialized in monthly magazines (meaning that only one chapter would be released at a time), and Dickens had a public who eagerly awaited each installment. Some of the most notable are: *Oliver Twist* (1837-39), *Nicholas Nickleby* (1838-39), *Martin Chuzzlewit* (1843-1844), *David Copperfied* (1849-50), *A Tale of Two Cities* (1859), and *Great Expectations* (1860-61).

Dickens was also widely regarded for the Christmas stories he produced almost every year from 1843 to 1867. The first, and most popular of these stories was *A Christmas Carol,* reportedly conceived and written in only a few weeks. According to Encyclopedia Britannica, it was "the one great Christmas myth of modern literature."[7] With time, Dickens' view of life would come to be described as his "Christmas philosophy"[8] (the idea that the Christmas spirit of kindness and generosity should prevail throughout the year), and Dickens himself came to be intimately associated with Christmas. According to Encyclopedia Britannica:

"His great attachment to Christmas (in his family life as well as his writings) is indeed significant and has contributed to his popularity. 'Dickens dead?' exclaimed a London girl in 1870. 'Then will Father Christmas die too?'— a tribute both to his association with Christmas and to the mythological status of the man as well as of his work."[9]

Dickens' love for Christmas was probably influenced in part by his affection for children, and in *A Christmas Carol*, he tenderly wrote, "For it is good to be children sometimes, and never better than at Christmas, when its mighty Founder was a child himself."

As his own children grew, they began to show interest in theater, and Dickens' attention returned to his old hobby. By 1851, Dickens was writing, directing, and acting with his children and friends. Often his productions were intended to raise money for those in need.

Dickens' theater experience gradually led to public readings of his writing, and he proved to be a master of performance. Dickens' fame as a public reader grew to nearly equal his reputation as a writer, and from 1858 until his death, he completed a number of wonderfully successful tours. According to Encyclopedia Britannica:

"He was a magnificent performer, and important elements in his art—the oral and dramatic qualities—were demonstrated in these renderings. His insight and skill revealed nuances in the narration and characterization that few readers had noticed."[10]

One of Dickens most popular readings was *A Christmas Carol* (for which audiences would sit captivated for three hours). Altogether Dickens performed about 471 times, and as a result, he wrote much less during the last ten years of his life. However, it seems he had discovered his true passion. He loved to see and delight audiences, and he gloried in their admiration. According to Encyclopedia Britannica:

"No important author (at least, according to reviewers, since Homer) and no English author since who has had anything like his stature has devoted so much time and energy to this activity. The only comparable figure is his contemporary, Mark Twain, who acknowledged Dickens as the pioneer."[11]

Dickens was just as popular in the United States as he was in his native country of England. His reading tour in America (1867-1868) only served to strengthen the admiration of his many fans and increase his reputation. Sadly, Dickens' active and demanding performance schedule probably contributed to his early death in 1870, but he died as a dearly loved man on both sides of the Atlantic.

Though Dickens' writing has been attacked for its sentimentality, even the harshest critics acknowledge his talent. For many, "He is second only to Shakespeare as the greatest English writer" of all time.[12] Interestingly, G.K. Chesterton (1874-1936), one of the most distinguished writers of the next generation in England, so highly regarded Dickens' work that he wrote prefaces for many of them; these were later collected in *Appreciations and Criticisms of the Works of Charles Dickens* (1911). Dickens' tombstone in Poet's Corner of Westminster Abbey, London, succinctly summarizes his life: "He was a sympathiser to the poor, the suffering, and the oppressed; and by his death, one of England's greatest writers is lost to the world."[13]

The following excerpt is the final chapter ("The End of It") of *A Christmas Carol.* The familiar story begins on Christmas Eve with the bad-tempered Ebenezer Scrooge spending his day, among other things, abusing his clerk, Bob Cratchit (the father of crippled Tiny Tim), rejecting his nephew Fred's invitation to dinner and coldly sending away men who were raising money for the poor.

That night, the ghost of Scrooge's late business partner Jacob Marley visits him. Marley expresses his remorse for failing to be more charitable during his life, and he informs Scrooge that other spirits will appear who might actually offer him a chance for reform. The three spirits who visit Scrooge are: the Ghost of Christmas Past, the Ghost of Christmas Present and the Ghost of Christmas Yet to Come.

During the visit of the last spirit, the Ghost of Christmas Yet to Come, Scrooge witnesses his own funeral. Sadly, nobody mourns his death, and people actually joke about his stinginess. Furthermore, Scrooge learns that young Tiny Tim dies, because his family cannot afford the medical attention that he needs. When Scrooge wakes up, he is a changed man. It is here that the excerpt begins.

[1] Smith, Grahame. "Charles Dickens." The Literary Encyclopedia. January 8, 2001. Retrieved October 19, 2008: http://www.litencyc.com/php/speople.php?rec=true&UID=5085. Much of the biography for Charles Dickens is drawn from this source.

[2] Smith, Grahame.

[3] Smith, Grahame.

[4] Merriman, C.D., "Charles Dickens." Biography written for Jalic Inc. Retrieved October 19, 2008: http://www.online-literature.com/dickens/.

[5] Smith, Grahame.

[6] Smith, Grahame.

[7] Encyclopedia Britannica. "Charles Dickens." Retrieved October 19, 2008 from Encyclopedia Britannica Online: http://www.britannica.com/EBchecked/topic/162141/Charles-Dickens.

[8] Encyclopedia Britannica.

[9] Encyclopedia Britannica.

[10] Encyclopedia Britannica.

[11] Encyclopedia Britannica.

[12] Smith, Grahame.

[13] Merriman, C.D.

The Story
Reading Time: 12 minutes

Yes! And the bedpost was his own. The bed was his own, the room was his own. Best and happiest of all, the Time before him was his own, to make amends in!

"I will live in the Past, the Present, and the Future!" Scrooge repeated, as he scrambled out of bed. "The Spirits of all Three shall strive within me. Oh Jacob Marley! Heaven, and the Christmas Time be praised for this. I say it on my knees, old Jacob, on my knees!"

He was so fluttered and so glowing with his good intentions, that his broken voice would scarcely answer to his call. He had been sobbing violently in his conflict with the Spirit, and his face was wet with tears.

"They are not torn down!" cried Scrooge, folding one of his bed-curtains in his arms, "they are not torn down, rings and all. They are here — I am here — the shadows of the things that would have been, may be dispelled. They will be! I know they will."

His hands were busy with his garments all this time; turning them inside out, putting them on upside down, tearing them, mislaying them, making them parties to every kind of extravagance.

"I don't know what to do!" cried Scrooge, laughing and crying in the same breath; and making a perfect Laocoon of himself with his stockings. "I am as light as a feather, I am as happy as an angel, I am as merry as a schoolboy. I am as giddy as a drunken man. A merry Christmas to every-body! A happy New Year to all the world! Hallo here! Whoop! Hallo!"

He had frisked into the sitting-room, and was now standing there: perfectly winded.

"There's the saucepan that the gruel was in!" cried Scrooge, starting off again, and frisking round the fireplace. "There's the door, by which the Ghost of Jacob Marley entered. There's the corner where the Ghost of Christmas Present sat. There's the window where I saw the wandering Spirits. It's all right, it's all true, it all happened. Ha ha ha!"

Really, for a man who had been out of practice for so many years, it was a splendid laugh, a most illustrious laugh. The father of a long, long line of brilliant laughs.

"I don't know what day of the month it is," said Scrooge. "I don't know how long I've been among the Spirits. I don't know anything. I'm quite a baby. Never mind. I don't care. I'd rather be a baby. Hallo! Whoop! Hallo here!"

He was checked in his transports by the churches ringing out the lustiest peals he had ever heard. Clash, clang, hammer; ding, dong, bell! Bell, dong, ding; hammer, clang, clash! Oh, glorious, glorious!

Running to the window, he opened it, and put out his head. No fog, no mist; clear, bright, jovial, stirring, cold; cold, piping for the blood to dance to; Golden sunlight; Heavenly sky; sweet fresh air; merry bells. Oh, glorious. Glorious!

"What's to-day?" cried Scrooge, calling downward to a boy in Sunday clothes, who perhaps had loitered in to look about him.

"Eh?" returned the boy, with all his might of wonder.

"What's to-day, my fine fellow?" said Scrooge.

"To-day?" replied the boy. "Why, Christmas Day."

"It's Christmas Day!" said Scrooge to himself. "I haven't missed it. The Spirits have done it all in one night. They can do anything they like. Of course they can. Of course they can. Hallo, my fine fellow!"

"Hallo!" returned the boy.

"Do you know the Poulterer's, in the next street but one, at the corner?" Scrooge inquired.

"I should hope I did," replied the lad.

"An intelligent boy!" said Scrooge. "A remarkable boy! Do you know whether they've sold the prize Turkey that was hanging up there — Not the little prize Turkey: the big one?"

"What, the one as big as me?" returned the boy.

"What a delightful boy!" said Scrooge. "It's a pleasure to talk to him. Yes, my buck."

"It's hanging there now," replied the boy.

"Is it?" said Scrooge. "Go and buy it."

"Walk-ER!" exclaimed the boy.

"No, no," said Scrooge, "I am in earnest. Go and buy it, and tell them to bring it here, that I may give them the direction where to take it. Come back with the man, and I'll give you a shilling. Come back with him in less than five minutes and I'll give you half-a-crown."

The boy was off like a shot. He must have had a steady hand at a trigger who could have got a shot off half so fast.

"I'll send it to Bob Cratchit's!" whispered Scrooge, rubbing his hands, and splitting with a laugh. "He shan't know who sends it. It's twice the size of Tiny Tim. Joe Miller never made such a joke as sending it to Bob's will be!"

The hand in which he wrote the address was not a steady one, but write it he did, somehow, and went down-stairs to open the street door, ready for the coming of the poulterer's man. As he stood there, waiting his arrival, the knocker caught his eye.

"I shall love it, as long as I live!" cried Scrooge, patting it with his hand. "I scarcely ever looked at it before. What an honest expression it has in its face. It's a wonderful knocker. — Here's the Turkey. Hallo! Whoop! How are you? Merry Christmas!"

It *was* a Turkey! He never could have stood upon his legs, that bird. He would have snapped them short off in a minute, like sticks of sealing-wax.

"Why, it's impossible to carry that to Camden Town," said Scrooge. "You must have a cab."

The chuckle with which he said this, and the chuckle with which he paid for the Turkey, and the chuckle with which he paid for the cab, and the chuckle with which he recompensed the boy, were only to be exceeded by the chuckle with which he sat down breathless in his chair again, and chuckled till he cried.

Shaving was not an easy task, for his hand continued to shake very much; and shaving requires attention, even when you don't dance while you are at it. But if he had cut the end of his nose off, he would have put a piece of sticking-plaister over it, and been quite satisfied.

He dressed himself all in his best, and at last got out into the streets. The people were by this time pouring forth, as he had seen them with the Ghost of Christmas Present; and walking with his hands behind him, Scrooge regarded every one with a delighted smile. He looked so irresistibly pleasant, in a word, that three or four good-humoured fellows said, "Good morning, sir. A merry

Christmas to you." And Scrooge said often afterwards, that of all the blithe sounds he had ever heard, those were the blithest in his ears.

He had not gone far, when coming on towards him he beheld the portly gentleman, who had walked into his counting-house the day before, and said, "Scrooge and Marley's, I believe." [This man was attempting to raise money for the poor but was sent cruelly sent away by Scrooge.] It sent a pang across his heart to think how this old gentleman would look upon him when they met; but he knew what path lay straight before him, and he took it.

"My dear sir," said Scrooge, quickening his pace, and taking the old gentleman by both his hands. "How do you do. I hope you succeeded yesterday. It was very kind of you. A merry Christmas to you, sir!"

"Mr. Scrooge?"

"Yes," said Scrooge. "That is my name, and I fear it may not be pleasant to you. Allow me to ask your pardon. And will you have the goodness" — here Scrooge whispered in his ear.

"Lord bless me!" cried the gentleman, as if his breath were taken away. "My dear Mr. Scrooge, are you serious?"

"If you please," said Scrooge. "Not a farthing less. A great many back-payments are included in it, I assure you. Will you do me that favour?"

"My dear sir," said the other, shaking hands with him. "I don't know what to say to such munificence."

"Don't say anything please," retorted Scrooge. "Come and see me. Will you come and see me?"

"I will!" cried the old gentleman. And it was clear he meant to do it.

"Thank you," said Scrooge. "I am much obliged to you. I thank you fifty times. Bless you!"

He went to church, and walked about the streets, and watched the people hurrying to and fro, and patted children on the head, and questioned beggars, and looked down into the kitchens of houses, and up to the windows, and found that everything could yield him pleasure. He had never dreamed that any walk — that anything — could give him so much happiness. In the afternoon he turned his steps towards his nephew's house.

He passed the door a dozen times, before he had the courage to go up and knock. But he made a dash, and did it.

"Is your master at home, my dear?" said Scrooge to the girl. Nice girl. Very.

"Yes, sir."

"Where is he, my love?" said Scrooge.

"He's in the dining-room, sir, along with mistress. I'll show you up-stairs, if you please."

"Thank you. He knows me," said Scrooge, with his hand already on the dining-room lock. "I'll go in here, my dear."

He turned it gently, and sidled his face in, round the door. They were looking at the table (which was spread out in great array); for these young housekeepers are always nervous on such points, and like to see that everything is right.

"Fred!" said Scrooge.

Dear heart alive, how his niece by marriage started. Scrooge had forgotten, for the moment, about her sitting in the corner with the footstool, or he wouldn't have done it, on any account.

"Why bless my soul!" cried Fred, "who's that?"

"It's I. Your uncle Scrooge. I have come to dinner. Will you let me in, Fred?"

Let him in! It is a mercy he didn't shake his arm off. He was at home in five minutes. Nothing could be heartier. His niece looked just the same. So did Topper when he came. So did the plump sister when she came. So did every one when they came. Wonderful party, wonderful games, wonderful unanimity, won-der-ful happiness! But he was early at the office next morning. Oh he was early there. If he could only be there first, and catch Bob Cratchit coming late! That was the thing he had set his heart upon.

And he did it; yes, he did. The clock struck nine. No Bob. A quarter past. No Bob. He was full eighteen minutes and a half behind his time. Scrooge sat with his door wide open, that he might see him come into the tank.

His hat was off, before he opened the door, his comforter too. He was on his stool in a jiffy, driving away with his pen, as if he were trying to overtake nine o'clock.

"Hallo," growled Scrooge, in his accustomed voice, as near as he could feign it. "What do you mean by coming here at this time of day?"

"I'm very sorry, sir," said Bob. "I *am* behind my time."

"You are?" repeated Scrooge. "Yes. I think you are. Step this way, if you please."

"It's only once a year, sir," pleaded Bob, appearing from the tank. "It shall not be repeated. I was making rather merry yesterday, sir."

"Now, I'll tell you what, my friend," said Scrooge, "I am not going to stand this sort of thing any longer. And therefore," he continued, leaping from his stool, and giving Bob such a dig in the waistcoat that he staggered back into the tank again — "and therefore I am about to raise your salary."

Bob trembled, and got a little nearer to the ruler. He had a momentary idea of knocking Scrooge down with it, holding him, and calling to the people in the court for help and a strait-waistcoat.

"A merry Christmas, Bob," said Scrooge, with an earnestness that could not be mistaken, as he clapped him on the back. "A merrier Christmas, Bob, my good fellow, than I have given you for many a year. I'll raise your salary, and endeavour to assist your struggling family, and we will discuss your affairs this very afternoon, over a Christmas bowl of smoking bishop, Bob. Make up the fires, and buy another coal-scuttle before you dot another *i*, Bob Cratchit!"

Scrooge was better than his word. He did it all, and infinitely more; and to Tiny Tim, who did not die, he was a second father. He became as good a friend, as good a master, and as good a man, as the good old city knew, or any other good old city, town, or borough, in the good old world. Some people laughed to see the alteration in him, but he let them laugh, and little heeded them; for he was wise enough to know that nothing ever happened on this globe, for good, at which some people did not have their fill of laughter in the outset; and knowing that such as these would be blind anyway, he thought it quite as well that they should wrinkle up their eyes in grins, as have the malady in less attractive forms. His own heart laughed, and that was quite enough for him.

He had no further intercourse with Spirits, but lived upon the Total Abstinence Principle, ever afterwards; and it was always said of him, that he knew how to keep Christmas well, if any man alive possessed the knowledge. May that be truly said of us, and all of us! And so, as Tiny Tim observed, God Bless Us, Every One!

A Harmony of
the Nativity Story

The Background
Matthew, Luke and John
Biblical Text, First Century Story

Four different authors (Matthew, Mark, Luke and John) give an account of the life of Jesus in the Bible. However, only two of them, Matthew and Luke, give any details about his birth. Mark makes no mention of Jesus' life before his baptism, and John gives only an ethereal account of how "the Word became flesh" (John 1:14).

Divinely, God willed that a variety of authors would contribute to his Word, the Bible. Frequently, each author offers a unique perspective on the same event. For example, Matthew was a Jew. His gospel focuses heavily on how Jesus fulfilled the Old Testament prophecy about the Jewish Messiah. On the other hand, Luke was probably a Gentile. He uses literary devices that suggest a Greek background and a high level of education. He takes care to explain Jewish customs and traces the genealogy of Jesus all the way back to Adam.

In some cases, these authors are accused of contradicting each other. One of the most obvious "discrepancies" in the Nativity story is the difference in the genealogies of Jesus as given by Matthew and Luke. Matthew's list begins with Abraham and descends to Jesus, whereas Luke's list begins with Jesus and ascends to Adam. This does not present a significant problem until the succession from David begins (see Genealogy table on pp. 326-327).

The first problem is that Matthew lists 26 generations between David and Jesus and Luke lists 41, but this incongruity is fairly easy to resolve. According to *A Harmony of the Gospels* by Robert L. Thomas and Stanley N. Gundry:

> "Omission of generations in biblical genealogies is not unique to this case, and Jews are known to have done this freely. The purpose of a genealogy was not to account for every generation but to establish the fact of an undoubted succession, including especially the more important ancestors."[1]

The second problem is more difficult to resolve. Between Matthew and Luke's genealogies, other than Shealtiel and Zerubbabel, every descendant after David is different. Though at first this appears to be an irreconcilable problem in Scripture, further research reveals that it is actually an intriguing fulfillment of prophecy.

In order to understand the genealogies, we must first look back to the Old Testament when God made an unconditional promise to King David:

> "'When your days are over and you rest with your fathers, I will raise up your offspring to succeed you, who will come from your own body, and I will establish his kingdom. He is the one who will build a house for my Name, and I will establish the throne of his kingdom

forever. I will be his father, and he will be my son. . . Your house and your kingdom will endure forever before me; your throne will be established forever'" (2 Samuel 7:12-16).

God promised that David's own offspring would reign forever, and several generations later, his descendant Jeconiah, also called Jehoiakim, sat on his throne as king of Judah. But Jeconiah was an evil man and was cursed by God as a result:

"This is what the LORD says: 'Record this man as if childless, a man who will not prosper in his lifetime, for none of his offspring will prosper, none will sit on the throne of David or rule anymore in Judah'" (Jeremiah 22:30).

This creates a dilemma. Jeconiah and his descendants had a legal right to the throne of David, but God declared that his offspring would never rule again. How could God's promise to David and his curse on Jeconiah both be fulfilled? Look to the genealogies of Jesus to understand.

First, Matthew traces Jesus' descent through Joseph to reveal that he had a "legal" right to David's throne. But since Joseph was a descendant of Jeconiah, Matthew is careful to show that Jesus was not actually Joseph's offspring. He calls Joseph "the husband of Mary, of whom was born Jesus, who is called Christ" (Matthew 1:16). The word "whom" in Greek is feminine singular in form and clearly refers back to Mary. Scholars Thomas and Gundry summarize this fact:

"As to human parentage, Jesus was born of Mary alone, though Joseph was his legal father. As Jesus' legal father, Joseph's legal claim passed to Jesus. But because Jesus was not actually of Jeconiah's seed . . . Jesus escaped the curse."[2]

Next, Luke undertakes the task of tracing Jesus' actual physical descent. This is important in light of God's promise to David that Messiah would come from his own body. But the fact that Jesus had no human father creates a unique challenge for Luke. His solution is to record Mary's genealogy; however, he is careful to conform to custom by not mentioning her name. In effect, Luke removes Joseph from the genealogy by saying of Jesus, "He was the son, so it was thought, of Joseph" (Luke 1:23). Thomas and Gundry explain:

"By this device Joseph's name is shown to be not properly part of the genealogy. Jesus was only thought to be his son. This would make Jesus the son (i.e., grandson or descendant) of Eli, Mary's progenitor, and is consistent with Luke's account of Jesus' conception, which makes clear that Joseph was not his physical father."[3]

In summary, the gospels record two different genealogies for Jesus. Matthew traces Joseph's line and confirms Jesus' right to David's throne through his legal father. Luke traces Mary's line to reveal that, though Jesus was a physical descendant of David, he avoided the curse placed on

The Genealogy of Jesus Christ

Luke 3:23-38
(Jesus' Natural Lineage Through Mary)

Adam
Seth
Enosh
Kenan
Mahalalel
Jared
Enoch
Methuselah
Lamech
Noah
Shem
Arphaxad
Cainan
Shelah
Eber
Peleg
Reu
Serug
Nahor
Terah

Matthew 1:1-17
(Jesus' Legal Lineage Through Joseph)

Matthew 1:1-17	Luke 3:23-38
Abraham	Abraham
Isaac	Isaac
Jacob	Jacob
Judah (and Tamar)	Judah
Perez	Perez
Hezron	Hezron
Ram	Ram
Amminadab	Amminadab
Nahson	Nahshon
Salmon (and Rahab)	Salmon
Boaz (and Ruth)	Boaz
Obed	Obed
Jesse	Jesse
King David (and Bathsheba)	David
King Solomon	Nathan
King Rehoboam	Mattatha
King Abijah	Menna
King Asa	Melea
King Jehoshaphat	Eliakim
King Jehoram	Jonam
King Uzziah	Joseph
King Jotham	Judah
King Ahaz	Simeon
King Hezekiah	Levi
King Manasseh	Matthat
King Amon	Jorim
King Josiah	Eliezer
King Jeconiah	Joshua
Shealtiel	Er
Zerubbabel	Elmadam
Abiud	Cosam
Eliakim	Addi
Azor	Melki
Zadok	Neri
Akim	Shealtiel
Eliud	Zerubbabel
Eleazar	Rhesa

Genealogy is continued on the next page.

The Genealogy of Jesus (Continued)	**Luke 3:23-38** (Jesus' Natural Lineage Through Mary)	*Genealogy continued from* *"Rhesa" on previous page.* Joanan Joda Josech Semein Mattathias Maath Naggai Esli Nahum Amos Mattathias Joseph Jannai Melki Levi Matthat Heli
Matthew 1:1-17 (Jesus' Legal Lineage Through Joseph)	*Genealogy continued from* *"Eleazar" on previous page.* Matthan Jacob	
	Joseph (the husband of Mary) **JESUS**	Joseph **JESUS** (the son, so it was thought, of Joseph)

Jeconiah. The common names found in the genealogies, Shealtiel and Zerubbabel, do not represent the same people.

One other point in regard to Jesus' ancestry is worth mentioning. Luke 1:5 records that Elizabeth, Mary's relative, was a descendant of Aaron. This implies that Mary may also have come from the line of Aaron. In Exodus 29:9, God proclaims that the priesthood of Israel belongs to Aaron and his sons by "lasting ordinance." This is intriguing in light of Jesus' ministry as a priest. Hebrews 2:17 says, "For this reason he had to be made like his brothers in every way, in order that he might become a merciful and faithful high priest in service to God, and that he might make atonement for the sins of the people."

The following account of Christ's birth is considered "A Harmony of the Nativity Story." It begins with the introduction to John's gospel and then combines the story as told by the gospel writers Matthew and Luke. Every word of the harmony comes directly from the Bible.

---

[1] Thomas, Robert T. and Gundry, Stanley N. *A Harmony of the Gospels with Explanations and Essays*. Harper Collins, 1978, p. 315.

[2] Thomas, Robert T. and Gundry, Stanley N., p. 318.

[3] Thomas, Robert T. and Gundry, Stanley N., p. 317.

The Story
Reading Time: 20 minutes

The Word Became Flesh (John 1:1-18)

In the beginning was the Word, and the Word was with God, and the Word was God. He was with God in the beginning.

Through him all things were made; without him nothing was made that has been made. In him was life, and that life was the light of men. The light shines in the darkness, but the darkness has not understood it.

There came a man who was sent from God; his name was John. He came as a witness to testify concerning that light, so that through him all men might believe. He himself was not the light; he came only as a witness to the light. The true light that gives light to every man was coming into the world.

He was in the world, and though the world was made through him, the world did not recognize him. He came to that which was his own, but his own did not receive him. Yet to all who received him, to those who believed in his name, he gave the right to become children of God — children born not of natural descent, nor of human decision or a husband's will, but born of God.

The Word became flesh and made his dwelling among us. We have seen his glory, the glory of the One and Only, who came from the Father, full of grace and truth.

John testifies concerning him. He cries out, saying, "This was he of whom I said, 'He who comes after me has surpassed me because he was before me.'" From the fullness of his grace we have all received one blessing after another. For the law was given through Moses; grace and truth came through Jesus Christ. No one has ever seen God, but God the One and Only, who is at the Father's side, has made him known.

The Birth of John the Baptist Foretold (Luke 1: 5-23)

In the time of Herod king of Judea there was a priest named Zechariah, who belonged to the priestly division of Abijah; his wife Elizabeth was also a descendant of Aaron. Both of them were upright in the sight of God, observing all the Lord's commandments and regulations blamelessly. But they had no children, because Elizabeth was barren; and they were both well along in years.

Once when Zechariah's division was on duty and he was serving as priest before God, he was chosen by lot, according to the custom of the priesthood, to go into the temple of the Lord and burn incense. And when the time for the burning of incense came, all the assembled worshipers were praying outside.

Then an angel of the Lord appeared to him, standing at the right side of the altar of incense. When Zechariah saw him, he was startled and was gripped with fear. But the angel said to him: "Do not be afraid, Zechariah; your prayer has been heard. Your wife Elizabeth will bear you a son, and you are to give him the name John. He will be a joy and delight to you, and many will rejoice because of his birth, for he will be great in the sight of the Lord. He is never to take wine or other fermented drink, and he will be filled with the Holy Spirit even from birth. Many of the people of Israel will he bring back to the Lord their God. And he will go on before the Lord, in the spirit and power of Elijah, to turn the hearts of the fathers to their children and the disobedient to the wisdom of the righteous—to make ready a people prepared for the Lord."

Zechariah asked the angel, "How can I be sure of this? I am an old man and my wife is well along in years."

The angel answered, "I am Gabriel. I stand in the presence of God, and I have been sent to speak to you and to tell you this good news. And now you will be silent and not able to speak until the day this happens, because you did not believe my words, which will come true at their proper time."

Meanwhile, the people were waiting for Zechariah and wondering why he stayed so long in the temple. When he came out, he could not speak to them. They realized he had seen a vision in the temple, for he kept making signs to them but remained unable to speak.

When his time of service was completed, he returned home. After this his wife Elizabeth became pregnant and for five months remained in seclusion. "The Lord has done this for me," she said. "In these days he has shown his favor and taken away my disgrace among the people."

The Birth of Jesus Foretold, *The Annunciation* (Luke 1:26-38)

In the sixth month, God sent the angel Gabriel to Nazareth, a town in Galilee, to a virgin pledged to be married to a man named Joseph, a descendant of David. The virgin's name was Mary. The angel went to her and said, "Greetings, you who are highly favored! The Lord is with you."

Mary was greatly troubled at his words and wondered what kind of greeting this might be. But the angel said to her, "Do not be afraid, Mary, you have found favor with God. You will be with child and give birth to a son, and you are to give him the name Jesus. He will be great and will be called the Son of the Most High. The Lord God will give him the throne of his father David, and he will reign over the house of Jacob forever; his kingdom will never end."

"How will this be," Mary asked the angel, "since I am a virgin?"

The angel answered, "The Holy Spirit will come upon you, and the power of the Most High will overshadow you. So the holy one to be born will be called the Son of God. Even Elizabeth your relative is going to have a child in her old age, and she who was said to be barren is in her sixth month. For nothing is impossible with God."

"I am the Lord's servant," Mary answered. "May it be to me as you have said." Then the angel left her.

Mary Visits Elizabeth (Luke 1:39-45)

At that time Mary got ready and hurried to a town in the hill country of Judea, where she entered Zechariah's home and greeted Elizabeth. When Elizabeth heard Mary's greeting, the baby leaped in her womb, and Elizabeth was filled with the Holy Spirit. In a loud voice she exclaimed: "Blessed are you among women, and blessed is the child you will bear! But why am I so favored, that the mother of my Lord should come to me? As soon as the sound of your greeting reached my ears, the baby in my womb leaped for joy. Blessed is she who has believed that what the Lord has said to her will be accomplished!"

Mary's Song, *The Magnificat* (Luke 1:46-56)

And Mary said:

> "My soul glorifies the Lord and my spirit rejoices in God my Savior,
>> for he has been mindful of the humble state of his servant.
> From now on all generations will call me blessed,
>> for the Mighty One has done great things for me — holy is his name.
> His mercy extends to those who fear him,
>> from generation to generation.
> He has performed mighty deeds with his arm;
>> he has scattered those who are proud in their inmost thoughts.
> He has brought down rulers from their thrones
>> but has lifted up the humble.
> He has filled the hungry with good things
>> but has sent the rich away empty.
> He has helped his servant Israel,
>> remembering to be merciful to Abraham and his descendants forever,
>> even as he said to our fathers."

Mary stayed with Elizabeth for about three months and then returned home.

The Birth of John the Baptist (Luke 1:57-66)

When it was time for Elizabeth to have her baby, she gave birth to a son. Her neighbors and relatives heard that the Lord had shown her great mercy, and they shared her joy.

On the eighth day they came to circumcise the child, and they were going to name him after his father Zechariah, but his mother spoke up and said, "No! He is to be called John."

They said to her, "There is no one among your relatives who has that name."

Then they made signs to his father, to find out what he would like to name the child. He asked for a writing tablet, and to everyone's astonishment he wrote, "His name is John." Immediately his mouth was opened and his tongue was loosed, and he began to speak, praising God. The neighbors were all filled with awe, and throughout the hill country of Judea people were talking about all these things. Everyone who heard this wondered about it, asking, "What then is this child going to be?" For the Lord's hand was with him.

Zechariah's Song (Luke 1:67-80)

His father Zechariah was filled with the Holy Spirit and prophesied:

"Praise be to the Lord, the God of Israel,
    because he has come and has redeemed his people.
He has raised up a horn of salvation for us
    in the house of his servant David
(as he said through his holy prophets of long ago),
salvation from our enemies
    and from the hand of all who hate us—
to show mercy to our fathers
    and to remember his holy covenant,
    the oath he swore to our father Abraham:
to rescue us from the hand of our enemies,
    and to enable us to serve him without fear
    in holiness and righteousness before him all our days.
And you, my child, will be called a prophet of the Most High;
    for you will go on before the Lord to prepare the way for him,
to give his people the knowledge of salvation
    through the forgiveness of their sins,
because of the tender mercy of our God,
    by which the rising sun will come to us from heaven
to shine on those living in darkness
    and in the shadow of death,
to guide our feet into the path of peace."

And the child grew and became strong in spirit; and he lived in the desert until he appeared publicly to Israel.

An Angel Appears to Joseph (Matthew 1:18-25)

This is how the birth of Jesus Christ came about: His mother Mary was pledged to be married to Joseph, but before they came together, she was found to be with child through the Holy Spirit. Because Joseph her husband was a righteous man and did not want to expose her to public disgrace, he had in mind to divorce her quietly.

But after he had considered this, an angel of the Lord appeared to him in a dream and said, "Joseph son of David, do not be afraid to take Mary home as your wife, because what is conceived in her is from the Holy Spirit. She will give birth to a son, and you are to give him the name Jesus, because he will save his people from their sins."

All this took place to fulfill what the Lord had said through the prophet: "The virgin will be with child and will give birth to a son, and they will call him Immanuel" [Isaiah 7:14] — which means, "God with us."

When Joseph woke up, he did what the angel of the Lord had commanded him and took Mary home as his wife. But he had no union with her until she gave birth to a son. And he gave him the name Jesus.

Jesus' Legal Lineage Through Joseph (Matthew 1:1-17)

A record of the genealogy of Jesus Christ the son of David, the son of Abraham:

Abraham was the father of Isaac,
    Isaac the father of Jacob,
    Jacob the father of Judah and his brothers,
    Judah the father of Perez and Zerah, whose mother was Tamar,
    Perez the father of Hezron,
    Hezron the father of Ram,
    Ram the father of Amminadab,
    Amminadab the father of Nahshon,
    Nahshon the father of Salmon,
    Salmon the father of Boaz, whose mother was Rahab,
    Boaz the father of Obed, whose mother was Ruth,
    Obed the father of Jesse,
    and Jesse the father of King David.

David was the father of Solomon, whose mother had been Uriah's wife,
    Solomon the father of Rehoboam,
    Rehoboam the father of Abijah,
    Abijah the father of Asa,

Asa the father of Jehoshaphat,
Jehoshaphat the father of Jehoram,
Jehoram the father of Uzziah,
Uzziah the father of Jotham,
Jotham the father of Ahaz,
Ahaz the father of Hezekiah,
Hezekiah the father of Manasseh,
Manasseh the father of Amon,
Amon the father of Josiah,
and Josiah the father of Jeconiah and his brothers at the time of the exile to Babylon.

After the exile to Babylon:
Jeconiah was the father of Shealtiel,
Shealtiel the father of Zerubbabel,
Zerubbabel the father of Abiud,
Abiud the father of Eliakim,
Eliakim the father of Azor,
Azor the father of Zadok,
Zadok the father of Akim,
Akim the father of Eliud,
Eliud the father of Eleazar,
Eleazar the father of Matthan,
Matthan the father of Jacob,
and Jacob the father of Joseph, the husband of Mary, of whom was born Jesus, who is
  called Christ.

Thus there were fourteen generations in all from Abraham to David, fourteen from David to the exile to Babylon, and fourteen from the exile to the Christ

Jesus' Natural Lineage Through Mary (Luke 3:23–37)

Now Jesus . . . was the son, so it was thought, of Joseph,

the son of Heli, the son of Matthat,
the son of Levi, the son of Melki,
the son of Jannai, the son of Joseph,
the son of Mattathias, the son of Amos,
the son of Nahum, the son of Esli,
the son of Naggai, the son of Maath,

the son of Mattathias, the son of Semein,
the son of Josech, the son of Joda,
the son of Joanan, the son of Rhesa,
the son of Zerubbabel, the son of Shealtiel,
the son of Neri, the son of Melki,
the son of Addi, the son of Cosam,
the son of Elmadam, the son of Er,
the son of Joshua, the son of Eliezer,
the son of Jorim, the son of Matthat,
the son of Levi, the son of Simeon,
the son of Judah, the son of Joseph,
the son of Jonam, the son of Eliakim,
the son of Melea, the son of Menna,
the son of Mattatha, the son of Nathan,
the son of David, the son of Jesse,
the son of Obed, the son of Boaz,
the son of Salmon, the son of Nahshon,
the son of Amminadab, the son of Ram,
the son of Hezron, the son of Perez,
the son of Judah, the son of Jacob,
the son of Isaac, the son of Abraham,
the son of Terah, the son of Nahor,
the son of Serug, the son of Reu,
the son of Peleg, the son of Eber,
the son of Shelah, the son of Cainan,
the son of Arphaxad, the son of Shem,
the son of Noah, the son of Lamech,
the son of Methuselah, the son of Enoch,
the son of Jared, the son of Mahalalel,
the son of Kenan, the son of Enosh,
the son of Seth, the son of Adam,
the son of God.

The Birth of Jesus (Luke 2:1-7)

In those days, Caesar Augustus issued a decree that a census should be taken of the entire Roman world. (This was the first census that took place while Quirinius was governor of Syria.) And everyone went to his own town to register.

So Joseph also went up from the town of Nazareth in Galilee to Judea, to Bethlehem the town of David, because he belonged to the house and line of David. He went there to register with Mary, who was pledged to be married to him and was expecting a child. While they were there, the time came for the baby to be born, and she gave birth to her firstborn, a son. She wrapped him in cloths and placed him in a manger, because there was no room for them in the inn.

The Shepherds and the Angels (Luke 2:8-20)

And there were shepherds living out in the fields nearby, keeping watch over their flocks at night. An angel of the Lord appeared to them, and the glory of the Lord shone around them, and they were terrified. But the angel said to them, "Do not be afraid. I bring you good news of great joy that will be for all the people. Today in the town of David a Savior has been born to you; he is Christ the Lord. This will be a sign to you: You will find a baby wrapped in cloths and lying in a manger."

Suddenly a great company of the heavenly host appeared with the angel, praising God and saying,

"Glory to God in the highest,
   and on earth peace to men on whom his favor rests."

When the angels had left them and gone into heaven, the shepherds said to one another, "Let's go to Bethlehem and see this thing that has happened, which the Lord has told us about."

So they hurried off and found Mary and Joseph, and the baby, who was lying in the manger. When they had seen him, they spread the word concerning what had been told them about this child, and all who heard it were amazed at what the shepherds said to them. But Mary treasured up all these things and pondered them in her heart. The shepherds returned, glorifying and praising God for all the things they had heard and seen, which were just as they had been told.

Jesus Presented in the Temple (Luke 2:21-38)

On the eighth day, when it was time to circumcise him, he was named Jesus, the name the angel had given him before he had been conceived.

When the time of their purification according to the Law of Moses had been completed, Joseph and Mary took him to Jerusalem to present him to the Lord (as it is written in the Law of the Lord, "Every firstborn male is to be consecrated to the Lord") [Exodus 13:2,12], and to offer a sacrifice in keeping with what is said in the Law of the Lord: "a pair of doves or two young pigeons" [Leviticus 12:8].

Now there was a man in Jerusalem called Simeon, who was righteous and devout. He was waiting for the consolation of Israel, and the Holy Spirit was upon him. It had been revealed to him by the Holy Spirit that he would not die before he had seen the Lord's Christ. Moved by the Spirit, he went into the temple courts. When the parents brought in the child Jesus to do for him what the custom of the Law required, Simeon took him in his arms and praised God, saying:

"Sovereign Lord, as you have promised,
　　you now dismiss your servant in peace.
For my eyes have seen your salvation,
　　which you have prepared in the sight of all people,
a light for revelation to the Gentiles
　　and for glory to your people Israel."

The child's father and mother marveled at what was said about him. Then Simeon blessed them and said to Mary, his mother: "This child is destined to cause the falling and rising of many in Israel, and to be a sign that will be spoken against, so that the thoughts of many hearts will be revealed. And a sword will pierce your own soul too."

There was also a prophetess, Anna, the daughter of Phanuel, of the tribe of Asher. She was very old; she had lived with her husband seven years after her marriage, and then was a widow until she was eighty-four. She never left the temple but worshiped night and day, fasting and praying. Coming up to them at that very moment, she gave thanks to God and spoke about the child to all who were looking forward to the redemption of Jerusalem.

The Visit of the Magi (Matthew 2:1-12)

After Jesus was born in Bethlehem in Judea, during the time of King Herod, Magi from the east came to Jerusalem and asked, "Where is the one who has been born king of the Jews? We saw his star in the east and have come to worship him."

When King Herod heard this he was disturbed, and all Jerusalem with him. When he had called together all the people's chief priests and teachers of the law, he asked them where the Christ was to be born. "In Bethlehem in Judea," they replied, "for this is what the prophet has written:

'But you, Bethlehem, in the land of Judah,
　　are by no means least among the rulers of Judah;
for out of you will come a ruler
　　who will be the shepherd of my people Israel'" [Micah 5:2].

Then Herod called the Magi secretly and found out from them the exact time the star had appeared. He sent them to Bethlehem and said, "Go and make a careful search for the child. As soon as you find him, report to me, so that I too may go and worship him."

After they had heard the king, they went on their way, and the star they had seen in the east went ahead of them until it stopped over the place where the child was. When they saw the star, they were overjoyed. On coming to the house, they saw the child with his mother Mary, and they bowed down and worshiped him. Then they opened their treasures and presented him with gifts of gold and of incense and of myrrh. And having been warned in a dream not to go back to Herod, they returned to their country by another route.

The Escape to Egypt (Matthew 2:13-18)

When they had gone, an angel of the Lord appeared to Joseph in a dream. "Get up," he said, "take the child and his mother and escape to Egypt. Stay there until I tell you, for Herod is going to search for the child to kill him."

So he got up, took the child and his mother during the night and left for Egypt, where he stayed until the death of Herod. And so was fulfilled what the Lord had said through the prophet: "Out of Egypt I called my son" [Hosea 11:1].

When Herod realized that he had been outwitted by the Magi, he was furious, and he gave orders to kill all the boys in Bethlehem and its vicinity who were two years old and under, in accordance with the time he had learned from the Magi. Then what was said through the prophet Jeremiah was fulfilled:

"A voice is heard in Ramah,
    weeping and great mourning,
Rachel weeping for her children
    and refusing to be comforted,
because they are no more" [Jeremiah 31:15].

The Return to Nazareth (Matthew 2:19-23)

After Herod died, an angel of the Lord appeared in a dream to Joseph in Egypt and said, "Get up, take the child and his mother and go to the land of Israel, for those who were trying to take the child's life are dead."

So he got up, took the child and his mother and went to the land of Israel. But when he heard that Archelaus was reigning in Judea in place of his father Herod, he was afraid to go there. Having been warned in a dream, he withdrew to the district of Galilee, and he went and lived in a town called Nazareth. So was fulfilled what was said through the prophets: "He will be called a Nazarene."

(Luke 2:39-40)

When Joseph and Mary had done everything required by the Law of the Lord, they returned to Galilee to their own town of Nazareth. And the child grew and became strong; he was filled with wisdom, and the grace of God was upon him.

Christmas Every Day

The Background
William Dean Howells, 1837-1920
Fairy Tale, 19ᵗʰ Century

Williams Dean Howells was the son of a country printer and newspaper editor. His father moved the family regularly throughout the state of Ohio as he sought new economic opportunities and tried to stay in the center of political activism. This nomadic life prevented Howells from obtaining a conventional education. However, he learned a great deal about the literary world as he helped his father in the printing shop. By age nine, he was typesetting, and not long after, he began proof-reading. Eventually, he became a contributing editor.

By age nineteen, Howells began publishing in the reputable *Cicinnati Gazette*. Soon thereafter, his work was being published in newspapers across the state. As a strong opponent of slavery, Howells affiliated himself with the Republican party and was soon commissioned to write a campaign biography, the *Lives and Speeches of Abraham Lincoln and Hannibal Hamlin* (1860).

After a Republican victory in November, Howells' reputation grew, and on a trip to New England, he got to interact with some of America's greatest literary men: Ralph Waldo Emerson, James Russell Lowell, Oliver Wendell Holmes, Henry Wadsworth Longfellow, Henry David Thoreau and Nathaniel Hawthorne. Many years later, Howells published an account of this trip, *Literary Friends and Acquaintance* (1900), and his work is now considered a major contribution to American cultural history.

Soon after his New England trip, Howells traveled to Italy to serve as the American consul in Venice. On Christmas Eve 1862, he married Elinor Mead at the American embassy in Paris. Once the Civil War ended, Howells and his wife returned to the U.S. and settled in New England. In 1866, he became the assistant editor of the *Atlantic,* the nation's foremost literary magazine, and by 1871, he became the chief editor. Howells' opinions were greatly respected in literary circles, and he developed a close friendship with both Mark Twain and Henry James.[1]

With a growing family to support, Howells also began to write novels. According to *The Literary Encyclopedia*:

"With almost incessant regularity, Howells composed at least one novel annually for almost fifty years, beginning with *Their Wedding Journey* (1872) and ending with the posthu-mously-published *Vacation of the Kelwyns* (1920). To this already bulging bibliography he added an editor's considerable day-work of book reviews, prefaces, critical essays, travel sketches, and parlor theatricals. His was truly a writing life."[2]

Throughout his life, Howells was a passionate advocate of literary realism. He believed that authors should depict life as it really is, rather than "romanticizing" it. Sadly, Howells' realism probably contributed to his agnosticism. Many realists of his time began to view God as a "romantic" creation of bygone days. Regardless, Howells' writing was not devoid of moral and biblical themes.

Perhaps, a remnant of his Quaker roots remained in him even though his father had left the church when Howells was a young boy.

Howells' realism is evident in his classic story "Christmas Every Day" (published in an 1892 collection called *Christmas Every Day and Other Stories*). Though told in the form of a playful and humorous fairy tale, Howells does not hesitate to address some of humanity's more ignoble traits like greed and bad tempers.

Howells appeals to the familiar Christmas season in which children (and really the child in every person) want the gifts, fun and festivities to continue indefinitely, failing to consider that there are consequences for such indulgences. On the other hand, Howells more subtly reveals the adult tendency to be easily irritated by the work and the stress associated with Christmas. In the end, Howells' short story gives a lesson in moderation, and it serves as a reminder to cherish the special day that comes only once a year.

---

[1] Encyclopedia Brittanica. "William Dean Howells." Retrieved August 29, 2008 from Encyclopedia Britannica Online: http://www.britannica.com/EBchecked/topic/273557/William-Dean-Howells.

[2] Anesko, Michael. "William Dean Howells." *The Literary Encyclopedia.* Retrieved October 12, 2008 from: http://www.litencyc.com/php/speople.php?rec=true&UID=2237. Much of the biographical information for Howells is drawn from this source.

The Story
Reading Time: 10 minutes

The little girl came into her papa's study, as she always did Saturday morning before breakfast, and asked for a story. He tried to beg off that morning, for he was very busy, but she would not let him. So he began:

"Well, once there was a little pig —"

She stopped him at the word. She said she had heard little pig-stories till she was perfectly sick of them.

"Well, what kind of story shall I tell, then?"

"About Christmas. It's getting to be the season."

"Well!" Her papa roused himself. "Then I'll tell you about the little girl that wanted it Christmas every day in the year. How would you like that?"

"First-rate!" said the little girl; and she nestled into comfortable shape in his lap, ready for listening.

"Very well, then, this little pig—Oh, what are you pounding me for?"

"Because you said little pig instead of little girl."

"I should like to know what's the difference between a little pig and a little girl that wanted it Christmas every day!"

"Papa!" said the little girl warningly. At this her papa began to tell the story.

Once there was a little girl who liked Christmas so much that she wanted it to be Christmas every day in the year, and as soon as Thanksgiving was over she began to send postcards to the old Christmas Fairy to ask if she mightn't have it. But the old Fairy never answered, and after a while the little girl found out that the Fairy wouldn't notice anything but real letters sealed outside with a monogram—or your initial, anyway. So, then, she began to send letters, and just the day before Christmas, she got a letter from the Fairy, saying she might have it Christmas every day for a year, and then they would see about having it longer.

The little girl was excited already, preparing for the old-fashioned, once-a-year Christmas that was coming the next day. So she resolved to keep the Fairy's promise to herself and surprise everybody with it as it kept coming true, but then it slipped out of her mind altogether.

She had a splendid Christmas. She went to bed early, so as to let Santa Claus fill the stockings, and in the morning she was up the first of anybody and found hers all lumpy with packages of candy, and oranges and grapes, and rubber balls, and all kinds of small presents. Then she waited until the rest of the family was up, and she burst into the library to look at the large presents laid out on the library table—books, and boxes of stationery, and dolls, and little stoves, and dozens of handkerchiefs, and inkstands, and skates, and photograph frames, and boxes of watercolors, and dolls' houses—and the big Christmas tree, lighted and standing in the middle.

She had a splendid Christmas all day. She ate so much candy that she did not want any breakfast, and the whole forenoon the presents kept pouring in that had not been delivered the night before, and she went round giving the presents she had got for other people, and came home and ate turkey and cranberry for dinner, and plum pudding and nuts and raisins and oranges, and then went out and coasted, and came in with a stomachache crying, and her papa said he would see if his house was turned into that sort of fool's paradise another year, and they had a light supper, and pretty early everybody went to bed cross.

The little girl slept very heavily and very late, but she was wakened at last by the other children dancing around her bed with their stockings full of presents in their hands. "Christmas! Christmas! Christmas!" they all shouted.

"Nonsense! It was Christmas yesterday," said the little girl, rubbing her eyes sleepily.

Her brothers and sisters just laughed. "We don't know about that. It's Christmas today, anyway. You come into the library and see."

Then all at once it flashed on the little girl that the Fairy was keeping her promise, and her year of Christmases was beginning. She was dreadfully sleepy, but she sprang up and darted into the library. There it was again! Books, and boxes of stationery, and dolls, and so on.

There was the Christmas tree blazing away, and the family picking out their presents, and her father looking perfectly puzzled, and her mother ready to cry. "I'm sure I don't see how I'm to dispose of all these things," said her mother, and her father said it seemed to him they had had something just like it the day before, but he supposed he must have dreamed it. This struck the little girl as the best kind of a joke, and so she ate so much candy she didn't want any breakfast, and went round carrying presents, and had turkey and cranberry for dinner, and then went out and coasted, and came in with a stomachache, crying.

Now, the next day, it was the same thing over again, but everybody getting crosser, and at the end of a week's time so many people had lost their tempers that you could pick up lost tempers anywhere, they perfectly strewed the ground. Even when people tried to recover their tempers they usually got somebody else's, and it made the most dreadful mix.

The little girl began to get frightened, keeping the secret all to herself, she wanted to tell her mother, but she didn't dare to, and she was ashamed to ask the Fairy to take back her gift, it seemed ungrateful and ill-bred. So it went on and on, and it was Christmas on St. Valentine's Day and Washington's Birthday, just the same as any day, and it didn't skip even the First of April, though everything was counterfeit that day, and that was some little relief.

After a while turkeys got to be awfully scarce, selling for about a thousand dollars apiece. They got to passing off almost anything for turkeys—even half-grown hummingbirds. And cranberries— well they asked a diamond apiece for cranberries. All the woods and orchards were cut down for Christmas trees. After a while they had to make Christmas trees out of rags. But there were plenty of rags, because people got so poor, buying presents for one another, that they couldn't get any new clothes, and they just wore their old ones to tatters. They got so poor that everybody had to go to the poorhouse, except the confectioners, and the storekeepers, and the book-sellers, and they all got so rich and proud that they would hardly wait upon a person when he came to buy. It was perfectly shameful!

After it had gone on about three or four months, the little girl, whenever she came into the room in the morning and saw those great ugly, lumpy stockings dangling at the fireplace, and the disgusting presents around everywhere, used to sit down and burst out crying. In six months she was perfectly exhausted, she couldn't even cry anymore.

And how it was on the Fourth of July! On the Fourth of July, the first boy in the United States woke up and found out that his firecrackers and toy pistol and two-dollar collection of fireworks were nothing but sugar and candy painted up to look like fireworks. Before ten o'clock every boy in the United States discovered that his July Fourth things had turned into Christmas things and was so mad. The Fourth of July orations all turned into Christmas carols, and when anybody tried to read the Declaration of Independence, instead of saying, "When in the course of human events it becomes necessary," he was sure to sing, "God rest you merry, gentlemen." It was perfectly awful.

About the beginning of October the little girl took to sitting down on dolls wherever she found them—she hated the sight of them so, and by Thanksgiving she just slammed her presents across the room. By that time people didn't carry presents around nicely anymore. They flung them over the fence or through the window, and, instead of taking great pains to write "For dear Papa," or "Mama" or "Brother," or "Sister," they used to write, "Take it, you horrid old thing!" and then go and bang it against the front door.

Nearly everybody had built barns to hold their presents, but pretty soon the barns overflowed, and then they used to let them lie out in the rain, or anywhere. Sometimes the police used to come and tell them to shovel their presents off the sidewalk or they would arrest them.

Before Thanksgiving came it had leaked out who had caused all these Christmases. The little girl had suffered so much that she had talked about it in her sleep, and after that hardly anybody would play with her, because if it had not been for her greediness it wouldn't have happened. And now, when it came Thanksgiving, and she wanted them to go to church, and have turkey, and show their gratitude, they said that all the turkeys had been eaten for her old Christmas dinners and if she would stop the Christmases, they would see about the gratitude. And the very next day the little girl began sending letters to the Christmas Fairy, and then telegrams, to stop it. But it didn't do any good, and then she got to calling at the Fairy's house, but the girl that came to the door always said, "Not at home," or "Engaged," or something like that, and so it went on till it came to the old once-a-year Christmas Eve. The little girl fell asleep, and when she woke up in the morning –

"She found it was all nothing but a dream," suggested the little girl.

"No indeed!" said her papa. "It was all every bit true!"

"What did she find out, then?"

"Why, that it wasn't Christmas at last, and wasn't ever going to be, anymore. Now it's time for breakfast."

The little girl held her papa fast around the neck.

"You shan't go if you're going to leave it so!"

"How do you want it left?"

"Christmas once a year."

"All right," said her papa, and he went on again.

Well, with no Christmas ever again, there was the greatest rejoicing all over the country. People met together everywhere and kissed and cried for joy. Carts went around and gathered up all the candy and raisins and nuts, and dumped them into the river, and it made the fish perfectly sick. And the whole United States, as far out as Alaska, was one blaze of bonfires, where the children were burning up their presents of all kinds. They had the greatest time!

The little girl went to thank the old Fairy because she had stopped its being Christmas, and she said she hoped the Fairy would keep her promise and see that Christmas never, never came again. Then the Fairy frowned, and said that now the little girl was behaving just as greedily as ever, and she'd better look out. This made the little girl think it all over carefully again, and she said she would be willing to have it Christmas about once in a thousand years, and then she said a hundred, and then she said ten, and at last she got down to one. Then the Fairy said that was the good old way that had pleased people ever since Christmas began, and she was agreed. Then the little girl said, "What're your shoes made of?" And the Fairy said, "Leather." And the little girl said, "Bargain's done forever," and skipped off, and hippity-hopped the whole way home, she was so glad.

"How will that do?" asked the papa.

"First-rate!" said the little girl, but she hated to have the story stop, and was rather sober. However, her mama put her head in at the door and asked her papa:

"Are you never coming to breakfast? What have you been telling that child?"

"Oh, just a tale with a moral." The little girl caught him around the neck again.

"We know! Don't you tell what, papa! Don't you tell what!"

Good King Wenceslas

The Background
The Life of a Saint, 907-929/935 AD

Wenceslas is the Germanized form of "Václav the Good." He was born to the first Christian Duke of Bohemia (part of the modern day Czech Republic) and became Duke himself at age 18. His brother murdered him in either 929 or 935 (sources vary), and he was soon thereafter honored as a saint.

Though Wenceslas was well known in his native land, he was virtually unknown in the English speaking world until John Mason Neale (see pp. 208-209), translator of the carols "Good Christian Men Rejoice" and "O Come, O Come Emmanuel," popularized his story in the song "Good King Wenceslas." Neale was a Latin scholar who patiently researched the records of European lands in order to bring the great music and traditions of the past to England.

Since Neale devoted himself to the needs of the poor and oppressed, he was understandably intrigued by the gracious and generous life of Wenceslas. Though Neale is best known for his work as a translator, his lyrics for "Good King Wenceslas" were an original work. He set his words to a 14th century tune, *Tempest adest floridum,* which was formerly sung in the spring and means "the time has arrived for flowers to bloom." Neale's song, however, was first published in *Carols for Christmastide* (1853). Though the song is set on St. Stephen's Day, December 26, and though there is no mention of Christmas, Neale wrote it at a time when the greatest celebrations of Christmas took place on the 12 days following the holiday. Thus, as the song gained popularity, King Wenceslas came to be intimately associated with Christmas. The words of Neale's song tell a beautiful story and are as follows:

"Good King Wenceslas looked out,
On the feast of Stephen,
When the snow lay round about,
Deep and crisp and even:
Brightly shone the moon that night,
Though the frost was cruel,
When a poor man came in sight,
Gathering winter fuel.

"'Hither page and stand by me,
If thou know'st it, telling —
Yonder peasant, who is he?
Where and what his dwelling?'
'Sire, he lives a good league hence,
Underneath the mountain,

Right against the forest fence,
By Saint Agnes' fountain.'

"'Bring me flesh and bring me wine!
Bring me pine logs hither!
Thou and I will see him dine,
When we bear them thither.'
Page and monarch forth they went,
Forth they went together;
Though the rude winds wild lament,
And the bitter weather.

"'Sire, the night is darker now,
And the wind blows stronger;
Fails my heart, I know not how,
I can go no longer.'
'Mark my footsteps, good my page,
Tread thou in them boldly:
Thou shalt find the winter's rage
Freeze thy blood less coldly.'

"In his master's steps he trod,
Where the snow lay dinted;
Heat was in the very sod
Which the saint had printed.
Therefore, Christian men, be sure,
Wealth or rank possessing,
Ye who now will bless the poor,
Shall yourselves find blessing."

It should be noted that though Wenceslas was a duke, the title of "king" was conferred on him after his death by Otto the Great, who was crowned Holy Roman Emperor in 962.

Today, most Americans are only vaguely familiar with the story of King Wenceslas, if at all. However, his life is a model for Christian living, and the traits for which he is honored, kindness and generosity, are qualities that are especially valued during the Christmas season.

Without doubt, Wenceslas was a historical ruler and a faithful Christian. However, the details of his life exist mainly in oral tradition. The following story is woven into the known history of the era and is drawn from both the Catholic Encyclopedia[1] and the Oxford Dictionary of Saints.[2]

[1] Mershman, Francis. "St. Wenceslaus." Catholic Encyclopedia. Robert Appleton Company, 1912. Retrieved October 4, 2008 from New Advent: http://www.newadvent.org/cathen/15587b.htm and Ott, Michael. "St. Ludmilla." Robert Appleton Company, 1910. Retrieved October 4, 2008 from New Advent: http://www. newadvent.org/cathen/09416a.htm.

[2] Farmer, David Hugh. *The Oxford Dictionary of Saints*. Oxford University Press, 2004, pp. 534-535.

The Story
Reading Time: 5 minutes

Though born of the same parents within moments of each other, Wenceslas and Boleslaus, twin brothers, could not have been more different. From infancy, Wenceslas was full of warmth and smiles; Boleslaus, on the other hand, was cold and aloof.

Wenceslas' pleasant nature and early interest in things of God won him special favor in the eyes of Ludmilla, his paternal grandmother. Ludmilla had converted to Christianity in her youth through the influence of Saint Cyril and Saint Methodius, two brothers from Thessalonica, who served as missionaries to the Slavic people. Ludmilla and her husband Boriwoi, the first Christian Duke of Bohemia, withstood great difficulties on account of their faith, since there were very few believers in their pagan land. Yet, these trials only served to increase Ludmilla's faith, and she committed to raise her family up in the Lord. Unfortunately, her son Wratislaw married a woman who only pretended to be a Christian. Drahomira was the daughter of a pagan tribal chief and was baptized into Christianity so she could marry into a powerful family.

When Wratislaw died, his boys, Wenceslas and Boleslaus, were only 8 years old. Devastated by the loss of her son, Ludmilla devoted herself all the more to her beloved grandson, Wenceslas. The growing intimacy between Ludmilla and Wenceslas sparked bitter jealousy in the heart of his mother Drahomira. Furthermore, she began to openly oppose Christianity. Seizing on tensions between believers and non-believers, Drahomira incited two noblemen to murder Ludmilla. Though her life on earth ended, Ludmilla's influence on Wenceslas remained. Christian friends continued to encourage him in his faith and to educate him in the things of God.

Meanwhile, the ambitious Drahomira was acting as regent in Bohemia, and her evil reign caused unhappiness and discord throughout the land. When Wenceslas, the older of her twins, turned 18, he easily took the reigns of government from her.

Wenceslas proved to be a capable young leader, and he initiated many changes for the benefit of his people. For example, he reduced the arbitrary power of judges in order to create a system of justice for all, and he worked hard to establish good relations with surrounding nations. Yet, of all Wenceslas' efforts on behalf of his nation, the most striking involved his personal acts on behalf of the poor. He was known to carry provisions on his own shoulders and travel through difficult weather in order to provide for his people. Every year, as Christmas ushered in the cold season, a time that could devastate the poor, Wenceslas would exert his greatest effort to supply the poor with basic necessities. As a result, Wenceslas was an extremely popular ruler among his people, and the Lord used him to draw many pagans to Christianity.

However, Wenceslas' Christian influence was not welcome by all, particularly by those of the noble class. He was known to encourage the work of German missionaries in their efforts to Christianize Bohemia. And furthermore, in order to prevent war, Wenceslas agreed to pay a tribute to Germany for the protection of his people. This was very unpopular among the noble and nationalistic Bohemians, and it gave Drahomira the opportunity to start building alliances within the kingdom on behalf of her other son, Boleslaus.

Drahomira exercised great influence over Boleslaus, and though he loved Wenceslas, Drahomira spent many years and used many persuasive words to incite him against his brother. By 935, believing that he was doing what was best for his country, Boleslaus submitted to his mother's evil plan. He invited Wenceslas to a religious feast, and on the way to church, he had his brother murdered.

When Boleslaus arrived on the scene, his dying brother looked mercifully into his eyes and said, "Dear brother, may God forgive you and may you seek him that I might see you again in heaven." As Wenceslas breathed his last, Boleslaus was overcome with remorse and wept bitterly over his brother's dead body. Within hours, Boleslaus received news of the birth of his own son. Ominously, he named him "Strachkvas" meaning "a dreadful feast."

Though his murder earned him the title "Boleslaus the Cruel," his reign (929-967) was marked by acts of repentance. He trained his children in the Christian faith and even sent his daughter Mlada (a nun) to Rome requesting permission to allow a bishop the authority to govern Prague. His son who succeeded him as Duke of Bohemia came to be known as Boleslaus II the Pious.

Boleslaus was also largely responsible for establishing Wenceslas' place in history. He set up a memorial for his brother at St. Vitus' Cathedral in Prague, and he encouraged the people of Bohemia to remember Wenceslas' good and generous life. By 985, a feast for Wenceslas celebrated him as a martyr of the faith, and by the early 11[th]century, he became the patron saint of Bohemia. His picture was engraved on coins, and his crown became a symbol of the Czech nation.

In the Great Walled Country

The Background
Raymond Macdonald Alden, 1873-1924
Fairy Tale, 20th Century

Raymond Macdonald Alden was born in New York to Gustavus Rossenberg Alden and Isabella Macdonald, both committed Christians. His father was a pastor and his mother was a well-known author who dedicated her pen "to the direct and continuous effort to win others for Christ and help others to closer fellowship with him."[1]

Alden's mother began writing at an early age and used the pseudonym "Pansy," a pet name given to her by her father. Soon after Raymond's birth, she started a weekly children's magazine that she affectionately titled "The Pansy." Though it began as a small Sunday School publication, it quickly grew into a full subscription magazine. It included fictional stories, illustrations, news of new inventions, and updates on missionary endeavors.[2] This magazine gave Raymond's mother the opportunity to train him, as well as his cousin Grace Livingston Hill (1865-1947), in writing; Hill would later become a famous Christian romance novelist.

As a young teen, Raymond began contributing stories to the magazine using the pen name "Paranete." One year, in response to his mother's request for a Christmas story, he produced "Why the Chimes Rang" (a story that would later establish itself as a classic).[3] In 1908, it was published in a book with the same name along with ten additional children's stories, one of which is his other Christmas classic "In the Great Walled Country." Though Alden published two books full of children's stories during the course of his life, he spent the majority of his career as a literary scholar.

In 1894, Alden graduated from the University of Pennsylvania as valedictorian. He obtained an M.A. from Harvard and then returned to the University of Pennsylvania to earn a Ph.D. In 1899, Alden was hired to teach at Stanford, and with the exception of a three year-leave when he headed the English department at the University of Illinois, he remained at Stanford throughout his career.[4]

In 1904, Alden married Barbara Hitt, and eventually they had five children together. Despite the demands of a large family, Alden excelled in his work. He wrote more than a dozen scholarly works and was recognized as an authority on Shakespeare, Tennyson and Thoreau. The Academic Council of Stanford University said that Alden's original research was "thorough and judicious"; his literary criticism showed "sympathy and finesse"; his fiction showed "cleverness and feeling," and his writing of verses showed a "sense of beauty and sincerity."[5] In addition to his literary talents, Alden was also a gifted pianist. Yet, of all his accomplishments, his associates at Stanford noted the following in a memorial resolution written after Alden's death:

"One of the chief moving forces of his nature was strong religious convictions and emotions, and he was a conscientious and orthodox, though liberal, Christian. None of his qualities were more conspicuous than his courage, which was put to a severe test during the suffering tedium and discouragement of long and distressing illnesses."[6]

Alden's illness ultimately claimed his life, and he passed away in 1924. However, his legacy in literature remains alive and well. His writing continues to inspire a variety of readers, from children to scholars.

Alden's Christian commitment is evident in the following story, "The Great Walled Country." It is a Christmas fairy tale that creatively brings to life the biblical lesson: "Do nothing out of selfish ambition or vain conceit, but in humility consider others better than yourselves. Each of you should look not only to your own interests, but also to the interests of others" (Galatians 2:3-4).

---

[1] Alden, Isabella Macdonald. Edited by Grace Livingston Hill. *Memories of Yesterdays*. J.P. Lippincott, 1931.

[2] Creel, Daena. "About Pansy." Retrieved October 19, 2008: http://www.isabellamacdonaldalden.com/about.html.

[3] Creel, Daena. "Dr. Raymond Macdonald Alden, 'Paranete.'" Retrieved October 19, 2008: http://www.isabella-macdonaldalden.com/rma.html. Most of the basic biographical data for Alden is drawn from this source.

[4] The Academic Council of Stanford University. "Memorial Resolution, Raymond M. Alden (1873-1927)." Retrieved October 19, 2008: http://histsoc.stanford.edu/pdfmem/AldenR.pdf.

[5] The Academic Council of Stanford University.

[6] The Academic Council of Stanford University.

The Story
Reading Time: 12 minutes

Away at the northern end of the world, farther than men have ever gone with their ships or their sleds, and where most people suppose that there is nothing but ice and snow, is a land full of children, called The Great Walled Country. This name is given because all around the country is a great wall, hundreds of feet thick and hundreds of feet high. It is made of ice, and never melts, winter or summer; and of course it is for this reason that more people have not discovered the place.

The land, as I said, is filled with children, for nobody who lives there ever grows up. The king and the queen, the princes and the courtiers, may be as old as you please, but they are children for all that. They play a great deal of the time with dolls and tin soldiers, and every night at seven o'clock have a bowl of bread and milk and go to bed. But they make excellent rulers, and the other children are well pleased with the government.

There are all sorts of curious things about the way they live in The Great Walled Country, but this story is only of their Christmas season. One can imagine what a fine thing their Christmas must be, so near the North Pole, with ice and snow everywhere; but this is not all. Grandfather Christmas lives just on the north side of the country, so that his house leans against the great wall and would tip over if it were not for its support. Grandfather Christmas is his name in The Great Walled Country;

353

no doubt we should call him Santa Claus here. At any rate, he is the same person, and, best of all the children in the world, he loves the children behind the great wall of ice.

One very pleasant thing about having Grandfather Christmas for a neighbor is that in The Great Walled Country they never have to buy their Christmas presents. Every year, on the day before Christmas, before he makes up his bundles for the rest of the world, Grandfather Christmas goes into a great forest of Christmas trees, that grows just back of the palace of the king of The Great Walled Country, and fills the trees with candy and books and toys and all sorts of good things. So when night comes, all the children wrap up snugly, while the children in all other lands are waiting in their beds, and go to the forest to gather gifts for their friends. Each one goes by himself, so that none of his friends can see what he has gathered; and no one ever thinks of such a thing as taking a present for himself. The forest is so big that there is room for every one to wander about without meeting the people from whom he has secrets, and there are always enough nice things to go around.

So Christmas time is a great holiday in that land, as it is in all the best places in the world. They have been celebrating it in this way for hundreds of years, and since Grandfather Christmas does not seem to grow old any faster than the children, they will probably do so for hundreds of years to come.

But there was once a time, so many years ago that they would have forgotten all about it if the story were not written in their Big Book and read to them every year, when the children in The Great Walled Country had a very strange Christmas. There came a visitor to the land. He was an old man, and was the first stranger for very many years that had succeeded in getting over the wall. He looked so wise, and was so much interested in what he saw and heard, that the king invited him to the palace, and he was treated with every possible honor.

When this old man had inquired about their Christmas celebration, and was told how they carried it on every year, he listened gravely, and then, looking wiser than ever, he said to the king:

"That is all very well, but I should think that children who have Grandfather Christmas for a neighbor could find a better and easier way. You tell me that you all go out on Christmas Eve to gather presents to give to one another the next morning. Why take so much trouble, and act in such a round about way? Why not go out together, and every one get his own presents? That would save the trouble of dividing them again, and every one would be better satisfied, for he could pick out just what he wanted for himself. No one can tell what you want as well as you can."

This seemed to the king a very wise saying, and he called all his courtiers and counselors about him to hear it. The wise stranger talked further about his plan, and when he had finished they all agreed that they had been very foolish never to have thought of this simple way of getting their Christmas gifts.

"If we do this," they said, "no one can ever complain of what he has, or wish that some one had taken more pains to find what he wanted. We will make a proclamation, and always after this follow the new plan."

So the proclamation was made, and the plan seemed as wise to the children of the country as it had to the king and the counselors. Every one had at some time been a little disappointed with his Christmas gifts; now there would be no danger of that.

On Christmas Eve they always had a meeting at the palace, and sang carols until the time for going to the forest. When the clock struck ten every one said, "I wish you a Merry Christmas!" to the person nearest him, and then they separated to go their ways to the forest. On this particular night it seemed to the king that the music was not quite so merry as usual, and that when the children spoke to one another their eyes did not shine as gladly as he had noticed them in other years; but there could be no good reason for this, since every one was expecting a better time than usual. So he thought no more of it.

There was only one person at the palace that night who was not pleased with the new proclamation about the Christmas gifts. This was a little boy named Inge, who lived not far from the palace with his sister. Now his sister was a cripple, and had to sit all day looking out of the window from her chair; and Inge took care of her, and tried to make her life happy from morning till night. He had always gone to the forest on Christmas Eve and returned with his arms and pockets loaded with pretty things for his sister, which would keep her amused all the coming year. And although she was not able to go after presents for her brother, he did not mind that at all, especially as he had other friends who never forgot to divide their good things with him.

But now, said Inge to himself, what would his sister do? For the king had ordered that no one should gather any presents except for himself, or any more than he could carry away at once. All of Inge's friends were busy planning what they would pick for themselves, but the poor crippled child could not go a step toward the forest. After thinking about it a long time, Inge decided that it would not be wrong if, instead of taking gifts for himself, he took them altogether for his sister. This he would be very glad to do; for what did a boy who could run about and play in the snow care for presents, compared with a little girl who could only sit still and watch others having a good time? Inge did not ask the advice of any one, for he was a little afraid others would tell him he must not do it; but he silently made up his mind not to obey the proclamation.

And now the chimes had struck ten, and the children were making their way toward the forest, in starlight that was so bright that it almost showed their shadows on the sparkling snow. As soon as they came to the edge of the forest, they separated, each one going by himself in the old way, though now there was really no reason why they should have secrets from one another.

Ten minutes later, if you had been in the forest, you might have seen the children standing in dismay with tears on their faces, and exclaiming that there had never been such a Christmas Eve before. For as they looked eagerly about them to the low-bending branches of the evergreen trees, they saw nothing hanging from them that could not be seen every day in the year. High and low they searched, wandering farther into the forest than ever before, lest Grandfather Christmas might have chosen a new place this year for hanging his presents; but still no presents appeared. The king called his counselors about him, and asked them if they knew whether anything of this kind had happened before, but they could tell him nothing. So no one could guess whether Grandfather Christmas had forgotten them, or whether some dreadful accident had kept him away.

As the children were trooping out of the forest, after hours of weary searching, some of them came upon little Inge, who carried over his shoulder a bag that seemed to be full to overflowing. When he saw them looking at him, he cried:

"Are they not beautiful things? I think Grandfather Christmas was never so good to us before."

"Why, what do you mean?" cried the children. "There are no presents in the forest."

"No presents!" said Inge. "I have my bag full of them." But he did not offer to show them, because he did not want the children to see that they were all for his little sister instead of for himself.

Then the children begged him to tell them in what part of the forest he had found his presents, and he turned back and pointed them to the place where he had been. "I left many more behind than I brought away," he said. "There they are! I can see some of the things shining on the trees even from here."

But when the children followed his footprints in the snow to the place where he had been, they still saw nothing on the trees, and thought that Inge must be walking in his sleep, and dreaming that he had found presents. Perhaps he had filled his bag with the cones from the evergreen trees.

On Christmas Day there was sadness all through The Great Walled Country. But those who came to the house of Inge and his sister saw plenty of books and dolls and beautiful toys piled up about the little cripple's chair; and when they asked where these things came from, they were told, "Why, from the Christmas-tree forest." And they shook their heads, not knowing what it could mean.

The king held a council in the palace, and appointed a committee of his most faithful courtiers to visit Grandfather Christmas, and see if they could find what was the matter. In a day or two more the committee set out on their journey. They had very hard work to climb the great wall of ice that lay between their country and the place where Grandfather Christmas lived, but at last they reached the top. And when they came to the other side of the wall, they were looking down into the top of his chimney. It was not hard to go down this chimney into the house, and when they reached the bottom of it they found themselves in the very room where Grandfather Christmas lay sound asleep.

It was hard enough to waken him, for he always slept one hundred days after his Christmas work was over, and it was only by turning the hands of the clock around two hundred times that the committee could do anything. When the clock had struck twelve times two hundred hours, Grandfather Christmas thought it was time for his nap to be over, and he sat up in bed, rubbing his eyes.

"Oh, sir!" cried the prince who was in charge of the committee, "we have come from the king of The Great Walled Country, who has sent us to ask why you forgot us this Christmas, and left no presents in the forest."

"No presents!" said Grandfather Christmas. "I never forget anything. The presents were there. You did not see them, that's all."

But the children told him that they had searched long and carefully, and in the whole forest there had not been found a thing that could be called a Christmas gift.

"Indeed!" said Grandfather Christmas. "And did little Inge, the boy with the crippled sister, find none?"

Then the committee was silent, for they had heard of the gifts at Inge's house, and did not know what to say about them.

"You had better go home," said Grandfather Christmas, who now began to realize that he had been awakened too soon, "and let me finish my nap. The presents were there, but they were never intended for children who were looking only for themselves. I am not surprised that you could not see them. Remember that not everything that wise travelers tell you is wise." And he turned over and went to sleep again.

The committee returned silently to The Great Walled Country, and told the king what they had heard. The king did not tell all the children of the land what Grandfather Christmas had said, but, when the next December came, he made another proclamation, bidding every one to seek gifts for others, in the old way, in the Christmas-tree forest. So that is what they have been doing ever since; and in order that they may not forget what happened, in case any one should ever ask for another change, they have read to them every year from their Big Book the story of the time when they had no Christmas gifts.

Kate's Choice

The Background
Louis May Alcott, 1832-1888
Classic, 19ᵗʰ Century Story

Louisa May Alcott began her life in Pennsylvania. Her mother Abigail came from a prominent Boston family (the Mays) who were active in abolitionism, prison reform and other social causes. Alcott's father, Bronson, was the self-educated son of a Connecticut farmer and mechanic, and despite his lack of formal education, he proved to have a sharp intellect.

By age twenty-four, Bronson began a career in teaching, and shortly after marrying Abigail, he founded a school based on his unique philosophical ideas. The Temple School was briefly famous, having admitted the children of many notable people; however, Bronson was forced to close it down in 1839 after a storm of controversy. He was accused of being blasphemous because of his transcendental views (see p. 262 for more on transcendentalism), obscene because he allowed discussion on topics like childbirth and circumcision, and ridiculous because of his unique teaching methods.

Unfortunately, the school's failure left the family virtually bankrupt, and they were forced to accept assistance from friends and family. Interestingly, the noted writer and philosopher, Ralph Waldo Emerson, was one of the Alcott's main benefactors. With Emerson's support, Bronson was able to pursue another unique project — the creation of a commune called Fruitlands in Harvard, Ma. According to biographer Helena Maragou:

> "Like Bronson Alcott's other ventures, Fruitlands proved short-lived. It dissolved in only eight months after its members failed to produce a crop and, most importantly, to create harmonious relationships with one another. The Fruitlands experiment was Bronson's last serious attempt to assume the responsibilities of the family provider. From 1844 on, the role of the breadwinner was assumed partly by Louisa's mother and sisters, and principally (and finally exclusively) by Louisa herself."[1]

Alcott's early efforts to contribute to the family finances consisted of sewing, teaching and even working in domestic service. However, she began to experiment with writing, and by 1851 she published her first poem, "Sunlight" in *Peterson's* magazine. The following year, her first piece of fiction, "The Rival Painters: A Tale of Rome," appeared in a Boston publication called the *Olive Branch*. Alcott's first book, *Flower Fables*, was published in 1854. It was a collection of fairy tales about flowers that she wrote (when she was only sixteen years old) for Emerson's daughter Ellen. Though the income was modest, the popularity of the book encouraged Alcott to more actively pursue a career in literature. She tirelessly wrote poems, short stories, and reviews for newspapers.

By the early 1860's, Alcott was able to focus exclusively on writing. Her first major literary success was *Hospital Sketches* in 1863. The previous year, she had worked as a Civil War nurse in Washington D.C. However, after only a few months, she became seriously ill and had to return home. Maragou records:

"The experience bore significant personal fruit. She transformed letters she wrote home from Washington into an autobiographical narrative giving vivid details of her life as a Civil War nurse. The little volume became immediately popular in the North because of its intimate depiction of the drama of war behind the battle lines."[2]

It was later discovered that Alcott's illness was caused by mercury poisoning, and she would suffer from its effects for the rest of her life.[3] Regardless, she continued to write, and in addition to her novels she anonymously, or pseudonymously, published a variety of thrillers filled with villains, vengeful plots and even murder. Though they did not contribute to her reputation, these thrillers proved to be financially rewarding.

In 1867, Alcott became the editor of a girl's magazine called *Merry's Museum*. In addition to editing, she contributed poems, stories, and even an advice column under the pseudonym "Aunt Wee."[4] During this time, an editor from Roberts Brothers, a publishing company, asked Alcott to write a novel for girls. In 1868, the first part of the story, called *Little Women*, was published, and the second part was completed the following year. According to Maragou:

"The tremendous success of *Little Women* transformed the author into a veritable celebrity and gave her career a decisive turn toward juvenile fiction. Alcott's financial rewards were plentiful, and fans pursued both her and her works with unrelenting enthusiasm."[5]

Over the course of the 1870's, Alcott devoted almost all of her time to writing for children, and she affectionately became known as "The Children's Friend." At this point in her life, it appears that she abandoned the transcendental views of her father in favor of traditional Christianity. However, we are left to deduce Alcott's personal belief system largely from her works of fiction. In an effort to honor her father, she carefully weeded out any personal records that clearly conflicted with his philosophical system. According to biographer Martha Saxton, "She got rid of most of her diaries and condensed events into snippets and remarks."[6] Yet after Bronson passed away, Alcott admitted, "His philosophy I have never understood."[7]

Alcott's juvenile stories are generally filled with Christian themes, and several of them are set during every child's favorite holiday, Christmas. There is even a prominent Christmas scene in *Little Women*. The sheer volume of wonderful Christmas stories by Alcott made it difficult to choose just one. However, "Kate's Choice" offers a unique lesson about taking care of our own families.

Though the Christmas season generally has the positive affect of inspiring generosity toward strangers in want, often there are needs within one's own extended family that remain unmet. The Bible offers a harsh rebuke for this: "If anyone does not provide for his relatives, and especially for his immediate family, he has denied the faith and is worse than an unbeliever" (1 Timothy 5:8).

"Kate's Choice" is about a forgotten family member whose needs, though not material, go unnoticed. It is Alcott's endearing character, Kate, who teaches others about the significance of taking care of family. Consider what the world might look like if every family looked after its own — physically, emotionally, and spiritually.

---

[1] Maragou, Helena. "Louisa May Alcott." *The Literary Encyclopedia.* February 9, 2004. Retrieved October 12, 2008: http://www.litencyc.com/php/speople.php?rec=true&UID=62. Much of the biography for Louisa May Alcott is drawn from this source.

[2] Maragou, Helena.

[3] Saxton, Martha. *Louisa May Alcott, A Modern Biography.* Farrar, Straus and Giroux, 1995, p. 1.

[4] Maragou, Helena.

[5] Maragou, Helena.

[6] Saxton, Martha, p. 367.

[7] Saxton, Martha, p. 367.

The Story
Reading Time: 30 minutes

"Well, what do you think of her?"
"I think she's a perfect dear, and not a bit stuck up with all her money."
"A real little lady, and ever so pretty."
"She kissed me lots, and doesn't tell me to run away, so I love her."

The group of brothers and sisters standing round the fire laughed as little May finished the chorus of praise with these crowning virtues.

Tall Alf asked the question, and seemed satisfied with the general approval of the new cousin just come from England to live with them. They had often heard of Kate, and rather prided themselves on the fact that she lived in a fine house, was very rich, and sent them charming presents. Now pity was added to the pride, for Kate was an orphan, and all her money could not buy back the parents she had lost. They had watched impatiently for her arrival, had welcomed her cordially, and after a day spent in trying to make her feel at home they were comparing notes in the twilight, while Kate was having a quiet talk with Mamma.

"I hope she will choose to live with us. You know she can go to any of the uncles she likes best," said Alf.

"We are nearer her age than any of the other cousins, and Papa is the oldest uncle, so I guess she will," added Milly, the fourteen-year-old daughter of the house.

"She said she liked America," said quiet Frank.

"Wonder if she will give us a lot of her money?" put in practical Fred, who was always in debt.

"Stop that!" commanded Alf. "Mind now, if you ever ask her for a penny I'll shake you out of your jacket."

"Hush! She's coming," cried Milly, and a dead silence followed the lively chatter.

A fresh-faced bright-eyed girl of fifteen came quietly in, glanced at the group on the rug, and paused as if doubtful whether she was wanted.

"Come on!" said Fred encouragingly.

"Shall I be in the way?"

"Oh! Dear, no, we were only talking," answered Milly, drawing her cousin nearer with an arm about her waist.

"It sounded like something pleasant," said Kate, not exactly knowing what to say.

"We were talking about you," began little May, when a poke from Frank made her stop to ask, "What's that for? We *were* talking about Kate, and we all said we liked her, so it's no matter if I do tell."

"You are very kind," and Kate looked so pleased that the children forgave May's awkward frankness.

"Yes, and we hoped you'd like us and stay with us," said Alf, in the lofty and polite manner which he thought became the young lord of the house.

"I am going to try all the uncles in turn, and then decide; Papa wished it," answered Kate, with a sudden tremble of the lips, for her father was the only parent she could remember, and had been unusually dear for that reason.

"Can you play billiards?" asked Fred, who had a horror of seeing girls cry.

"Yes, and I'll teach you."

"You had a pony-carriage at your house, didn't you?" added Frank, eager to help on the good work.

"At Grandma's — I had no other home, you know," answered Kate.

"What shall you buy first with your money?" asked May, who *would* ask improper questions.

"I'd buy a grandma if I could," and Kate both smiled and sighed.

"How funny! We've got one somewhere, but we don't care much about her," continued May, with the inconvenient candor of a child.

"Have you? Where is she?" and Kate turned quickly, looking full of interest.

"Papa's mother is very old, and lives ever so far away in the country, so of course we don't see much of her," explained Alf.

"But Papa writes sometimes, and Mamma sends her things every Christmas. We don't remember her much, because we never saw her but once, ever so long ago; but we do care for her, and May mustn't say such rude things," said Milly.

"I shall go and see her. I can't get on without a grandmother," and Kate smiled so brightly that the lads thought her prettier than ever. "Tell me more about her. Is she a dear old lady?"

"Don't know. She is lame, and lives in the old house, and has a maid named Dolly, and — that's all I can tell you about her," and Milly looked a little vexed that she could say no more on the subject that seemed to interest her cousin so much.

Kate looked surprised, but said nothing, and stood looking at the fire as if turning the matter over in her mind, and trying to answer the question she was too polite to ask — how could they live without a grandmother? Here the tea-bell rang, and the flock ran laughing downstairs; but, though she said no more, Kate remembered that conversation, and laid a plan in her resolute little mind which she carried out when the time came.

According to her father's wish she lived for a while in the family of each of the four uncles before she decided with which she would make her home. All were anxious to have her, one because of her money, another because her great-grandfather had been a lord, a third hoped to secure her for his son, while the fourth and best family loved her for herself alone. They were worthy people, as the world goes — busy, ambitious, and prosperous; and everyone, old and young, was fond of bright, pretty, generous Kate. Each family was anxious to keep her, a little jealous of the rest, and very eager to know which she would choose.

But Kate surprised them all by saying decidedly when the time came:

"I must see Grandma before I choose. Perhaps I ought to have visited her first, as she is the oldest. I think Papa would wish me to do it. At any rate, I want to pay my duty to her before I settle anywhere, so please let me go."

Some of the young cousins laughed at the idea, and her old-fashioned, respectful way of putting it, which contrasted strongly with their free-and-easy American speech. The uncles were surprised, but agreed to humor her whim, and Uncle George, the eldest, said softly:

"I ought to have remembered that poor Anna was Mother's only daughter, and the old lady would naturally love to see the girl. But, my dear, it will be desperately dull. Only two old women and a quiet country town. No fun, no company, you won't stay long."

"I shall not mind the dullness if Grandma likes to have me there. I lived very quietly in England, and was never tired of it. Nursey can take care of me, and I think the sight of me will do the dear old lady good, because they tell me I am like Mamma."

Something in the earnest young face reminded Uncle George of the sister he had almost forgotten, and recalled his own youth so pleasantly that he said, with a caress of the curly head beside him:

"So it would, I'm sure of it, and I've a great mind to go with you and 'pay my duty' to Mother, as you prettily express it."

"Oh, no, please don't, sir; I want to surprise her, and have her all to myself for a little while. Would you mind if I went quite alone with Nursey? You can come later."

"Not a bit; you shall do as you like, and make sunshine for the old lady as you have for us. I haven't seen her for a year, but I know she is well and comfortable, and Dolly guards her like a dragon. Give her my love, Kitty, and tell her I send her something she will value a hundred times more than the very best tea, the finest cup, or the handsomest tabby that ever purred."

So, in spite of the lamentations of her cousins, Kate went gaily away to find the Grandma whom no one else seemed to value as she did.

You see, Grandpa had been a farmer, and lived contently on the old place until he died; but his four sons wanted to be something better, so they went away one after the other to make their way in the world. All worked hard, got rich, lived splendidly, and forgot as far as possible the old life and the dull old place they came from. They were good sons in their way, and had each offered his mother a home with him if she cared to come. But Grandma clung to the old home, the simple ways, and quiet life, and, thanking them gratefully, she had remained in the big farmhouse, empty, lonely, and plain though it was, compared to the fine homes of her sons.

Little by little the busy men forgot the quiet, uncomplaining old mother, who spent her years thinking of them, longing to see and know their children, hoping they would one day remember how she loved them all, and how solitary her life must be.

Now and then they wrote or paid her a hasty visit, and all sent gifts of far less value to her than one loving look, one hour of dutiful, affectionate companionship.

"If you ever want me, send and I'll come. Or, if you ever need a home, remember the old place is here always open, and you are always welcome," the good old lady said. But they never seemed to need her, and so seldom came that the old place evidently had no charm for them.

It was hard, but the sweet old lady bore it patiently, and lived her lonely life quietly and usefully, with her faithful maid Dolly to serve and love and support her.

Kate's mother, her one daughter, had married young, gone to England, and, dying early, had left the child to its father and his family. Among them little Kate had grown up, knowing scarcely anything of her American relations until she was left an orphan and went back to her mother's people. She had been the pet of her English grandmother, and, finding all the aunts busy, fashionable women, had longed for the tender fostering she had known, and now felt as if only grandmothers could give.

With a flutter of hope and expectation she approached the old house after the long journey was over. Leaving the luggage at the inn, and accompanied by faithful Nurse, Kate went up the village street, and, pausing at the gate looked at the home where her mother had been born.

A large, old-fashioned farmhouse, with a hospitable porch and tall trees in front, an orchard behind, and a capital hill for black-berries in summer, and coasting in winter, close by. All the upper windows were curtained, and made the house look as if is was half asleep. At one of the lower windows sat a portly puss, blinking in the sun, and at the other appeared a cap, a regularly grandmotherly old cap, with a little black bow perked up behind. Something in the lonely look of the house and the pensive droop of the cap made Katy hurry up the walk and tap eagerly at the antique knocker. A brisk little old woman peered out, as if startled at the sound, and Kate asked, smiling, "Does Madam Coverley live here?"

"She does, dear. Walk right in," and throwing wide the door, the maid trotted down a long, wide hall, and announced in a low tone to her mistress:

"A nice, pretty little girl wants to see you, mum."

"I shall love to see a young face. Who is it, Dolly?" asked a pleasant voice.

"Don't know, mum."

"Grandma must guess," and Kate went straight up to the old lady with both hands out, for the first sight of that sweet old face won her heart.

Lifting her spectacles, Grandma looked silently a minute, then opened her arms without a word, and in the long embrace that followed Kate felt assured that she was welcome to the home she wanted.

"So like my Anna! And this is her little girl? God bless you, my darling! So good to come and see me!" said the old lady when she could speak.

"Why, Grandma, I couldn't get on without you, and as soon as I knew where to find you I was in a fidget to be off; but had to do my other visits first, because the uncles had planned it so. This is Dolly, I am sure, and that is my good nurse. Go and get my things please, Nursey. I shall stay here until Grandma sends me away."

"That will never be, dearie. Now tell me everything. It is like an angel coming to see me all of a sudden. Sit close, and let me feel sure it isn't one of the dreams I make to cheer myself when I'm lonesome."

Kate sat on a little stool at Grandma's feet, and, leaning on her knee, told all her little story, while the old lady fed her hungry eyes with the sight of the fresh young face, listened to the music of a loving voice, and felt the happy certainty that someone had remembered her, as she longed to be remembered.

Such a happy day as Kate spent talking and listening, looking at her new home, which she found delightful, and being petted by the two old women, who would hardly let Nursey do anything for her. Kate's quick eyes read the truth of Grandma's lonely life very soon; her warm heart was full of tender pity, and she resolved to devote herself to making the happiness of the dear old lady's few remaining years. For at eighty, one should have the prop of loving children, if ever.

To Dolly and madam it really did seem as if an angel had come, a singing, smiling, chattering sprite, who danced all over the old house, making blithe echoes in the silent rooms, and brightening every corner she entered. Kate opened all the shutters and let in the sun, saying she must see which room she liked best before she settled.

She played on the old piano, that wheezed and jangled, all out of tune; but no one minded, for the girlish voice was as sweet as a lark's. She invaded Dolly's sacred kitchen, and messed to her heart's content, delighting the old soul by praises of her skill, and petitions to be taught all she knew. She pranced to and fro in the long hall, and got acquainted with the lives of painted ancestors hanging there in big wigs or short-waisted gowns. She took possession of Grandma's little parlor, and make it so cozy the old lady felt as if she was bewitched, for cushioned armchairs, fur footstools, soft rugs, and delicate warm shawls appeared like magic. Flowers bloomed in the deep, sunny window-seats, pictures of lovely places seemed to break out on the oaken walls, a dainty work-basket took its place near Grandma's quaint one, and, best of all, the little chair beside her own was seldom empty now.

The first thing in the morning a kiss waked her, and the beloved voice gave her a gay "Good morning, Grandma dear!" All day Anna's child hovered about her with willing hands and feet to serve her, loving heart to return her love, and the tender reverence which is the beautiful tribute the young should pay the old. In the twilight, the bright head always was at her knees; and, in either listening to the stories of the past or making lively plans for the future, Kate whiled away the time that used to be so sad.

Kate never found it lonely, seldom wished for other society, and grew every day more certain that here she could find the cherishing she needed, and do the good she hoped.

Dolly and Nurse got on capitally; each tried which could sing "Little Missy's" praises loudest, and spoil her quickest by unquestioning obedience to every whim or wish. A happy family, and the dull November days went by so fast that Christmas was at hand before they knew it.

All the uncles had written to ask Kate to pass the holidays with them, feeling sure she must be longing for a change. But she had refused them all, saying she should stay with Grandma, who could not go anywhere to join other people's merrymakings, and must have one of her own at home. The uncles urged, the aunts advised, and the cousins teased; but Kate denied them all, yet offended no one, for she was inspired by a grand idea, and carried it out with help from Dolly and Nurse, unsuspected by Grandma.

"We are going to have a little Christmas fun up here among ourselves, and you mustn't know about it until we are ready. So just sit all cozy in your corner, and let me riot about as I like. I know you won't mind, and I think you'll say it is splendid when I've carried out my plan," said Kate, when the old lady wondered what she was thinking about so deeply, with her brows knit and her lips smiling.

"Very well, dear, do anything you like, and I shall enjoy it, only don't get tired, or try to do too much," and with that Grandma became deaf and blind to the mysteries that went on about her.

She was lame, and seldom left her own rooms; so Kate, with her devoted helpers, turned the house topsy-turvy, trimmed up halls and parlors and the great dining room with shining holly and evergreen, laid fires ready for kindling the hearths that had been cold for years, and had beds made up all over the house.

What went on in the kitchen, only Dolly could tell; but such delicious odors as stole out made Grandma sniff the air, and think of merry Christmas revels long ago. Up in her own room Kate wrote lots of letters, and sent orders to the city that made Nursey hold up her hands. More letters came in reply, and Kate had a rapture over every one. Big bundles were left by the express, who came so often that the gates were opened and the lawns soon full of sleigh tracks. The shops in the village were ravaged by Mistress Kate, who laid in stores of gay ribbons, toys, nuts, and all manner of queer things.

"I really think she's lost her mind," said the postmaster as she flew out of the office one day with a handful of letters.

"Pretty critter! I wouldn't say a word against her, not for a mint of money. She's so good to old Mrs. Coverley," answered his fat wife, smiling as she watched Kate ride up the village street on an ox-sled.

If Grandma had thought the girl out of her wits, no one could have blamed her; for on Christmas day she really did behave in the most singular manner.

"You are going to church with me this morning, Grandma. It's all arranged. A closed carriage is coming for us, the sleighing is lovely, the church all trimmed up, and I must have you see it. I shall wrap you in fur, and we will go and say our prayers together, like good girls, won't we?" said Kate, who was in a queer flutter, while her eyes shone, her lips were all smiles, and her feet kept dancing in spite of her.

"Anywhere you like, my darling. I'd start for Australia tomorrow, if you wanted me to go with you," answered Grandma, who obeyed Kate in all things, and seemed to think she could do no wrong.

So they went to church, and Grandma did enjoy it; for she had many blessings to thank God for, chief among them the treasure of a dutiful, loving child. Kate tried to keep herself quiet, but the odd little flutter would not subside, and seemed to get worse and worse as time went on. It increased rapidly as they drove home, and, when Grandma was safe in her little parlor again, Kate's hands trembled so she could hardly tie the strings of the old lady's state and festival cap.

"We must take a look at the big parlor. It is all trimmed up, and I've got my presents in there. Is it ready, Doll?" asked Kate, as the old servant appeared, looking so excited that Grandma said, laughing:

"We have been quiet so long, poor Dolly don't know what to make of a little gaiety."

"Lord bless us, my dear mum! It's all so beautiful and kinder surprisin', I feel as ef merrycles had come to pass agin," answered Dolly, actually wiping away tears with her best white apron.

"Come, Grandma," and Kate offered her arm. "Don't she look sweet and dear?" she added, smoothing the soft, silken shawl about the old lady's shoulders, and kissing the placid old face that beamed at her from under the new cap.

"I always said madam was the finest old lady a-goin', ef folks only knew it. Now, Missy, ef you don't make haste, that parlor door will bust open, and spoil the surprise; for they are just boilin' over in there," with which mysterious remark Dolly vanished, giggling.

Across the hall they went, but at the door Kate paused, and said with a look Grandma never forgot:

"I hope I have done right. I hope you'll like my present, and not find it too much for you. At any rate, remember I meant to please you and give you the thing you need and long for most, my dear old Grandma."

"My good child, don't be afraid. I shall like anything you do, and thank you for your thought of me. What a curious noise! I hope the fire hasn't fallen down."

Without another word, Kate threw open the door and led Grandma in. Only a step or two — for the old lady stopped short and stared about her, as if she didn't know her own best parlor. No wonder she didn't, for it was full of people, and such people! All her sons, their wives and children, rose as she came in, and turned to greet her with smiling faces. Uncle George went up and kissed her, saying, with a choke in his voice, "A merry Christmas, Mother!" and everybody echoed the words in a chorus of goodwill that went straight to the heart.

Poor Grandma could not bear it, and sat down in her big chair, trembling, and sobbing like a little child. Kate hung over her, fearing the surprise had been too much; but joy seldom kills, and presently the old lady was calm enough to look up and welcome them all by stretching out her feeble hands and saying, brokenly yet heartily:

"God bless you, my children! This *is* a merry Christmas, indeed! Now tell me all about it, and who everybody is; for I don't know half the little ones."

Then Uncle George explained that it was Kate's plan, and told how she had made everyone agree to it, pleading so eloquently for Grandma that all other plans were given up. They had arrived while she was at church, and had been with difficulty kept from bursting out before the time.

"Do you like your present?" whispered Kate, quite calm and happy now that the grand surprise was safely over.

Grandma answered with a silent kiss that said more than the warmest words, and then Kate put everyone at ease by leading up the children, one by one, and introducing each with some lively speech. Everybody enjoyed this and got acquainted quickly; for Grandma thought the children the most remarkable she had ever seen, and the little people soon made up their minds that an old lady who had such a very nice, big house, and such a dinner waiting for them (of course they had peeped everywhere), was a most desirable and charming Grandma.

By the time the first raptures were over, Dolly and Nurse and Betsey Jane (a girl hired for the occasion) had got dinner on the table; and the procession, headed by Madam proudly escorted by her eldest son, filed into the dining room where such a party had not met for years.

It would be quite impossible to do justice to that dinner: pen and ink are not equal to it. I can only say that everyone partook copiously of everything; that they laughed and talked, told stories, and sang songs; and when no one could do any more, Uncle George proposed Grandma's health, which was drunk standing, and followed by three cheers. Then up got the old lady, quite rosy and young, excited and gay, and said in a clear strong voice —

"I give you in return the best of grandchildren, little Kate."

I give you my word the cheer they gave Grandma was nothing to the shout that followed these words; for the old lady led off with amazing vigor, and the boys roared so tremendously that the sedate tabby in the kitchen flew off her cushion, nearly frightened into a fit.

After that, the elders sat with Grandma in the parlor, while the younger part of the flock trooped after Kate all over the house. Fires burned everywhere, and the long unused toys of their fathers were brought out for their amusement. The big nursery was full of games, and here Nursey collected the little ones when the larger boys and girls were invited by Kate to go out and coast. Sleds had been provided, and until dusk they kept it up, the city girls getting as gay and rosy as Kate herself in this healthy sport, while the lads frolicked to their hearts' content, building snow forts, pelting one another, and carousing generally without any policeman to interfere or any stupid old ladies to get upset, as at home in the park.

A cozy tea and a dance in the long hall followed, and they were just thinking what they would do next, when Kate's second surprise came.

There were two great fireplaces in the hall: up the chimney of one roared a jolly fire, but the other was closed by a tall fire-board. As they sat about, resting after a brisk contra dance, a queer rustling and tapping was heard behind this fire-board.

"Rats!" suggested the girls, jumping up into the chairs.

"Let's have 'em out!" added the boys, making straight for the spot, intent on fun.

But before they got there, a muffled voice cried, "Stand from under!" and down went the board with a crash, out bounced Santa Claus, startling the lads as much as the rumor of rats had the girls.

A jolly old saint he was, all in fur, with sleigh-bells jingling from his waist and the point of his high cap, big boots, a white beard, and a nose as red as if Jack Frost had had a good tweak at it. Giving himself a shake that set all the bells ringing, he stepped out upon the hearth, saying in a half-gruff, half-merry tone:

"I call this a most inhospitable way to receive me! What do you mean by stopping up my favorite chimney? Never mind, I'll forgive you, for this is an unusual occasion. Here, some of you fellows, lend a hand and help me out with my sack."

A dozen pair of hands had the great bag out in a minute, and, lugging it to the middle of the hall, left it beside St. Nick, while the boys fell back into the eager, laughing crowd that surrounded the newcomer.

"Where's my girl? I want my Kate," said the saint, and when she went to him he took a base advantage of his years, and kissed her in spite of the bread.

"That's not fair," whispered Kate, as rosy as the holly berries in her hair.

"Can't help it — must have some reward for sticking in that horrid chimney so long," answered Santa Claus, looking as roguish as any boy. Then he added aloud, "I've got something for everybody, so make a big ring, and the good fairy will hand round the gifts."

With that he dived into his bag and brought out treasure after treasure, some fine, some funny, many useful, and all appropriate, for the good fairy seemed to have guessed what each one wanted. Shouts of laughter greeted the droll remarks of the jolly saint, for he had a joke about everything, and people were quite exhausted by the time the bottom of the sack was reached.

"Now, then, a rousing good game of blind man's buff, and then this little family must go to bed, for it's past eleven."

As he spoke, the saint cast off his cap and beard, fur coat, and big boots, and proceeded to dance a double shuffle with great vigor and skill; while the little ones, who had been thoroughly mystified, shouted, "Why, it's Alf!" and fell upon him *en masse* as the best way of expressing their delight at his successful performance of that immortal part.

The game of blind man's buff that followed was a "rouser" in every sense of the word, for the gentlemen joined, and the children flew about like a flock of chickens when hawks are abroad. Such peals of laughter, such shouts of fun, and such racing and scrambling that old hall had never seen before. Kate was so hunted that she finally took refuge behind Grandma's chair, and stood there looking at the lively scene, her face full of happiness as she remembered that it was her work.

The going to bed that night was the best joke of all; for, though Kate's arrangements were peculiar, everyone voted that they were capital. There were many rooms, but not enough for all to have one apiece. So the uncles and aunts had the four big chambers, all the boys were ordered into the great playroom, where beds were made on the floor, and a great fire blazing that the camping out might be as comfortable as possible. The nursery was devoted to the girls, and the little ones were sprinkled round wherever a snug corner was found.

How the riotous flock were ever got into their beds no one knows. The lads caroused until long past midnight, and no knocking on the walls of paternal boots, or whispered entreaties of maternal voices through keyholes, had any effect, for it was impossible to resist the present advantages for a grand Christmas rampage.

The girls giggled and gossiped, told secrets, and laid plans more quietly; while the small things tumbled into bed, and went to sleep at once, quite used up with the festivities of this remarkable day.

Grandma, down in her own cozy room, sat listening to the blithe noises with a smile on her face, for the past seemed to have come back again, and her own boys and girls to be frolicking above there, as the used to do forty years ago.

"It's all so beautiful I can't go to bed, Dolly, and lose any of it. They'll go away tomorrow, and I may never see them any more," she said, as Dolly tied on her nightcap and brought her slippers.

"Yes, you will, mum. That dear child has made it so pleasant they can't keep away. You'll see plenty of 'em, if they carry out half the plans they have made. Mrs. George wants to come up and pass the summer here; Mr. Tom says he shall send his boys to school here, and every girl among them has promised Kate to make her a long visit. The thing is done, mum, and you'll never be lonely any more."

"Thank God for that!" and Grandma bent her head as if she had received a great blessing. "Dolly, I want to go and look at those children. It seems so like a dream to have them here, I must be sure of it," said Grandma, folding her wrapper about her, and getting up with great decision.

"Massy on us, mum, you haven't been up them stairs for months. The dears are all right, warm as toasts, and sleepin' like dormice, I'll warrant," answered Dolly, taken aback at this new whim of old madam's.

But Grandma would go, so Dolly gave her an arm, and together the two old friends hobbled up the wide stairs, and peeped in at the precious children. The lads looked like a camp of weary warriors reposing after a victory, and Grandma went laughing away when she had taken a proud survey of this promising portion of the rising generation. The nursery was like a little convent full of rosy nuns sleeping peacefully; while a pictured Saint Agnes, with her lamb, smiled on them from the wall, and the firelight flickered over the white figures and sweet faces, as if the sight were too fair to be lost in darkness. The little ones lay about promiscuously, looking like dissipated Cupids with sugar hearts and faded roses still clutched in their chubby hands.

"My darlings!" whispered Grandma, lingering fondly over them to cover a pair of rosy feet, put back a pile of tumbled curls, or kiss a little mouth still smiling in its sleep.

But when she came to the coldest corner of the room, where Kate lay on the hardest mattress, under the thinnest quilt, the old lady's eyes were full of tender tears; and, forgetting the stiff joints that bent so painfully, she knelt slowly down, and, putting her arms about the girl, blessed her in silence for the happiness she had given one old heart.

Kate woke at once, and started up, exclaiming with a smile:

"Why, Grandma, I was dreaming about an angel, and you look like one with your white gown and silvery hair!"

"No, dear, you are the angel in this house. How can I ever give you up?" answered madam, holding fast the treasure that came to her so late.

"You never need to, Grandma, for I have made my choice."

Little Piccola

The Background
Celia Thaxter, 1835-1894
Classic, 19th Century Poem (Adapted into a story in 1914 by Frances Jenkins Olcott)

Celia Thaxter was the daughter of a lighthouse keeper on the Isles of the Shoals, a small group of islands situated near the New England coast. Growing up in an isolated environment gave Celia time to freely enjoy the beauty of the landscape that surrounded her, and she cherished her island world.

After living on both White Island and Smuttynose Island, Celia's family settled on Appledore Island, the largest of the Isles of the Shoals.[1] Her father built a large resort hotel, and hired a man named Levi Thaxter to manage it. Levi also worked as a tutor to Celia, and though he was fifteen years old than her, they married in 1851. Celia was only sixteen.

After settling in Massachusetts in 1856, the Thaxter marriage began to suffer. Celia was nostalgic for the islands and worried about her husband's financial extravagance.[2] She found expression in verse, and one of her poems (titled "Land-Locked" by an editor) was printed without her knowledge in the prestigious *Atlantic Monthly* in 1861. It expressed her longing for the "caressing murmur of the wave that breaks in tender music on the shore."[3]

Realizing that her poetry could contribute to the family finances, Celia began to devote more time to writing, and her work was accepted by a variety of publications. Unfortunately, her success seemed only to further tension with her husband who resented her growing popularity. Though the couple had three sons together,[4] they began to live separate lives. They never divorced; however, Celia would often travel back to Appledore Island and spend long periods of time there.

Celia proved to be a popular hostess at her father's hotel. She welcomed and entertained some of the most notable literary people of her day including Ralph Waldo Emerson, Henry David Thoreau, and Harriet Beecher Stowe. Though Celia was always self-conscious about her lack of formal education, these reputable visitors undoubtedly considered Celia to be their literary equal.

Celia felt at home on Appledore Island. A significant part of her time there was spent with her mother, so she was completely devastated when her mother passed away in 1877. However, this loss turned her to God for the first time, and her later works reflected this change. Her poem titled "Submission," in the book *Drift-Weed* (1878), speaks of "groping to find hope" in "death's awful mystery" and "reaching empty arms above" to "clasp God's hand."[5]

In 1884, Celia published *Poems for Children* in which she included a poem called "Piccola." The poem beautifully illustrates God's provision for a poor girl on Christmas Day. The Bible speaks frequently about God's concern for those in need, and Celia's use of a bird in her poem calls to mind two different passages that quote the words of Jesus. The first is about worry:

"Therefore I tell you, do not worry about your life, what you will eat or drink; or about your body, what you will wear. Is not life more important than food, and the body more important than clothes? Look at the birds of the air; they do not sow or reap or store away in barns, and yet your heavenly Father feeds them. Are you not much more valuable than they? Who of you by worrying can add a single hour to his life?" (Matthew 6:25-27).

The second is about fear:

"Are not two sparrows sold for a penny? Yet not one of them will fall to the ground apart from the will of your Father. And even the very hairs of your head are all numbered. So don't be afraid; you are worth more than many sparrows" (Matthew 10:29-31).

Celia's poem presents a lovely example of God's tender concern for the poor, and another great author, Frances Jenkins Olcott (1873-1963), recognized its worth. Olcott adapted Thaxter's poem into story form for her collection of *Good Stories for Great Holidays* (1914). In addition to writing many children's books herself, Olcott was head of the Children's department at Carnegie Library. She is widely known for her effort to distribute children's literature throughout the United States.

---

[1] McHenry, Robert. *Famous American Women: A Biographical Dictionary from Colonial Times to the Present.* Courier Dover Publications, 1983, p. 410.

[2] Walker, Cheryl, editor. *American Women Poets of the Nineteenth Century, An Anthology.* Rutgers University Press, 1992, p. 294. Much of the biography for Thaxter is drawn from this source.

[3] Thaxter, Celia. *Poems.* Hurd and Houghton, 1874, p. 10.

[4] Johnson, Rossiter, editor. *The Twentieth Century Biographical Dictionary of Notable Americans.* The Biographical Society, 1904, entry on "Celia Thaxter."

[5] Thaxter, Celia. *Drift-Weed.* Houghton, Mifflin and Company, 1894, p. 90.

The Story
Reading Time: 3 minutes

In the sunny land of France there lived many years ago a sweet little maid named Piccola. Her father had died when she was a baby, and her mother was very poor and had to work hard all day in the fields for a few sous [coins].

Little Piccola had no dolls and toys, and she was often hungry and cold, but she was never sad nor lonely.

What if there were no children for her to play with! What if she did not have fine clothes and beautiful toys! In summer there were always the birds in the forest, and the flowers in the fields and meadows — the birds sang so sweetly, and the flowers were so bright and pretty!

In the winter when the ground was covered with snow, Piccola helped her mother, and knit long stockings of blue wool.

The snow-birds had to be fed with crumbs, if she could find any, and then, there was Christmas Day.

But one year her mother was ill and could not earn any money. Piccola worked hard all the day long, and sold the stockings which she knit, even when her own little bare feet were blue with the cold.

As Christmas Day drew near she said to her mother, "I wonder what the good Saint Nicholas will bring me this year. I cannot hang my stocking in the fireplace, but I shall put my wooden shoe on the hearth for him. He will not forget me, I am sure."

"Do not think of it this year, my dear child," replied her mother. "We must be glad if we have bread enough to eat."

But Piccola could not believe that the good saint would forget her. On Christmas Eve she put her little wooden patten on the hearth before the fire, and went to sleep to dream of Saint Nicholas.

As the poor mother looked at the little shoe, she thought how unhappy her dear child would be to find it empty in the morning, and wished that she had something, even if it were only a tiny cake, for a Christmas gift. There was nothing in the house but a few sous, and these must be saved to buy bread.

When the morning dawned Piccola awoke and ran to her shoe.

Saint Nicholas had come in the night. He had not forgotten the little child who had thought of him with such faith.

See what he had brought her. It lay in the wooden patten, looking up at her with its two bright eyes, and chirping contentedly as she stroked its soft feathers.

A little swallow, cold and hungry, had flown into the chimney and down to the room, and had crept into the shoe for warmth.

Piccola danced for joy, and clasped the shivering swallow to her breast.

She ran to her mother's bedside. "Look, look!" she cried. "A Christmas gift, a gift from the good Saint Nicholas!" And she danced again in her little bare feet.

Then she fed and warmed the bird, and cared for it tenderly all winter long; teaching it to take crumbs from her hand and her lips, and to sit on her shoulder while she was working.

In the spring she opened the window for it to fly away, but it lived in the woods near by all summer, and came often in the early morning to sing its sweetest songs at her door.

One Solitary Life

The Background
James Allan Francis, 1864-1928
Sermon Excerpt, 20th Century

Dr. James Allan Francis was born in Nova Scotia, Canada. He became a pastor at age twenty-one and served in ministry for the remainder of his life. His first pastorate was in New York City at the Riverside Baptist Church, and after serving in other varied pastorates in the East, he came to Los Angeles in 1914.[1]

Though he had a busy life as a pastor, Francis was able to publish a handful of books: *Drops from a Living Fountain* (1895), *Christ's Mould of Prayer* (1924), and *Christ is All And Other Sermons* (1928). His publications are full of passionate encouragement for Christians to know their Lord, to rely on him, and to follow his example.

Francis' most famous words, now known as "One Solitary Life," originated as part of a sermon that he delivered on July 11, 1926 to the Baptist Young People's Union at a Los Angeles Convention.[2] A friend transcribed the message titled "Arise, Sir Knight," and Dr. Francis published it that same year in a collection called *The Real Jesus and Other Sermons.*

Since one section of the sermon was particularly popular, minor changes were made to the original words in order to circulate them independently. This adapted version was first published around 1930 by The American Baptist Publication Society and was titled "Jesus — A Brief Life." This is the version that follows.

Over time, Francis' powerful description of Christ came to be known as "One Solitary Life" (the last words of the passage), and it was most often circulated during the Christmas season. Truly, it is remarkable to consider how Christ's birth proved to be predictive of how he would spend the rest of his life on earth — in great humility.

Interestingly, Francis' passage was so widely circulated that, along the way, it's authorship fell into obscurity. In fact, to this day, the words continue to be credited to an anonymous author. Perhaps this anonymity is fitting. After all, Francis' purpose was to turn attention to one particular man and his "one solitary life."

---

[1] "Historian Tracks Down Description of Christ." *Los Angeles Times*. December 1, 1973, p. 32.

[2] Francis, James Allan. *The Real Jesus and Other Sermons*. The Judson Press, 1926, p.121.

The Story

Reading Time: 2 minutes

Here is a man who was born in an obscure village as the child of a peasant woman. He grew up in another obscure village.

He worked in a carpenter shop until he was thirty and then for three years was an itinerant preacher.

He never wrote a book.

He never held an office.

He never owned a home.

He never had a family.

He never went to college.

He never put his foot inside a big city.

He never traveled two hundred miles from the place where he was born.

He never did one of the things that usually accompany greatness.

He had no credentials but himself.

He had nothing to do with this world except the naked power of his divine manhood.

While still a young man the tide of popular opinion turned against him.

His friends ran away.

One of them denied him.

Another betrayed him.

He was turned over to his enemies.

He went through the mockery of a trial.

He was nailed upon the cross between two thieves.

His executioners gambled for the only piece of property he had on earth while he was dying, and that was his coat.

When he was dead, he was taken down and laid in a borrowed grave through the pity of a friend.

Nineteen wide centuries have come and gone and today he is the center of the human race and the leader of the column of progress.

I am far within the mark when I say that all the armies that ever marched, and all the navies that were ever built, and all the parliaments that ever sat and all the kings that ever reigned, put together, have not affected the life of man upon the earth as powerfully as has this one solitary life.

Saint Lucy

The Background
The Life of a Saint, 283-304 AD

St. Lucy (or Lucia), whose name means "light," was a contemporary of St. Nicholas. She lived in Syracuse, Sicily during the reign of the Roman Emperor Diocletian who initiated a great persecution against Christians in 303 AD. Though many of the details of Lucy's life are unknown, she is celebrated for her commitment to purity, as well as for her generosity. She was, without question, a godly young woman who died for her faith in 304 AD.

Shortly after Lucy's death, she was honored as a saint. An inscription dating back to 400 AD has been found in Syracuse, and references to her are found in early Roman documents. Furthermore, according to Encyclopedia Britannica, "As evidence of her early fame, two churches are known to have been dedicated to her in Britain before the 8th century, at a time when the land was largely pagan."[1]

St. Lucy's day is observed on December 13. In Scandinavian countries, it is one of the most popular celebrations of the year and marks the beginning of the Christmas season. Young girls dress in white and wear a crown of lights on their head in honor of Lucy. Reportedly, the tradition is based on a belief that Lucy wore a lighted wreath on her head when she delivered provisions to persecuted Christians in the underground catacombs of Syracuse. Carrying lights on her head allowed her to fill her arms with as many goods as possible. Interestingly, the Scandinavian celebrations of St. Lucy's day may in fact mark the first distinctly Christian use of lighted wreaths (see p. 166 for more detail).

The following story is drawn mainly from Alban Butler's *The Lives of the Fathers, Martyrs, and Other Principal Saints* (1866), a source that relies heavily on both the *Acta* (a fifth century record) and St. Aldhelm (around 639-709 AD).[2] Most of the dialogue is drawn from either Aelfric's *Lives of Saints*, written by Aelfric of Eynsham (around 955-1010 AD)[3] or *The Golden Legend* by Jacobus de Voragine (around 1230 – 1298).[4]

---

[1] Encyclopedia Britannica. "Saint Lucy." Retrieved September 30, 2008 from Encyclopedia Britannica Online: http://www.britannica.com/EBchecked/topic/350717/Saint-Lucy.

[2] Butler, Alban. *The Lives of the Fathers, Martyrs, and Other Principal Saints*. J. Duffy, 1866, pp. 201-203.

[3] Aelfric of Eynsham. *Aelfric's Lives of Saints*. Walter W. Skeat edition. Early English Text Society, N. Trübner & Co., 1881, pp. 211-218.

[4] de Voragine, Jacobus. *The Golden Legend*. Translated and Adapted by Granger Ryan and Helmut Ripperger, Ayer Company Publishers, Inc., 1969.

The Story
Reading Time: 8 minutes

Lucy was admired for her pleasant features since her birth; yet throughout her childhood, her eyes carried a quiet grief. Though Lucy had been born into honor and wealth in the city of Syracuse, Sicily, and though her mother Eutychia was loving and attentive, Lucy had lost her father in infancy, and she longed for his love. Lucy had been raised in the Christian faith from her cradle, but she had never pursued God as her first and greatest love – as the only one who could satisfy her longing for a father and fill the emptiness in her soul.

As Lucy grew into a young woman, she committed to seeking God, and she gradually became acquainted with him. With time, her eyes began to sparkle and her life began to shine with good deeds. Surely Lucy came to embody her name, which means "light," and the change was evident to all. Lucy's mother, in particular, was overjoyed to see her daughter's newfound happiness.

There was only one secret that Lucy kept from her mother Eutychia — she committed her virginity to God and determined to remain unmarried for the rest of her life. Ignorant of Lucy's vow, her mother continually persuaded her to marry. Lucy was successful in avoiding the pressure for several years, partly because her mother became distracted by a medical condition – a continual flow of blood.

After four troublesome years and many attempts at finding a remedy, Eutychia began to lose hope of recovering. Fearing that her health would prevent her from caring for herself and protecting her precious daughter, Eutychia consented to give Lucy's hand in marriage to a noble pagan suitor.

Lucy was devastated to hear news of the betrothal, but she trusted that God would provide a way out for her. As she devoted herself to prayer, she felt led to make a pilgrimage with her mother to Cantania, a city less than 50 miles away. Word had traveled to Syracuse that a great many miracles were taking place there. Lucy persuaded Eutychia to travel with her, and they hastily set out on their journey.

Shortly after arriving in Cantania, Lucy and Eutychia attended Mass. The Scripture reading for the day was from the gospel of Luke about Jesus healing a woman who had "been subject to bleeding for twelve years" (Luke 8:43). Lucy felt certain that God intended to heal her mother, and she committed to praying throughout the night for God's grace. She prayed for many hours before falling asleep exhausted. In a dream she had a vision of Agatha, the patron saint of Cantania, among a host of angels.

Agatha, a virgin who had been killed for her Christian faith over 50 years prior, said, "My sister Lucy, God has heard your prayers. Your holy faith has helped your mother. Look! She is entirely healed through Christ. Take her back to Syracuse, and be not afraid of the trials that await you there. Christ, your groom, desires to honor you with the glorious robes of martyrdom."

Lucy rose trembling from the bright vision she had seen and said to her mother, "You are mightily healed! Now I pray that you will never give me to any bridegroom but the one who has restored your health. Furthermore, as for the property you intended to give me for my marriage, allow me to use it for my Lord."

Eutychia replied, "Dearest daughter, you know my wealth and how I have carefully increased your father's property since his death. First close my eyes, then do as you please with all of our goods."

Lucy said, "Mother, whatever you give away at your death, you give because you cannot take it with you. Give now while you are healthy, and you will have reward in the world to come."

After returning to Syracuse, Lucy frequently exhorted her mother to give away all of their goods to the poor, to widows and to orphans. And when a great persecution of Christians broke out during the reign of Diocletian, the Roman Emperor, their generosity extended to exiles.

During this time, many Christians went into hiding in underground burial places called catacombs. These believers were suffering greatly for lack of food and clothing. Furthermore, they spent their days in darkness. As the Christmas season approached, young Lucy determined to seek out these brothers and sisters to bring them desperately needed provisions.

The cold season was setting in, and it was no easy task to travel secretly to the catacombs and then make a way through the darkness. Moreover, Lucy desired to bring as many goods as she could carry. She did not dare relinquish an arm in order to carry a light. Thus, she designed a wreath for her head in which to place candles. The sight of young Lucy crowned with light was like a heavenly vision to the exiles in the catacombs. She was indeed a light in their darkness, and she earned a permanent place in their hearts.

Meanwhile, ever since Lucy's suitor learned how she despised his love, his wrath toward her had been growing. Once the persecution of Christians was in full force, he found the opportunity to avenge his pride by denouncing her to his friend Paschasius, the Governor of Sicily.

Paschasius immediately summoned Lucy and commanded her to offer sacrifices to idols. But Lucy answered him, "The sacrifice which is pleasing to God is to visit the poor and to help them in their time of need. And since I have nothing else to offer, I shall offer myself to the Lord."

Paschasius responded, "Your words are fit to be spoken to ignorant people like yourself, but to me, who keeps the decrees of the emperor, you speak them in vain."

Lucy answered, "You keep the decrees of your master, and I, for my part, wish to keep the law of my God. You fear your master, and I fear God. You are careful not to offend him; I am conscious of offending God. You desire to please the emperor, and I wish to please Christ. Do then what you think is right in your eyes, for I do what is right before God."

Then Paschasius said, "You speak like a fool. Furthermore, you have behaved like a vile woman by squandering your father's riches on seducers."

Lucy replied, "As to my father's riches, I have invested them wisely, and never have I allowed near me any seducers, either of the body or of the soul."

"And who are the seducers of the body and the soul of whom you speak?" Paschasius asked.

"You and those like you are the seducers of the soul, because you lead men to turn away from their Creator; as for seducers of the body, they are those who would have us put fleshly pleasures ahead of eternal joys."

"Your words will cease when you feel the blow of the lash," roared Paschasius.

"The words of God will never cease."

"Do you pretend to be God?" Paschasius asked scornfully.

Lucy answered, "I am the handmaid of God, who said to his disciples, 'You will be brought before governors and kings as witnesses to them. . . . Do not worry about what to say or how to say it. At that time you will be given what to say, for it will not be you speaking, but the Holy Spirit speaking through you."

Then Paschasius asked, "Do you claim to have the Holy Spirit in you?"

"Whoever lives chastely is the temple of the Holy Spirit," said Lucy.

"Then I will send you to a house of ill repute where your body will be violated, and you will lose the Holy Spirit."

Lucy responded, "The body is not polluted unless the soul consents. If my body is ravished against my wishes, my chastity will thereby be doubled. You cannot change my will. As for my body, here it is, ready for every torture."

Paschasius summoned men to drag Lucy away to a loathsome house, and told the men, "Invite the crowd to have their way with this woman until she dies." But, try as they might, the Holy Spirit made Lucy so heavy that she could not be moved.

In anger, Paschasius demanded an explanation, "What witchcraft is this that so many men are unable to move a lone maiden?"

Lucy replied, "It is not witchcraft, it is the power of Christ. You could add another thousand men, and they would still be unable to move me."

At this point, Paschasius was beside himself with rage, and he commanded that a great fire be built around Lucy and that pitch, resin and boiling oil be thrown upon her.

Lucy said, "I have obtained from Christ in prayer the assurance that deadly fire will have no power over me so that you will be put to shame. Furthermore, my example is intended to free the faithful from their fear of suffering and deprive unbelievers of their cruel joy."

Paschasius was so furious that he could not be appeased. His friends urged him to kill her quickly, and one hastily plunged a sword into her throat. But, far from losing the power of speech, Lucy spoke many words of encouragement to believers before she died, and she admonished them to be strong and courageous in the Lord.

As Lucy breathed her last, her eyes were filled with light. She must have been gazing on the Lord in all his glory, because the reflection in her eyes was so radiant that those people who were near her had to turn away. Though believers greatly mourned the loss of Lucy's light on earth that day, they rejoiced over her birth into heaven. Furthermore, because of her example, they were greatly strengthened in faith during the next several years of persecution. Soon after Lucy's death, she was honored as a saint and remains so to this day.

Sir Gawain and the Green Knight

The Background
Medieval Legend, Adapted and Abridged

Sir Gawain was the nephew of the famous King Arthur, and his adventures with the Green Knight were set during the Christmas seasons of two consecutive years. In medieval times, the greatest holiday celebrations took place on the days after Christmas and included the New Year. The following story helps shed light on how medieval nobility may have spent their Christmas holiday. Moreover, it gives insight into the connotations that were attached to various Christmas symbols like holly, stars and the color green.

As with most Arthurian legends, the story emphasizes characteristics like honor, chivalry and integrity; it is distinct, however, in that the hero, noble as he is, fails to adhere to some of his own grand values. This uniqueness makes the story all the more appropriate for Christmas. As we all recognize our tendency to fall short of perfect virtue, we better understand the need for Christ as our Savior.

The oldest known manuscript of the story of the Green Knight is dated around 1400 AD. By this time, the legends of Arthur had been passed down in oral form for some six centuries. Though the anonymous author may have simply retold a story that had been known for many years and in many places, he told it particularly well – with both style and humor.

The author, the "Gawain poet" (or the "Pearl poet" as he is often called), wrote the story in an alliterative verse form. Instead of using rhyme, each individual line of the story used words that started with the same syllable. For example, here is an attempt to preserve, in modern English, the alliterative form of lines 37 and 38:

The <u>k</u>ing lay at <u>C</u>amelot upon <u>Ch</u>ristmas
With many <u>l</u>ovely <u>l</u>ords and <u>l</u>adies

The original poem is made up of 2,530 lines and reveals that the author had an extensive vocabulary from which to draw. Though his identity is unknown, much can be learned about him from his writing. According to Dr. W. R. J. Barron, research fellow at the University of Exeter:

"We do not know who he was, but from his own work we can see that he was widely read in the most sophisticated literature of the age, religious and secular, English, French and Latin. He was a provincial, writing in the dialect of his region and in the alliterative verse traditional there, but on the evidence of his poetry he had an intimate knowledge of aristocratic life, architecture, etiquette, hunting, feasting, dress and armour, and the terms of courtly conversation. He may well have lived in one of the great castles of Lancashire, Staffordshire or Derbyshire. . . . One thing, however, is certain: he was a writer of genius. Of his four poems, two, the biblical homilies *Purity* and *Patience*, rank high in Middle

English literature, and two amongst the masterpieces of any period. One is *Sir Gawain*, the other is the religious poem *Pearl*."[1]

Interestingly J. R. R. Tolkien, best known for his *Lord of the Ring* series, is often erroneously ascribed as the author of *Sir Gawain and the Green Knight*. As a Middle English scholar, Tolkien, and his friend E. V. Gordon, published an academic edition of the "Gawain poet" text (along with extensive notes) in 1925. Tolkien also spent many years working to translate the story for a broader audience while still maintaining its unique literary form. When his popular translation was finally published in 1975, a few years after his death, it listed him as the author rather than the translator. As a result, the story continues to be attributed to him. There were, however, a variety of other modern English translations of *Sir Gawain and the Green Knight* before Tolkien's.

The following is an abridged version of the story. It excludes various details about hunting trips but otherwise closely resembles the original. It relies heavily on two translations. The first is a 1900 translation by Jessie L. Weston, who noted in the preface that she made "an attempt to render [the poem] more accessible to the general public, by giving it a form that shall be easily intelligible, and at the same time preserve as closely as possible the style of the author."[2] The second source is an excellent revised edition of a 1974 book by W. R .J. Barron, who provides the original text side by side with a literal translation.[3] The original "Gawain poet" manuscript is known as *Cotton Nero A.x, art 3*, following a naming system used by one of its owners, Robert Cotton, a collector of Medieval English texts.

Enjoy the traditional "flowery" language of this wonderful Arthurian legend!

---

[1] Barron, W.R.J. *Sir Gawain and the Green Knight*. Text and facing translation edited by W. R. J. Barron. Manchester University Press, 2004, pp. 3-4.

[2] Weston, Jessie Laidlay. *Sir Gawain and the Green Knight: A Middle-English Arthurian Romance Retold in Modern Prose, with Introduction & Notes*. Translated by Jessie Laidlay Weston. D. Nutt, 1900. p. vi.

[3] Barron, W.R.J.

The Story
Reading Time: 30 minutes

If you think that the following story sounds strange and unbelievable, I can only tell you that magical things were known to happen during the reign of the great King Arthur. If you listen for a little while, I will tell you a tale just as I have heard it told.

Every Christmas, the king and his knights would gather in Camelot for a great celebration. The most famous knights in Christendom and the fairest ladies who ever lived would gather together for feasting and merry-making. And he who held court was the most handsome and the most noble of men, King Arthur.

After many days of feasting, the New Year arrived, and all of the court gathered to celebrate Christmas anew. Following Mass, gifts were joyfully exchanged and the merriment continued until dinner. Once all the guests were seated, Arthur appealed to his stately company to share a tale of some great adventure or act of chivalry. He would not eat until he heard a new and exciting story that he could believe. This was his custom at every significant feast, because he was a noble man who became restless with idle talk.

And so, as food was being served to his guests, Arthur stood in his place and listened graciously to various stories. He had not yet taken his food when an awesome figure entered the room on a horse. The man was so large that he may have been half-giant. He was quite handsome except that he was bright green all over. His clothes, his hair, his beard and his skin were all green. Even his horse, stirrups and saddle were green. He was decorated with green jewels and gold so that he gleamed and sparkled all over. His glance was bright as fire, and it seemed that no man could possibly survive a blow from him.

Yet, the green knight had no helmet, no armor, no spear and no shield. In one of his hands he carried only a sprig of holly, which is at its greenest when the woods are bare. In the other hand he carried an enormous green axe. He asked, "Where is the ruler of this company?"

For a long moment the knights and ladies simply stared at him. They had seen many marvels before but never one such as this. They were silent not so much due to fear, but partly out of curiosity and partly out of deference to their king.

King Arthur, of course, was not at all afraid. He said, "Sir, you are truly welcome here. I am Arthur, the head of this house. Please dismount and join our feast. Whatever your errand, we can learn of it later."

"No," replied the Green Knight. "It is not my intent to stay. However, I have come here because of your renown and the reputation of your knights as the bravest and noblest in the land. You may be assured that I come in peace by the holly branch that I carry, and if you are as good as men say, you will graciously grant me the sport that I request."

King Arthur answered, "Courteous knight, if you desire a single combat, you will not fail to get one here."

"No, I do not desire a fight," said the Green Knight. "What I ask is for a Christmas game. If anyone here is so bold, let him fearlessly strike one blow for another. I will give him my axe to use as he pleases, and I will undergo the first blow unarmed. I will remain unmoved on this spot to receive the first blow, provided that I may reserve the right to deal the next blow in a year."

Arthur's court sat stunned, and when no one spoke, the Green Knight laughed and mocked them, "What? Is this the court of Arthur that is known so well throughout the realm? Are you cowering in fear?"

At this Arthur took offense and boldly rose to his feet to accept the challenge. But his nephew, Gawain, begged that the contest might be his. He said, "Uncle, it seems to me that when a foolish challenge is made so arrogantly in your court, it is not fitting for you to accept it — especially when there are so many here that are eager to serve you. Furthermore, since I am the least among the court, my life would be the smallest loss. I am esteemed only because you are my uncle. For I have not yet had opportunity to demonstrate virtue on my own."

As the nobles discussed the matter, they all agreed that Arthur should be exempt from the foolish challenge and that the contest should be given to Gawain. With Arthur's permission, Gawain arose from his seat and approached the Green Knight. After taking the axe in his hand, Arthur gave him God's blessing and urged him to have a resolute heart and a steady hand.

The Green Knight took his stance, bending his head a little and exposing the flesh of his neck. Gawain boldly lifted the axe and brought it down so precisely that the head was cleanly severed from his body. Yet, the Green Knight neither staggered nor fell. Instead, he picked up his head and mounted his horse. Holding his head in his hands, the mouth of the Green Knight spoke thus, "See to it, Gawain, that in a year and a day, you seek me out in the Green Chapel. I am known by many to reside there, and I will be waiting to repay your blow." With that, he dashed out of the door.

Then King Arthur said aloud to his fair queen Guinevere, "Let nothing disturb you today. Such things are proper at Christmas time. Furthermore, I can now take my meal, for I have seen a marvelous thing." He turned to Gawain and said, "Put your axe on the wall as a reminder of the bold adventure that awaits you, and take courage; God will be with you!" Then the court joined together to celebrate the New Year and praise Gawain for his good courage.

The following seasons past quickly, and by All Saint's Day on November 1, King Arthur held a feast in honor of Gawain. Though all of the court spoke of pleasant things, they were secretly distressed in their hearts on account of the journey that lay before Gawain. But the knight himself remained cheerful, and he began his preparations the following day.

When Gawain was ready to depart, he came to the king to request his leave of the noble lords and ladies of the court. They kissed him, escorted him out and commended him to Christ. Gawain and his horse, Gryngolet, were both wonderfully dressed, and as Gawain prepared to mount, he was presented with a stunning shield. It was bright red with a pentangle, or five-pointed star, of gold. And just why the pentangle was appropriate for this noble lord, I must tell, though it will delay me.

First, Gawain was proved faultless in his five senses. Second, he was never at fault with his five fingers. Third, he drew strength from the suffering of Christ and his five wounds (the piercing of his two hands, two feet and side). Fourth, he drew happiness from the five joys of Christ (the Annunciation, the Nativity, the Resurrection, the Ascension and the Assumption). Fifth, he displayed the five great virtues of knighthood: generosity, love, purity, courtesy and compassion.

So as Gawain set on his way, the people watched with tears in their eyes. They lamented that such a noble knight should perish on account of a strange and magical man. For it seemed to them that Gawain should live a long and prosperous life and bring further renown to his God and king and country.

As Gawain rode through the woods and hills seeking the Green Chapel, he spent many nights alone; he had no company save his horse. Furthermore, he traveled through terrain where the people loved neither God nor man. Everywhere he went, he inquired whether anyone had heard of the Green Knight of the Green Chapel, but they all denied it.

For many weeks, the good knight suffered the greatest hardships, enduring discomforts and perils of all kinds. When at last Christmas Eve arrived, Gawain was distressed that he might not manage to see Mass and celebrate that birth of the Lord, who on Christmas day was born of a virgin to end our troubles. He prayed that God would provide a way for him.

Just then, hidden among many massive trees, he came upon the fairest castle he had ever seen. When he observed that the drawbridge was up and that the gates were firmly shut, he called aloud to make himself known. At once, a courteous porter came to inquire of his business.

"Good sir," said Gawain, "Would you deliver my request for shelter to the master of this house?"

The porter quickly returned with many servants to receive the noble knight. They attended him well, and the lord of the house came to greet him.

"You are welcome here. Treat everything here as your own," said the lord.

Gawain accepted the warmth of the fire and the abundance of fine food with deep gratitude. For, he had suffered from cold and hunger for many weeks. And when the lord and his household learned the identity of Gawain, they were greatly pleased. For they had heard of him, and of Arthur and of the Round Table, and they were anxious to profit from Gawain's good breeding. They desired to hear his polished phrases of courtly discourse and watch his masterly display of good manners.

When the meal was finished, everyone made his or her way to the chapel for the solemn evening service of the festive season. Afterward, Gawain was introduced to the lady of the house, the wife of the lord, whom he thought fairer than even Guinevere.

On the following day, when all men celebrated that the Lord God was born to die for our good, joy could be found in homes all over the earth. And so it could be found in the house of the lord; it was full of delights. Yet among all the amusements of the day, Gawain found particular pleasure in the company of the fair lady; together they enjoyed courteous conversation that was free of impropriety.

For three days, the lord and his many guests made merry with drinking, singing and dancing to carols. But at last, all those who were not of the household prepared to depart. When Gawain said his goodbyes, the lord seized hold of him and led him to his private quarters. He spoke of his gratitude for having such an honored guest during the festival of God, and he earnestly endeavored to detain the knight longer. Gawain replied that though he was duty-bound to the lord in matters great and small, and though he desired to do whatever the lord asked of him, he could by no means remain.

This led the lord to inquire about what dreadful task had driven Gawain away from the royal court during the festive season. Gawain relayed that he had made a solemn covenant with the Knight of the Green Chapel and that he must urgently seek him, for he only had three days left before the new year. Gawain said, "I would rather be struck down dead than fail in my errand."

The lord replied, "Ah, then you must stay. The Green Chapel is not two miles from here."

So Gawain agreed to stay, and there was much joy in the house for the remainder of the day. As the time came to retire, the lord said to Gawain, "You told me that you were duty-bound to me in matters great and small. Will you agree to do whatever I ask?"

Gawain answered, "While I remain in your castle, I will be obedient to your every command."

The lord told Gawain that he desired for him to rise at his ease the next day and come to the table whenever he liked. He, on the other hand, intended to rise early and go hunting. Furthermore, the lord requested the following agreement: Whatever he brought back from the hunt he would give to Gawain in exchange for whatever good or ill Gawain gained in his home that day.

"By God," said Gawain. "I agree to do so if such a sport will please you."

So the lord rose early the next day and departed for his hunt. Meanwhile, Gawain lay dozing on his fair bed until the light of day shone brightly on the walls. As he drifted in and out of sleep, he heard the door gently open, and he saw the beautiful lady enter his room. Feeling surprised and embarrassed, Gawain pretended to be asleep. But the lady sat softly on his bed waiting for him to wake. He determined that he must face her boldly, yet courteously. When he opened his eyes, he acted startled and crossed himself with his hand as if to protect himself by prayer.

But the lady spoke amiably and said she only desired conversation with the knight whom the whole world revered. So they talked of many things until morning passed; all the while, Gawain acted with both restraint and politeness. When at last the lady rose to take her leave, Gawain consented. But then she surprised him by criticizing his manners: "Does the noble Gawain remain so long with a lady and not beg a kiss out of courtesy?"

"I shall kiss at your command in the way befitting of a knight lest I displease you," said Gawain.

At that the lady took him in her arms and kissed him on the cheek. They commended one another to Christ, and Gawain went out to Mass with an easy mind. Afterward, he went to his meal and enjoyed further conversation with the fair lady.

In the late evening, the hunting party returned and sounded many proud calls on their horns. The lord gathered the entire household together in the hall, and as his part of the agreement, he presented Gawain with the fine meat of a successful hunt.

Gawain graciously thanked him and said, "And by the terms of our arrangement, I will give to you what I have honorably gained in your house today." And with all the grace he could contrive, he gave a kiss to the lord. "There, take my winnings. I give it freely and have gained nothing else today."

"Hah!" said the lord. "It may be an even better prize if I knew where you gained this treasure."

"That was not in the agreement, so ask me no more," said Gawain.

With that, they laughed and made merry and enjoyed the abundance of fresh deer meat from the hunt. After much choice wine, and amid their jesting, Gawain and the lord agreed to the same terms for the following day – whatever the lord brought back from his hunt would be exchanged for whatever Gawain earned in the home.

Once again, the lord rose before dawn to leave for his hunt. And once again, his lady quietly entered the quarters of Gawain. At once, she scolded him for forgetting his lesson from the previous day. When he claimed ignorance, she reminded him that it befits every knight who practices chivalry to give a kiss to any lady that could properly claim one.

"My lady, I would not dare do so," said Gawain. "If I were denied, I would indeed be at fault for having made an advance. However, I am at your disposal to kiss when you please."

At that the fair lady kissed his cheek with propriety and sat down to discourse with him. She cheerfully asked him to teach her something of the art of love, since his reputation in chivalry was so great. To this, Gawain replied that she certainly had more skill in the art than he, and he carefully avoided her tests and temptations. So skillful was Gawain with his words that the lady took no offense at him, and there was no impropriety on either side. After much amusement, the lady took her leave and kissed Gawain courteously.

Once again Gawain attended Mass and then sat for a splendid meal. Later that evening, the lord returned exhausted from a difficult hunt, but his fatigue was subdued by the excitement and pride of presenting a slain boar to Gawain. In order to honor the lord, Gawain expressed horror at the sight of the enormous boar head. Then the lord said, "In respect of our agreement, the boar is yours."

"And just as faithfully, I will give you my winnings in exchange," said Gawain. He clasped the Lord and kissed him courteously.

"Hah!" said the lord. "You are the wisest man I know Gawain, and you will surely be rich if you continue on with such a trade."

That evening was spent eating the fresh meat of the boar, singing songs, dancing and enjoying every possible amusement. All the while, the lady sat at Gawain's side. Though her attention and looks of favor began to trouble his heart, his good manners prevented him from rebuking her. He behaved with complete courtesy toward her.

Before the party retired, the lord summoned Gawain to his private quarters. They drank and chatted, and the lord encouraged Gawain to abide by their agreement once more. For, the following day was New Year's Eve. When Gawain begged leave to depart on the morrow, in order to uphold his pledge to the Green Knight, the lord prevailed on him to stay just one more day.

"On my honor," said the lord, "I give you my word that you will reach the Green Chapel by the dawn of the New Year, in time to do your business. Lie in your room tomorrow and relax. I will hunt in the wood again and return to make our exchange in the evening. For I have tested you twice and have found you trustworthy. The third time will pay for all; remember that tomorrow."

After further conversation, both the lord and Gawain retired to bed, and the lord rose early again for his hunt. While Gawain was deep in a troubled sleep, wondering what fate would befall him when he met the Green Knight, the lady entered his room. She came toward him and kissed his face gracefully. Gawain welcomed her cheerfully, and when he saw her so beautifully dressed, so faultless in features and so fair in complexion, joy welled up in his heart. At once, they fell into pleasant conversation. Yet, all the while, there was great peril between them, should Gawain not be mindful of temptation.

Then the fair lady began to boldly press Gawain to the limit – that he either accept her love then and there or refuse it offensively. Though he determined to remain courteous, he was greatly distressed at the thought of betraying the lord of the castle. Moreover, he was fearful of committing a sin against God. So he attempted, with good-natured laughter, to deflect the words of the lady.

But she persisted, "Gawain, you deserve blame if you do not hold this lady who sits beside you above all else in the world, unless you already hold another lady more dear. I pray you tell me straightly. Is there another lady to whom you hold a firm faith?"

"I have no such love," said Gawain, "nor do I intend to have one at present."

"That is the worst that I could hear," said the lady, "but indeed I have my answer. Kiss me now courteously, and I will go away as a maiden whose love was despised."

After kissing him graciously on the cheek, she asked, "Will you grant me just one consolation? Will you give me some gift, even if just a glove, so that the reminder of you will ease my grief?"

"Dear lady," said Gawain, "for your sake, I wish I had packed my dearest possessions. However, since I am here on a mission, I have nothing of value with me. Forgive me lady, but I dare not give you something of little worth as a love token."

"Oh noble knight," said the lady, "then you shall have something of mine." She offered him a splendid ring, but Gawain refused it saying, "I cannot accept a gift from you fair lady, for I have nothing to offer in return."

She pressed him until he swore not to take it. Then, thinking that he would not accept her gift because of its cost, she insisted that he take her green silk sash instead. She begged him to take it since it was of little value. Again, Gawain refused saying that he would not accept anything until God granted him grace to accomplish the task that lay before him.

"Do not refuse this piece of silk, dear knight," said the lady, "though it is of little value of itself, it carries a special quality. Whoever wraps this sash closely about him cannot be killed; no man, no magic, no strategy of any kind can harm him."

It occurred to Gawain that this might be the very thing that would save him from his eminent danger, so he allowed her to speak on. At last, he consented to her urging, and he promised, for her sake, never to reveal it to anyone. Then she kissed him and took her leave.

When the lady had gone, Gawain set off for the chapel where he quietly confessed all his sins to a priest. He left feeling a sense of peace, and he spent the remainder of the day happily chatting with the noble ladies of the house. When the lord returned from his hunt, Gawain approached him saying, "This time I shall be the first to fulfill the terms of our agreement." He embraced the Lord and kissed him for the third time

"Ah!" said the lord. "I have but a poor return for the precious thing you have bestowed on me. I have hunted all day and have nothing but a fox skin."

Then all the household enjoyed a meal together. They ate and talked and laughed late into the night. When Gawain humbly took his leave, he graciously thanked the lord for his exceptional hospitality. He asked just one more favor — that the lord would assign a servant to show him the way to the Green Chapel in the morning. This the lord did willingly.

Gawain did not sleep much that night, and he rose before dawn. He dressed in his splendid armor and privately wrapped the sash of green silk around his waist. Then he mounted his good horse Gryngolet, and commended both the castle and all of its inhabitants to Christ.

The lord's servant faithfully led Gawain on the path to the Green Chapel. But as they got nearer, the servant halted. Out of love for Gawain, he counseled the knight to leave by some other path. For he knew that the Green Chapel was a perilous place and that the man who lived there was ruthless. He promised Gawain with many oaths that he would never utter a word about him running away from the cruel man.

"I thank you for wishing the best for me," said Gawain, "and I am certain that you would faithfully keep your promise. However, if I took flight out of fear, I would be a cowardly knight; there would be no excuse for me. I intend to go to the chapel no matter what may happen there, good or bad. And however grim the Green Knight may be, God is surely able to protect his servants."

Seeing that Gawain was determined, the servant directed him to the chapel and then galloped away. Feeling utterly alone, Gawain said to himself, "I will neither weep nor moan; rather, I commend myself to God and yield completely to his will." Then he continued on his journey down a rugged slope to the bottom of the valley. Strangely, he saw nothing like a chapel in any direction. He saw nothing but a small hill with a hole in it. It was overgrown with grass and sat on the side of a slope by the water's edge. The channel of a stream flowed there, and the water foamed in such a way that it looked like it was boiling.

"Can this be the Green Chapel?" Gawain asked himself. "The Devil may well recite his prayers here. It is an evil looking place, and I feel in my whole being that it is the Evil One himself who has brought me here to destroy me. This is the most unholy church that I have ever seen."

Then Gawain heard a terrible sound, as if someone were sharpening a blade upon a grindstone.

Over and over the screeching echoed through the valley. Gawain felt certain it was meant to make his courage falter. But he drew strength from God and called out loudly, "Who is the master in this place? Gawain is here, true to his word. If any man desires something of me, let him come quickly, now or never."

"Wait," said someone up on the hillside, "and you shall quickly have what I promised you."

The horrible sound continued for a time until the man made his way down the hill. When he finally appeared, Gawain saw that he was arrayed in green just like before and he carried a massive axe in his hand. Gawain greeted the Green Knight, but his bow was by no means a low one.

"So, good sir, you can be trusted to keep a pledge," said the Green Knight. "God keep you, Gawain. You have faithfully timed your journey and have so far honored the terms arranged between us. Now take off your helmet and receive what is due to you. And make no more resistance than I offered you when you cut off my head in a single blow."

"I will not resist," said Gawain. "And by God who gave me life, I will not begrudge you, whatever harm befalls me. I only ask that you limit yourself to one stroke."

Then Gawain bowed down and exposed the white skin of his neck. He acted as though he feared nothing. But as the Green Knight swung back the axe to deal his blow, Gawain slightly flinched. The Green Knight stopped the blade with a sudden jerk and then rebuked Gawain with many haughty words, "You cannot be Gawain, the knight who is known throughout the land for his bravery. You are flinching for fear before feeling any harm. I have never heard of a knight with such cowardice. I neither flinched nor budged when you struck me in King Arthur's court, even as my head fell at my feet. Therefore, you ought to acknowledge me as the better man."

Sir Gawain replied, "I flinched once, but I will do so no more. And consider that if my head falls on the stones, I cannot restore it as you did yours. But let us get on with our business. Hurry and deal out my fate."

This time, the Green Knight swung the axe fiercely at Gawain, but he stopped his hand before it could do any harm. Gawain did not flinch in any limb but stood still as a stone. Then the Green Knight spoke approvingly, "So now that you have regained your courage, I really must strike you. May the exalted order of your knighthood preserve you now."

Gawain said furiously, "Strike at once and cease delay. You have threatened for so long, that I believe you have struck fear into your own heart."

At that, the Green Knight lifted the axe and let it down skillfully so that it grazed Gawain's neck. Though his blood poured onto the snow, Gawain knew that he had received only a minor wound. He jumped to his feet, armed himself, and said, "Cease your attack! I have taken your blow without resistance, and if you give any more, I will return them promptly."

When the Green Knight saw how Gawain faced him fearlessly, his heart was pleased. Then he said, "Bold knight, you need not be so fierce. No man here has done you wrong, or will do you wrong, according to the covenant made at Arthur's court. I promised you one blow, and you have received it. Consider yourself paid in full. If I desired to do so, I could have given you a more severe blow. Instead, on my first attempt, I only pretended to harm you, thus treating you fairly in accordance with our first agreement made in my house. On that evening, you were true to your word and gave me your winnings like a loyal and honest man. On my second attempt, I pretended again to harm you; for, on the second day of our agreement, when you kissed my wife, you were faithful to give me these kisses as well. For both of these days, no harm was done. However, on the third day, you failed in one respect – for that you received a trifling wound. For it is my green sash that you are wearing. Moreover, I know all about your conduct with my wife, for I sent her to test you. And truly, you have proved to be the most faultless knight who ever lived. You are like a pearl among dried white peas; you are of far greater value than most. Your only fault was this: You accepted the sash not because of its value or because of my wife's persuasion, but because you loved your life."

Gawain was overcome with shame and cried, "A curse upon cowardice and covetousness, for in them is the destruction of virtue." Then he loosened the sash and flung it before the Green Knight. "There is the token of my falsehood. Because I feared your blow, I allowed cowardice and covetousness to possess me, and I forsook the virtues that are proper for knights. For now I myself am found false, though I have always despised treachery and lies. Do with me as you will, and hereafter, I will always be on guard against the sin that crouches at my door."

The Green Knight laughed and said, "Noble Gawain, your atonement is complete. Your penance was done at the edge of my blade, and you are made clean by your free confession. And take back my sash to remind you of this adventure at the Green Chapel." Then the Green Knight urged Gawain to come back to the castle for the remainder of the Christmas season. He desired that Gawain be reconciled to his wife, who had acted as his ardent opponent.

"No, indeed," said Gawain. "Though you have shown me the greatest kindness, I am now anxious to return home. But may God bless you and reward you with good things. Please commend me to your wife, the lady who so cleverly deceived me. And since I am in the company of a great many noble men, like Adam, Solomon, Samson and David, who were made fools by women, perhaps I will be excused. As for the sash, I will keep it willingly as a sign of my frailty. If I ever sense pride welling up in my heart as I ride with the noble knights of Arthur, I will look upon this sash and be humbled by it. Lastly, please permit me to be bold and ask one more thing of you. What is your proper name?"

"I am called Bertilak de Hautdesert," said the Green Knight. "And whatever magic you may attribute to me comes rather from your aunt, Morgan le Fay. She learned her skill from Merlin, who you know well. It was Morgan who sent me to Arthur's court last year to see if what was rumored about the great renown of the Round Table was true. She will surely be pleased to embrace you now that you have completed your mission. I entreat you to come back with me to see her; for, she is in my home. Furthermore, you are greatly loved by those in my household. Even I bear more good will to you than to any other man on earth because of your integrity."

But Gawain was determined to return to Camelot. So he and Bertilak embraced and commended each other to God before they parted. Gawain had many adventures on his way home that I do not have time to recount. As he traveled, the wound on his neck gradually healed, and every day, he faithfully wore the green sash over it — slinging it diagonally across his chest and fastening it at his side.

When Gawain arrived home safely, there was great joy in Arthur's court. It seemed wonderful to all the knights and ladies that he had returned. And when they asked him about his adventure, he told them the details of the amazing story and confessed all of his faults. He uncovered his neck to reveal the wound given by the hand of the Green Knight for his disloyalty, and he suffered torment when he spoke of it; the blood rushed to his face for shame. He showed them the sash also and said, "This is the badge that I received for the cowardice and covetousness to which I fell prey. I will wear it for as long as I live. For, though I might conceal my sin from others, I cannot undo it; it will be ever before me."

The king consoled the knight, and the court laughed loudly at the tale. All agreed that, for friendship's sake, every member of the Round Table should wear a bright green sash across his chest, just like Gawain, in remembrance of his strange Christmas adventure. And the good repute of the Round Table came to be associated with this mark of humility, and those who wore it were greatly honored.

Thus befell this adventure in the days of Arthur, and all the chronicles of Britain bear record to it. Now may he who humbly bore the crown of thorns for our sin bring us to his bliss!

AMEN

The Christmas Cuckoo

The Background
Frances Browne, 1816-1879
Classic, 19ᵗʰ Century Story (Adapted in 1914 by Frances Jenkins Olcott)

The story of "The Christmas Cuckoo" is one of seven fairy tales told in the book *Granny's Wonderful Chair.* Irish poet and novelist Frances Browne first published it in 1856. The book is full of charm, and Browne masterfully paints vivid pictures with her words making it surprising to learn that she was blind. A brief biography in the preface of a 1916 publication of her book describes Browne as follows:

"That she was a poet the story tells on every page, but of her blindness it tells not a word. From beginning to end it is filled with pictures; each little tale has its own picturesque setting, its own vividly realised scenery. Her power of visualisation would be easy to under-stand had she become blind in the later years of her life, when the beauties of the physical world were impressed on her mind; but Frances Browne was blind from infancy. The pictures she gives us in her stories were created, in darkness, from material which came to her only through the words of others. In her work are no blurred lines or uncertainties . . . . It would seem that the completeness of her calamity created, within her, that serenity of spirit which contrives the greatest triumphs in Life and in Art."[1]

Frances was born into poverty as the seventh of twelve children in County Donegal, Ireland. Nevertheless, she secured her own education by bribing her brothers and sisters to read to her in exchange for doing their household chores. And her biographer tells us:

"When the usual bribe failed, she invented stories for them, and, in return for these, books were read to her which, while they seemed dull and uninteresting enough to the readers, built up for the eager listener those enchanted steps by which she was to climb into her intellectual kingdom."[2]

By 1840, Browne began writing and publishing poems. One of her sisters served as her secretary, writing down the words that Browne dictated.[3] Seven years later, after achieving some fame as a poet, Browne left her mountain village to begin a literary career in Edinburgh, Scotland. Despite working fervently and publishing regularly, Browne's income was modest. And though she was poor herself, she financially supported her mother.

After five years in Scotland, Browne relocated to London, England. She had the good fortune of receiving a generous sum of money from a nobleman, and this allowed her to write without the pressures of generating regular income. She was able to expand her literary efforts to include novels and children's stories, the most popular of which is *Granny's Wonderful Chair*. The story is about a poor girl named Snowflower whose grandmother tells her the secret of her magic chair. All Snowflower had to do was sit in the chair and imagine a place that she would like to visit. The chair would travel wherever she wished or tell a story whenever she asked. Snowflower requests that the chair take her to the court of King Winwealth, and there the chair tells stories before a grand audience. The first of these stories is "The Christmas Cuckoo."

The tale is about two poor brothers, Scrub and Spare, who unknowingly bring a cuckoo (one of the most common birds found in western Europe) into their home on Christmas day. When they discover the bird tucked in their firewood, they agree to let it stay until spring. When it comes time for the cuckoo to set off and "shout its spring cry throughout the world," it offers to bring back a gift. Essentially, the brothers are allowed to choose between riches or contentment. Their contrasting choices call to mind the followings verses:

"But godliness with contentment is great gain. For we brought nothing into the world, and we can take nothing out of it. But if we have food and clothing, we will be content with that. People who want to get rich fall into temptation and a trap and into many foolish and harmful desires that plunge men into ruin and destruction. For the love of money is a root of all kinds of evil. Some people, eager for money, have wandered from the faith and pierced themselves with many griefs" (1 Timothy 6:6-10).

Since Christmas is a time of gift giving, there tends to be an unfortunate focus on material things. This story serves as a reminder that contentment is of much greater value that the riches of the world.

The following text is an adapted version of the story as found in *Good Stories for Great Holidays* by Frances Jenkins Olcott (1873-1963). In addition to writing many children's books herself, Olcott was head of the Children's department at Carnegie Library. She is widely known for her efforts to distribute children's literature throughout the United States.

---

[1] Browne, Francis. *Granny's Wonderful Chair.* Biography written by D. R. E. P. Dutton and Company, 1916, Preface.

[2] Browne, Francis, Preface by D.R.

[3] Montgomery, Elizabeth Rider. *The Story Behind Great Stories.* Robert M. McBride & Company, 1947, p. 68.

The Story
Reading Time: 15 minutes

Once upon a time there stood in the midst of a bleak moor, in the North Country, a certain village. All its inhabitants were poor, for their fields were barren, and they had little trade; but the poorest of them all were two brothers called Scrub and Spare, who followed the cobbler's craft. Their hut was built of clay and wattles. The door was low and always open, for there was no window. The roof did not entirely keep out the rain and the only thing comfortable was a wide fireplace, for which the brothers could never find wood enough to make sufficient fire. There they worked in most brotherly friendship, though with little encouragement.

On one unlucky day a new cobbler arrived in the village. He had lived in the capital city of the kingdom and, by his own account, cobbled for the queen and the princesses. His awls were sharp, his lasts were new; he set up his stall in a neat cottage with two windows. The villagers soon found out that one patch of his would outwear two of the brothers'. In short, all the mending left Scrub and Spare, and went to the new cobbler.

The season had been wet and cold, their barley did not ripen well, and the cabbages never half- closed in the garden. So the brothers were poor that winter, and when Christmas came they had nothing to feast on but a barley loaf and a piece of rusty bacon. Worse than that, the snow was very deep and they could get no firewood.

Their hut stood at the end of the village; beyond it spread the bleak moor, now all white and silent. But that moor had once been a forest; great roots of old trees were still to be found in it, loosened from the soil and laid bare by the winds and rains. One of these, a rough, gnarled log, lay hard by their door, the half of it above the snow, and Spare said to his brother, "Shall we sit here cold on Christmas while the great root lies yonder? Let us chop it up for firewood, the work will make us warm."

"No," said Scrub, "it's not right to chop wood on Christmas; besides, that root is too hard to be broken with any hatchet."

"Hard or not, we must have a fire," replied Spare. "Come, brother, help me in with it. Poor as we are there is nobody in the village will have such a yule log as ours."

Scrub liked a little grandeur, and, in hopes of having a fine yule log, both brothers strained and strove with all their might till, between pulling and pushing, the great old root was safe on the hearth, and beginning to crackle and blaze with the red embers.

In high glee the cobblers sat down to their bread and bacon. The door was shut, for there was nothing but cold moonlight and snow outside; but the hut, strewn with fir boughs and ornamented with holly, looked cheerful as the ruddy blaze flared up and rejoiced their hearts.

Then suddenly from out the blazing root they heard: "Cuckoo! cuckoo!" as plain as ever the spring-bird's voice came over the moor on a May morning.

"What is that?" said Scrub, terribly frightened; "it is something bad!"

"Maybe not," said Spare.

And out of the deep hole at the side of the root, which the fire had not reached, flew a large, gray cuckoo, and lit on the table before them. Much as the cobblers had been surprised, they were still more so when it said, "Good gentlemen, what season is this?" "It's Christmas," said Spare.

"Then a merry Christmas to you!" said the cuckoo. "I went to sleep in the hollow of that old root one evening last summer, and never woke till the heat of your fire made me think it was summer again. But now since you have burned my lodging, let me stay in your hut till the spring comes round — I only want a hole to sleep in, and when I go on my travels next summer be assured I will bring you some present for your trouble."

"Stay and welcome," said Spare, while Scrub sat wondering if it were something bad or not.

"I'll make you a good warm hole in the thatch," said Spare. "But you must be hungry after that long sleep — here is a slice of barley bread. Come help us to keep Christmas!"

The cuckoo ate up the slice, drank water from a brown jug, and flew into a snug hole which Spare scooped for it in the thatch of the hut. Scrub said he was afraid it wouldn't be lucky; but as it slept on and the days passed he forgot his fears.

So the snow melted, the heavy rains came, the cold grew less, the days lengthened, and one sunny morning the brothers were awakened by the cuckoo shouting its own cry to let them know the spring had come.

"Now I'm going on my travels," said the bird, "over the world to tell men of the spring. There is no country where trees bud, or flowers bloom, that I will not cry in before the year goes round. Give me another slice of barley bread to help me on my journey, and tell me what present I shall bring you at the twelvemonth's end."

Scrub would have been angry with his brother for cutting so large a slice, their store of barley being low, but his mind was occupied with what present it would be most prudent to ask for.

"There are two trees hard by the well that lies at the world's end," said the cuckoo; "one of them is called the golden tree, for its leaves are all of beaten gold. Every winter they fall into the well with a sound like scattered coin, and I know not what becomes of them. As for the other, it is always green like a laurel. Some call it the wise, and some the merry, tree. Its leaves never fall, but they that get one of them keep a blithe heart in spite of all misfortunes, and can make themselves as merry in a hut as in a palace."

"Good master cuckoo, bring me a leaf off that tree!" cried Spare.

"Now, brother, don't be a fool!" said Scrub; "think of the leaves of beaten gold! Dear master cuckoo, bring me one of them!"

Before another word could be spoken the cuckoo had flown out of the open door, and was shouting its spring cry over moor and meadow.

The brothers were poorer than ever that year. Nobody would send them a single shoe to mend, and Scrub and Spare would have left the village but for their barley-field and their cabbage-garden. They sowed their barley, planted their cabbage, and, now that their trade was gone, worked in the rich villagers' fields to make out a scanty living.

So the seasons came and passed; spring, summer, harvest, and winter followed each other as they have done from the beginning. At the end of the latter Scrub and Spare had grown so poor and ragged that their old neighbors forgot to invite them to wedding feasts or merrymakings, and the brothers thought the cuckoo had forgotten them, too, when at daybreak on the first of April they heard a hard beak knocking at their door, and a voice crying, "Cuckoo! cuckoo! Let me in with my presents!"

Spare ran to open the door, and in came the cuckoo, carrying on one side of its bill a golden leaf larger than that of any tree in the North Country; and in the other side of its bill, one like that of the common laurel, only it had a fresher green.

"Here," it said, giving the gold to Scrub and the green to Spare, "it is a long carriage from the world's end. Give me a slice of barley bread, for I must tell the North Country that the spring has come."

Scrub did not grudge the thickness of that slice, though it was cut from their last loaf. So much gold had never been in the cobbler's hands before, and he could not help exulting over his brother.

"See the wisdom of my choice," he said, holding up the large leaf of gold. "As for yours, as good might be plucked from any hedge, I wonder a sensible bird would carry the like so far."

"Good master cobbler," cried the cuckoo, finishing its slice, "your conclusions are more hasty than courteous. If your brother is disappointed this time, I go on the same journey every year, and for your hospitable entertainment will think it no trouble to bring each of you whichever leaf you desire."

"Darling cuckoo," cried Scrub, "bring me a golden one."

And Spare, looking up from the green leaf on which he gazed as though it were a crown-jewel, said, "Be sure to bring me one from the merry tree."

And away flew the cuckoo.

"This is the feast of All Fools, and it ought to be your birthday," said Scrub. "Did ever man fling away such an opportunity of getting rich? Much good your merry leaves will do in the midst of rags and poverty!"

But Spare laughed at him, and answered with quaint old proverbs concerning the cares that come with gold, till Scrub, at length getting angry, vowed his brother was not fit to live with a respectable man; and taking his lasts, his awls, and his golden leaf, he left the wattle hut, and went to tell the villagers.

They were astonished at the folly of Spare, and charmed with Scrub's good sense, particularly when he showed them the golden leaf, and told that the cuckoo would bring him one every spring.

The new cobbler immediately took him into partnership; the greatest people sent him their shoes to mend. Fairfeather, a beautiful village maiden, smiled graciously upon him; and in the course of that summer they were married, with a grand wedding feast, at which the whole village danced except Spare, who was not invited, because the bride could not bear his low-mindedness, and his brother thought him a disgrace to the family.

As for Scrub he established himself with Fairfeather in a cottage close by that of the new cobbler, and quite as fine. There he mended shoes to everybody's satisfaction, had a scarlet coat and a fat goose for dinner on holidays. Fairfeather, too, had a crimson gown, and fine blue ribbons; but neither she nor Scrub was content, for to buy this grandeur the golden leaf had to be broken and parted with piece by piece, so the last morsel was gone before the cuckoo came with another.

Spare lived on in the old hut, and worked in the cabbage-garden. (Scrub had got the barley-field because he was the elder.) Every day his coat grew more ragged, and the hut more weather-beaten; but people remarked that he never looked sad or sour. And the wonder was that, from the time any one began to keep his company, he or she grew kinder, happier, and content.

Every first of April the cuckoo came tapping at their doors with the golden leaf for Scrub, and the green for Spare. Fairfeather would have entertained it nobly with wheaten bread and honey, for she had some notion of persuading it to bring two golden leaves instead of one; but the cuckoo flew away to eat barley bread with Spare, saying it was not fit company for fine people, and liked the old hut where it slept so snugly from Christmas till spring.

Scrub spent the golden leaves, and remained always discontented; and Spare kept the merry ones. I do not know how many years passed in this manner, when a certain great lord, who owned that village, came to the neighborhood. His castle stood on the moor. It was ancient and strong, with high towers and a deep moat. All the country as far as one could see from the highest turret belonged to its lord; but he had not been there for twenty years, and would not have come then only he was melancholy. And there he lived in a very bad temper. The servants said nothing would please him, and the villagers put on their worst clothes lest he should raise their rents.

But one day in the harvest-time His Lordship chanced to meet Spare gathering water-cresses at a meadow stream, and fell into talk with the cobbler. How it was nobody could tell, but from that hour the great lord cast away his melancholy. He forgot all his woes and went about with a noble train, hunting, fishing, and making merry in his hall, where all travelers were entertained, and all the poor were welcome.

This strange story spread through the North Country, and great company came to the cobbler's hut — rich men who had lost their money, poor men who had lost their friends, beauties who had grown old, wits who had gone out of fashion — all came to talk with Spare, and, whatever their troubles had been, all went home merry.

The rich gave him presents; the poor gave him thanks. Spare's coat ceased to be ragged, he had bacon with his cabbage, and the villagers began to think there was some sense in him.

By this time his fame had reached the capital city, and even the court. There were a great many discontented people there; and the king had lately fallen into ill humor because a neighboring princess, with seven islands for her dowry, would not marry his eldest son.

So a royal messenger was sent to Spare, with a velvet mantle, a diamond ring, and a command that he should repair to court immediately.

"Tomorrow is the first of April," said Spare, "and I will go with you two hours after sunrise."

The messenger lodged all night at the castle, and the cuckoo came at sunrise with the merry leaf.

"Court is a fine place," it said, when the cobbler told it he was going, "but I cannot come there; they would lay snares and catch me; so be careful of the leaves I have brought you, and give me a farewell slice of barley bread."

Spare was sorry to part with the cuckoo, little as he had of its company, but he gave it a slice which would have broken Scrub's heart in former times, it was so thick and large. And having sewed up the leaves in the lining of his leather doublet, he set out with the messenger on his way to court.

His coming caused great surprise there. Everybody wondered what the king could see in such a common-looking man; but scarcely had His Majesty conversed with him half an hour, when the princess and her seven islands were forgotten and orders given that a feast for all comers should be spread in the banquet hall.

The princes of the blood, the great lords and ladies, the ministers of state, after that discoursed with Spare, and the more they talked the lighter grew their hearts, so that such changes had never been seen at court.

The lords forgot their spites and the ladies their envies, the princes and ministers made friends among themselves, and the judges showed no favor.

As for Spare, he had a chamber assigned him in the palace, and a seat at the king's table. One sent him rich robes, and another costly jewels; but in the midst of all his grandeur he still wore the leathern doublet, and continued to live at the king's court, happy and honored, and making all others merry and content.

The First
Christmas Tree

The Background
Henry van Dyke, 1852-1933
Historical Fiction, 8th Century Story

Henry van Dyke was born in Pennsylvania to a prominent Presbyterian minister. As a child, he spent a great deal of time outdoors with his father who instilled in him a love of nature. Van Dyke carried this passion for God's creation throughout this life, and it appeared in much of his later writing.

Van Dyke was also academically inclined. He earned a B.A. from Princeton University in 1873, an M.A. in 1876, and a seminary degree in 1877. He then traveled to Germany to study for two years at the University of Berlin. When he returned to America in 1879, he was ordained as a Presbyterian minister. His first pastorate was at United Congregational Church in Newport, Rhode Island, and during his time there, he married Ellen Reid (with whom he had nine children).

In 1883, van Dyke accepted a position as pastor of the Brick Presbyterian Church in New York City, where he remained for the next 17 years. While pastoring, he also published several books, mostly on topics of religion. One book, however, was devoted to literature, *The Poetry of Tennyson* (1889). This publication was eventually considered van Dyke's greatest contribution to scholarship, and according to biographer Juliet Iwelumor, it established him as "an outstanding figure in the literary world."[1]

Though van Dyke had a wonderful family and an adoring church congregation, he experienced a time of great personal grief around the year 1892.[2] He described it as a year "full of sickness and sorrow" and many sleepless nights.[3] Most likely, the loss of his father, a man whose counsel and companionship he cherished into adulthood, was a significant source of van Dyke's grief. Yet during this difficult period, one of his best-known stories, *The Story of the Other Wise Man* (1896), came to his mind. It is a Christmas story about a fictional character named Artaban who fails to meet up with his companions (the Wise Men), because he stops to help a man in need. Artaban then has to journey alone to find the King of the Jews, but he is prevented time and again when he pauses to assist others. As Artaban is about to die after many years of searching, he hears the heavenly voice of Jesus confirming that through his service to others, he served Christ himself. "His treasures were accepted" and he "had found the King."[4]

Van Dyke gives the following account in his preface to *The Story of the Other Wise Man*:

"[Though the story] came to me suddenly and without labor, there was a great deal of study and toil to be done before it could be written down. An idea arrives without effort; a form can only be wrought out by patient labor. If your story is worth telling, you ought to love it enough to be willing to work over it until it is true – true not only to the ideal, but also to the real. The light is a gift; but the local color can only be seen by one who looks for it long and steadily. Artaban went with me while I toiled through a score of volumes of ancient history and travel. I saw his figure while I journeyed on the motionless sea of desert and in the strange cities of the East."[5]

In the end, van Dyke's labor produced a beautiful piece of historical fiction. His careful research is evident in every detail of his story. Furthermore, his work prepared him for a subsequent Christmas when he created his next great piece of historical fiction, *The First Christmas Tree* (1897). Both stories were first made public when he read them aloud to his congregation in New York as sermons.

By all accounts, van Dyke was a teacher at heart, and in 1900, he accepted a position as a professor of English literature at Princeton University. With the exception of various overseas assignments, van Dyke taught until he retired in 1923. While at Princeton, he remained active with his denomination. He chaired the committee that wrote the first Presbyterian printed liturgy, *The Book of Common Worship of 1906*, and in 1907, he wrote the wonderful hymn "Joyful, Joyful We Adore Thee" set to the music of Beethoven's *Ninth Symphony*. The hymn was first published in the *Presbyterian Hymnal* in 1911 and also appeared in van Dyke's collection of poems that same year. The words beautifully illustrate van Dyke's appreciation of God's creation. Here are the first two stanzas of the "Hymn of Joy":

"Joyful, joyful, we adore Thee, God of glory, Lord of love;
Hearts unfold like flowers before Thee, praising Thee their sun above.
Melt the clouds of sin and sadness; drive the dark of doubt away;
Giver of immortal gladness, fill us with the light of day!

"All Thy works with joy surround Thee, earth and heaven reflect Thy rays,
Stars and angels sing around Thee, center of unbroken praise.
Field and forest, vale and mountain, blooming meadow, flashing sea,
Chanting bird and flowing fountain, call us to rejoice in Thee."[6]

In addition to his contributions to literature and to the church in America, van Dyke was also a gracious representative of his country overseas. In 1908, van Dyke traveled to the University of Paris to work as a visiting lecturer. By 1913, President Woodrow Wilson, a friend and former class-mate of van Dyke, appointed him as the ambassador to the Netherlands and Luxemborg. Shortly thereafter, World War I broke out, and American citizens throughout Europe rushed to Holland seeking refuge. Van Dyke was well suited for the job of comforting these distraught Americans and caring for their spiritual well being. Furthermore, according to the biography by Iwelumor, "Although he was inexperienced as an ambassador, van Dyke conducted himself with the skill of a trained diplomat, maintaining the rights of all American refugees in Europe and organizing work for their relief."[7] As the war came to a close in 1918, van Dyke returned to the U.S. and joined the chaplain's corps of the U.S. Naval Reserve. He served as lieutenant commander and wrote an introduction to the Navy Chaplain's manual (1918).

Van Dyke returned to Princeton in 1919 and continued teaching until his retirement in 1923. When he passed away 10 years later, he left behind a vibrant legacy, not only in print, but in the lives of thousands of people who were personally touched by his leadership as a pastor, a teacher or an ambassador. Furthermore, the people who knew him most intimately, his family, only served to confirm the excellence of his character. His son, Tertius, published a biography in 1935 to honor his father's memory. Tertius wrote, "The outstanding qualities of the man were courage, sensitiveness, sympathy. He was alive all the time . . . . His career was subsidiary to his life."[8]

The following excerpt is from Henry van Dyke's historical fiction story, *The First Christmas* (1897). It recounts one of the most famous events in the life of Winfried (around 672 – 754), a man who served as a missionary to pagan Germanic tribes. History records that Winfried (named Boniface in 719 by Pope Gregory II) boldly confronted the pagan god Thor by challenging him to strike him dead if he cut down Thor's holy oak tree.[9] As Winfried started to chop down the oak, a great wind miraculously blew it over. When the people saw that Thor did not harm Winfried, they accepted his message about the one true God. This "felling of Thor's Oak" is commonly regarded as the beginning of German Christianization beyond the borders of the Roman Empire; it is also widely associated with the origin of the Christmas tree. Van Dyke's careful historical research is evident in this dramatic fictional account. The excerpt begins after Winfried and his companions, less than 20 men, have traveled through difficult terrain in a fervent attempt to reach a pagan tribe by Christmas Eve. They arrive at Thor's oak tree just in time.

---

[1] Iwelumor, Juliet. "Henry van Dyke." Pennsylvania State University Library, Biographies. Retrieved October 17, 2008: http://pabook.libraries.psu.edu/palitmap/bios/Van_Dyke__Henry.html. Much of the biography for van Dyke is drawn from this source.

[2] Montgomery, Elizabeth Rider. *The Story Behind Great Stories*. Robert M. McBride & Company, 1947, p. 194.

[3] Van Dyke, Henry. *The Story of the Other Wise Man*. Paraclete Press, 1984, Preface, p. x.

[4] Van Dyke, Henry. *The Story of the Other Wise Man*, p. 48.

[5] Van Dyke, Henry. *The Story of the Other Wise Man*, Preface, p. xii.

[6] Van Dyke, Henry. *The Poems of Henry van Dyke*. C. Scribner's Sons, 1913, p. 332.

[7] Iwelumor, Juliet.

[8] Van Dyke, Tertius. *Henry Van Dyke, A Biography*. Harper and Brothers Publishers, 1935, p. 424.

[9] Farmer, David. *Oxford Dictionary of Saints*. Oxford University Press, 2003, p. 66.

The Story
Reading Time: 20 minutes

Withered leaves still clung to the branches of the oak, torn and faded banners of the departed summer. The bright crimson of autumn had long since disappeared, bleached away by the storms and the cold. But tonight these tattered remnants of glory were red again, ancient blood-stains against the dark blue sky. For an immense fire had been kindled in front of the tree. Tongues of ruddy flame, fountains of ruby sparks, ascended through the spreading limbs and flung a fierce illumination upward and around. The pale, pure moonlight that bathed the surrounding forests was quenched and eclipsed here. Not a beam of it sifted through the branches of the oak. It stood like a pillar of cloud between the still light of heaven and the crackling, flashing fire of earth.

But the fire itself was invisible to Winfried and his companions. Great throngs of people were gathered around it in a half-circle, their backs to the open glade, their faces toward the oak. Seen against that glowing background, it was but the silhouette of a crowd, vague, black, formless, mysterious.

The travelers paused for a moment at the edge of the thicket, and took counsel together.

"It is the assembly of the tribe," said one of the foresters, "the great night of the council. I heard of it three days ago, as we passed through one of the villages. All who swear by the old gods have been summoned. They will sacrifice a steed to the god of war, and drink blood, and eat horseflesh to make them strong. It will be at the peril of our lives if we approach them. At least we must hide the cross if we want to escape death."

"Do not hide the cross," cried Winfried, lifting his staff, "for I have come to show it, and to make these blind folk see its power. There is more to be done here tonight than the slaying of a steed, and a greater evil to be stayed than the shameful eating of meat sacrificed to idols. I have seen it in a dream. Here the cross must stand and be our banner."

At his command the sled was left in the border of the wood, with two of the men to guard it, and the rest of the company moved forward across the open ground. They approached unnoticed, for all the multitude were looking intently toward the fire at the foot of the oak.

Then Winfried's voice rang out, "Hail, sons of the forest! A stranger claims the warmth of your fire in the winter night."

Swiftly, and as with a single motion, a thousand eyes were bent upon the speaker. The semi-circle opened silently in the middle; Winfried entered with his followers; it closed again behind them.

Then, as they looked round the curving ranks, they saw that the hue of the assemblage was not black, but white — dazzling, radiant, solemn. White, the robes of the women clustered together at the points of the wide crescent; white, the glittering chainmail of the warriors standing in close ranks; white, the fur mantles of the aged men who held the central place in the circle; white, with the shimmer of silver ornaments and the purity of lamb's-wool, the raiment [clothing] of a little group of children who stood close by the fire; white, with awe and fear, the faces of all who looked at them;

411

and over all the flickering, dancing radiance of the flames played and glimmered like a faint, vanishing tinge of blood on snow.

The only figure untouched by the glow was the old priest, Hunrad, with his long, spectral robe, flowing hair and beard, and dead-pale face, who stood with his back to the fire and advanced slowly to meet the strangers.

"Who are you? From where do you come, and what do you seek here?" His voice was as heavy and toneless as a muffled bell.

"I am your kinsman, of the German brotherhood," answered Winfried, "and from England, beyond the sea, have I come to bring you a greeting from that land, and a message from the All-Father, whose servant I am."

"Welcome, then," said Hunrad, "welcome, kinsman, and be silent; for what passes here is too high to wait, and must be done before the moon crosses the middle heaven, unless, indeed, you have some sign or token from the gods. Can you work miracles?"

The question came sharply, as if a sudden gleam of hope had flashed through the tangle of the old priest's mind. But Winfried's voice sank lower and a cloud of disappointment passed over his face as he replied: "No, miracles have I never performed, though I have heard of many; but the All-Father has given no power to my hands save such as belongs to common man."

"Stand still, then, you common man," said Hunrad, scornfully, "and behold what the gods have called us hither to do. This night is the death-night of the sun-god, Baldur the Beautiful, beloved of gods and men. This night is the hour of darkness and the power of winter, of sacrifice and mighty fear. This night the great Thor, the god of thunder and war, to whom this oak is sacred, is grieved for the death of Baldur, and angry with this people because they have forsaken his worship. Long is it since an offering has been laid upon his altar, long since the roots of his holy tree have been fed with blood. Therefore its leaves have withered before the time, and its boughs are heavy with death. Therefore the Slavs and the Wends have beaten us in battle. Therefore the harvests have failed, and the wolf hordes have ravaged the folds, and the strength has departed from the bow, and the wood of the spear has broken, and the wild boar has slain the huntsman. Therefore the plague has fallen on our dwellings, and the dead are more than the living in all our villages. Answer me, my people, are not these things true?"

A hoarse sound of approval ran through the circle. A chant, in which the voices of the men and women blended, like the shrill wind in the pine trees above the rumbling thunder of a waterfall, rose and fell in rude cadences.

O Thor, the Thunderer
Mighty and merciless,
Spare us from smiting!
Heave not thy hammer,
Angry, aginst us;
Plague not thy people.

Take from our treasure
Richest of ransom.
Silver we send thee,
Jewels and javelins,
Goodliest garments,
All our possessions,
Priceless, we proffer.
Sheep will we slaughter,
Steeds will we sacrifice;
Bright blood shall bathe
O tree of Thunder,
Life-floods shall lave thee,
Strong wood of wonder.
Mighty, have mercy,
Smite us no more,
Spare us and save us,
Spare us, Thor! Thor!

With two great shouts the song ended, and stillness followed so intense that the crackling of the fire was heard distinctly. The old priest stood silent for a moment. His shaggy brows swept down over his eyes like ashes quenching flame. Then he lifted his face and spoke.

"None of these things will please the god. More costly is the offering that shall cleanse your sin, more precious the crimson dew that shall send new life into this holy tree of blood. Thor claims your dearest and your noblest gift."

Hunrad moved nearer to the group of children who stood watching the fire and the swarms of spark-serpents darting upward. They had heeded none of the priest's words, and did not notice now that he approached them, so eager were they to see which fiery snake would go highest among the oak branches. Foremost among them, and most intent on the pretty game, was a boy like a sunbeam, slender and quick, with blithe brown eyes and laughing lips. The priest's hand was laid upon his shoulder. The boy turned and looked up in his face.

"Here," said the old man, with his voice vibrating as when a thick rope is strained by a ship swinging from her moorings, "here is the chosen one, the eldest son of the Chief, the darling of the people. Hearken, Bernhard, will you go to Valhalla, where the heroes dwell with the gods, to bear a message to Thor?"

The boy answered, swift and clear: "Yes, priest, I will go if my father bids me. Is it far away? Shall I run quickly? Must I take my bow and arrows for the wolves?"

The boy's father, the chieftain Gundhar, standing among his bearded warriors, drew his breath deep, and leaned so heavily on the handle of his spear that the wood cracked. And his wife, Irma, bending forward from the ranks of women, pushed the golden hair from her forehead with one hand.

The other dragged at the silver chain about her neck until the rough links pierced her flesh, and the red drops fell unheeded on her breast.

A sigh passed through the crowd, like the murmur of the forest before the storm breaks. Yet no one spoke save Hunrad:

"Yes, my Prince, both bow and spear you shall have, for the way is long, and you are a brave huntsman. But in darkness you must journey for a little space, and with eyes blindfolded. Are you afraid?"

"I fear nothing," said the boy, "neither darkness, nor the great bear, nor the were-wolf. For I am Gundhar's son, and the defender of my people."

Then the priest led the child in his garment of lamb's wool to a broad stone in front of the fire. He gave him his little bow tipped with silver, and his spear with shining head of steel. He bound the child's eyes with a white cloth, and bade him kneel beside the stone with his face to the cast. Unconsciously the wide arc of spectators drew inward toward the centre, as the ends of the bow draw together when the cord is stretched. Winfried moved noiselessly until he stood close behind the priest.

The old man stooped to lift a black hammer of stone from the ground — the sacred hammer of the god Thor. Summoning all the strength of his withered arms, he swung it high in the air. It poised for an instant above the child's fair head—then turned to fall.

One keen cry shrilled out from where the women stood: "Me! Take me! Not Bernhard!"

The flight of the mother toward her child was swift as the falcon's swoop. But swifter still was the hand of the deliverer.

Winfried's heavy staff thrust mightily against the hammer's handle as it fell. Sideways it glanced from the old man's grasp, and the black stone, striking on the altar's edge, split in two. A shout of awe and joy rolled along the living circle. The branches of the oak shivered. The flames leaped higher. As the shout died away the people saw the lady Irma, with her arms clasped round her child, and above them, on the altar-stone, Winfried, his face shining like the face of an angel.

Like a swift mountain-flood rolling down its channel, a huge rock tumbling from the hill-side and falling in mid-stream, and the baffled waters, broken and confused, pausing in their flow, dashing high against the rock, foaming and murmuring, with divided impulse, uncertain whether to turn to the right or the left: Even so Winfried's bold deed fell into the midst of the thoughts and passions of the council. They were at a standstill. Anger and wonder, reverence and joy and confusion surged through the crowd. They knew not which way to move: to resent the intrusion of the stranger as an insult to their gods, or to welcome him as the rescuer of their darling prince.

The old priest crouched by the altar, silent. Conflicting counsels troubled the air. Let the sacrifice go forward; the gods must be appeased. No, the boy must not die; bring the chieftain's best horse and slay it in his stead — it will be enough; the holy tree loves the blood of horses. Not so, there is a better counsel yet: Seize the stranger whom the gods have led hither as a victim and make his life pay the forfeit of his daring.

The withered leaves on the oak rustled and whispered overhead. The fire flared and sank again. The angry voices clashed against each other and fell like opposing waves. Then the chieftain Gundhar struck the earth with his spear and gave his decision.

"All have spoken, but none are agreed. There is no voice of the council. Keep silence now, and let the stranger speak. His words shall give us judgment, whether he is to live or to die."

Winfried lifted himself high upon the altar, drew a roll of parchment from his bosom, and began to read.

"A letter from the great Bishop of Rome, who sits on a golden throne, to the people of the forest, Hessians and Thuringians, Franks and Saxons. *In nomine Domini, sanctae et individuae Trinitatis, amen!*"

A murmur of awe ran through the crowd. "It is the sacred tongue of the Romans, the tongue that is heard and understood by the wise men of every land. There is magic in it. Listen!"

Winfried went on to read the letter, translating it into the speech of the people.

"We have sent unto you our Brother Boniface, and appointed him your bishop, that he may teach you the only true faith, and baptize you, and lead you back from the ways of error to the path of salvation. Hearken to him in all things like a father. Bow your hearts to his teaching. He does not come for earthly gain, but for the gain of your souls. Depart from evil works. Do not worship the false gods, for they are devils. Offer no more bloody sacrifices, nor eat the flesh of horses, but do as our Brother Boniface commands you. Build a house for him that he may dwell among you, and a church where you may offer your prayers to the only living God, the Almighty King of Heaven."

It was a splendid message: proud, strong, peaceful, loving. The dignity of the words imposed mightily upon the hearts of the people. They were quieted as men who have listened to a lofty strain of music.

"Tell us, then," said Gundhar, "what is the word that you bring to us from the Almighty? What is your counsel for the tribes of the woodland on this night of sacrifice?"

"This is the word, and this is the counsel," answered Winfried. "Not a drop of blood shall fall tonight, except that which pity has drawn from the breast of your princess, in love for her child. Not a life shall be blotted out in the darkness tonight; but the great shadow of the tree that hides you from the light of heaven shall be swept away. For this is the birth night of the Christ, the son of the All-Father and the Savior of mankind. He is fairer than Baldur the Beautiful, greater than Odin the Wise, kinder than Freya the Good. Since he has come to earth the bloody sacrifices must cease. The dark Thor, on whom you vainly call, is dead. Deep in the shades of Niffelheim he is lost forever. His power in the world is broken. Will you serve a helpless god? See, my brothers, you call this tree his oak. Does he dwell here? Does he protect it?"

A troubled voice of assent rose from the throng. The people stirred uneasily. Women covered their eyes. Hunrad lifted his head and muttered hoarsely, "Thor! Take vengeance! Thor!"

Winfried beckoned to Gregor. "Bring the axes, yours and one for me. Now, young woodsman, show your craft! The king-tree of the forest must fall, and swiftly, or all is lost!"

The two men took their places facing each other, one on each side of the oak. Their cloaks were flung aside, their heads bare. Carefully they felt the ground with their feet, seeking a firm grip of the earth. Firmly they grasped the axe handles and swung the shining blades.

"Tree-god!" cried Winfried, "Are you angry? This is how we smite you!"

"Tree-god!" answered Gregor, "Are you mighty? This is how we fight you!"

Clang! Clang! The alternate strokes beat time upon the hard, ringing wood. The axe-heads glittered in their rhythmic flight, like fierce eagles circling about their quarry.

The broad flakes of wood flew from the deepening gashes in the sides of the oak. The huge trunk quivered. There was a shuddering in the branches. Then the great wonder of Winfried's life came to pass.

Out of the stillness of the winter night, a mighty rushing noise sounded overhead.

Was it the ancient gods on their white battle-steeds, with their black hounds of wrath and their arrows of lightning, sweeping through the air to destroy their foes?

A strong, whirling wind passed over the treetops. It gripped the oak by its branches and tore it from its roots. Backward it fell, like a ruined tower, groaning and crashing as it split asunder in four great pieces.

Winfried let his axe drop, and bowed his head for a moment in the presence of almighty power.

Then he turned to the people, "Here is the timber," he cried, "already felled and split for your new building. On this spot shall rise a chapel to the true God and his servant St. Peter."

"And here," said he, as his eyes fell on a young fir tree, standing straight and green, with its top pointing toward the stars, amid the divided ruins of the fallen oak, "here is the living tree, with no stain of blood upon it, that shall be the sign of your new worship. See how it points to the sky. Call it the tree of the Christ-child. Take it up and carry it to the chieftain's hall. You shall go no more into the shadows of the forest to keep your feasts with secret rites of shame. You shall keep them at home, with laughter and songs and rites of love. The Thunder-oak has fallen, and I think the day is coming when there shall not be a home in all Germany where the children are not gathered around the green fir-tree to rejoice in the birth night of Christ."

So they took the little fir from its place, and carried it in joyous procession to the edge of the glade, and laid it on the sled. The horses tossed their heads and drew their load bravely, as if the new burden had made it lighter.

When they came to the house of Gundhar, he ordered them to throw open the doors of the hall and set the tree in the midst of it. They kindled lights among the branches until it seemed to be tangled full of fireflies. The children encircled it, wondering, and the sweet odor of the balsam filled the house.

Then Winfried stood beside the chair of Gundhar, on the dais at the end of the hall, and told the story of Bethlehem, of the babe in the manger, of the shepherds on the hills, of the host of angels and their midnight song. All the people listened, charmed into stillness.

But the boy Bernhard, on Irma's knee, folded in her soft arms, grew restless as the story lengthened and began to prattle softly at his mother's ear.

"Mother," whispered the child, "why did you cry out so loud, when the priest was going to send me to Valhalla?"

"Oh, hush, my child," answered the mother, and pressed him closer to her side.

"Mother," whispered the boy again, laying his finger on the stains upon her breast, "see, your dress is red! What are these stains? Did someone hurt you?"

The mother closed his mouth with a kiss. "Dear, be still, and listen!"

The boy obeyed. His eyes were heavy with sleep. But he heard the last words of Winfried as he spoke of the angelic messengers flying over the hills of Judea and singing as they flew. The child wondered and dreamed and listened. Suddenly his face grew bright. He put his lips close to Irma's cheek again.

"Oh, mother!" he whispered very low, "do not speak. Do you hear them? Those angels have come back again. They are singing now behind the tree."

And some say that it was true; but others say that it was only Gregor and his companions at the lower end of the hall, chanting their Christmas hymn:

All glory be to God on high,
And on the earth be peace!
Good-will, henceforth, from heaven to man,
Begin and never cease.

The Gift of the Magi

The Background
O. Henry, 1862-1910
Classic, 20th Century Story

O. Henry is the pen name for William Sydney Porter. He was born in North Carolina to a physician father and a mother who died of tuberculosis when he was only three years old. After his mother's passing, his aunt (a teacher) and his paternal grandmother raised him. His aunt, in particular, helped to instill in him an early love for literature. Though he read constantly, he was restless with school, and at age 15, he began a career working in his uncle's drugstore.

Five years later, Porter moved to Texas hoping to relieve a persistent cough that he feared might be the first sign of tuberculosis. Fortunately, his health improved, and he eventually left the ranch for Austin. However, his experience on the ranch made a lasting impression. He learned customs and mannerisms that would show up later in his many western stories.[1]

Porter worked a variety of jobs in Austin, and in 1887, he married Athol Estes. Their first child, a son, died shortly after childbirth, but by 1889, a daughter, Margaret, was born. To support his growing family, Porter took a position as a teller at the First National Bank of Austin. On the side, he spent his time writing for various publications. His passion for writing led him to resign from the bank in 1894 and create his own humorous weekly publication called *The Rolling Stone*. Unfortunately, this entrepreneurial effort failed, so he took a position as a reporter and columnist with the *Houston Post*.

By 1895, Porter's previous work as a bank teller came back to haunt him. Though charges of embezzlement were initially dropped, a persistent bank examiner pressed the issue until Porter was indicted in 1896. Porter chose to flee the country rather than face a trial, but he was forced to return when he learned of his wife's failing health. He was present for her death in 1897. The following year, he was convicted of embezzling money and was sentenced to five years in an Ohio penitentiary.

Though Porter's attempt to avoid his trial did not help to support a case for his innocence, there has been much debate over his actual guilt. Apparently, his bank had very informal policies and was negligent about record keeping. Porter maintained that he was innocent of wrong-doing and believed that he was a scapegoat for lax banking practices.[2] There has also been speculation that Porter may have used funds, with the support of a bank official, to finance *The Rolling Stone* – a "loan" that he intended to repay.

Whether he was guilty or not, Gale's Literary Database records, "In the Ohio State Penitentiary, Porter became familiar with many of the men whose stories he would later create in fiction."[3] Furthermore, he had time to focus on and develop his writing. Though he used a variety of pseudonyms, his first story written in prison, "Whistling Dick's Christmas," published in McClure's in 1899, was signed "O. Henry." This name would remain with him the rest of his life.

In a New York Times interview, Porter described how he chose his pen name:

"I said to a friend: 'I'm going to send out some stuff. I don't know if it amounts to much, so I want to get a literary alias. Help me pick out a good one.' He suggested that we get a newspaper and pick a name from the first list of notables that we found in it. In the society columns we found the account of a fashionable ball. 'Here we have our notables,' said he. We looked down the list and my eye lighted on the name Henry, 'That'll do for a last name,' said I. 'Now for a first name. I want something short. None of your three-syllable names for me.' 'Why don't you use a plain initial letter, then?' asked my friend. 'Good,' said I, 'O is about the easiest letter written, and O it is.'"[4]

Understandably, Porter made no mention of the fact that his pseudonym was chosen during his days in prison. It was a period of his life that he tried to hide, even from his daughter. However, the penitentiary had a significant affect on him as a person and as a writer. He developed a love and sympathy for people there. This may give credibility to the theory that the pen name "O. Henry" was actually drawn from the letters in "Ohio Penitentiary."

Porter emerged from prison in 1901 after having his sentence reduced to three years for good behavior. In 1902, he moved to New York City and spent "hours talking with characters of the city – gangsters, shopgirls, hobos, prostitutes, actors – and transmuting them into fiction that he sold at a rapid rate to magazines and newspapers."[5]

Between 1903 and 1906, Porter had an arrangement with New York's *World* publication to produce one story per week. The classic tale "The Gift of the Magi" was first published in the 1905 Christmas issue of *World*. The editor decided to feature a Porter story on the front page with a large, full color illustration. However, as usual, Porter was late in submitting his story. Reportedly, the illustrator, Dan Smith, went to beg Porter for some indication as to what he should draw. Porter, "having no plot in his conscious mind," described a room with two people in it – a man with a watch in his hand and a girl with beautiful long hair.[6] The story later developed in Henry's mind, and no one ever suspected that it had been written after the picture was drawn.

Porter spent the next five years publishing at a frenzied pace. But by 1920, he "was suffering from nervous exhaustion and ill health, as well as financial desperation caused by his own generosity and financial irresponsibility."[7] He died that same year.

At the time of his death, Porter had published 10 collections and over 600 short stories. He was considered the most popular short story writer in the world, and the term "O. Henry style" is still used to describe stories, generally humorous, with ironic twists or surprise endings.[8] "The Gift of the Magi" is a perfect example of Porter's unique style. Full of both humor and wit, the story also offers insight into the true wisdom of generosity. As Proverbs teaches, "A generous man will prosper; he who refreshes others will himself be refreshed" (Proverbs 11:25).

[1] *Contemporary Authors.* "William Sydney Porter." Gale, 2002. Retrieved October 15, 2008 from Gale Literary Databases. Much of the biography for Porter is drawn from this source.

[2] *Contemporary Authors.*

[3] *Contemporary Authors.*

[4] *New York Times.* "'O. Henry' on Himself, Life, and Other Things." April 4, 1909, Page SM9. Retrieved October 16, 2008: http://www.greensboro-nc.gov/departments/Library/ohenry/Public+Library/on+himself. htm.

[5] *Contemporary Authors.*

[6] Montgomery, Elizabeth Rider. *The Story Behind Great Stories.* Robert M. McBride & Company, 1947, p. 201.

[7] *Contemporary Authors.*

[8] *Contemporary Authors.*

The Story

Reading Time: 10 minutes

One dollar and eighty-seven cents. That was all. And sixty cents of it was in pennies. Pennies saved one and two at a time by bulldozing the grocer and the vegetable man and the butcher until one's cheeks burned with the silent imputation of parsimony that such close dealing implied. Three times Della counted it. One dollar and eighty-seven cents. And the next day would be Christmas.

There was clearly nothing to do but flop down on the shabby little couch and howl. So Della did it. Which instigates the moral reflection that life is made up of sobs, sniffles, and smiles, with sniffles predominating.

While the mistress of the home is gradually subsiding from the first stage to the second, take a look at the home. A furnished flat at $8 per week. It did not exactly beggar description, but it certainly had that word on the lookout for the mendicancy squad.

In the vestibule below was a letter-box into which no letter would go, and an electric button from which no mortal finger could coax a ring. Also appertaining thereunto was a card bearing the name "Mr. James Dillingham Young."

The "Dillingham" had been flung to the breeze during a former period of prosperity when its possessor was being paid $30 per week. Now, when the income was shrunk to $20, though, they were thinking seriously of contracting to a modest and unassuming D. But whenever Mr. James Dillingham Young came home and reached his flat above he was called "Jim" and greatly hugged by Mrs. James Dillingham Young, already introduced to you as Della. Which is all very good.

Della finished her cry and attended to her cheeks with the powder rag. She stood by the window and looked out dully at a gray cat walking a gray fence in a gray backyard. Tomorrow would be

Christmas Day, and she had only $1.87 with which to buy Jim a present. She had been saving every penny she could for months, with this result. Twenty dollars a week doesn't go far. Expenses had been greater than she had calculated. They always are. Only $1.87 to buy a present for Jim. Her Jim. Many a happy hour she had spent planning for something nice for him. Something fine and rare and sterling—something just a little bit near to being worthy of the honor of being owned by Jim.

There was a pier-glass between the windows of the room. Perhaps you have seen a pierglass in an $8 flat. A very thin and very agile person may, by observing his reflection in a rapid sequence of longitudinal strips, obtain a fairly accurate conception of his looks. Della, being slender, had mastered the art.

Suddenly she whirled from the window and stood before the glass. Her eyes were shining brilliantly, but her face had lost its color within twenty seconds. Rapidly she pulled down her hair and let it fall to its full length.

Now, there were two possessions of the James Dillingham Youngs' in which they both took a mighty pride. One was Jim's gold watch that had been his father's and his grandfather's. The other was Della's hair. Had the queen of Sheba lived in the flat across the airshaft, Della would have let her hair hang out the window some day to dry just to depreciate Her Majesty's jewels and gifts. Had King Solomon been the janitor, with all his treasures piled up in the basement, Jim would have pulled out his watch every time he passed, just to see him pluck at his beard from envy.

So now Della's beautiful hair fell about her rippling and shining like a cascade of brown waters. It reached below her knee and made itself almost a garment for her. And then she did it up again nervously and quickly. Once she faltered for a minute and stood still while a tear or two splashed on the worn red carpet.

On went her old brown jacket; on went her old brown hat. With a whirl of skirts and with the brilliant sparkle still in her eyes, she fluttered out the door and down the stairs to the street.

Where she stopped the sign read: "Mne. Sofronie. Hair Goods of All Kinds." One flight up Della ran, and collected herself, panting. Madame, large, too white, chilly, hardly looked the "Sofronie."

"Will you buy my hair?" asked Della.

"I buy hair," said Madame. "Take yer hat off and let's have a sight at the looks of it."

Down rippled the brown cascade.

"Twenty dollars," said Madame, lifting the mass with a practised hand.

"Give it to me quick," said Della.

Oh, and the next two hours tripped by on rosy wings. Forget the hashed metaphor. She was ransacking the stores for Jim's present.

She found it at last. It surely had been made for Jim and no one else. There was no other like it in any of the stores, and she had turned all of them inside out. It was a platinum fob chain simple and chaste in design, properly proclaiming its value by substance alone and not by meretricious ornamentation—as all good things should do. It was even worthy of The Watch. As soon as she saw it she knew that it must be Jim's. It was like him. Quietness and value—the description applied to both. Twenty-one dollars they took from her for it, and she hurried home with the 87 cents. With that chain on his watch Jim might be properly anxious about the time in any company. Grand as the watch was, he sometimes looked at it on the sly on account of the old leather strap that he used in place of a chain.

When Della reached home her intoxication gave way a little to prudence and reason. She got out her curling irons and lighted the gas and went to work repairing the ravages made by generosity added to love. Which is always a tremendous task, dear friends—a mammoth task.

Within forty minutes her head was covered with tiny, close-lying curls that made her look wonderfully like a truant schoolboy. She looked at her reflection in the mirror long, carefully, and critically.

"If Jim doesn't kill me," she said to herself, "before he takes a second look at me, he'll say I look like a Coney Island chorus girl. But what could I do—oh! what could I do with a dollar and eighty-seven cents?"

At 7 o'clock the coffee was made and the frying-pan was on the back of the stove hot and ready to cook the chops.

Jim was never late. Della doubled the fob chain in her hand and sat on the corner of the table near the door that he always entered. Then she heard his step on the stair away down on the first flight, and she turned white for just a moment. She had a habit of saying a little silent prayer about the simplest everyday things, and now she whispered: "Please God, make him think I am still pretty."

The door opened and Jim stepped in and closed it. He looked thin and very serious. Poor fellow, he was only twenty-two—and to be burdened with a family! He needed a new overcoat and he was without gloves.

Jim stopped inside the door, as immovable as a setter at the scent of quail. His eyes were fixed upon Della, and there was an expression in them that she could not read, and it terrified her. It was not anger, nor surprise, nor disapproval, nor horror, nor any of the sentiments that she had been prepared for. He simply stared at her fixedly with that peculiar expression on his face.

Della wriggled off the table and went for him.

"Jim, darling," she cried, "don't look at me that way. I had my hair cut off and sold because I couldn't have lived through Christmas without giving you a present. It'll grow out again—you won't mind, will you? I just had to do it. My hair grows awfully fast. Say 'Merry Christmas!' Jim, and let's be happy. You don't know what a nice—what a beautiful, nice gift I've got for you."

"You've cut off your hair?" asked Jim, laboriously, as if he had not arrived at that patent fact yet even after the hardest mental labor.

"Cut it off and sold it," said Della. "Don't you like me just as well, anyhow? I'm me without my hair, ain't I?"

Jim looked about the room curiously.

"You say your hair is gone?" he said, with an air almost of idiocy.

"You needn't look for it," said Della. "It's sold, I tell you—sold and gone, too. It's Christmas Eve, boy. Be good to me, for it went for you. Maybe the hairs of my head were numbered," she went on with sudden serious sweetness, "but nobody could ever count my love for you. Shall I put the chops on, Jim?"

Out of his trance Jim seemed quickly to wake. He enfolded his Della. For ten seconds let us regard with discreet scrutiny some inconsequential object in the other direction. Eight dollars a week or a million a year—what is the difference? A mathematician or a wit would give you the wrong answer. The magi brought valuable gifts, but that was not among them. This dark assertion will be illuminated later on.

Jim drew a package from his overcoat pocket and threw it upon the table.

"Don't make any mistake, Dell," he said, "about me. I don't think there's anything in the way of a haircut or a shave or a shampoo that could make me like my girl any less. But if you'll unwrap that package you may see why you had me going a while at first."

White fingers and nimble tore at the string and paper. And then an ecstatic scream of joy; and then, alas! a quick feminine change to hysterical tears and wails, necessitating the immediate employment of all the comforting powers of the lord of the flat.

For there lay The Combs—the set of combs, side and back, that Della had worshipped long in a Broadway window. Beautiful combs, pure tortoise shell, with jeweled rims—just the shade to wear in the beautiful vanished hair. They were expensive combs, she knew, and her heart had simply craved and yearned over them without the least hope of possession. And now, they were hers, but the tresses that should have adorned the coveted adornments were gone.

But she hugged them to her bosom, and at length she was able to look up with dim eyes and a smile and say: "My hair grows so fast, Jim!"

And then Della leaped up like a little singed cat and cried, "Oh, oh!"

Jim had not yet seen his beautiful present. She held it out to him eagerly upon her open palm. The dull precious metal seemed to flash with a reflection of her bright and ardent spirit.

"Isn't it a dandy, Jim? I hunted all over town to find it. You'll have to look at the time a hundred times a day now. Give me your watch. I want to see how it looks on it."

Instead of obeying, Jim tumbled down on the couch and put his hands under the back of his head and smiled.

"Dell," said he, "let's put our Christmas presents away and keep 'em a while. They're too nice to use just at present. I sold the watch to get the money to buy your combs. And now suppose you put the chops on."

The magi, as you know, were wise men — wonderfully wise men — who brought gifts to the Babe in the manger. They invented the art of giving Christmas presents. Being wise, their gifts were no doubt wise ones, possibly bearing the privilege of exchange in case of duplication. And here I have lamely related to you the uneventful chronicle of two foolish children in a flat who most unwisely sacrificed for each other the greatest treasures of their house. But in a last word to the wise of these days let it be said that of all who give gifts these two were the wisest. Of all who give and receive gifts, such as they are wisest. Everywhere they are wisest. They are the magi.

The Legend
of Befana

The Background
Legend, Italian

The legend of Befana predates Christianity and most likely has its origin in Rome. Befana is traditionally characterized as an old woman who travels the world to find children; she rewards the good ones and penalizes the bad ones.

As Christianity began to take root in Italy, the story of Befana developed a connection with the Wise Men and was infused with biblical themes. The most popular versions of the story recount how the Wise Men stayed in Befana's home during their journey to find Christ. When they invited Befana to join them, she declined (believing that her work was more important than going to see Christ). Her story is reminiscent of Martha in Luke 10:38-42, who, instead of sitting at the Lord's feet, was distracted by trivial work.

After the Wise Men continued on their journey, Befana had a change of heart; she decided to set off and find the infant King. Unfortunately, she left too late and was doomed to look for the Christ child forever.

In Italy, Befana is said to visit children on the eve of Epiphany (January 6), the day that the Wise Men first saw Jesus, in the hope of finding Christ. Good children are rewarded with candy and sweets; bad children receive stones and charcoal. Befana is generally depicted with a broom in hand and, being the good housekeeper that she is, she sweeps the floor before she leaves.

The following story serves as a reminder to "seek first his kingdom," and "do not worry about tomorrow" (Matthew 6:33-34). Had Befana heeded these words, she may have been a part of the most important event in history.

The Story
Reading Time: 5 minutes

Befana was beautiful as a young woman. She was also very particular about the details of her life. Her appearance, her home, her garden, etc. were always in precise order. Yet, despite her perfectionism, Befana was not disagreeable at all. In fact, most people liked her. Many young ladies sought her friendship, though none of them ever felt quite free enough to call her a friend. Befana also had many suitors in her youth, but none of them ever felt confident enough of her affection to propose marriage.

So Befana had grown old with no husband, no children and no intimate friends. Yet, she remained kind as she aged, and people still liked her. Befana's parents had provided for her, their only child, until their death. Once they passed away, Befana converted the family home into an inn, thus assuring her own financial independence. She enjoyed having visitors and proved to be a fine hostess. Word spread of the immaculate quarters, the enjoyable conversation and the fine food available at her inn.

One evening, stately men from the East arrived seeking lodging. Befana showed warm hospitality to their party, and she chatted late into the evening with them about the intent of their journey. The wise guests spoke of marvelous things. They told of prophecies that had been handed down for over 700 years about this very generation in which a King would be born in Israel. They also recounted the signs in the heavens that confirmed the time had come. They wanted to be among the first to honor and worship the infant King.

Befana was captivated and asked many questions of the Wise Men. Seeing her interest, they invited her to join them on their journey. Befana sensed that she should go. She even felt an excitement that she had not experienced since childhood. But the emotion was stifled as she thought of her inn. Who would attend to the cleaning, the cooking and the guests? How could she possibly leave? If she closed down for business, could she ever regain her reputation as an innkeeper? As her heart struggled, her hands floundered to pick up a broom, and she began to sweep.

One of the Wise Men, Gaspar, rose from his seat and pointedly asked, "Befana, will you come to see the newborn King?"

"I cannot go," she replied. "Who would care for the inn?"

Gaspar said, "Surely you can close the inn for a time. We have left important work behind and traveled a great distance, because we know that the birth of this King is a matter of great significance."

Befana paused but did not respond as thoughts raced through her mind.

Next Balthasar rose, "Befana, will you come to see the infant of whom the prophets have foretold?"

"I cannot go," she replied. "Besides taking care of the inn, I am old and have never been far from home."

The Wise Men assured her that they would provide for all of her needs and would even assign a handmaiden to attend her. With much admonition, they attempted to convince her. But as the hour got late, they retired to bed without success.

The next day, the Wise Men rose early to start on their journey. As they prepared their camels, they realized that Befana had already watered them. Moreover, she had laid out a lovely breakfast. Broom in hand, she was sweeping again.

This time Melchoir spoke, "Befana, surely we will respect your wishes, but we must ask again: Will you not come see the great King of whom all the heavens proclaim?"

"I cannot go," she replied. "Besides the inn and my age, I have no gift worthy of a great King."

Melchoir said, "This is no ordinary King. Perhaps you can serve him with your kindness and hospitality as you have graciously served us."

But Befana assured them that her mind was made up and could not be altered. Though her words were firm, her heart wavered. Somehow she felt that she should go. But all of her worries overcame her, and she remained. She watched the Wise Men until they were specks in a small cloud of dust kicked up by their camels. She felt uneasy, and knew no other way to deal with her emotion than to pour herself into her work.

She swept, cleaned and organized with great energy that day, and she felt a sense of satisfaction when her work was done. But a strange thing happened when she went to put her broom away in the closet. She caught sight of a bag that had been there for many years. It was full of items that her mother had kept since her childhood (clothes, toys, etc.). It was meant for her to pass down to her children, but she had none. Then the thought struck her that she should deliver them to the infant King.

Yes, she would go. God had given her a sign. But she had many arrangements to make before she could travel and catch up with the Wise Men. After several days of preparation and the packing of many provisions, Befana finally set off on her journey. She stopped at many inns along the way to Israel, and as she made inquiries, she felt confident that she was traveling in the path of the Wise Men. But when she finally arrived in Jerusalem, she learned that the Wise Men had vanished after traveling to Bethlehem. Of course, the people of Bethlehem were loath to talk with her, a stranger, about the whereabouts of the King that she sought. They had recently endured a great tragedy on account of this King. In seeking to destroy any rival to his throne, Herod had ordered the murder of every infant boy in Bethlehem. There were rumors that the infant King had escaped, but no one knew where.

So Befana continued on in her search. It is said that she still seeks the infant King, and as she travels from place to place, she distributes her many provisions to children along the way in the hope that she will one day find the one she seeks. And knowing no other way to deal with her regrets, she continues to clean; she sweeps every home before she leaves.

The Legend
of the Poinsettia

The Background
Legend, Mexican

When Mexico was Christianized in the 16th century through the influence of Spain, the poinsettia (or "star flower" in the language of the Aztec people) came to be associated with Christmas (see pp. 126-128). A charming legend was spread throughout Mexico telling of how a simple weed was miraculously transformed into the first poinsettia plant on Christmas Eve. The plant came to be known in Mexico as the *Flores de Noche Buena* (Flowers of the Holy Night).

There are several variations of the legend of the poinsettia. Most include a poor young girl in Mexico who was distraught over the fact that she had nothing but a weed to present to the Lord at a Christmas Eve service. But the weed was miraculously transformed into a brilliant poinsettia plant. The following account adds several details to the story in order to build the characters. It highlights how God often chooses "the poor in the eyes of the world to be rich in faith and to inherit the kingdom he promised those who love him" (James 2:5). Enjoy this retelling of "The Legend of the Poinsettia."

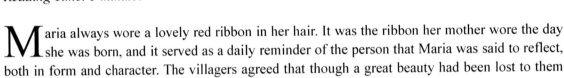

The Story
Reading Time: 5 minutes

Maria always wore a lovely red ribbon in her hair. It was the ribbon her mother wore the day she was born, and it served as a daily reminder of the person that Maria was said to reflect, both in form and character. The villagers agreed that though a great beauty had been lost to them when Maria's mother died, it had blossomed again in Maria.

The children in particular adored Maria. She was kind to them and patiently instructed them in the trade of her small village in Mexico, weaving beautiful blankets. Among the children, Maria had a special affection for Ana, a child 7 years her junior. Ana's mother had died at birth as had Maria's. Their fathers, to whom they were particularly devoted, raised them, and neither girl had any other siblings.

Maria was a diligent worker. She worked hard weaving blankets to sell at the market. Since she had no mother, she also managed her home and cared for her father. The little spare time afforded to Maria was dedicated to working on an elegant tapestry. Maria had spent several years working on a Nativity design, and it was her desire to present it to the Lord on the Christmas Eve following her 15th birthday.

For many in the village, presenting a gift at church on Christmas Eve was a bit of a competition. It seemed that each year the gifts had become more elaborate. Though many simply tried to out-do their neighbor, Maria's work was a true labor of love. She sincerely desired to please the Lord with the care and attention she put into the tapestry.

When the long awaited Christmas Eve finally came, Maria spent the morning looking and re-looking over the tapestry to make sure it was perfect. Just as she had carefully placed it in her bag, she heard Ana's voice in the distance. Ana was running frantically toward her and spoke almost unintelligibly when she finally arrived. With great care, Maria extracted that Ana's father had fallen dangerously ill. The village doctor had sent Ana to a visiting merchant in a hurried effort to reach him before he left with the rare herbs that were required for treatment. Ana attempted to buy the herbs, but the merchant refused to accept any of her fine blankets in trade. He claimed the herbs were far more valuable than any of the blankets made in her village. Though the thought pained her, Maria knew exactly what the merchant would accept as a fair trade . . . the tapestry. Maria made haste to complete the exchange.

Hours later, after Maria had obtained the herbs and delivered them to Ana's father, the village doctor announced that the danger had passed. Though little Ana had been so brave throughout the trial of her father's life, she sobbed when she heard the news. Maria held her as she cried.

Both girls were stunned when Ana's father spoke. Weakly, he asked that Ana deliver his gift to the church service that evening. He had worked all year on a wood carving, and considering the events of the day, he especially wanted to express his gratitude to God for sparing his life. Ana and Maria looked to the doctor who nodded approvingly and assured them that he would remain with his patient throughout the night.

Maria had completely forgotten about the Christmas Eve service. She rushed home to dress. As she hurried along the path alone, she was filled with joy at how God had saved Ana's father on this special night. Yet her heart ached over the fact that she had no tapestry to present to the Lord. In fact, she had nothing to give. Maria and her father, though poor themselves, had given all they had to neighbors in greater need.

At that moment a plant caught Maria's eye. She had never noticed it before. As she surveyed it, she determined that the green leaves were quite lovely. A brief hesitation filled her heart. Surely the other villagers would scoff at her for presenting a weed to the Lord, but she reasoned that if he himself had created it, than it would be a worthy, though humble gift. She would bear the scoffing. If only she had a ribbon to tie around it. Though tempted to ignore the thought that she ought to use the ribbon in her hair, Maria knew somehow that it would please the Lord. It pained her to think of giving away the only tangible connection that she had to her mother. Surely the Lord, more than anyone, knew how precious the ribbon was to her, but it seemed to her that it was he who filled her with the strength to loosen it from her hair and fasten it to the leaves.

On arriving at the Christmas Eve service, Maria's ears rang with the boasting of villagers in regard to their various gifts. One by one, she watched as each laid their gift before the Christ Child of the Nativity scene. A wave of doubt filled Maria. Would she offend the Lord if she presented such a gift? She prayed quietly as she approached the statue and thanked God in faith that he knew her heart. Maria heard whispers all around her and once more, nearly lost heart. But as she glanced down at the plant, she gasped. Bright red leaves in the shape of a star had burst open. The ribbon that had added such vibrant color to the green plant now paled in comparison to the brilliance of the red leaves.

The villagers all praised God for his magnificent creation — it seemed like the perfect flower to honor the birth of Christ. With much celebration, the flower was planted outside Maria's church, and it soon grew into a plant of marvelous size. It produced an abundant display of flowers every Christmas season. Many were given to visiting merchants who carried the flowers throughout Mexico and spread the story of the miracle that had taken place in Maria's village. The flowers came to be known as the *Flores de Noche Buena*, or Flowers of the Holy Night.

The Parable of the Birds

The Background
Louis Cassels, 1922-1974
Parable, 20th Century

Louis Cassels was born and raised in South Carolina. After graduating from Duke University in 1942, he joined the Air Force to serve during World War II. Over the course of his three years in the army, Cassels worked as a communications officer and then a first lieutenant. Soon after the war ended, he took a position as a correspondent with United Press International. He served in this capacity for twenty years before becoming senior editor in 1967, a position he held for the remainder of his life.

From 1955-1974, Cassels authored the popular column "Religion in America."[1] Cassels was a devoted Christian, and in the last ten years of his life, he wrote over a dozen books that were all dedicated to issues of faith. Some of his notable publications were: *Your Bible* (1967), *The Real Jesus: How He Lived and What He Taught (*1968), and *The Reality of God* (1971).

Throughout his career in journalism, Cassel's earned a variety of prestigious awards, and his coverage of religious news earned him respect from people of all different faiths. Yet, he never compromised his conviction that truth in religion really mattered. In 1965, he wrote a book titled, *What's the Difference? A Comparison of the Faiths Men Live By*, in which he carefully outlined the core doctrines of many religions. In his final chapter, "Does It Matter What You Believe?" he wrote:

"Does it really matter in the long run whether you're a Christian, a Jew, a Moslem, or a Buddhist? Millions of people today, including many nominal members of Christian churches, are inclined to answer in the negative. They believe that all religions are basically the same, and that 'one pathway to Truth is as good as another.' This sounds like a wonderfully broad-minded attitude, and people who hold it usually think they are being quite modern in their approach to religion. In fact, they are simply subscribing to a very old type of religion called syncretism.

"We encounter syncretism repeatedly in the Old Testament of the Bible. When the prophets proclaimed that there is no other God than Jehovah, they were resisting the syncretism of the Babylonian civilization that surrounded Israel. Then, as now, syncretism presented itself as an extremely tolerant and reasonable kind of faith. Babylon was perfectly willing to add Jehovah to its idol-cluttered altars, if the Jews would abandon their claim that He was the only god. Had the Jews not been — in the eyes of their Babylonian neighbors — narrow-minded and fanatical in rejecting these terms, the religion of Judaism would have been simply swallowed up without a trace five thousand years ago.

"Christianity also encountered the temptation of syncretism in its infancy. The Roman civilization into which the Church was born was proud of its open-minded attitude toward all religions. As the historian Edward Gibbon has put it, 'The various *modi* of worship which prevailed in the Roman world were all considered by the people equally useful.' The Romans felt, in other words, that it didn't matter what a man believed so long as he believed something that would comfort him in battle and keep him reasonably honest. When Christianity first reached Rome, it was accorded a warm reception. The emperor Alexander Severus added a statue of Jesus to his private chapel, which already contained figures of numerous pagan gods. Rome began to persecute the Christian Church only when it fought off the smothering embrace of syncretism, and stubbornly insisted that 'there is no other name under heaven than Jesus Christ whereby men may be saved.'" [2]

Cassels went on to say, "The heart of the Christian faith is the assertion that God has revealed himself in history in the person of Jesus Christ."[3] Truly, the idea that God became a man and walked among his creation is one of the most profound claims of Christianity. In an effort to explain God's remarkable act, Cassels followed the example of Jesus, who used parables to teach challenging spiritual truths.

Cassels wrote "The Parable of the Birds" and distributed it through UPI (United Press International) in December of 1959. The story appeared in newspapers and on radio broadcasts across the country. It was so popular that it was (and continues to be) reproduced every Christmas. One of the most notable voices to introduce the story on the air was Paul Harvey (the master storyteller of 20th century radio).

In his parable, Cassels addresses some of the significant reasons why God chose to come into the world as a man – to demonstrate his love for people, to show his intimate understanding of human life and to personally deliver the message of salvation. Enjoy this moving story.

---

[1] *Contemporary Authors.* "Louis Cassels." Gale, 2002. Retrieved October 15, 2008 from Gale Literary Databases. Much of the biography for Louis Cassels is drawn from this source.

[2] Cassels, Louis. *What's the Difference? A Comparison of the Faiths Men Live By.* Doubleday & Company, Inc., 1965, pp. 211-212.

[3] Cassels, Louis, pp. 215-216.

The Story
Reading Time: 3 minutes

Now the man to whom I'm going to introduce you was not a scrooge; he was a kind, decent, mostly good man. He was generous to his family and upright in his dealings with other men. But he just didn't believe all that stuff about God becoming a man, which the churches proclaim at Christmas time. It just didn't make sense, and he was too honest to pretend otherwise.

"I'm truly sorry to distress you," he told his wife, "but I'm not going with you to church this Christmas Eve." He said he'd feel like a hypocrite and that he would much rather just stay at home. And so he stayed, and they went to the midnight service.

Shortly after the family drove away in the car, snow began to fall. He went to the window to watch the flurries getting heavier and heavier. Then he went back to his fireside chair to read his newspaper. Minutes later he was startled by a thudding sound. Then another and another — sort of a thump or a thud. At first he thought someone must have been throwing snowballs against his living room window.

But when he went to the front door to investigate, he found a flock of birds huddled miserably in the snow. They'd been caught in the storm and, in a desperate search for shelter, had tried to fly through his large landscape window. Well, he couldn't let the poor creatures lie there and freeze, so he remembered the barn where his children stabled their pony. That would provide a warm shelter, if he could direct the birds to it.

Quickly he put on a coat and galoshes and then he tramped through the deepening snow to the barn. He opened the doors wide and turned on a light, but the birds did not come in. He figured food would entice them. So he hurried back to the house, fetched breadcrumbs and sprinkled them on the snow. He made a trail to the brightly lit, wide-open doorway of the stable. But to his dismay, the birds ignored the breadcrumbs and continued to flap around helplessly in the snow.

He tried catching them. He tried shooing them into the barn by walking around them and waving his arms. Instead, they scattered in every direction, except into the warm, lighted barn. And then he realized that they were afraid of him. To them, he reasoned, I am a strange and terrifying creature. If only I could think of some way to let them know that they can trust me — that I am not trying to hurt them but to help them. But how?

Any move he made tended to frighten and confuse them. They just would not follow. They would not be led or shooed, because they feared him.

"If only I could be a bird," he thought to himself, "and mingle with them and speak their language. Then I could tell them not to be afraid. Then I could show them the way to the safe warm barn. But I would have to be one of them so they could see and hear and understand."

At that moment the church bells began to ring. The sound reached his ears above the sounds of the wind. And he stood there listening to the bells pealing the glad tidings of Christmas. And he sank to his knees in the snow.

"Now I understand," he whispered. "Now I see why you had to do it."

'Twas the Night Before
Christmas, A Visit
From St. Nicholas

The Background
Clement Clarke Moore, 1779-1863 or Henry Livingston, Jr., 1748-1828
Classic Poem, 19th Century

Clement Clarke Moore was born in New York City as the only child of Benjamin Moore and Charity Clarke. Moore's father, who tutored his son at home until college, faithfully imparted his interests to his son in both academic life and ministry.[1] As a graduate of King's College, Moore's father worked as its acting president during the first year of the American Revolution and was later appointed to the presidency of Columbia College (now Columbia University). Moore's father was also active in the Episcopal Church throughout his life and served as the second bishop of the Diocese of New York.

When Moore entered Columbia College, he proved to be a capable student. He graduated in 1798 "at the head of his class, as his father had, thirty years earlier," and by 1801, he had earned an M.A. degree.[2] Moore was uniquely gifted in language, and he devoted most of the next several years to producing a massive two-volume Hebrew Lexicon, *A Compendious Lexicon of the Hebrew Language* (1809). He also taught language and literature courses at Columbia College.

In 1813, Moore married Catharine Elizabeth Taylor, with whom he would eventually have nine children. Despite the responsibilities of a growing family, Moore remained active in scholarship and ministry over the next several years. He was instrumental in helping to create the first Episcopal Seminary in America (the General Theological Seminary), and in 1821, he became one of its first professors. He also donated a large portion of land onto which the seminary would eventually relocate. Moore remained at the seminary until he retired in 1850.

Reportedly, in 1822, Moore wrote the poem "A Visit from St. Nicholas" (now known as "'Twas the Night Before Christmas") for his children (he had six at the time). This delightful poem has since been credited with popularizing the fantasy surrounding St. Nicholas and giving uniformity to American Christmas traditions.

Most likely, the poem developed out of ideas that were already circulating through the U.S. For example, in 1809, Washington Irving (a famous American writer) had published a satire on Dutch immigrants and their traditions called *History of New York*. Though Irving characterized St. Nicholas as an old man in dark robes who rode a flying horse, he depicted elderly Dutch men as jolly and fat with white beards and smoking pipes. He also characterized them as wearing wide leather belts and leather boots. By 1822, it appears that St. Nicholas had evolved into one of Irving's jolly old Dutch men. Furthermore, as evidence that reindeer had already come to be associated with Saint Nicholas (or Santa Claus) in America, a poem published in 1821, "The Children's Friend," said the following:

Old Santeclaus with much delight
His reindeer drives this frosty night.
O'er chimney tops, and tracks of snow,
To bring his yearly gifts to you.[3]

There are various accounts about how the poem "A Visit From St. Nicholas" came to appear anonymously in the *Troy Sentinel* on December 23, 1823. Reportedly, a relative copied the verses during her stay at the Moore home, from which a copy was made by Sarah Harriet Butler (a friend). Sarah's father, Rev. David Butler, was apparently so impressed with the poem that he gave it to the editor of the *Sentinel*. Once the poem was printed, it was an immediate success and would appear in publications across the country in subsequent years.

Though "A Visit From St. Nicholas" was attributed to Moore in *The New York Book of Poetry* in 1837,[4] Moore did not personally claim authorship until 1844, when he published his collection of *Poems*. Some say that because Moore was a serious scholar, he did not have much interest in identifying himself as the writer of a fairy tale poem. However, others claim that Moore did not identify himself earlier, because he did not actually write the famous poem. The family of writer Henry Livingston, Jr. maintains that long before the poem was first published in the *Sentinel* (probably 1808), their ancestor was reading it to his children every Christmas Eve.[5]

The most convincing case in favor of Livingston's authorship is made by Don Foster in his book *Author Unknown, On the Trail of the Anonymous*. Foster is an English professor who has served as a textual analyst in several high profile criminal cases; his specialty is author identity. After carefully reviewing Livingston's work, Foster noted that a distinct aspect of his style was the way he used the word "all" as an adverb, and this can be seen throughout the Christmas poem: "all through the house," "all snug in their beds," "all dressed in fur," etc. Additionally, the poem is characteristically Dutch in its view of St. Nicholas. Whereas Moore was of English descent, Livingston was Dutch. Furthermore, Moore repeated an editor's correction that changed two of the reindeer names from *Dunder* and *Blixem*, the Dutch words for "thunder" and "lightening," to *Donder* and *Blitzen*.* Lastly, before Moore claimed authorship of the work in his publication of *Poems*, he apparently wrote to the *Sentinel* to see if anyone could remember its origin, but no one could.[6]

After researching the work of both Livingston and Moore, Foster also drew some interesting conclusions about their respective characters. Whereas he perceived Livingston (a father of 12) to be warm, tender-hearted, and playful, he inferred that Moore was cold, judgmental and self-righteous. Foster argues that "'Twas the Night Before Christmas" is "as different from Moore's other children's verse [which were more preachy than they were playful] as Christmas cookies from steamed spinach."[7]

Regardless, there are still many scholars who hold passionately to the belief that Moore wrote the poem. Historian Stephen Nissenbaum highlights the following fact as evidence:

"In 1829 that same Troy newspaper [that had first printed the verses in 1823] reprinted the poem . . . but this time the newspaper's editor added some tantalizing hints about the identity of the poem's author: he was a New York City man 'by birth and residence,' and 'a gentleman of more merit as a scholar and writer than many of more noisy pretensions.'"[8]

Nissenbaum concludes, "While keeping up the aura of genteel anonymity, these words [from the editor of the *Troy Sentinel*] pointed pretty clearly to Moore."[9] Henry Livingston, who had recently passed away, was neither a scholar nor a resident of New York City.

Though the editorial comment certainly does not confirm Moore's authorship, it does imply that the editor of the *Sentinel* credited the poem to him six years after it was first printed. However, if Moore himself was not acknowledging authorship at this point, it is easy to imagine how rumors and speculation could fill the void. It is not so easy, on the other hand, to imagine how Moore's name can now be separated from a poem that has been published in his name millions of times around the world.

But what if Livingston was in fact the true author? Well, who can blame Moore for wanting to claim a bit of the warm Christmas spirit that so permeated Livingston's life and the lines of "'Twas the Night Before Christmas"?

---

[1] Dictionary of Literary Biography. "Clement Clarke Moore." Retrieved on October 18, 2008: http://www.bookrags.com/biography/clement-clarke-moore-dlb/. Much of the biography for Clement Clarke Moore is drawn from this source.

[2] Patterson, Samuel White. *The Poet of Christmas Eve: A Life of Clement Clarke Moore, 1779-1863.* Morehouse-Gorham Co., 1956, p. 45.

[3] Patterson, Samuel White, p. 12.

[4] Hoffman, Charles Fenno. *The New York Book of Poetry.* G. Dearborn, 1837, pp. 217-219.

[5] Van Deusen, Mary. "Major Henry Livingston, Jr., The Christmas Poem." Retrieved October 18, 2008: http://www.iment.com/maida/familytree/henry/index.htm.

[6] Foster, Don. *Author Unknown: On the Trail of the Anonymous.* Henry Holt, 2000, pp. 259-266.

[7] Foster, Don, p. 261.

[8] Nissenbaum, Stephen. "There Arose Such a Clatter: Who Really Wrote 'The Night before Christmas'? And Why Does It Matter?" Retrieved October 18, 2008: http://www.historycooperative. org/journals/cp/vol-01/no-02/moore/moore-2.shtml.

[9] Nissenbaum, Stephen.

*The editor actually changed "Blixem" to "Blixen" for better rhyme. Moore, who was familiar with German (but not Dutch), changed it to "Blitzen."

The Story
Reading Time: 3 minutes

'Twas the night before Christmas, when all thro' the house
Not a creature was stirring, not even a mouse;
The stockings were hung by the chimney with care,
In hopes that St. Nicholas soon would be there;

The children were nestled all snug in their beds,
While visions of sugar-plums danc'd in their heads;
And Mama in her 'kerchief, and I in my cap,
Had just settled our brains for a long winter's nap —

When out on the lawn there arose such a clatter,
I sprang from the bed to see what was the matter.
Away to the window I flew like a flash,
Tore open the shutters and threw up the sash.

The moon on the breast of the new fallen snow
Gave the lustre of mid-day to objects below;
When, what to my wondering eyes should appear,
But a miniature sleigh, and eight tiny rein-deer,

With a little old driver, so lively and quick,
I knew in a moment it must be St. Nick.
More rapid than eagles his coursers they came,
And he whistled, and shouted, and called them by name;

"Now! Dasher, now! Dancer, now! Prancer, and Vixen,
On! Comet, on! Cupid, on! Dunder and Blixem;
To the top of the porch! to the top of the wall!
Now dash away! dash away! dash away all!"

As dry leaves before the wild hurricane fly,
When they meet with an obstacle, mount to the sky;
So up to the house-top the coursers they flew,
With the sleigh full of Toys — and St. Nicholas too:

And then in a twinkling, I heard on the roof
The prancing and pawing of each little hoof.
As I drew in my head, and was turning around,
Down the chimney St. Nicholas came with a bound:

He was dress'd all in fur, from his head to his foot,
And his clothes were all tarnish'd with ashes and soot;
A bundle of toys was flung on his back,
And he look'd like a peddler just opening his pack:

His eyes — how they twinkled! his dimples how merry,
His cheeks were like roses, his nose like a cherry;
His droll little mouth was drawn up like a bow,
And the beard of his chin was as white as the snow;

The stump of a pipe he held tight in his teeth,
And the smoke it encircled his head like a wreath.
He had a broad face, and a little round belly
That shook when he laugh'd, like a bowlful of jelly:

He was chubby and plump, a right jolly old elf,
And I laugh'd when I saw him in spite of myself;
A wink of his eye and a twist of his head
Soon gave me to know I had nothing to dread;

He spoke not a word, but went straight to his work,
And fill'd all the stockings; then turn'd with a jerk,
And laying his finger aside of his nose
And giving a nod, up the chimney he rose.

He sprung to his sleigh, to his team gave a whistle,
And away they all flew, like the down of a thistle:
But I heard him exclaim, ere he drove out of sight --
"Happy Christmas to all, and to all a good night."

'Twas the Night Before
Christmas, A Visit
From Christ

The Background
Angie Mosteller, Contemporary
A New Christ Centered Poem

On the night before Christmas, most of us are so distracted by the details associated with a visit from St. Nicholas that we forget about the much more important visit of God, who miraculously entered the world as a man over 2,000 years ago. This "visit" lasted over 30 years as God walked on earth teaching, loving and healing countless people. Ultimately, he gave up his life in order to offer salvation to whoever believed in him. Truly, this is the greatest gift known to man.

Though the following poem uses the famous first line of the classic, its purpose is to turn attention to Jesus and the true significance of Christmas. The book, *Fifth Seal*, by Bodie and Brock Thoene, inspired the words of the last verse of this poem. The story gives a fictional, though historical, account of the birth of Christ, and depicts what Joseph's first words to Jesus may have been. Here is the excerpt from *Fifth Seal* (note that *Yosef* is the Hebrew name for "Joseph" and *Yeshua* is the Hebrew name for "Jesus"):

"'Shalom, little one,' Yosef whispered. To the carpenter, who had little experience with newborns, the infant looked for all the world like a partially unwrapped Torah scroll. When a synagogue's ark was opened to deliver the Word of God to a reverent, adoring congregation, the scroll's royal covering of blue, purple, and scarlet was first laid aside, revealing the humbler, inner wrapping . . . just like now.

Yosef the Tzadik [righteous], a worshipful congregation of one, adored what he saw and rubbed the corner of his eye on his robe's sleeve . . . .

With a bit of wiggling and squirming, Yeshua freed one hand from the confines of the swaddling. A tiny fist emerged and went to His mouth.

Instinctively, Yosef reached his own calloused hand toward the child's. Partway there, struck by sudden hesitation, Yosef paused, but the baby's eyes had already spotted the motion.

A moment later baby Yeshua's right hand closed around Yosef's little finger. Yosef's eyes overflowed onto his cheeks and down into his beard.

'Shalom,' he whispered again. 'Welcome to our –' Stopping, the carpenter corrected himself. 'Welcome to your world. You are loved.'"

Through Jesus "all things were made" (John 1:3). The whole world belongs to him, yet he chose to enter it as a helpless infant for our sake. May this poem lead you to reflect on God's amazing love for us!

The Story
Reading Time: 2 minutes

'Twas the night before Christmas, and all through the earth,
Every creature was stirring, awaiting a birth.
The time for Messiah was certainly near,
The prophets foretold it; the Bible was clear.

From the book of beginnings, the very first sin,
God's word made it clear how His grace entered in.
Born of a virgin, He'd come as a man.
The Creator among us, the time was at hand.

The stars were arranged to show marvelous things,
Setting Wise Men to journey and find the true King.
Shepherds in Bethlehem gazed on the sky,
Longing to see him, their Lord the Most High.

How could they know that the very next night
An angel of God would speak words of delight?
How the Savior was born, it was news of great joy.
In a cloth and a manger they'd find the dear boy.

And a heavenly host would soon join to sing
Of the glory of God and of wonderful things.
He entered creation, set position aside
To show us how deeply his love did abide.

Sin sent us away from our almighty Lord.
He became one of us that we might be restored.
He's the Prince of our Peace; He's the one who makes whole.
He is Wisdom Incarnate, a Shepherd of Souls.

He's the Author of Life; He's the Ruler of All.
He can offer salvation, on His name we call.
The shepherds and Wise Men would bow to adore
Holy God among men, our greatest reward.

All glory and honor is due to this King.
Let all join in worship; let every tongue sing.
Jesus is Lord, all creation proclaims.
He's the first and last, He is always the same.

History turned on the first Christmas day,
When God became man in a humble display.
As we think of the manger in which He was laid,
Let our hearts welcome Him to the world He made!

Where Love Is, God Is

The Background
Leo Tolstoy, 1828-1910
Legend, French

Count Lev Nikolayevich Tolstoy (commonly known as Leo Tolstoy) was born into a distinguished family of old Russian nobility. Though both of his parents died while he was young, he had female relatives who committed to raising him.

By age 16, Tolstoy entered a local university. But formal education did not suit him, and he left without graduating in 1847. Having inherited the estate where he had been born, Tolstoy spent the next few years recklessly seeking fulfillment in gambling and romantic relationships. Yet, despite his debauched lifestyle, his interest in literature began to grow. He kept an extensive diary of "thoughts, actions and high-minded resolutions."[1] He also translated a popular 1768 English novel, *A Sentimental Journey Through France and Italy*, and attempted his first short story, "A History of Yesterday" (1851). But by the time he completed these literary pursuits, he was buried in debt and feeling that his life was useless and empty. As a result, he decided to join the Russian army.

During his time in the army, Tolstoy wrote a largely autobiographical narrative called *Childhood*, which was published in 1852. Its popularity led to the sequels *Boyhood* (1854) and *Youth* (1857). Yet, of his early successes, the greatest was *Sebastopol Sketches* (1855-1856), a series that detailed Tolstoy's experiences while leading men under fire during the Crimean War. According to biographer A.D.P. Briggs in *The Literary Encyclopedia*:

"The authenticity of his first-hand account enabled him to captivate his readers, and in doing so to undermine the false glamour of warfare; some of the scenes are worthy of *War and Peace*, which they clearly anticipate."[2]

The Crimean War (1854-1856) was the result of major European powers attempting to gain influence over the territories of the declining Ottoman Empire. The war was unique in that it was considered the first modern conflict to introduce technology that could significantly impact the outcome. Tolstoy was able to offer an eye witness account of the dreadful new ways of war. Once the conflict ended, Tolstoy retired from the army.

In 1857, Tolstoy traveled abroad to Geneva and Paris. When he returned to Russia, he was a more mature man, and he was ready to make a significant contribution to society. His first endeavor was the establishment of a school for peasant children on his estate. He also determined to write on challenging topics. He published *Family Happiness* (1859) in which he addressed the difficulties of marriage for women who must replace "romantic idealism by submission to duty, humdrum housekeeping, and the pleasures of raising children."[3] He also addressed the complexities of death in *Three Deaths* (1859).

In 1860, Tolstoy traveled to Paris again. This time, he went to visit his dying brother, Nikolai. Though Tolstoy had lost many loved ones in his life, namely his parents, the loss of his brother was particularly devastating to him. His experience was later recreated in his famous work *Anna Karenina* (published in installments from 1873-1877) and in other works such as *The Death of Ivan Il'ich* (1886).

The 1860's produced one of Tolstoy's greatest works, *War and Peace*, an ambitious historical novel about the French invasion of Russia in 1812. The first draft was completed in 1863, but not being satisfied with the ending, Tolstoy spent 1866 -1869 rewriting his work. This same decade also produced a fruitful marriage. In 1862, Sophia Bers became Tolstoy's wife. Though only eighteen years old when they married, Sophia proved to be an effective manager of their estate. She also bore Tolstoy thirteen children (nine boys and four girls) over the next several years; sadly, four of them died young. In addition to the demands of a full house, Sophia dedicated her evenings to transcribing Tolstoy's work. According to Briggs, she may even "have been responsible for much serious editing of his manuscripts that has never been fully explored or acknowledged."[4]

Though Tolstoy produced another gigantic masterpiece, *Anna Karenina*, in the 1870's, Briggs records that he became "increasingly obsessed with problems of religious belief, death and morality; he became an unhappy man, difficult to live with."[5] Ultimately, a spiritual crisis that almost led Tolstoy to suicide culminated instead in a conversion experience that he described in *A Confession* (1882). He explained that, though he abandoned his Christian faith as a young man, he could find no fulfillment in any other philosophy or religion. Thus he decided to return to the teaching of Jesus, though he remained critical of the organized church, which he thought promoted "a great deal of superstition alongside Christian truths."[6]

After his conversion, Tolstoy's writing took a decided turn toward religious and moral teaching. Though his views on socialism and pacifism attracted interest from all over the world, they largely alienated him from his family, his government and his national church. His wife, in particular, thought his socialistic ideas (namely giving up their possessions when they had such a large family to raise) were absurd. Tolstoy also provoked his government in Russia with accusations of violence, oppression and corruption; they banned his work *The Kingdom of God Is Within You* (1894) saying that Tolstoy's endorsement of pacifism was dangerous. Lastly, the Russian Orthodox Church was hostile toward Tolstoy's criticism of organized religion, and he was excommunicated in 1901.

By 1905, Tolstoy was openly condemning the revolutionary violence that was spreading across Russia. He opposed both Marxist materialism and Imperial repression, advocating spiritual reform instead.[7] Had Tolstoy's counsel been heeded, Russia's future may have taken a very different course. Instead, Marxist communism took hold and reigned for most of the 20th century. Since Tolstoy died in 1910, he never witnessed the dramatic political change that overtook his country after the last Russian Czar, Nicholas II, abdicated his reign in 1917. However, Tolstoy's work lived on, and according to Briggs, it was the "biggest and richest individual contribution to the treasure house of Russian culture" during the 19th century.

Tolstoy wrote "Where Love Is, God Is" in 1885 after his conversion experience. Since he was fluent in French, it comes as no surprise that his story is based on an old French legend. Though his story was originally written in Russian, it has been translated into many languages and has popularized the French legend throughout the world. The following English translation was published by Aylmer and Louise Maude in a 1906 collection of Tolstoy's work, *Twenty-Three Tales*. The Maudes (a husband and wife team) were personal friends of Tolstoy and are widely recognized for the quality of their translation work. Furthermore, in 1902, Tolstoy personally authorized Aylmer Maude to write his biography.

The story "Where Love Is, God Is" portrays a beautiful example of how serving others is like serving Christ himself. It seems especially appropriate for the Christmas season of generosity.

[1] Public Broadcasting Service. *Classic Masterpiece.* "A Tolstoy Timeline." Retrieved October 14, 2008: http://www.pbs.org/wgbh/masterpiece/anna/timeline_text.html.

[2] Briggs, A.D.P. "Lev Nikolaevich Tolstoy". *The Literary Encyclopedia.* April 19, 2004. Retrieved October 14, 2008: http://www.litencyc.com/php/speople.php?rec=true&UID=4413, accessed 26 September 2008. Much of the biography for Tolstoy is drawn from this source.

[3] Briggs, A.D.P.

[4] Briggs, A.D.P.

[5] Briggs, A.D.P.

[6] Tolstoy, Leo. *A Confession and Other Religious Writings.* Translated by Jane Kentish. Penguin Classics, 1987, p. 58.

[7] Public Broadcasting Service.

The Story
Reading Time: 25 minutes

In a certain town there lived a cobbler, Martin Avdéitch by name. He had a tiny room in a basement, the one window of which looked out on to the street. Through it one could only see the feet of those who passed by, but Martin recognized the people by their boots. He had lived long in the place and had many acquaintances. There was hardly a pair of boots in the neighborhood that had not been once or twice through his hands, so he often saw his own handiwork through the window. Some he had re-soled, some patched, some stitched up, and to some he had even put fresh uppers. He had plenty to do, for he worked well, used good material, did not charge too much, and could be relied on. If he could do a job by the day required, he undertook it; if not, he told the truth and gave no false promises; so he was well known and never short of work.

Martin had always been a good man; but in his old age he began to think more about his soul and to draw nearer to God. While he still worked for a master, before he set up on his own account, his wife had died, leaving him with a three-year old son. None of his elder children had lived, they had all died in infancy. At first Martin thought of sending his little son to his sister's in the country, but then he felt sorry to part with the boy, thinking: "It would be hard for my little Kapit n to have to grow up in a strange family; I will keep him with me."

Martin left his master and went into lodgings with his little son. But he had no luck with his children. No sooner had the boy reached an age when he could help his father and be a support as well as a joy to him, than he fell ill and, after being laid up for a week with a burning fever, died. Martin buried his son, and gave way to despair so great and overwhelming that he murmured against God. In his sorrow he prayed again and again that he too might die, reproaching God for having taken the son he loved, his only son while he, old as he was, remained alive. After that Martin left off going to church.

One day an old man from Martin's native village who had been a pilgrim for the last eight years, called in on his way from Tritsa Monastery. Martin opened his heart to him, and told him of his sorrow.

"I no longer even wish to live, holy man," he said. "All I ask of God is that I soon may die. I am now quite without hope in the world."

The old man replied: "You have no right to say such things, Martin. We cannot judge God's ways. Not our reasoning, but God's will, decides. If God willed that your son should die and you should live, it must be best so. As to your despair? that comes because you wish to live for your own happiness."

"What else should one live for?" asked Martin.

"For God, Martin," said the old man. "He gives you life, and you must live for Him. When you have learnt to live for Him, you will grieve no more, and all will seem easy to you."

Martin was silent awhile, and then asked: "But how is one to live for God?"

The old man answered: "How one may live for God has been shown us by Christ. Can you read? Then buy the Gospels, and read them: there you will see how God would have you live. You have it all there."

These words sank deep into Martin's heart, and that same day he went and bought himself a Testament in large print, and began to read.

At first he meant only to read on holidays, but having once begun he found it made his heart so light that he read every day. Sometimes he was so absorbed in his reading that the oil in his lamp burnt out before he could tear himself away from the book. He continued to read every night, and the more he read the more clearly he understood what God required of him, and how he might live for God. And his heart grew lighter and lighter. Before, when he went to bed he used to lie with a heavy heart, moaning as he thought of his little Kapit n; but now he only repeated again and again: "Glory to Thee, glory to Thee, O Lord! Thy will be done!"

From that time Martin's whole life changed. Formerly, on holidays he used to go and have tea at the public house, and did not even refuse a glass or two of vodka. Sometimes, after having had a drop with a friend, he left the public house not drunk, but rather merry, and would say foolish things:

shout at a man, or abuse him. Now, all that sort of thing passed away from him. His life became peaceful and joyful. He sat down to his work in the morning, and when he had finished his day's work he took the lamp down from the wall, stood it on the table, fetched his book from the shelf, opened it, and sat down to read. The more he read the better he understood, and the clearer and happier he felt in his mind.

It happened once that Martin sat up late, absorbed in his book. He was reading Luke's Gospel; and in the sixth chapter he came upon the verses:

"To him that smiteth thee on the one cheek offer also the other; and from him that taketh away thy cloak withhold not thy coat also. Give to every man that asketh thee; and of him that taketh away thy goods ask them not again. And as ye would that men should do to you, do ye also to them likewise."

He also read the verses where our Lord says:

"And why call ye me, Lord, Lord, and do not the things which I say? Whosoever cometh to me, and heareth my sayings, and doeth them, I will shew you to whom he is like: He is like a man which built an house, and digged deep, and laid the foundation on a rock: and when the flood arose, the stream beat vehemently upon that house, and could not shake it: for it was founded upon a rock. But he that heareth and doeth not, is like a man that without a foundation built an house upon the earth, against which the stream did beat vehemently, and immediately it fell; and the ruin of that house was great."

When Martin read these words his soul was glad within him. He took off his spectacles and laid them on the book, and leaning his elbows on the table pondered over what he had read. He tried his own life by the standard of those words, asking himself:

"Is my house built on the rock, or on sand? If it stands on the rock, it is well. It seems easy enough while one sits here alone, and one thinks one has done all that God commands; but as soon as I cease to be on my guard, I sin again. Still I will persevere. It brings such joy. Help me, O Lord!"

He thought all this, and was about to go to bed, but was loth to leave his book. So he went on reading the seventh chapter about the centurion, the widow's son, and the answer to John's disciples, and he came to the part where a rich Pharisee invited the Lord to his house; and he read how the woman who was a sinner, anointed his feet and washed them with her tears, and how he justified her. Coming to the forty-fourth verse, he read:

"And turning to the woman, he said unto Simon, Seest thou this woman? I entered into thine house, thou gavest me no water for my feet: but she hath wetted my feet with her tears, and wiped them with her hair. Thou gavest me no kiss; but she, since the time I came in, hath not ceased to kiss my feet. My head with oil thou didst not anoint: but she hath anointed my feet with ointment."

He read these verses and thought: "He gave no water for his feet, gave no kiss, his head with oil he did not anoint?" And Martin took off his spectacles once more, laid them on his book, and pondered.

"He must have been like me, that Pharisee. He too thought only of himself, how to get a cup of tea, how to keep warm and comfortable; never a thought of his guest. He took care of himself, but for his guest he cared nothing at all. Yet who was the guest? The Lord himself! If he came to me, should I behave like that?"

Then Martin laid his head upon both his arms and, before he was aware of it, he fell asleep.

"Martin!" he suddenly heard a voice, as if some one had breathed the word above his ear.

He started from his sleep. "Who's there?" he asked.

He turned round and looked at the door; no one was there. He called again. Then he heard quite distinctly: "Martin, Martin! Look out into the street to-morrow, for I shall come."

Martin roused himself, rose from his chair and rubbed his eyes, but did not know whether he had heard these words in a dream or awake. He put out the lamp and lay down to sleep.

Next morning he rose before daylight, and after saying his prayers he lit the fire and prepared his cabbage soup and buckwheat porridge. Then he lit the samovár [Russian teapot], put on his apron, and sat down by the window to his work. As he sat working Martin thought over what had happened the night before. At times it seemed to him like a dream, and at times he thought that he had really heard the voice. "Such things have happened before now," thought he.

So he sat by the window, looking out into the street more than he worked, and whenever any one passed in unfamiliar boots he would stoop and look up, so as to see not the feet only but the face of the passer-by as well. A house-porter passed in new felt boots; then a water-carrier. Presently an old soldier of Nicholas' reign came near the window, spade in hand. Martin knew him by his boots, which were shabby old felt ones, galoshed with leather. The old man was called Stepánitch: a neighboring tradesman kept him in his house for charity, and his duty was to help the house-porter. He began to clear away the snow before Martin's window. Martin glanced at him and then went on with his work.

"I must be growing crazy with age," said Martin, laughing at his fancy. "Stepánitch comes to clear away the snow, and I must needs imagine it's Christ coming to visit me. Old dotard that I am!"

Yet after he had made a dozen stitches he felt drawn to look out of the window again. He saw that Stepánitch had leaned his spade against the wall, and was either resting himself or trying to get warm. The man was old and broken down, and had evidently not enough strength even to clear away the snow.

"What if I called him in and gave him some tea?" thought Martin. "The samovár is just on the boil."

He stuck his awl in its place, and rose; and putting the samovár on the table, made tea. Then he tapped the window with his fingers. Stepánitch turned and came to the window. Martin beckoned to him to come in, and went himself to open the door.

"Come in," he said, "and warm yourself a bit. I'm sure you must be cold."

"May God bless you!" Stepánitch answered. "My bones do ache to be sure." He came in, first shaking off the snow, and lest he should leave marks on the floor he began wiping his feet; but as he did so he tottered and nearly fell.

"Don't trouble to wipe your feet," said Martin "I'll wipe up the floor; it's all in the day's work. Come, friend, sit down and have some tea."

Filling two tumblers, he passed one to his visitor, and pouring his own out into the saucer, began to blow on it.

Stepánitch emptied his glass, and, turning it upside down, put the remains of his piece of sugar on the top. He began to express his thanks, but it was plain that he would be glad of some more.

"Have another glass," said Martin, refilling the visitor's tumbler and his own. But while he drank his tea Martin kept looking out into the street.

"Are you expecting any one?" asked the visitor.

"Am I expecting any one? Well, now, I'm ashamed to tell you. It isn't that I really expect any one; but I heard something last night which I can't get out of my mind. Whether it was a vision, or only a fancy, I can't tell. You see, friend, last night I was reading the Gospel, about Christ the Lord, how he suffered, and how he walked on earth. You have heard tell of it, I dare say."

"I have heard tell of it," answered Stepánitch; "but I'm an ignorant man and not able to read."

"Well, you see, I was reading of how he walked on earth. I came to that part, you know, where he went to a Pharisee who did not receive him well. Well, friend, as I read about it, I thought now that man did not receive Christ the Lord with proper honor. Suppose such a thing could happen to such a man as myself, I thought, what would I not do to receive him! But that man gave him no reception at all. Well, friend, as I was thinking of this, I began to doze, and as I dozed I heard some one call me by name. I got up, and thought I heard someone whispering, 'Expect me; I will come tomorrow.' This happened twice over. And to tell you the truth, it sank so into my mind that, though I am ashamed of it myself, I keep on expecting him, the dear Lord!"

Stepánitch shook his head in silence, finished his tumbler and laid it on its side; but Martin stood it up again and refilled it for him.

"Here drink another glass, bless you! And I was thinking too, how he walked on earth and despised no one, but went mostly among common folk. He went with plain people, and chose his disciples from among the likes of us, from workmen like us, sinners that we are. 'He who raises himself,' he said, 'shall be humbled and he who humbles himself shall be raised. You call me Lord,' he said, 'and I will wash your feet. He who would be first,' he said, 'let him be the servant of all; because,' he said, 'blessed are the poor, the humble, the meek, and the merciful.'"

Stepánitch forgot his tea. He was an old man easily moved to tears, and as he sat and listened the tears ran down his cheeks.

"Come, drink some more," said Martin. But Stepánitch crossed himself, thanked him, moved away his tumbler, and rose.

"Thank you, Martin Avdéitch," he said, "you have given me food and comfort both for soul and body."

"You're very welcome. Come again another time. I am glad to have a guest," said Martin.

Stepánitch went away; and Martin poured out the last of the tea and drank it up. Then he put away the tea things and sat down to his work, stitching the back seam of a boot. And as he stitched he kept looking out of the window, waiting for Christ, and thinking about him and his doings. And his head was full of Christ's sayings.

Two soldiers went by: one in government boots, and the other in boots of his own; then the master of a neighboring house, in shining galoshes; then a baker carrying a basket. All these passed on. Then a woman came up in worsted stockings and peasant-made shoes. She passed the window, but stopped by the wall. Martin glanced up at her through the window, and saw that she was a stranger, poorly dressed, and with a baby in her arms. She stopped by the wall with her back to the wind, trying to wrap the baby up, though she had hardly anything to wrap it in. The woman had only summer clothes on, and even they were shabby and worn. Through the window Martin heard the baby crying, and the woman trying to soothe it, but unable to do so. Martin rose and going out of the door and up the steps he called to her.

"My dear, I say, my dear!"

The woman heard, and turned round.

"Why do you stand out there with the baby in the cold? Come inside. You can wrap him up better in a warm place. Come this way!"

The woman was surprised to see an old man in an apron, with spectacles on his nose, calling to her, but she followed him in.

They went down the steps, entered the little room, and the old man led her to the bed.

"There, sit down, my dear, near the stove. Warm yourself, and feed the baby."

"Oh, I haven't got any milk. I have eaten nothing myself since early morning," said the woman, but still she took the baby to her breast.

Martin shook his head. He brought out a basin and some bread. Then he opened the oven door and poured some cabbage soup into the basin. He took out the porridge pot also but the porridge was not yet ready, so he spread a cloth on the table and served only the soup and bread.

"Sit down and eat, my dear, and I'll mind the baby. Why, bless me, I've had children of my own; I know how to manage them."

The woman crossed herself, and sitting down at the table began to eat, while Martin put the baby on the bed and sat down by it. He chucked and chucked, but having no teeth he could not do it well and the baby continued to cry. Then Martin tried poking at him with his finger; he drove his finger straight at the baby's mouth and then quickly drew it back, and did this again and again. He did not let the baby take his finger in its mouth, because it was all black with cobbler's wax. But the baby first grew quiet watching the finger, and then began to laugh. And Martin felt quite pleased.

The woman sat eating and talking, and told him who she was, and where she had been.

"I'm a soldier's wife," said she. "They sent my husband somewhere, far away, eight months ago, and I have heard nothing of him since. I had a place as cook till my baby was born, but then they would not keep me with a child. For three months now I have been struggling, unable to find a place, and I've had to sell all I had for food. I tried to go as a wet-nurse, but no one would have me; they said I was too starved-looking and thin. Now I have just been to see a tradesman's wife (a woman from our village is in service with her) and she has promised to take me. I thought it was all settled at last, but she tells me not to come till next week. It is far to her place, and I am fagged out, and baby is quite starved, poor mite. Fortunately our landlady has pity on us, and lets us lodge free, else I don't know what we should do."

Martin sighed. "Haven't you any warmer clothing?" he asked.

"How could I get warm clothing?" said she. "Why I pawned my last shawl for sixpence yesterday."

Then the woman came and took the child, and Martin got up. He went and looked among some things that were hanging on the wall, and brought back an old cloak.

"Here," he said, "though it's a worn-out old thing, it will do to wrap him up in."

The woman looked at the cloak, then at the old man, and taking it, burst into tears. Martin turned away, and groping under the bed brought out a small trunk. He fumbled about in it, and again sat down opposite the woman. And the woman said:

"The Lord bless you, friend. Surely Christ must have sent me to your window, else the child would have frozen. It was mild when I started, but now see how cold it has turned. Surely it must have been Christ who made you look out of your window and take pity on me, poor wretch!"

Martin smiled and said, "It is quite true; it was he made me do it. It was no mere chance made me look out."

And he told the woman his dream, and how he had heard the Lord's voice promising to visit him that day.

"Who knows? All things are possible," said the woman. And she got up and threw the cloak over her shoulders, wrapping it round herself and round the baby. Then she bowed, and thanked Martin once more.

"Take this for Christ's sake," said Martin, and gave her sixpence to get her shawl out of pawn. The woman crossed herself, and Martin did the same, and then he saw her out.

After the woman had gone, Martin ate some cabbage soup, cleared the things away, and sat down to work again. He sat and worked, but did not forget the window, and every time a shadow fell on it he looked up at once to see who was passing. People he knew and strangers passed by, but no one remarkable.

After a while Martin saw an apple-woman stop just in front of his window. She had a large basket, but there did not seem to be many apples left in it; she had evidently sold most of her stock. On her back she had a sack full of wood chips, which she was taking home. No doubt she had gathered them at some place where building was going on. The sack evidently hurt her, and she wanted to shift it from one shoulder to the other, so she put it down on the footpath and, placing her basket on a post, began to shake down the chips in the sack. While she was doing this a boy in a tattered cap ran up, snatched an apple out of the basket, and tried to slip away; but the old woman noticed it, and turning, caught the boy by his sleeve. He began to struggle, trying to free himself, but the old woman held on with both hands, knocked his cap off his head, and seized hold of his hair. The boy squawked and the old woman scolded him. Martin dropped his awl, not waiting to stick it in its place, and rushed out of the door. Stumbling up the steps, and dropping his spectacles in his hurry, he ran out into the street. The old woman was pulling the boy's hair and scolding him, and threatening to take him to the police. The lad was struggling and protesting, saying, "I did not take it. What are you beating me for? Let me go!"

Martin separated them. He took the boy by the hand and said, "Let him go, Granny. Forgive him for Christ's sake."

"I'll pay him out, so that he won't forget it for a year! I'll take the rascal to the police!"

Martin began entreating the old woman.

"Let him go, Granny. He won't do it again. Let him go for Christ's sake!"

The old woman let go, and the boy wished to run away, but Martin stopped him.

"Ask the Granny's forgiveness!" said he. "And don't do it another time. I saw you take the apple."

The boy began to cry and to beg pardon.

"That's right. And now here's an apple for you," and Martin took an apple from the basket and gave it to the boy, saying, "I will pay you, Granny."

"You will spoil them that way, the young rascals," said the old woman. "He ought to be whipped so that he should remember it for a week."

"Oh, Granny, Granny," said Martin, "that's our way but it's not God's way. If he should be whipped for stealing an apple, what should be done to us for our sins?"

The old woman was silent.

And Martin told her the parable of the lord who forgave his servant a large debt, and how the servant went out and seized his debtor by the throat. The old woman listened to it all, and the boy, too, stood by and listened.

"God bids us forgive," said Martin, "or else we shall not be forgiven. Forgive every one; and a thoughtless youngster most of all."

The old woman wagged her head and sighed.

"It's true enough," said she, "but they are getting terribly spoilt."

"Then we old ones must show them better ways," Martin replied.

"That's just what I say," said the old woman. "I have had seven of them myself, and only one daughter is left." And the old woman began to tell how and where she was living with her daughter, and how many grandchildren she had. "There now," she said, "I have but little strength left, yet I work hard for the sake of my grandchildren; and nice children they are, too. No one comes out to meet me but the children. Little Annie, now, won't leave me for any one. It's 'grandmother, dear grandmother, darling grandmother.'" And the old woman completely softened at the thought. "Of course, it was only his childishness, God help him," said she, referring to the boy.

As the old woman was about to hoist her sack on her back, the lad sprang forward to her, saying, "Let me carry it for you, Granny. I'm going that way."

The old woman nodded her head, and put the sack on the boy's back, and they went down the street together, the old woman quite forgetting to ask Martin to pay for the apple. Martin stood and watched them as they went along talking to each other.

When they were out of sight Martin went back to the house. Having found his spectacles unbroken on the steps, he picked up his awl and sat down again to work. He worked a little, but could soon not see to pass the bristle through the holes in the leather; and presently he noticed the lamplighter passing on his way to light the street lamps.

"Seems it's time to light up," thought he. So he trimmed his lamp, hung it up, and sat down again to work. He finished off one boot and, turning it about, examined it. It was all right. Then he gathered his tools together, swept up the cuttings, put away the bristles and the thread and the awls, and, taking down the lamp, placed it on the table. Then he took the Gospels from the shelf. He meant to open them at the place he had marked the day before with a bit of morocco, but the book opened at another place. As Martin opened it, his yesterday's dream came back to his mind, and no sooner had he thought of it than he seemed to hear footsteps, as though some one were moving behind him. Martin turned round, and it seemed to him as if people were standing in the dark corner, but he could not make out who they were. And a voice whispered in his ear: "Martin, Martin, don't you know me?"

"Who is it?" muttered Martin.

"It is I," said the voice. And out of the dark corner stepped Stepánitch, who smiled and vanishing like a cloud was seen no more.

"It is I," said the voice again. And out of the darkness stepped the woman with the baby in her arms and the woman smiled and the baby laughed, and they too vanished.

"It is I," said the voice once more. And the old woman and the boy with the apple stepped out and both smiled, and then they too vanished.

And Martin's soul grew glad. He crossed himself, put on his spectacles, and began reading the Gospel just where it had opened; and at the top of the page he read:

"I was a hungered, and ye gave me meat: I was thirsty, and ye gave me drink: I was a stranger, and ye took me in."

And at the bottom of the page he read:

"Inasmuch as ye did it unto one of these my brethren even these least, ye did it unto me."

And Martin understood that his dream had come true; and that the Savior had really come to him that day, and he had welcomed him.

Suggestions

RECOMMENDATIONS FOR FURTHER READING

The following books are recommended for further reading:

CHILDREN'S BOOKS (Few Words Per Page For Younger Children)

Only a Star
Margery Facklam, Author
Nancy Carpenter, Illustrator

On the night that Jesus was born, there were no Christmas ornaments – only the light of a star. But this star transformed the humble manger scene into glistening beauty fit for the newborn King. This wonderfully illustrated story contrasts modern Christmas decorations with the magnificence of nature.

Saint Nicholas, The Real Story of the Christmas Legend
Julie Stiegemeyer, Author
Chris Ellison, Illustrator

This book retells one of the most popular stories about St. Nicholas – how he supplied money to three young women without dowries. The story helps children to understand that St. Nicholas was a real person who loved and honored God. Furthermore, he set an excellent example of generosity. This book is beautifully illustrated with pictures that are true to life.

The Christmas Story
From the Gospels of Matthew and Luke
Cathy Ann Johnson, Illustrator

All of the text in this little book comes directly from the *International Children's Bible*. Combined with lovely illustrations, this is a great tool to teach children the true story of Christmas.

The Pine Tree Parable
Liz Curtis Higgs, Author
Nancy Munger, Illustrator

This is a simple and beautiful story about how one family sacrifices for another in need. Liz Curtis Higgs has written several popular parables for holidays, and she includes relevant Scripture on every page. The illustrations are colorful and inviting.

CHILDREN'S BOOKS (Many Words Per Page For Older Children)

Jotham's Journey, A Storybook for Advent
Arnold Ytreeide, Author

Jotham is a ten-year-old boy who is separated from his family. His search for them is full of adventures across the land of Israel. Ultimately, he meets up with them, as well as the newborn Savior in Bethlehem. This creative story is divided up into short chapters for each day of Advent and includes a daily discussion on Biblical themes. This book can help to start a wonderful tradition of storytelling for Advent.

One Wintry Night
Ruth Bell Graham, Author
Richard Jesse Watson, Illustrator

Set during the Christmas season, a young boy gets caught in a storm and seeks shelter in the home of a woman who spends the next evening telling him the Christmas story. Beginning with creation, God's work throughout history is revealed – culminating in Jesus' birth, death and resurrection. The Gospel message is creatively presented and complimented by marvelous illustrations.

The Kingfisher Book of Classic Christmas Stories
Ian Whybrow, Editor
Various Illustrators

This collection of 14 stories includes many of the great tales and legends of Christmas. Each story is illustrated by a different artist, which adds a unique variety to the book. It is a great addition to a Christmas library for children.

The Very First Christmas
Paul L. Maier, Author
Francisco Ordaz, Illustrator

When a young boy asks his mom to tell him a "real" story instead of a fairy tale, she proceeds to narrate the story of the first Christmas according to the gospel of Luke. Interesting historical details are woven through the story as the young boy asks questions about the setting of the first century. The illustrations are fantastic.

COLLECTIONS

A Louisa May Alcott Christmas
Raina Moore, Editor

Louisa May Alcott is best known today for her novel *Little Women*. During her life, she also wrote several charming short stories set during the Christmas season. This collection includes 20 of Alcott's holiday tales. Each story uniquely incorporates biblical themes like giving, selflessness, etc., and every selection is suitable for the whole family. For more on Louisa May Alcott, see p. 360-362.

Christmas Stories for the Heart
Alice Gray, Compiler

This book is a treasury of great short stories that inspire the spirit of Christmas. Most of the selections are just a few pages long and are perfect for reading together as a family during the Christmas season.

EVANGELISTIC BOOKS

The Case for Christ
Lee Strobel, Author

This book challenges readers to consider why Christmas matters. In true journalistic fashion, best-selling author Lee Stobel seeks out experts in various fields to identify the facts concerning Jesus. This short (about 90 pages) and enjoyable read is a perfect gift for the skeptic of Christianity.

Why a Manger? or *Why a Shepherd?*
Bodie and Brock Thoene, Authors

This husband and wife team is exceptionally talented at incorporating history and Bible teaching into their writing. *Why a Manger?* explores the significance of Jesus' humble birth. *Why a Shepherd?* addresses the implications of Jesus being called the "Good Shepherd." Each book is designed for outreach purposes. They are short (about 80 pages each) and easy to read in a single sitting.

HISTORICAL FICTION

Fifth Seal
Bodie and Brock Thoene, Authors

This is the fifth book in a series of historical fiction about Jesus' life. This one focuses on the details surrounding the birth of Jesus. The Thoenes have a unique ability to bring the New Testament to life, and their writing is captivating. It is an added bonus to learn that every detail of history is carefully researched. After finishing this book about the period during Christ's birth, you will surely want to read the entire series. For more on Bodie and Brock Thoene, see p. 308.

The Story of the Other Wise Man
Henry van Dyke, Author

This moving story introduces a fictional Wise Man who fails to meet up with his companions, because he stops to help a man in need. As he journeys alone to find the King of the Jews, he is prevented time and again by pausing to assist others. As this "other" Wise Man is about to die after many years of searching, he hears the heavenly voice of Jesus confirming that through his service to others, he had served Christ. "His treasures were accepted" and he "had found the King." Henry van Dyke carefully researched the historical setting and the details of travel in the first century to create this story. For more on van Dyke, see pp. 408-409.

SCHOLARLY BOOKS

In the Fullness of Time
Paul L. Maier, Author

Historian Paul L. Maier offers an intriguing look at the details surrounding Christmas. He truly brings the story of Jesus' birth to life as he carefully examines the world of the first century. Maier is a skillful narrator and provides fascinating information for people who enjoy history. This book also includes sections on Easter and the Early Church.

St. Nicholas, A Closer Look at Christmas
Joe Wheeler and Jim Rosenthal, Authors

This is an excellent resource for those seeking more information on St. Nicholas and the various traditions surrounding his life. The book will satisfy the most intellectual person with its detailed history, and it will please nearly everyone with its many beautiful depictions of St. Nicholas from regions around the world. It is a great choice for display on a coffee table during the Christmas season.

The Origins of Christmas
Joseph F. Kelly, Author

Scholar Joseph F. Kelly is an expert on the origin of Christmas, and he provides an intriguing look at ancient sources to describe how the celebration of Christmas developed. Parts of the "Source" section of this book (pp. 22-26) relied heavily on Kelly's work.

The Star of Bethlehem
Mark Kidger, Author

This book is perfect for amateur astronomers who are curious about the details surrounding the Star of Bethlehem. Professional astronomer Mark Kidger is a careful researcher and a clear communicator. He will surely captivate your attention. The discussion on the "Star of Bethlehem" (pp. 150-154) relied heavily on Kidger's work.

The World Encyclopedia of Christmas
Gary Bowler, Author

This encyclopedia is an excellent resource for those seeking reliable information on literally anything related to Christmas worldwide. Author Gary Bowler (a history professor) uniquely combines careful research with humor and wit. His work includes entries in alphabetical order on over 1000 topics (terms, customs, historical events, carols, movies, etc.). You will be hard pressed to think up a subject related to Christmas that is not addressed in this book.

For more recommendations, visit www.celebratingholidays.com.

Summary

CONCLUSION

The Purpose of Jesus' Birth

> "For God so loved the world that he gave his one and only Son, that whoever believes
> in him shall not perish but have eternal life" (John 3:16)

Over 2,000 years ago, an angel appeared to shepherds near Bethlehem and said: "Do not be afraid, I bring you good news of great joy that will be for all the people" (Luke 1:10). Why is the birth of Jesus such good news? Why is it cause for great joy? . . . Because only Jesus can meet the deepest need of humanity — forgiveness of sin. He is the only one who can offer peace with God and eternal life.

In order to understand the need for forgiveness, we must first recognize the critical issue of sin in our lives. To have a relationship with God and to ultimately spend eternity with him, we need to follow his laws perfectly — in our hearts and in our actions. Sadly, we human beings have failed miserably at our attempts to live sinless lives. The Bible teaches, "All have sinned and fall short of the glory of God" (Romans 3:23).

The consequence of sin is death, eternal separation from our Creator. When the first human beings, Adam and Eve, sinned against God by eating the forbidden fruit in the Garden of Eden, they brought death into the world. Since man was the source of death, man would also have to be the solution in overcoming it. Herein lies the dilemma; only God himself could live a sinless life and conquer death, but God was not a man. The death of a perfect human was required to reverse the consequence of human sin. For this reason, and beyond all comprehension, God determined from the beginning of time to become a man. Ultimately, Jesus was born to die so that we might live!

But we must come to him. Jesus said: "Come to me all you who are weary and burdened, and I will give you rest. Take my yoke upon you and learn from me, for I am gentle and humble in heart, and you will find rest for your souls" (Matthew 11:28-29). This is what it means to be a Christian: to recognize our sin and then come to Jesus, to seek forgiveness through him and then follow him as the shepherd of our soul. When writing to Christians in the Early Church about their lives before coming to Jesus, Peter said, "For you were like sheep going astray, but now you have returned to the Shepherd and Overseer of your souls" (1 Peter 2:25). How fitting that the announcement of Jesus' birth was made to shepherds and was followed by a host of angels who proclaimed, "Glory to God in the highest, and on earth peace to men on whom his favor rests" (Luke 2:14). The Good Shepherd was born to bring peace, true spiritual peace with God, to those who would follow him.

When Jesus said, "I tell you the truth, no one can see the kingdom of God unless he is born again," he was speaking of a spiritual birth. To be "born again" means to be born spiritually and to live eternally as a citizen of God's kingdom. Have you been born spiritually? If not, what better time to celebrate your spiritual birth than during the season in which we celebrate the birth of the one who makes it possible – Jesus. You can ask God, even now, through prayer, for a new birth. Prayer is talking to God, out loud or in your heart. He made you, and he knows you intimately; he can certainly hear you. Here is a sample prayer to follow or to put in your own words:

"Dear Lord, I recognize that I have sinned. I come to you seeking forgiveness. I desire peace with you and rest for my soul. I surrender my life to you. I want to follow Jesus as the Shepherd and Overseer of my soul. I accept the gift of eternal life. Please help me to demonstrate my gratitude by living in a way that honors you. In the name of Jesus I pray. Amen."

Though some aspects of our relationship with God are meant to be private, a decision to be "born again" and to follow Jesus is not. Becoming a Christian is the beginning of a new life in which we enter into a family of other believers. Our brothers and sisters in Christ can greatly encourage us to grow in our faith, and they can help us to better understand his Word, the Bible. If you need help finding Christians in your area, please send an email to info@celebratingholidays.com.

BIBLIOGRAPHY OF SOURCES

Abbey, John Charles. *Religious Thought in Old English Verse*. Sampson Low, 1892.

Aelfric of Eynsham. *Aelfric's Lives of Saints*. Walter W. Skeat edition. Early English Text Society, N. Trübner & Co., 1881.

Alden, Isabella Macdonald. Edited by Grace Livingston Hill. *Memories of Yesterdays*. J.P. Lippincott, 1931.

Allen, Alexander Viets Griswold. *Life and Letters of Phillips Brooks*, V2. E.P. Dutton and Co., 1900.

"An Appreciation and Explanation of Handel's Oratorio Messiah." Antipas Christadelphians: http://www.antipas.org/handel/midipage.html.

Anderson, Doug, editor. Various articles retrieved from Hymns and Carols of Christmas: http://www.hymnsandcarolsofchristmas.com.

Anesko, Michael. "William Dean Howells." The Literary Encyclopedia: http://www.litencyc.com/php/speople.php?rec=true&UID=2237.

Archer, Robert. "Euphorbia." PlantZAfrica: http://www.plantzafrica.com/plantefg/euphorbia.htm.

Armstrong, Mary Frances, Ludlow, Helen Wilhelmina, and Fenner, Thomas P. *Hampton and Its Students*. G.P. Putnam's Sons, 1874.

Arvin, Newton. *Longfellow: His Life and Work*. Boston: Little, Brown and Company, 1963.

Augustine. *An Augustine Synthesis*. Arranged by Erich Przywara. Harper, 1958.

Baker, Robert, and Landers, John M. *A Summary of Christian History.* B&H Publishing Group, 2005.

Bailey, Albert Edward. *The Gospel in Hymns: Backgrounds and Interpretations*. Scribner, 1950.

Barbour, Philip L., editor. *The Complete Works of Captain John Smith (1580-1631)*, Volume I. University of North Carolina Press, 1986.

Barron, W.R.J. *Sir Gawain and the Green Knight.* Text and facing translation edited by W. R. J. Barron. Manchester University Press, 2004.

Coffman, Elesha. "Raising Cane." Christianity Today: http://www.christianitytoday.com/history/newsletter/christmas/cane.html.

Cohen, Hennig and Coffin, Tristram Potter, Editors. *The Folklore of American Holidays*, First Edition. Gale Research Company.

Collins, Ace. *Stories Behind the Great Traditions of Christmas.* Zondervan, 2003.

Contemporary Authors. Various articles from Gale Literary Database.

Corman, Brian. "Nahum Tate". The Literary Encyclopedia: http://www.litencyc.com/php/speople.php?rec=true&UID=4317.

Creel, Daena. "About Pansy" and "Dr. Raymond Macdonald Alden, 'Paranete.'" Isabella Macdonald Alden Website: http://www.isabellamacdonaldalden.com/.

Das Rauhe Haus, "History, From 1832-1881": http://www.rauheshaus.de/stiftung/geschichte.

Dawson, William Francis. *Christmas: Its Origin and Associations.* E. Stock, 1902.

de Voragine, Jacobus. *The Golden Legend.* Translated and Adapted by Granger Ryan and Helmut Ripperger, Ayer Company Publishers, Inc., 1969.

Delano, Sterling F. *The Harbinger and New England Transcendentalism: A Portrait of Associationism in America.* Fairleigh Dickinson University Press, 1984.

Dickens, Charles. *The Works of Charles Dickens.* Chapman and Hall, 1910.

Dictionary of Literary Biography. "Clement Clarke Moore": http://www.bookrags.com/biography/clement-clarke-moore-dlb/.

Durieu, René. L'auteur du "Minuit chrétiens." C. Lacour, 1997.

Elson, Louis Charles. *The History of American Music.* The Macmillan Company, 1915.

Encyclopedia Britannica Online, various articles: http://www.britannica.com/.

Eskew, Harry and McElrath, Hugh T. *Sing with Understanding.* Broadman Press, 1980.

Farley's and Sathers Candy Company. "Bob's": http://www.farleysandsathers.com/About/WhoWeAre.asp?BrandID=1.

Farmer, David Hugh. *The Oxford Dictionary of Saints.* Oxford University Press, 2004.

Feeney, Ann. "Biography of Adolphe Adam." All Music: http://www.allmusic.com/cg/amg.dll.

Fisk University. "History of Fisk": http://www.fisk.edu/page.asp?id=115.

Fountain, David Guy. *Isaac Watts Remembered.* Gospel Standard Publications, 1978.

Foster, Don. *Author Unknown: On the Trail of the Anonymous*. Henry Holt, 2000.

Francis, James Allan. *The Real Jesus and Other Sermons*. The Judson Press, 1926.

Frazer, James George. *The Golden Bough, A Study in Magic and Religion*. MacMillan, 1900.

Gilbert, Davies. *Some Ancient Christmas Carols*. John Nichols and Son, 1822.

Gill, John. *The New John Gill Exposition of the Entire Bible* (Commentary on Zech.14:20). Studylight: http://www.studylight.org/com/geb/view.cgi?book=zec&chapter=014&verse=020.

Gueranger, Abbot. *The Liturgical Year*. Translated by Laurence Shepherd. James Duffy, 1870.

Hatch, Jane M. *The American Book of Days*. H.W. Wilson Company, 1978.

Helmore, Thomas. *Accompanying Harmonies to The Hymnal Noted*. Novello, 1852.

Hill, Richard S. "Not So Far Away In A Manger, Forty-one Settings of an America Carol." Music Library Association, "Notes", December, 1945, Second Series, Vol. III, No. 1. Hymns and Carols of Christmas: http://www.hymnsandcarolsofchristmas.com/Hymns_and_Carols/Notes_On_Carols/away_in_a_manger.htm.

Hillquit, Morris. *History of Socialism in the United States*. Funk & Wagnalls Company, 1910.

Hoffman, Charles Fenno. *The New York Book of Poetry*. G. Dearborn, 1837, pp. 217-219.

Hopkins Jr., John Henry. *Carols, Hymns and Songs*. Church Book Depository, 1863.

Hopkins Jr., John Henry, editor. *Great Hymns of the Church*. James Portt & Company, 1887.

Hottes, Alfred Carl. *1001 Christmas Facts and Fancies* (1937). Kessinger Publishing, 2004.

Hughes, Charles W. *American Hymns Old and New*. Columbia University Press, 1980.

Husk, William Henry. *Songs of the Nativity: Being Christmas Carols, Ancient and Modern*. J.C. Hotten, 1884.

Iwelumor, Juliet. "Henry van Dyke." Pennsylvania State University Library, Biographies: http://pabook.libraries.psu.edu/palitmap/bios/Van_Dyke__Henry.html.

Johnson, Rossiter, editor. *The Twentieth Century Biographical Dictionary of Notable Americans*. The Biographical Society, 1904.

Julian, John, editor. *A Dictionary of Hymnology*. Dover Publications Inc., 1957.

Kaufmanis, Karlis. "The Star of Bethlehem." A Christmas Classic. Augsburg Fortress, 1999.

Keller, Phillip. *A Shepherd Looks at Psalm 23*. Zondervan, 2007.

Kelly, Joseph. *The Origins of Christmas*. Liturgical Press, 2004.

Kendall, Paul. "Mythology and Folklore of the Holly." Retrieved July 20, 2008 from Trees for Life: http://www.treesforlife.org.uk/forest/mythfolk/holly.html.

Keyte, Hugh and Parrott, Andrew, Editors. *The New Oxford Book of Carols*. Oxford University Press, 1992.

Kidger, Mark. *Star of Bethlehem*. Princeton University Press, 1999.

Kidner, Derek. "Genesis." Tyndale Old Testament Commentaries. Inter-Varsity Press, 1967.

Kitto, John and Alexander, William Lindsay, editors. The Encyclopedia of Biblical Literature, Volume 1. "Bell." Kessinger Publishing, 2003.

Knox, Thomas Francis. Translated by W. R. Inge. *The Life of Blessed Henry Suso by Himself*. Kessinger Publishing, 2006.

Kreeft, Peter. *Angels (and Demons), What Do We Really Know About Them?* Ignatius Press, 1995.

Lewis, C.S. *The Chronicles of Narnia, The Lion, The Witch and the Wardrobe*. Harper Collins Publishers, 1982.

Lewis, C.S. *The Screwtape Letters: With Screwtape Proposes a Toast*. HarperCollins, 1996.

Libbrecht, Ken. *Ken Libbrecht's Field Guide to Snowflakes*. Voyageur Press, 2006.

Libbrecht, Ken. *The Snowflake, Winter's Secret Beauty*. Voyageur Press.

Lloyd, A.L. *Folk Song in England*. International Publishers, 1967.

Longfellow, Henry Wadsworth. *The Poetical Works of Henry Wadsworth Longfellow*. Houghton, Mifflin and Company, 1886.

Los Angeles Times. "Historian Tracks Down Description of Christ." December 1, 1973.

MacArthur, John, Eareckson Tada, Wolgemuth, Robert and Bobbie. *O Come, All Ye Faithful*. Crossway Books, 2001.

Maier, Paul. *In the Fullness of Time*. Kregel Publications, 1997.

Maragou, Helena. "Louisa May Alcott." The Literary Encyclopedia: http://www.litencyc.com/php/speople.php?rec=true&UID=62.

Marek, George R. *Gentle Genius, The Story of Felix Mendelssohn*. Funk & Wagnalls, 1972.

Martindale, Cyril Charles. "Christmas." The Catholic Encyclopedia. Robert Appleton Company, 1908. Retrieved July 20, 2008 from New Advent: http://www.newadvent.org/cathen/03724b.htm.

Martyr, Justin. *Dialogue with Trypho,* Chapter LXXVIII. Christian Classics Ethereal Library: http://www.ccel.org/ccel/schaff/anf01.viii.iv.lxxviii.html.

Massachusetts Bay Colony. From the records of the General Court, May 11, 1659. *Massachusetts Travel Journal*: http://masstraveljournal.com/features/1101chrisban.html.

McClintock, John. *Cyclopedia of Biblical, Theological & Ecclesiastical Literature*, Yule. Harper & Brothers, 1889.

McCutchan, Robert Guy. *Hymn Tune Names, Their Sources and Significance*. Abingdon Press, 1957.

McHenry, Robert. *Famous American Women: A Biographical Dictionary from Colonial Times to the Present*. Courier Dover Publications, 1983.

McMahon, Arthur. "Blessed Henry Suso." The Catholic Encyclopedia. Robert Appleton Company, 1908. New Advent: http://www.newadvent.org/cathen/07238c.htm.

Merriman, C.D., "Charles Dickens." Biography written for Jalic Inc.: http:// www.online-literature.com/dickens/.

Mershman, Francis. "St. Wenceslaus." Catholic Encyclopedia. Robert Appleton Company, 1912. New Advent: http://www.newadvent.org/cathen/15587b.htm.

Mikkelson, Barbara. "Candy Cane." Snopes.com: http://www.snopes.com/holidays/christmas/candycane.asp.

Millar, Patrick. *The Story of the Church's Song*. Originally Published in 1927. Read Books, 2007.

Montgomery, Elizabeth Rider. *The Story Behind Great Stories*. Robert M. McBride & Company, 1947.

Montgomery, James. *The Poetical Works of James Montgomery: With a Memoir of the Author.* Memoir by Robert Carruthers. Little, Brown and Company, 1860.

Mullet, Mary. The American Magazine. "The Snowflake Man." Interview with Wilson Bentley, February 1925. Jericho Historical Society: http://snowflakebentley.com/mullet.htm.

Music, David. *Hymnology, A Collection of Source Readings*. The Scarecrow Press, 1996.

Myers, Robert J. *Celebrations, The Complete Book of American Holidays*. Doubleday and Company Inc, 1972, p. 333.

Myers, Robert Manson. *Handel's Messiah, A Touchstone of Taste*. Octagon Books, 1971.

Neale, John Mason. *Mediaeval Hymns and Sequences*. J. Masters, 1867.

Newton, William Wilberforce. *The Child and the Bishop: Together with Certain Memorabilia of the Rt. Rev. Phillips Brooks.* J.G. Cupples, 1894.

New York Times. "'O. Henry' on Himself, Life, and Other Things." April 4, 1909, Page SM9. Retrieved October 16, 2008: http://www.greensboro-nc.gov/departments/Library/ohenry/Public+Library/on+himself. htm.

Ninde, Edward Summerfield. *The Story of the American Hymn.* The Abingdon Press, 1921.

Nissenbaum, Stephen. "There Arose Such a Clatter: Who Really Wrote 'The Night before Christmas'? And Why Does It Matter?" History Cooperative: http://www.historycooperative. org/journals/cp/vol-01/no-02/moore/moore-2.shtml.

Nova, Claude. "Histoire du Minuit chrétiens." Nemausensis: http://www.nimausensis.com/Gard/MinuitChretienNova.pdf.

Osbeck, Kenneth W. *Amazing Grace.* Kregel Publications, 1990.

Osbeck, Kenneth. *Joy to the World! The Stories Behind Your Favorite Christmas Carols.* Kregel Publications, 1999.

Ott, Michael. "St. Ludmilla." Robert Appleton Company, 1910. New Advent: http://www.newadvent.org/cathen/09416a.htm.

Patterson, Samuel White. *The Poet of Christmas Eve: A Life of Clement Clarke Moore, 1779-1863.* Morehouse-Gorham Co., 1956.

Pennington, Edgar Legare. "John Freeman Young, Second Bishop of Florida." Church Missions Publishing Company, 1939.

Pohle, Joseph. "Sacrifice of the Mass." The Catholic Encyclopedia. Robert Appleton Company, 1911. New Advent: http://www.newadvent.org/cathen/10006a.htm.

Public Broadcasting Service. Classic Masterpiece. "A Tolstoy Timeline." PBS: http://www.pbs.org/wgbh/masterpiece/anna/timeline_text.html.

Ray, Steve. "Mary The Ark of the Covenant." Catholic Culture: http://www.catholicculture.org/library/view.cfm?RecNum=6811.

Robinson, Paschal. "St. Francis." The Catholic Encyclopedia. Robert Appleton Company, 1909. New Advent: http://www.newadvent.org/cathen/06221a.htm.

Routley, Erik. *The English Carol.* Oxford University Press, 1959

Sandys, William. *Christmas Carols, Ancient and Modern*. R. Beckley, 1833.

Saunders, William. "What are the 'O Antiphons'?" Arlington Catholic Herald: http://www.catholiceducation.org/articles/religion/re0374.html.

Saxton, Martha. *Louisa May Alcott, A Modern Biography*. Farrar, Straus and Giroux, 1995.

Sears, Edmund. *Regeneration*, 1854. Kessinger Publishing, 2003.

Sears, Edmund. *Sermons and Songs of the Christian Life*. Noyes, Holmes, 1875.

Shakespeare, William. *The Merry Wives of Windsor: A Comedy*. G. Bell and Sons, 1886.

Smith, Grahame. "Charles Dickens." The Literary Encyclopedia. January 8, 2001: http://www.litencyc.com/php/speople.php?rec=true&UID=5085.

Smith, John. Contributor: John Milliken Thompson. *The Journals of Captain John Smith: A Jamestown Biography*. National Geographic Society, 2007.

Sourcebook for Sundays and Seasons, An Almanac of Parish Liturgy. Liturgy Training, 2007.

Spurgeon, Charles Haddon. *Spurgeon's Sermons on Christmas and Easter*. Sermon Titled: "Immanuel – The Light of Life." Kregel Publicatoins, 1995.

Stille Nacht Gesellschaft (Silent Night Society) in Austria: http://www.stillenacht.at/en/.

Stocking, William, and Miller, Gordon K . *The City of Detroit*. Michigan, 1701-1922. S.J. Clarke Publishing Company, 1922.

Strong, James. *The New Strong's Exhaustive Concordance of the Bible*. Thomas Nelson Publishers, 1984.

Studwell, William. *The Christmas Carol Reader*. The Haworth Press, 1995.

Swartz Jr., B.K. *The Origin of American Christmas Myth and Customs*. Ball State University: http://www.bsu.edu/web/01bkswartz/xmaspub.html.

Tally, Thomas J. *The Origins of the Liturgical Year*. Liturgical Press, 1986.

Tenny-Brittian, Bill. "Why Is There One Pink Advent Candle?" Home Church Network Association: http://www.hcna.us/columns/pink_advent_candle.html.

Terry, Sir Richard R., editor. *Gilbert and Sandys' Christmas Carols*. Burns, Oates & Washbourne, 1932.

Tertullian. *The Ante-Nicene Fathers, On Idolatry.* Edited by Alexander Roberts and James Donaldson. C. Scribner's Sons, 1903.

Thaxter, Celia. *Drift-Weed.* Houghton, Mifflin and Company, 1894.

Thaxter, Celia. *Poems.* Hurd and Houghton, 1874.

The Academic Council of Stanford University. "Memorial Resolution, Raymond M. Alden (1873-1927)." Stanford University: http://histsoc.stanford.edu/pdfmem/AldenR.pdf.

The White House Historical Association. "White House Christmas Tree Themes." The White House Historical Association: http://www.whitehousehistory.org/whha_shows/holidays_christmas/index.html

Thoreau, Henry David. *The Writings of Henry David Thoreau.* Houghton, Mifflin and Company, 1887.

Thomas of Celano. *St. Francis of Assisi.* Translated from the Latin by Placid Herman. Franciscan Herald Press, 1963.

Thomas, Robert T. and Gundry, Stanley N. *A Harmony of the Gospels with Explanations and Essays.* Harper Collins, 1978.

Thompson, Sue Ellen. *Holiday Symbols.* Omnigraphics, 1988.

Thurston, Herbert. "Bells." Catholic Encyclopedia. Robert Appleton Company, 1907. New Advent: http://www.newadvent.org/cathen/02418b.htm

Tighe, William. *Calculating Christmas.* Touchstone Journal, December 2003 issue.

Tolkien, J.R.R. *The Father Christmas Letters.* Edited by Baillie Tolkien. Houghton Mifflin Company, 1976.

Tolstoy, Leo. *A Confession and Other Religious Writings.* Translated by Jane Kentish. Penguin Classics, 1987, p. 58.

Van Deusen, Mary. "Major Henry Livingston, Jr., The Christmas Poem." Van Deusen: http:// www.iment.com/maida/familytree/henry/index.htm.

Van Dyke, Henry. *The Poems of Henry van Dyke.* C. Scribner's Sons, 1913.

Van Dyke, Henry. *The Story of the Other Wise Man.* Paraclete Press, 1984.

Van Dyke, Tertius. *Henry Van Dyke, A Biography.* Harper and Brothers Publishers, 1935.

Virgil. *The Eclogues.* Kessinger Publishing, 2004.

Waggoner, Ben. "Carl Linnaeus." University of California Museum of Paleontology: http://www.ucmp.berkeley.edu/history/linnaeus.html.

Walker, Cheryl, editor. *American Women Poets of the Nineteenth Century, An Anthology.* Rutgers University Press, 1992.

Walsh, Joseph J. *Were They Wise Men or Kings? The Book of Christmas Questions.* Westminster John Knox Press, 2001.

Weiser, Francis X. *Handbook of Christian Feasts and Customs.* Harcourt, Brace and Company, Inc., 1958.

Wesley, Charles. Contributor John R. Tyson. *Charles Wesley: A Reader.* Oxford University Press, 1989.

Weston, Jessie Laidlay. *Sir Gawain and the Green Knight: A Middle-English Arthurian Romance Retold in Modern Prose, with Introduction & Notes.* Translated by Jessie Laidlay Weston. D. Nutt, 1900.

Wheeler, Joe and Rosenthal, Jim, *St. Nicholas, A Closer Look at Christmas.* Thomas Nelson, 2005.

Wilhelm, Joseph. "The Nicene Creed." The Catholic Encyclopedia, V 11. Robert Appleton Company, 1911. New Advent: http://www.newadvent.org/cathen/11049a.htm

Williams, Craven E. "Origins: Wesley and Handel." Greensboro College: http://www.gborocollege.edu/prescorner/handel.html.

Williard, Dallas. *The Divine Conspiracy: Rediscovering Our Hidden Life in God.* Harper Collins, 1998.

Willis, Richard Storrs. *Our Church Music: A Book for Pastors and People.* Dana, 1856.

Witvliet, John D. and Vroege, David. *Proclaiming the Christmas Gospel, Ancient Sermons and Hymns for Contemporary Christian Inspiration.* Baker Books, 2004.

Wolford, Ron. "The Poinsettia Pages." University of Illinois Extension: http://www.urbanext.uiuc.edu/poinsettia/.

Work, John Wesley. *Folk Song of the American Negro.* Fisk University, 1915.

Work III, John Wesley. *American Negro Songs: 230 Folk Songs and Spirituals, Religious and Secular.* Courier Dover Publications, 1998.

INDEX

LaVergne, TN USA
20 February 2011
217250LV00006B/58/P